Reds, Whites, and Blues

PRINCETON STUDIES IN CULTURAL SOCIOLOGY

Paul J. DiMaggio, Michèle Lamont, Robert J. Wuthnow, Viviana A. Zelizer, *series editors*

A list of titles in this series appears at the back of the book.

Reds, Whites, and Blues

Social Movements, Folk Music,
and Race in the United States

William G. Roy

PRINCETON UNIVERSITY PRESS

PRINCETON AND OXFORD

Published by Princeton University Press, 41 William Street,
Princeton, New Jersey 08540
In the United Kingdom: Princeton University Press, 6 Oxford Street,
Woodstock, Oxfordshire OX20 1TW

Grateful acknowledgment for permission to use lines from "The Anti-Slavery Harp" is
made to Uncle Tom's Cabin and Culture: A Multi-Media Archive (utc.oath.virginia.edu)

Grateful acknowledgement for permission to use lines from "Your Dog Loves My Dog,"
(lyrics by James Bevel and Bernard Lafayette) is made to Stormking Music, Inc.

Roy, William G., 1946–
   Reds, whites, and blues : social movements, folk music, and race in the United States /
William G. Roy.
      p. cm. — (Princeton studies in cultural sociology)
   Includes bibliographical references and index.
   ISBN 978-0-691-14363-7 (cloth : alk. paper)   1. Folk music—Political aspects—
United States—History—20th century.   2. Social movements—United States—History—
20th century.   3. Music and race—United States—History—20th century.   I. Title.
   ML3918.F65R69 2010
   306.4'84240973—dc22
2009049319

British Library Cataloging-in-Publication Data is available

This book has been composed in Sabon

Printed on acid-free paper. ∞

press.princeton.edu

Printed in the United States of America

10   9   8   7   6   5   4   3   2   1

For Chuck Tilly

Contents

Preface

For any readers who know my earlier work on large-scale American industrial corporations, the transition to the study of American folk music, social movements, and race may be curious. Indeed it is curious to me. The common thread in all my work is how social patterns and relations come to be historically. The original question that animated my choice of sociology as a career was how the American power structure described by C. Wright Mills and G. William Domhoff came into being. After deciding that the late nineteenth and early twentieth century was the critical turning point, I did a dissertation under the late Charles Tilly on the role of business in American foreign policy. That project revealed the critical role of corporations in particular and the surprising (to a young graduate student) discovery that large industrial corporations were quite rare until that period, when they suddenly blossomed to reign over the economy. Writing *Socializing Capital: The Rise of the Large Industrial Corporation in America* (1997, Princeton University Press) nurtured my interest in the broad question of how things that we now take for granted came to be. I began to tackle that general question in teaching undergraduate honors courses at UCLA, leading to *Making Societies: How Our World Came to Be* (2001, Pine Forge Press). Written for an undergraduate audience, it reflected on how several aspects of our taken-for-granted world in Western societies differ from other societies and how the Western understandings and practices came to be. Western societies have particular understandings of and practices embodying time, space, race, gender, class, and their intersections, which can be explained historically at particular times and places by the actions of specific actors. Through this project, my thinking was influenced by the cultural turn in sociology, especially the renewed interest in the arts, including music. Music has filled my life since childhood, but never in sociological terms. I participated in social movements in college and developed an unfulfilled scholarly commitment in graduate school. And my teaching helped focus an interest in the study of race. This project originally posed the question of how social movements helped shape the racial identity of American folk music, which began as explicitly and assertively white, and broadened to include all vernacular music by all Americans. But the 1960s commercial folk revival was, with few notable exceptions, distinctly white, though less by intention than default. As I investigated the role that social movements played in the development of folk music, I began to make note of the radically different social forms taken by different generations of movements in their musical activities. Sensitized by greater attention to social relations by musicologists such as Edward Small and music sociologists such as Tia DeNora, I became fascinated by the contrast between the Old Left, communist-inspired movement of the 1930s and 1940s and the civil rights movement of the 1960s. The Old Left's instrumental adoption of music as a weapon of propaganda was embedded in the familiar composer/performer/audience set of relations, even though musical leaders such as Pete Seeger aspired to build a singing movement. The civil rights movement, building on the repertoire and musical vision of the Old Left, used music as part of the collective action itself, singing on the picket line, freedom rides, even jail time. The line between composer, performer, and audience was blurred. Since both movements adopted folk music in part to reach across racial boundaries, I was especially interested in how the different social forms of music affected their relative success. That issue thus forms the agenda of this book.

Music and social movements have been widely celebrated as two catalysts that can elevate the human condition by lifting spirits and undermining subordination. Race has been one of the most pervasive forms of domination in the modern world, especially in America. While there is no pretense that music alone can fortify social movements to effectively confront the formidable structures and commitments that drive the engines of racial domination, examining the intersection of music, social movements, and race can hopefully deepen our understanding and appreciation for an important piece of the intricate and perplexing processes that improve the society we live in.

Most authors are acutely aware of what their books owe to others. A sociologist who studies how things come to be should be especially conscious. On a broad scale, this book is part of a stream of scholarship that intersects the study of social movements, cultural sociology, especially music sociology, and the study of race. Hopefully it will help each stream along. The study of social movements has increasingly included the role of culture and the arts. Not only do social movements have culture in the anthropological sense of shared understandings, they also do creative activity with music, art, drama, literature, and poetry. It is hoped that this book will contribute to that literature by exploring how the effects of the arts are as much a matter of the social relations within which they are embedded as their content. While social context is consequential for all the arts, the scholarship on music has more fully addressed issues of exactly how social relations of culture matter. Thus the book concludes with a discussion of how social movements *do* culture. The social dynamics of race have been central to American scholarship on social movements and the sociology of culture. Not only is race such a pervasive, puzzling, and profound dilemma for our society, the blossoming of social movement research in the last half century was sparked by a movement about race—the civil rights movement. This book has relatively little original to contribute to the sociology of race. Its contribution would be intended to reinforce that strand of scholarship that emphasizes the historically specific meaning and structures of race. As a historically constructed set of relationships, race is manifested in a particular bundle of rights, responsibilities, powers, and privileges that are encapsulated in the complex dynamics built on racially defined categorical difference. This bundle of rights, responsibilities, powers, and privileges—and thus race itself—changes as a result of particular actions by particular actors. Social movements have been important actors in the reshaping of race over the last two centuries, from the abolitionists forward. And the arts have been important in reinforcing racial boundaries or building bridges across them. This book builds on a growing literature revealing that process.

More immediately, particular individuals have inspired, informed, and improved this work. Most fundamentally, my graduate school advisor, Chuck Tilly, did all, though this particular project was far from what I could have imagined in that dim past. But as the project unfolded in my imagination, numerous conversations with him, along with a few drafts of early chapters (characteristically returned to me with terrific suggestions within days), helped me focus and think about it in new ways. Part of my motivation for this study was a desire, since I was a graduate student, to study social movements, a field that Tilly, as much as anyone, has shaped. Anyone who knew Chuck will know why a former student, even one thirty years from graduate school, would dedicate a book to him.

I began this project a novice in the sociology of music. A number of its leaders have taught me by example and in conversation. Tia DeNora has been a particular inspiration, in her brilliant scholarship, her stimulating conversation, and her generous reading of several chapters. Musicologists and ethnomusicologists at UCLA have graciously tutored me along, especially Lester Feder, Susan McClary, Tim Rice, Rob Waltzer, and Christopher Waterman. Other sociologists who have constructively commented on parts of the manuscript include Ron Aminzade, Howard Becker, Rogers Brubaker, Mary Ann Clawson, William Danaher, Timothy Dowd, Dick Flacks, David Grazian, David Halle, Nancy Hanrahan, Jennifer Lena, David McFarland, Richard (Pete) Peterson, Damon Philips, Vincent Roscigno, Rob Rosenthal, Gabriel Rossman, Violaine Roussell, Darby Southgate, and Peter Stamatov. Audiences at Emory University, UC Berkeley, and UCLA have made helpful suggestions. Folklorist Ronald Cohen has generously advised, encouraged, and helped me think through issues related to American folk music. I've been blessed with a series of talented, dedicated, and resourceful research assistants. On her way to a PhD in musicology, Barbara Moroncini began while an undergraduate and taught me expansively about music while helping lay the groundwork for the historical background. Jessica Read helped arrange interviews and dig through numerous archives. Gabrielle Raley helped elaborate historical issues and make the text more readable. Molly Jacobs shepherded the production process, especially the detail-work of securing permissions. The staff at the American Folklife Center of the Library of Congress, the Labadie Collection of American Radicalism at the University of Michigan, the Walter Reuther Library at Wayne State University, the Southern Folklife Collection at the University of North Carolina, and the Music Library at UCLA have all been exceptionally helpful. The research has been supported by grants from the Academic Senate of UCLA and the LeRoy Neiman Center for the Study of American Society and Culture at UCLA. Historical insight and details unavailable elsewhere were plentiful in interviews by the author with Guy and Candie Carawan, Barbara Dane, Archie Green, Bess Lomax Hawes, Joe Hickerson, Mike Seeger, Pete Seeger, and Irwin Silber. The editorial team at Princeton University Press has shepherded the production process expertly and congenially. The original editor on this project, Timothy Sullivan, helped shape the basic contours and provided encouragement at just the right time. His successor, Eric Schwartz, picked it up without a hitch and has had just the right mix of professionalism and support. Eric's assistant, Janie Chan, has helped with numerous details that authors try to avoid. Ellen Foos, the senior production editor, has executed the high production values for which Princeton is well known. Jennifer Backer has rescued the manuscript from many of the infelicities that I penned. Natalie Baan provided exacting and expert proofreading of the final page proofs and Rocio Rosales compiled the index with great care. My wife Alice has supported the project in every way imaginable—emotionally, intellectually, and editorially. It is a much better book for her contribution and I am a more balanced person. Remaining errors are, of course, my own.

Reds, Whites, and Blues

CHAPTER ONE

Social Movements, Music, and Race

On December 23, 1938, the left-wing magazine *New Masses* sponsored a concert in New York's Carnegie Hall titled "From Spirituals to Swing," featuring some of America's now-legendary African American performers, including Count Basie, Sister Rosetta Tharp, Sonny Terry, and the Golden Gate Quartet. The program notes put the music in social context: "It expresses America so clearly that its readiest recognition here has come from the masses, particularly youth. While the intelligentsia has been busy trying to water our scrawny cultural tree with European art and literary movements, this thing has come to maturity unnoticed" ("From Spirituals to Swing" program). One of the songs, "I'm on My Way," could be heard a quarter century later in freedom rallies in places like Albany, Georgia. Commentators again embraced the sounds of African American culture as the music of America. Other parallels are found. The 1938 concert and 1961 Albany musicking each occurred during a peak of social movement activity, the communist-led Old Left that resulted in the unionization of America's core industrial sector, and the civil rights movement that crippled the insidious system of legalized racial segregation. In both, African Americans and whites joined to make music, challenging the dominant racial order that infected all aspects of social life. The aspirations of both movements to bridge racial boundaries with music were explicit—wedding black music (spirituals) and black-inspired white music (swing) in one event and invoking a universal principle (freedom) in the other. And both were but one moment of many in larger cultural projects that have used music in pursuit of social change.

But the contrasts were equally important. Most important, "From Spirituals to Swing" was a performance. One group of people sang and played for another, who participated as an audience. As such it succeeded, parlaying the popularity of such stars as Benny Goodman to launch performers like the Golden Gate Quartet and inject popular music with African American sensibilities. Still, the larger leftist movement was not able to change the musical tastes of their core target constituency, the American working class. Freedom songs, on the other hand, though made familiar by media coverage of the movement, had relatively little commercial impact. They did, however, have a huge impact on the movement, affording racially diverse activists the opportunity to join together in a somatic experience of unity. This distinction is the theme of this book: the social form of music—specifically the relationship between those who sing and those who listen—reflects and shapes the social relationship between social movement leaders and participants, conditioning the effect that music can have on movement outcomes.

THE PROBLEM

I demonstrate the effects of the social relationships *within* music on the social effects *of* music with a comparison of the Old Left/communist-led movement of the 1930s and 1940s with the civil rights movement of the 1950s and 1960s. Both movements self-consciously adopted folk music as a cultural project, both motivated by the potential of folk music to bridge racial boundaries, but with very different effects. The Old Left succeeded in boosting folk music from an esoteric genre meaningful to academics and antiquarians into a genre of popular music familiar to ordinary Americans. But it was never embraced by their rank-and-file constituents, especially the African Americans they aspired to mobilize. The civil rights movement, in contrast, had little interest in putting freedom songs on the charts. Even those that eventually became universally known, such as "We Shall Overcome," were never commercial hits. But participating in the movement meant doing music. The impact of "We Shall Overcome" and other freedom songs was less important for their mass appeal than in the activity of blacks and whites joining arms and singing together. Thus the thesis of the book is that the effect of music on social movement activities and outcomes depends less on the meaning of the lyrics or the sonic qualities of the performance than on the social relationships within which it is embedded. This implies that music is fundamentally social. Accounts and perspectives that focus solely on textual meaning or sonic qualities disregard a profound sociological dimension of how music operates in social interaction. Music is a social relationship, and glossing over the interaction of people around music clouds over the explanatory power that sociological analysis can bring.

FOLK MUSIC IN AMERICAN CULTURE

Folk music has played a special role in twentieth-century politics and culture. In contrast to Europe, where folk music is characteristically associated with nationalist sentiment, American folk music carries a distinctively leftist tinge. If any American style is associated with the left as a genre, not just songs with radical lyrics, it is folk music. Alan Lomax, perhaps the most influential definer of what American folk music is, explained folk music's appeal: "first, in our longing for artistic forms that reflect our democratic and equalitarian political beliefs; and second, in our hankering after art that mirrors the unique life of this western continent—the life of the frontier, the great West, the big city. We are looking for a people's culture, a culture of the common man" (2003a: 86). These themes—the political, the nostalgic, and the populist—have been intertwined, weaving a consistent symbolic thread through the music's history. The combination is powerful. Many Old Leftists remember Woody Guthrie and Paul Robeson more vividly and fondly than any Communist Party official. Ask any graying veteran of the civil rights movement to recall the era and it is often the recollection of "We Shall Overcome" that makes him or her choke up.

The political meaning of folk music is based on its "ownership" by the left. The Old Left activists in the 1930s and 1940s and the civil rights activists of the 1960s claimed folk music as their own. As we shall see, American folk music had originally more of a nationalist, even racial connotation. The nostalgic meanings of folk music initially had more affinity with a conservative critique of modernism, affirming simple, rural life in the face of industrialization and urbanization. But the Old Left redefined the genre, tapping its populist overtones as "the people's music" on behalf of radicalism. This was music (supposedly) unspoiled by phonographs or radios, music from people who made a living by honest toil, who retained the pioneer spirit that made America great. It was music based not on the banalities of "June, croon, and spoon" but the rugged experiences of logging, sailing, children dying, and outlaws. And it was music that came from the heart and spoke to the heart. Rather than a song written to sell records, folk music was seen as music that reflected the real-life experiences of real people, singing about things that mattered. Ballads told stories of people's lives, work songs set the rhythm of toil, spirituals voiced sorrow and hope, and reels offered a respite from the toil.[1]

The meaning of folk music, its appeal, and the social relationships it reinforces or erodes are not inherent features of the genre. The concept of folk music is socially constructed, in the sense that its origins must be explained historically. It is the result of specific cultural projects—coordinated, self-conscious attempts by specific actors to create or reshape a genre. As elaborated below, the projects that shaped American folk music endowed it with a political message, appealed to a specific constituency, and set it within particular social relationships. Among the most contested issues was the definition of who constituted "the folk" of folk music. In the American context that means that race hovered over these projects, as activists struggled to include or exclude racial minorities, especially African Americans.

But before we get to the story, we need to clarify the issues at stake. The thesis that the Old Left was less successful than the civil rights movement at using folk music to bridge racial boundaries but more successful in making it a permanent part of American popular music intersects three areas of sociology: social movements, the sociology of music, and the sociology of race.

SOCIAL MOVEMENTS

A social movement can be defined as a form of contentious politics with three elements: (1) there are campaigns of collective claims against targets, usually powerful organizations like governments or corporations; (2) these campaigns draw on a widely shared repertoire of organizational forms, public meetings and demonstrations, marches, and so forth; and (3) the campaigns make public representations of their worthiness, unity, numbers, and commitment. Social movements are contentious insofar as they make claims, which if realized would adversely affect the interests of some other group (Tilly 2004b).

Sociologists began to pay serious attention to social movements after they, like just about everyone else, failed to anticipate the proliferation of social movements in the 1960s. The issue garnering the largest share of attention has been why social movements arise when and where they do and why people join them. In response to scholars who explained social movements as non-rational responses to social strain, most sociologists in the 1960s and 1970s emphasized organizational processes, the mobilization of resources, and the opportunities afforded by the political context. In the 1980s and 1990s scholars broadened the agenda to examine cultural factors (Alexander 1996; Eyerman and Jamison 1991; Jasper 1997; Johnston and Klandermans 1995; Kane 1997; Snow et al. 1986). But the agenda remained focused on why social movements arise and why people join them.

Less common until recently has been work on what social movements actually do, especially with culture, and what consequences have ensued. What social movements actually do comprises not just the activities such as demonstrations, marches, sit-ins, and strikes that presumably achieve goals but also the mundane activities of meeting, chatting, debating, and deliberating. Most of the literature on what social movements do assumes that activities are designed either to achieve the official goals of the movement, "social change" of some sort, or to recruit and retain members.[2] Scholars have long examined how internal relations affect the achievement of goals.[3]

While social movements do mobilize organizations to recruit members and carry out collective actions, much of the time is spent hanging out and meeting. As the title of Polletta's book on participatory democracy succinctly puts it, "freedom is an endless meeting." Polletta shows that social movements construct their internal social relationships on implicit or analogical templates of other social relationships. American movements that intentionally organized themselves around participatory democracy evoked familiar analogies to guide their practices. For some, a social movement was like a religious fellowship in which those with conscience were invited to deliberate until a consensus was achieved. Pacifist movements often followed this mode. Other movements followed a model of tutelage or tutorial, in which leaders or organizers elicited the concerns and aspirations of political novices to empower grassroots upheaval. Finally, many movements operated as groups of friends in which trust and personal commitment solidified the arduous work of setting goals and making decisions.

People who create social movements shape the social relations within them—both with constituents and with targets—on the basis of taken-for-granted templates from their experience tempered by the kinds of goals they are pursuing. Social movements are constructed not only in the image of other social movements but in the image of other institutions. Social movements can be modeled on quasi-political parties, churches, families, schools, clubs, armies, and even firms. These templates influence the kind of leadership, hierarchy, and authority, whether the movement organization has membership, and, if so, the openness of membership and obligations of membership.

These relationships within an organization are one of the main determinants of what social movements do with culture. A movement patterned after a political party is more likely to use culture to recruit and educate a targeted constituency than one patterned after a church, in which culture plays more of an expressive function reinforcing solidarity and commitment. When culture is used for recruitment and education, the emphasis is more on the political content than the form. In contrast, a movement using culture to fortify solidarity is more likely to attend to the social relations within the cultural practices. This is the pattern found in the use of music by the Old Left in the 1930s and 1940s and the civil rights movement in the 1960s. The former used music, as they used theater, dance, poetry, fiction, and art, as a weapon of propaganda, a vehicle to carry an ideological message. Even though the people who promoted music in that musical project hoped that members and constituents would fully participate in music and developed a new form of participatory music, the hootenanny, the social relations inside the movement did not foster broad cultural participation.[4] The fundamental relationship of culture remained performers and audiences. The musical activities of the Old Left were inspirational and supplied many of the songs for the civil rights movement, but they were refracted through a different set of social relations. The civil rights movement was rooted in a social institution used to doing music collectively, the church. The meetings where new members were recruited, where decisions were made, and where collective action was planned evoked religious services in both form and function. Most of the people were used to singing together when they gathered in groups. The social relationships were more like congregational singing than performers and audiences. Dr. Martin Luther King explicitly made the analogy between the movement and the church: "The invitational periods at the mass meetings, when we asked for volunteers, were much like those invitational periods that occur every Sunday morning in Negro churches, when the pastor projects the call to those present to join the church. By twenties and thirties and forties, people came forward to join our army" (1963: 59).

What does this tell us about social movements and music? First, it tells us that social movements mobilize around culture. Culture is not just something that movements have; it is something they do. What movements do with culture is just as important as the culture they have. Most of the literature on culture and social movements treats culture as a mental characteristic of the participants, asking either how the mental modes by which participants handle symbols affect their propensity to act or what meanings actions have for participants (Eyerman and Jamison 1991; Jasper 1997; Johnston and Klandermans 1995; Kane 1991; Steinberg 1999). Social movements develop identifiable organizations that bring people together, employ resources, and seek goals. Without organizations that have erected apparatuses and mobilized resources, social movements will either fail to develop culture or lose control of the culture, as happened with the New Left of the 1960s.

My concept of culture differs somewhat from the best-known book on the topic, Eyerman and Jamison's excellent *Music and Social Movements* (1998). They frame their analysis around the concept of "cognitive praxis," which they define as knowledge-producing activities that are carried out within social movements (1998: 7). This is consistent with their view that social movements are basically knowledge-bearing entities and that their main consequence is cultural change. Culture is treated as a symbolic and discursive realm existing at the social level but operationally found in individual expression. That is, culture is treated as something "out there" in the society but internalized in individuals, who provide a window on society. Insofar as culture is a system, it is a system of symbols and meanings. Analysis thus focuses on the content of that system more than the concrete social relations that embed it. Thus, cognitive praxis focuses on the relationship between the social movement and the mind of the activist.

Eyerman and Jamison open their book telling about a 1995 memorial celebration for folk music activist Ralph Rinzler at the Highlander Center (which is discussed in chapter 7): "We saw, and felt, how songs could conjure up long-lost social movements, and how music could provide an important vehicle for the diffusion of movement ideas into the broader culture" (1998: 1). This interpretation misses one of the most fundamental differences between the musical achievements of the Communist Party and those of the civil rights movement.

Diffusing cultural content or cultural forms is not the same as developing a rich cultural life within a movement. Movements vary in the extent to which they develop a distinctive cultural life in contrast to or at odds with the broader culture. Just as the literature on framing problematizes the consonance or dissonance of ideological or discursive worldviews between movements and broader audiences, analysts of culture must problematize the alignment of aesthetic content and form. A movement's ability to contribute to and even shape culture in the larger public is analytically and often empirically different from its ability to sustain a vibrant cultural world within its own ranks. Moreover, when movements do develop their own cultural vitality they differ in the extent to which their aesthetic tastes align with those of their constituencies. In contrast to the Communist Party, which was more successful at diffusing movement culture into the broader culture, the civil rights movement was more successful at facilitating music as an integral part of collective action that actually informed movement practice.

CULTURAL PROJECTS

The work that social movements do to use culture on behalf of movement goals can be called a cultural project. For social movements, a cultural project is a self-conscious attempt to use music, art, drama, dance, poetry, or other cultural materials, to recruit new members, to enhance the solidarity of members, or to persuade outsiders to adopt the movement's program.[5] Often carried out by specialists in the movement, they typically deliberately decide which genres to adopt, the cultural forms that are appropriate, how culture contributes to the goals of the movement, and what makes culture political. They also to some extent develop a cultural infrastructure, producing, distributing, and promoting their cultural work. Both the Old Left in the 1930s and 1940s and the civil rights movement in the 1960s adopted American folk music as a cultural project. They not only extolled the music but built organizational infra-structures and adopted specific practices to use folk music in their collec-tive action. But they did so in different social relations with different consequences.

Social movements have typically done cultural work for two purposes: to persuade outsiders to adopt new beliefs or ideologies while recruiting new members (culture-in-content), and to galvanize the solidarity of ex-isting members or deepen the boundaries between insiders and outsiders (culture-in-relations) (Denisoff 1983; Eyerman and Jamison 1998; Rosci-gno and Danaher 2004; Rosenthal and Flacks 2009). Scholars have ana-lyzed culture-in-content more closely, especially by examining the process of framing by which social movements align their messages with the broader culture and attempt to bring audiences closer to themselves (Ben-ford and Snow 2000; W. Gamson 1992; Snow et al. 1986; Tarrow 1998). The Old Left, especially the Communist Party, primarily conceived of culture as a propaganda weapon in an ideological war to jolt the working class out of their false consciousness.[6] The Composers Collective vividly demonstrated their orientation toward culture in their 1934 *Workers Songbook*.

> Music Penetrates Everywhere
> It Carries Words With It
> It Fixes Them In the Mind
> It Graves Them In the Heart
> Music is a Weapon in the Class Struggle
> (Lieberman 1995: 28)

The cultural work that enhances solidarity is often quite different from culture for recruitment because the dynamics of in-group and out-group affiliation can clash (Simmel 1955). In-group solidarity is often cultivated by engaging in practices that reinforce boundaries between members and non-members. Social movements, like all organizations, often find they can increase commitment by emphasizing how different (how much smarter, enlightened, moral, committed, or important) members are from others. Cultural work can thus take the form of rituals that are meaning-ful primarily to the initiated, with specialized symbols, language, and ac-tivities. This is one of the dynamics that facilitates the marginalization of sectarian organizations in which members become increasingly commit-ted and peripheral. It is a special problem in stigmatized movements that must offer members compensating structures of meaning to replace what their stigma has denied them. Lieberman has described the rich cultural life of Communist Party members in New York after World War II when membership often came at the price of friendship, jobs, housing, and even family ties. She has argued that the project of using culture to reach broader audiences for persuasion and recruitment increasingly turned inward to build solidarity within the movement (Denning 1996; Lieberman 1995; Reuss and Reuss 2000).[7] The civil rights movement had less need to convince people of the legitimacy of their goals than did the Old Left. The country was polarized between those who supported racial segregation and those who opposed it. The movement's constituency needed little persuasion to support the movement but much nurturing to become active and persevere against intimidation. Especially before it developed other cultural projects, music was absolutely critical to the movement.[8]

Different social movements not only adopt different genres for cultural projects and seek different goals through their projects; they do cultural work through different kinds of social relationships. To fully fathom how the social relations in the movement shaped the effect of their musical activities, it is necessary to determine what is sociological about music.

What Is Sociological about Music?

In a field as underdeveloped as the sociology of music, there is still little consensus about fundamental questions of theory and method. Scholarship conducted under the rubric of sociology of music draws on a broad variety of assumptions about how music enters into social interaction, how it relates to social boundaries such as race, gender, and class, how it expresses meaning (or does not), and even what we mean by music. The differences run deeper than the ordinary divisions between conventional schools of thought such as symbolic interactionism, identity-based theories, or network analysis because the nature of music itself is at stake.

The sociological salience of music can be framed in terms of three sets of questions. (1) Ontology: in terms of social relations, what *is* music? (2) Meaning: how do people create meaning from or in relationship to music? (3) Function: what does music do in social relationships and what do people do with music? While I cannot offer a grand theory of the sociology of music, it will help clarify the analysis of social movements, race, and music to concisely situate my perspective relative to others. The purpose is less to thoroughly vet, much less adjudicate, different perspectives than to frame my analysis within a broader context. The Old Left and the civil rights movement adopted very different implicit orientations toward these issues. While neither overtly theorized music in these terms, their different assumptions about the social nature of music help explain the different consequences of their doing music.

Ontology: What Music Is

At the most basic level scholars differ over what music is. Assumptions about what music is are related to what one does with music, the social relationships in which music is done, and the relationship between activity and context. Bohlman (1999) has identified three ontological approaches to music, conceptualizing music as an object, as a process, and as being embedded.[9]

First, most commonly, at least in the West, music is treated as an object, a *thing* that has the characteristics we attribute to objects, such as a moment of creation, stability of characteristics over its lifetime, stability of characteristics between contexts, and consistency of cause-and-effect relations. Rather than debating whether music should be treated as an object or not, it is more fruitful to problematize music's "objectness." Institutional settings that produce musical objects such as orchestras, record companies, publishers, and critics all continually render music as an object by asserting that what they are doing is independent of context. Institutional practices such as copyright and technologies such as notation and recording constrain musicians to concretize performances into singular, repeatable, named pieces of music called songs. Thus early blues singers, used to cobbling a performance from a standard repertoire of lines, riffs, and embellishments, were told by recording companies to perform "songs" that could be labeled on the records and copyrighted by the company. The institution of the market and the technology of recording then enabled the commodification of the music so that listening could become a specialized activity in a context independent from performance. In contrast, actors who explicitly embed music in contexts such as dancing, religion, sports events, or social movements weaken music's objectness.

The two social movements examined here treated music differently in terms of its objectness. While the Old Left emphatically rejected the extreme objectification of music embodied in the commercial definition that made music an item of property, and despite their ambitions to make music a spontaneously recurring event in the progressive movement, for the most part they treated music as an object, a set of songs distributed by the technologies of notated print and recorded sound. Their success in introducing folk music to broad audiences depended on the development of institutional structure with record companies, magazines, books, and live performances organizationally similar to commercial music. While the civil rights movement also treated music as a thing to some extent, codifying songs such as "We Shall Overcome" and distributing books and magazines, relative to the Old Left they treated music more as a process, training song leaders at places like the Highlander School, using "zipper songs" that could be adapted for the purpose at hand, and incorporating the folk process into their activities.

Bohlman's second ontological orientation to music is process. Rather than an object with fixed qualities, music can be treated as something always becoming that never achieves full objective status, something unbounded and open. When music is shared by a collectivity, its evolution is more readily observable and the mechanisms that objectify it are typically weaker. Shared music, as seen in the folk music process, passes from hand to hand and mouth to mouth, adapting, elaborating, unfolding, and simplifying. Christopher Small advocates treating music as a verb—*musicking*—rather than a noun, highlighting process in contrast to a noun's objectness.

> Music is not a thing at all but an activity, something that people do. The apparent thing "music" is a figment, an abstraction of the action, whose reality vanishes as soon as we examine it at all closely. This habit of thinking in abstractions, of taking from an action what appears to be its essence and of giving that essence a name, is probably as old as language; it is useful in the conceptualizing of our world but has its dangers. (1998: 2)

This perspective is more inherently sociological, shifting the agenda to what people are doing when they compose, perform, listen, discuss, dance to, worship to, or imagine music. It is especially germane to folk music, which is often treated in process terms, highlighting the folk process.

Even more sociological is Bohlman's third aspect of ontology, focusing on its embeddedness, treating it as part of another social activity, inseparable from it (1999). Here music is treated in terms of its function for a social activity. A hymn becomes something other than a hymn when taken out of a religious setting, as does a folk song when piped into an elevator.[10] Based on the ethnomethodological concern with problematizing how order is achieved, in this perspective music "is" what it does and its salient features are defined in terms of the social relationships within which it is embedded. Commercial music created, produced, and distributed through monetary exchange is treated as fundamentally different from religious music that fuses individual worshipers into a congregation collectively creating the social presence of a deity. The music is seen not only as influencing the event, as though the event could exist without it, but helping constitute the event itself. For many, a religious service without hymns does not feel fully like a religious service, nor does an aerobics class without music feel quite real. Music helps order the pace, feel, and energy of interaction that make the events "really" what they are. Thus music helps order the events both in the sense of providing a proper sequence (confession before redemption, warm-up before intense exercise) and the deeper sense of social order—how people relate to each other through precognitive structuring (DeNora 2000). Music thus *entrains* interaction, coordinating how people interact, whether the mutual silence of the classical concert, the cool ambiance of the jazz club, the solitary bubble of the student walking with earphones, dancers at the disco, or worshipers at a religious service (Blacking and Byron 1995; Clayton, Sager, and Will 2005).

Embeddedness is especially important for social movements. This book argues that the extent to which movements treat music as an object, a process, or an embedded activity helps constitute the movements themselves and affects what they achieve. The Old Left treated music primarily as an object, while being mindful of musical processes. Most often for them music meant performers singing for and with audiences to heighten consciousness and foster solidarity. The civil rights movement conceptualized music more as embedded in collective action and adopted processes to facilitate its use in such settings. Their vision was of people singing on picket lines and demonstrations, a vision shared by many Old Left activists but rarely achieved.

Meaning

Beyond the ontological question of what music *is*, the sociology of music presents distinctive challenges for questions of meaning, offering insights often neglected in sociological discussions of meaning in general. The question posed here is the extent to which meaning is to be located in the music, whether lyrics or sonic qualities, or in the context. And insofar as meaning is created in context, to what extent is it constructed in concrete social activities or in the discourse about it?[11] The analysis in this book runs against the grain of most musical scholarship, focusing on context more than the music itself.

Rather than engage in the voluminous debates about what meaning is, I will simply state my definition: meaning is the system of symbols by which people make sense of the world in the context of interaction. It is more a set of activities—interpretation, exchange, reflection—than a product. Meaning is fundamentally sociological insofar as it happens through interaction and makes interaction possible. I agree with DeNora (2003) that the question of *how* musical meaning is achieved is more sociologically interesting than the question of what it *is*.

The semiotic approach of analyzing musical meaning is typically studied by putting the analyst in the role of the listener, decoding meanings just as one does in language (Cooke 1959; Feld and Fox 1994; Shepherd and Wicke 1997; Treitler 1997). For some, the meaning is found in music's sonic qualities. Cerulo, for example, has offered a sociological account of how meaning can be interpreted from the semiotic structure of music in the relationship of notes to each other, simultaneously (harmony) and temporally (melody). In this perspective, "Music is a form of communication, and like other forms of communication—language, numbers, pictures—it is a symbol system by which senders convey thoughts, emotions, and information to receivers" (1995: 43–44).

When scholars discuss the political meaning of music, they typically refer to the lyrics. Political sentiments have often been expressed musically. People with political commitments have certainly turned to music as a means of expressing their ideals, often with the expectation that listeners might be persuaded by the lyrics. And movements have often embraced songs that crystallize their core beliefs.

There is increasing debate about how effectively lyrics carry messages and how persuasive they are, especially for people who do not agree with their message. Frith asserts that there is no evidence that the content of lyrics affects beliefs (or even reflects them). The words of songs, he says, are not about ideas but about expression: "It is not that love songs give people a false, sentimental, and fatalistic view of sexual relationships, but that romantic ideology requires such a view and makes love songs necessary" (1996: 164; Frith, Hall, and Du Gay 1996).[12]

This book has little to say about the lyrics of songs in the movements. To the extent that meaning matters, I believe sonic qualities are at least as important as lyrics, both because performers and listeners generally pay more attention to sound than words and because the impact of sound is deeper and less conscious than that of words.[13] The Old Left's greater focus on lyrics is part of the explanation for why their musicking less effectively bridged racial boundaries than did the civil rights movement. The music that energized collective action was not the music with the most meaningful lyrics but the music that fit its ritual use, from "Solidarity Forever" in the 1930s to "We Shall Overcome" in the 1960s. Many of the freedom songs in fact had little obvious political content.

The semiotic approach that finds meaning in music's sonic qualities or lyrics is challenged by contextualists, who argue that meaning resides less in the notes than in the social relations of those involved in doing music. DeNora, for example, charges that semiotic approaches "often conflate ideas about music's affect with the ways that music actually works for and is used by its recipients instead of exploring how such links are forged by situated actors" (2000: 22). Feld similarly advocates going beyond semiotic readings of music to investigate "the primacy of symbolic action in an ongoing intersubjective life world, and the ways engagement in symbolic action continually builds and shapes actors' perceptions and meanings" (1984: 383). The most explicit argument for a contextual view of music comes from Christopher Small.

The act of musicking establishes in the place where it is happening a set of relationships, and it is in those relationships that the meaning of the act lies. They are to be found not only between those organized sounds which are conventionally thought of as being the stuff of musical meaning but also between the people who are taking part, in whatever capacity, in the performance; and they model, or stand as metaphor for, ideal relationships as the participants in the performance imagine them to be: relationships between person and person, between individual and society, between humanity and the natural world and even perhaps the supernatural world. (1998: 13)

This implies that the meaning is never purely in the music because there is never *a* meaning. Meanings emerge in interaction as people do music (including listening and discussing) and are often about music. Political meanings develop from modes of musical interaction in composing, adapting, performing, listening, singing along with chanting, picketing, passing time in jail, and recollecting about music. Thus the meaning of "We Shall Overcome" is very different when sung at an organizing meeting in Albany, Georgia, in 1961, played as background music in a documentary about the civil rights movement, sung by Joan Baez on a commercial album, or played in a college class on twentieth-century American history. The sounds of the first two and last two examples may be identical, but the meaning is not because the relationship of the performers and audiences is very different. The kinds of social relationships within the various groups in the musical worlds of the Old Left and the civil rights movement embodied different modes of making meaning and different structures of mediating meaning to action.

For many people the meaning of music comes at least as much from talk about music as how they hear music. People do not just do music, they talk about it. They talk about it a great deal. The discourse about music is one of the most important ways that music is sociological, a social activity that cannot be explained from only the music itself, either the sonic qualities or the lyrics. The way that people talk about music—what they say, what it means to them, and how discourse underlies social relationships—is inseparable from how people hear music and what it means to them. Cruz, for example, describes how white abolitionists embraced slave spirituals in a discourse that reflected their ambivalence toward African Americans. In discourse studies, the social importance of music lies less in music itself than in how people talk about it. As he puts it, "Music is prophetic only in *post hoc* accounts, by after-the-fact outcomes that appear to validate human desires and anticipation. In such cases it is not music, but the social movements upon which music rides that matter. . . . It is not music's 'prophetic' capacities that warrant examination, but rather the complex processes by which social relations and social disruption are sounded and heard through music's noisiness" (1999: 64).

While musical discourse cannot be reduced to the music itself, discourse cannot be separated from the meaning or experience of music. DeNora emphasizes that discourse is not just *about* music but coproduces the meaning. Social significance is not pre-given but is apprehended within specific circumstances. She advocates a reflexive conception of meaning that considers aspects of the music itself, its context, and the discourse about it. Frith similarly discusses how the social bonds created by music come from talking about it and making judgments. Thus the racial and sexual connotations of rock and roll, he argues, arose more from the discourse around them than from the sonic qualities of sound. Blacks are discursively associated with the body and whites with the mind. Sonically the upbeat rhythms of rock and roll are less evocative of the sex act than is the lush sensation of seduction music. It was the racist discourse against rock and roll, he argues, more than the music itself that accounts for its sexual cultural connotation. Musical meaning is thus refracted through the discourse about it: "To grasp the meaning of a piece of music is to hear something not simply present to the ear. It is to understand a musical culture, to have 'a scheme of interpretation.' ... The 'meaning' of music describes, in short, not just an interpretive but a social process: musical meaning is not inherent (however 'ambiguously') in the text" (Frith 1996: 249–50).

Function

While meaning is essential to a sociological analysis of music, I will contend that the uses of music were more important than its meaning in explaining why the Old Left and civil rights movement had different effects.[14] But such programmatic statements still do not tell us what is sociological about how music is used. For that we turn to Schutz's concept of the precommunicative basis of interaction. By precommunicative interaction, he means interaction that is based not on the semantic content of symbols but on the temporally structured mutual orientation through gestures, coordination, turn taking, and so forth. To interact, people must orient toward others, not only in terms of intention but also in terms of what is going on. Precommunicative interaction is especially clear in nonverbal interaction such as team sports, dancing, walking on a busy sidewalk, making love, and doing music. "Tuning in" thus underlies the relationship in specific dimensions of time (Schutz 1964). By this logic music is not a non-social activity in social context but is context in and of itself (A. Seeger 2004). Just as turn taking, repairing interruptions, and the mutual reinforcement of grammatical rules make conversation possible, music is based on synchronized interaction and organization of sound. The interactions around musicking are critical not only to what it means but to what it does. Playing music, listening to it with others, dancing to it, or protesting with it are very different activities (DeNora 2000).

The social impact of music happens not only through a common understanding of it or the discourse around it but also through the experience of simultaneity. The mutual synchronizing of sonic and bodily experience creates a bond that is precommunicative and perhaps deeper than shared conscious meaning. This can happen through the interaction of composers and performers, performers and performers, performers and listeners, and listeners and listeners. The more involved a person is in doing music, whether in composing, performing, or listening, the tighter the bond is.

McNeill has documented the effects of temporally coordinated bodily activities on group functioning. Marching, calisthenics, chanting, singing, dancing, religious ritual, and other synchronized actions foster a form of solidarity richer and more robust than cognitive agreement: "Moving our muscles rhythmically and giving voice consolidate group solidarity by altering human feelings" (1995: viii). He describes his experience in basic training during World War II: "Words are inadequate to describe the emotion aroused by the prolonged movement in unison that drilling involved. A sense of pervasive well-being is what I recall; more specifically, a strange sense of personal enlargement; a sort of swelling out, becoming bigger than life, thanks to participation in collective ritual" (1995: 2). It was something felt, not talked about; that is, it was precommunicative. Emotion created a basis for social cohesion. The coordinated activities engendered a "boundary loss," the submergence of the self in the flow, the feeling of being part of a larger collectivity. Muscular bonding—whether the rigors of boot camp or making love—can fuse a relationship so deeply that people can be willing to risk life for it. McNeill even attributes the success of European armies over others partly to their drilling.

Thus bonds forged by musicking together can afford (but not necessarily create) other kinds of bonds. The bonds forged by musicking together may thus explain why the civil rights movement was more effective at bridging racial boundaries than was the Old Left.[15] Processes that redefine boundaries are especially important in situations involving conflict. Social movements attempt to redraw or reinforce boundaries. When redrawing boundaries they seek to eliminate cleavages of privilege, demarginalize the marginal, and bring together groups previously considered distinct. Whether they are redrawing or reinforcing boundaries, they seek to create solidarity among contenders, forge new identities, and enhance the feeling of belonging.

If music entrains social relations among people doing it, it is sociological, not just as a cultural object that people react to but as an activity that helps constitute other activities. As DeNora has discussed at length, we need to study what people do *to* music (do while musicking), what activities music is an element of. With music we play (in the sense of playing games, not playing music), shop, work, exercise, walk, make love, relax, dance, socialize, worship, drive, read, write, protest, and pass time (DeNora 2000). Small has ethnographically described how putatively "pure" listening in a classical concert is a carefully choreographed activity with precise expectations for its physical setting, the behavior of its performers, and the behavior of listeners, demanding a monopoly of everyone's body, if not their mind (1998). The experience for the audience involves not just hearing the sounds but sitting in neat rows as part of a crowd in an expansive, ornate hall, focusing on a conductor reproducing the intentions of the composer. All the actions we do *to* music involve interaction or the avoidance of interaction (passing time, working). We select music (or the music is selected for us) to do whatever we are doing the way we (or someone else) want to do it. You can shop quickly or leisurely, work intensely or at a steady pace, make love in frenzy or in lush sweetness, worship reflectively or magisterially. Music does not single-handedly determine the mood or the terms of interaction around activity, but it does, along with the physical context, interactive scripts, understanding of roles, and prior history, help shape the definition of what is being done and how it is done.

Three social functions of music are especially salient for this study: bounding, bridging, and ranking. The complex and at times paradoxical effects of music on reinforcing social distinctions, reaching across them, and facilitating or inverting hierarchy pose a challenge to sociology. "The trumpet's loud clangour / Excites us to arms," wrote Dryden in the seventeenth century, but Congreve rejoined that "Music has charms to soothe a savage breast." This duality is less a debate than a reflection of music's implication in a wide variety of social effects. Social distinctions are built and undermined; either process can, under different conditions, exacerbate or ease inequality. Music can play all these roles.

Bounding refers to the social mechanisms that create and sustain consequential categorical distinctions among people (Bowker and Star 1999; Lamont and Fournier 1992; Lamont and Molnár 2002; Roy 2001; Tilly 2004a; Zerubavel 1991). Music helps both create and mark consequential distinctions such as race, ethnicity, gender, class, generation, and region. The music that people perform and listen to, the way that they perform and listen, the meanings they attach to music and the contexts in which they do music are often signs that mark people as members of groups and that create or reinforce those distinctions. Anthony Seeger explains that for the Suyá of Brazil, music gives the individual identity, constitutes social relationships of village, and "re-creates, re-establishes, or alters the significance of singing and also of the persons, times, places, and audiences involved. It expresses the status, sex, and feelings of performers, and it brings these to the attention of the entire community" (2004: 65). It is not so very different in our society. Music does not just "reflect" race, gender, class, age, and so forth but helps create them. Part of doing race or doing gender is doing music, captured in the way that people perform, listen, and talk about music in particular ways that help make people white, black, Latino, or Asian, or male and female.

Music is equally important sociologically in its ability to reach across boundaries and bridge social relationships. It is not just Longfellow who has felt that "Music is the universal language of mankind." Some would explain music's universal qualities from its abstract form, assuming that it has no literal meaning that can link it to social groups. They would say that any racial, ethnic, gender, class, or generational meaning is arbitrary and relatively plastic. It is thus relatively easy for people to embrace music across boundaries, as seen in the diffusion of classical music beyond Europe or the popularity of World Music within it. Others find in music universal meaning—love, anguish, awe, beauty, and redemption.

Bounding and bridging are two mechanisms that shape a society's system of alignment between cultural boundaries (genre distinctions in arts, music, literature, etc.) and social boundaries. At one end of the continuum, a situation that can be described as heterology, we can imagine societies where genre distinctions have no relationship to non-cultural social distinctions.[16] Since heterology is merely a hypothetical possibility, sociologists have not addressed it. They have, however, widely discussed homology, the other end of the continuum (DeNora 2002; Frith 1996; Frith 1989; Lipsitz 2000; P. Martin 1995; Shepherd 1989; Shepherd and Wicke 1997). Homology is the principle that the structure of music parallels the structure of society.[17] The relationships between cultural distinctions like genres and social boundaries like race are said to be homologous to the extent that they align along similar dimensions of difference. If some genres are considered black, white, or Latino, or male or female, or high status or low status, or young or old, the cultural and social structures are homologous.

Because the groups that are bridged and bounded by music are rarely socially equal, music plays an important role in sustaining and reconfiguring social hierarchy. The relationship of music to social inequality has been the focus of some of the theoretically richest and most widely discussed sociological work on music. From mass society theory that dominated American sociology of culture in the 1950s and 1960s to more recent theories of cultural capital to a smaller literature on music as a form of social control, scholars have investigated the role that music plays in creating and sustaining inequality (Adorno 2000; Bourdieu 1984; Bryson 1996; DiMaggio 1982a; Levine 1988; McClary 2000; Peterson 1997b; C. Seeger 1957). But more recently sociologists have focused on how music can undermine hierarchy, breaching the cultural foundations of domination, inciting social movements, and at times turning social hierarchies on their heads.

Folk music inverts the conventional relationship between cultural and social hierarchy. The cultural elite of the folk project have valorized folk music precisely because it is the music of the common folk. The more marginal, humble, and unsophisticated the makers of music the better, at least from the perspective of the educated, urban folk enthusiasts. The very qualities that ordinarily would commend music as respectable are treated as shortcomings in folk music—sophistication, virtuosity, innovation, individuality, and refinement. As elaborated in later chapters, the inversion of cultural hierarchy in folk music, especially with its racial implications, was one of the factors that attracted left-wing activists to folk music. As the "people's music," folk music could be used to galvanize social movements and especially to bridge racial boundaries.

This is where the topic of social movements and the sociology of music come together. Rosenthal and Flacks identify three major functions that music can play for social movements: recruitment, mobilization, and serving the committed. Recruitment can be served by drawing potential recruits to movement events, exposing them to new ideas through lyrics, and helping form network ties that can serve to draw people in. As Joe Hill said, "A pamphlet, no matter how good, is never read but once, but a song is learned by heart and repeated over and over; and I maintain that if a person can put a few cold common sense facts in a song, and dress them up in a cloak of humor to take the dryness off of them he will succeed in reaching a great number of workers who are too unintelligent or too indifferent to read a pamphlet or an editorial on economic science" (quoted in Rosenthal and Flacks 2009: 27). Mobilization, their second function for social movements, refers to the ways that music can facilitate actual collective actions, both by reinforcing commitments and by energizing a group as it prepares for action. Their third function, serving the committed, refers to the way that music enhances solidarity, increases loyalty, reinforces identities, and gives content to ritual. One especially important function, also emphasized by Eyerman and Jamison (1998), is to keep movement culture alive in times of dormancy.[18]

Social movements are both a class of actors that use culture and a site where culture is enacted. As a site for cultural work, the kinds of social relationships including the degrees of hierarchy, the modes of decision-making, the social cleavages, especially race, gender, and class, and other features of interaction shape (and are affected by) the kind of cultural work that is done. As Eyerman and Jamison suggest, social movements also incubate social relationships and cultural content for the larger society. They are a site where people meet and where institutions interact, shaping both the form and content of culture (1998). For example, the American Communist Party (CP) helped develop institutions of political musicking where progressive musicians could come together to develop and disseminate a vibrant and far-reaching musical vitality. Like churches, schools, and community bands, the CP created noncommercial organizations to use music as a collective activity. In doing so, they bestowed American folk music not only as a popular genre but one with enduring left-wing political connotations (Lieberman 1995; Reuss and Reuss 2000).

RACE

While it is hoped that this book will substantially advance our understandings of music and social movements, its contribution to the sociology of race is more limited. But I would like to clarify where I stand on the meaning and social basis of race in America. By "race" I mean a systematic and hierarchical ideology and set of practices that categorize groups of people based on imputed correlations between physical inherited characteristics and social characteristics. It is not about skin color, shape of eyes, or structure of face but about social reactions to skin color, shape of eyes, and structure of face. It is not a characteristic of a person or a group of people but a characteristic of relations between people and the imputation of groupness. It is thus socially constructed, not in the sense of being the figment of people's imagination but in the sense of arising in particular times and places for particular social reasons (Roy 2001). Because it is socially constructed, it is a mutable object of contention. While the depth to which race permeates American social relations and institutions has made it disturbingly tenacious, there has been change. And while it pervades all aspects of life, there is variation in its operation and significance in different arenas of life.

Music has been one social arena that has been more inclusive than many other arenas in American society. Even in the depths of the Jim Crow South, black and white musicians interacted more frequently than non-musicians, learning each other's songs, teaching each other techniques, and sharing a struggle to eke it out on the margins (Frith, Hall, and Du Gay 1996; Levine 1977; Small 1987). Such inclusion is probably due less to any inherent tendency of music to bridge social boundaries than to specific historical conditions under slavery and after. Just as composers were considered house servants by pre-Romantic European patrons, plantation owners used slaves for entertainment. Music was one of the skills, along with smithing, carpentry, and tailoring, that slaves were groomed for. Many advertisements for slaves noted their musical talents, for example, a 1766 advertisement in the *Virginia Gazette*: "TO BE SOLD. A young healthy Negro fellow who has been used to wait on a Gentleman and plays extremely well on the French horn" (quoted in Southern 1983: 27). Notices of runaway slaves also frequently mentioned musical talents. Thus music was one of the first specifically human capacities that whites noted about slaves, leading to the persistent stereotype that blacks have a natural affinity for music. An article in *Dwight's Journal of Music* noted, "The Negro is a natural musician. He will learn to play on an instrument more quickly than a white man. They have magnificent voices and sing without instruction. . . . They go singing to their daily labors. The maid sings about the house, and the laborer sings in the field" (quoted in Levine 1977: 5). While much of the music played for the slave owners was European classical music, syncretic forms flourished, finding secure niches in minstrelsy and religion, springing forth into American popular music.

Analogous to the way that folk music inverts the association of refinement and high status, popular music inverts the ordinary hierarchy of race. "Black" is typically a term of affirmation, and "white" carries a connotation of lifelessness or dullness. Just as musical skills allowed talented slaves access to special privileges and benefits without unsettling the fundamental social relations of slavery, so the inversion of broader racial hierarchy has allowed some African Americans to achieve fame and, for a few, even wealth without threatening the basic racial hierarchy. This inversion of the dominant order is yet to be fully incorporated into prevailing sociological analyses of race. Insofar as theory is advanced by addressing anomalies that reigning theories cannot explain, this is an opportunity for the sociology of music to contribute something to our understanding of race.

One of the fundamental issues in thinking about the relationship between race and music is the extent to which music is a reflection of racial relations or a generative or transformative factor in constructing and reproducing racial relations. Insofar as music is a reflection of race, race is considered analytically and causally prior. Those studying it take racial relations as a given and show how music reflects them. This is the commonsense approach and the perspective found in most scholarly writing on race and music. The literatures on homology, appropriation, and exploitation tend to take this approach. It is assumed that people have a race and that they act on the basis of that race, selecting music, making music, borrowing music, and talking about music. Race is taken for granted and music is treated as malleable and shaped by racial dynamics (Courlander 1992; Filene 2000; Levine 1977; Lhamon 1998; Neal 1999; Negus and RománVelázquez 2002; Ramsey 2003; Small 1987; Southern 1983; Ward 1998).

Yet the converse relationship is also important. As a form of social interaction, music can also help constitute race, help change racial relations, or reinforce racial inequality. Embracing a certain kind of music not only "reflects" race but can also help define what it means to be a member of a racial group. Eschewing one's "own" music can make a person "less" a member of a race. When music is used to define what it means to belong to one race, it can take on an independent causative force. Radano, for example, argues that the examination of the relationship between race and music "will reveal not only music's expressive capacities but also its generative, constitutive effects" (2003: 4). He eloquently depicts how social relationships around music helped constitute a boundary, homogenizing how African Americans were viewed within the race and reifying the sense that they were different from whites. Cruz similarly shows how Northern abolitionists sought to humanize slaves for whites by displaying their musical talents singing spirituals. When whites were debating whether slaves were full human beings, few demonstrations were more effective with white audiences than showing blacks' capacity to make music. The viewpoint of whites was both empathetic and distanced, seeing slaves as human but different, creative but exotic, deserving of freedom though not necessarily equality. Thus were spirituals crystallized into a syncretic cultural form that combined inherited African sounds refracted through European tonal structures (Cruz 1999).

A theoretical goal of scholarship positing the reflexive relationship between race and music is overcoming essentialism, which Negus defines as "the notion that individuals of a particular social type possess certain essential characteristics and that these are *expressed* in particular cultural practices" (1996: 100).[19] It is the reflexive relationship of race and music that makes it possible to acknowledge the essentialism in the culture without falling into essentialism as scholars. Essentialism in the culture becomes something to explain, asking why it is that certain types of music are seen as essentially white, black, Latino, or other and why being a member of a racial group obligates a person to embrace a particular kind of music. Musical practices take place within a society permeated by race, and racial practices are often musical.

The two movements examined here—the Old Left and the civil rights movement—were each the most prominent force for racial justice for their time, but in very different ways. Both movements were essentialist in the sense that they assumed that there were naturally different kinds of people denoted by skin color. The goal of both was to reduce the saliency of that difference, to eliminate the hierarchical dimension of difference. For the Old Left, racial inequality was fundamentally economic. African Americans were seen as the most oppressed class, whose oppression divided and dragged down the working class. In 1925, the party sponsored the American Negro Labor Congress, "For the abolition of all discrimination, persecution and exploitation of the Negro race and working people generally; . . . to remove all bars and discrimination against Negroes and other races in the trade unions; . . . and to aid the general liberation of the darker races and the working people throughout all countries" (Solomon 1998: 94). It thereby followed that the strategy for racial justice centered on bringing blacks into the vanguard of the working class, especially by opening up industrial unions. With the Popular Front era of the late 1930s when the party adopted folk music as the people's music, race was a major issue for the party, especially in relationship to its CIO unions. CIO unions on the whole were much more racially inclusive than AFL unions (Stepan-Norris and Zeitlin 2003). But the movement's approach was not entirely economistic. Their International Labor Defense was very active in defending African Americans from legal abuse under Jim Crow judicial practices. Their role in the defense of the "Scottsboro Boys"— nine black teenagers accused of raping a white girl—brought to national attention the struggle for racial justice in the South.

In contrast, the civil rights movement's strategy focused on ending the legal system of segregation, assuming that economic equality would follow. Even when economic equality was sought, the primary strategy was through the political and judicial systems. Issues of class were muted at best, it being assumed that equal opportunity would benefit blacks rich and poor. When the initial goals of the movement were achieved in the end of de jure segregation, many movement activists, including Dr. King, turned to issues of economic injustice and jobs but never won the popular support, elite allies, or legislative victories of the first phase. The end of the movement against Jim Crow coincided with a radical change in the understanding of race itself. In place of an image that depicted race as a matter of skin color only, the black nationalist movement treated race as deeply cultural. Race became not just a marker by which people categorized each other but also a matter of identity, a sense of self that demanded personal and cultural expression. White culture, with its centuries of degradation of Africans and their descendants, was to be expunged by embracing the culture of the land their ancestors had been taken from.

For both movements, their conception of race was tied to their use of music. For the Old Left, subordinating race to class implied finding the music of the working class as a whole, that is, "the people's music." Rejecting genres such as country and western or rhythm and blues (R&B), which were identified with segments of the working class, they eventually found folk music, the closest thing America had to a true vernacular. They wanted a racially inclusive working class and sought out racially inclusive music. Because the civil rights movement was first and foremost a racial movement, activists could embed much of the same music found in African American social forms. Though both movements strategically aspired to a color-blind society, the Old Left tactically attempted to bring blacks into predominantly white unions while articulating a vision of racial justice to the broader community. The civil rights movement, in contrast, was recruiting whites to participate in integrated organizations in black communities. While music eventually helped recruit whites into the movement, its main function as a facilitator of collective action depended on the way that music was rooted in the community.

Thus neither side defined music with essential racial content but as something that could bridge racial boundaries, something that blacks and whites could share. But in some sense, the Old Left's faith in the power of music itself apart from its social form fit both their success and failure. Subordinating race to class, they thought that bringing black and white musicians together around putatively color-blind music that belonged to all the folks would help corrode racial walls. To a limited extent it did. And they helped popularize folk music, though with the connotation more of left-wing music than racially integrated music. In contrast, the civil rights movement's attention to the social form of music in collective action helped give it a connotation of racial inclusion, which became a liability when the movement bifurcated. Thus the racial dimension of music is intertwined in its use, in the kinds of social relations around doing music. Music and race are both constituted and become consequential through their doing.

Preview

The development of folk music as a genre is addressed in chapter 2. Genres—the categories that help organize the social relations around music—are often the result of particular cultural projects. Folk music is distinctive in two regards: it is categorized on the basis of who does it—the folk—rather than sonic qualities such as instrumentation, rhythm, harmony, or timbre, and it almost always refers to someone else's music. The scholars and gentlemen collectors who coined the concept, the activists who used it for nationalist or insurgent politics, and "folkies" who embrace its authenticity are rarely themselves "folk." This chapter reflects on what a sociology of genres might look like, emphasizing the musical and social context out of which new genres spring and the kind of agency required to hatch a new genre. The musical context, especially its racial dynamics, is highlighted, showing how the roots of American popular music grew from the complicated racial relations of minstrelsy, spirituals, and parlor music.

Chapter 3 focuses on the first folk project and addresses its origins. The concept of a musical genre that embodies the essential qualities and historical legacy of a people was originally part of European nationalizing projects. Scholars and gentlemen collectors "discovered" the premodern cultures of each of the major European nations, sacralizing and protecting from oblivion the culture of the national folk, in the process constructing boundaries along national lines. Because America lacked an ancient past and any remnant of a national peasantry, scholars initially doubted whether it had a folk culture. But as a wave of stigmatized immigrants began to diversify America in the late nineteenth century, scholars discovered what they identified as a remnant of English folk culture in remote southern mountains. American folk music was fashioned along racial lines. The "folk" of America were explicitly Anglo-Saxon. Like many other cultural constructions of the period, the first line of demarcation was between descendants of voluntary colonial settlers and everyone else. Yet the mythology of national purity contained the seeds of its own undoing. The legacy of vernacular popular music summarized in chapter 2 offered a glaring contrast to the evolving folk myth. The raw materials for a trenchant challenge to the first folk project were available for a new folk project to turn the myth of national racial purity on its head. The second folk project emerged from a most unlikely source.

In contrast to the conservative nationalist impulse that animated the first folk music project, a second project embraced folk music because they thought it could be racially inclusive. A few folklorists, most of them somewhat marginal to the original project, extended the boundaries of the folk beyond its Anglo-Saxon roots. And the correspondence of "folk" and "people" afforded the opportunity for activists to symbolically redraw the boundaries around the people by including new people in the folk. People associated with the Communist Party, searching for cultural means of mobilizing "the people," eventually settled on folk music as "the people's music." Chapter 4 tells the remarkable story of how America's most economistic social movement mounted a cultural project that painted the genre of folk music pink.

Chapter 5 describes how two generations of cultural entrepreneurs shaped the genre of American folk music as it continues to be understood today. The Lomaxes and Seegers, by working in the interstice of academic, government, educational, commercial, and social movement institutions demonstrated how consequential entrepreneurship can be in fashioning subculture.

Chapter 6 focuses on the organizational facet of the Old Left cultural project, especially People's Songs, Inc., a short-lived but immensely strategic culmination of communist-inspired musicking. Between the heyday of the Old Left and the rise of the civil rights movement the political uses of folk music may have receded from the eyes of the media, but they never disappeared. Not only did remnants of the communist movement keep the spirit alive in summer camps, hootenannies, and small outlets, but a number of other left-leaning institutions continued to use music in their activism, most notably the Highlander School of Monteagle, Tennessee. Inspired by Danish settlement schools, the Highlander was a catalyst for bottom-up community development in the South, first on behalf of unions and later for civil rights. Self-consciously aware of music's potential for bringing people together and forging solidarity, especially in a region where nearly everyone regularly participated in religious singing, they spread music like Johnny Appleseed spread apple trees.[20] Chapter 7 describes how the Highlander developed a distinctive style of musicking, highly suitable for bringing people together and empowering those seeking a better life through collective action.

Chapter 8 describes the third folk music project, the civil rights movement. In contrast to music in the Old Left, music in the civil rights movement was part of collective itself, not just a matter of performance for audiences. As part of a movement aspiring to end racial inequality, music was especially crucial for bridging racial difference, at least for a while. Facilitated by activities and leaders of the Highlander School, set into motion by local activists, and eagerly embraced by northerners who flocked to the South, freedom songs became a public face of the movement. For many it remains the standard against which musical activism is compared.

But the heyday was short-lived. Flush with the success of ending de jure segregation, strained by the maturation of a new generation of leaders pressing for deeper change, pressed by a hungry media seeking a news story more exciting than sit-ins or bus rides, and challenged by the different needs of an urban movement, the classic civil rights movement splintered. The cry of "Black Power" drowned out the ebbing echoes of "Freedom Now" as whites were asked to attend to the roots of injustice in their own communities. With new forms of collective action unsuitable for singing and a search for a specifically black culture, freedom songs became seen as irrelevant. Chapter 9 thus shows the denouement. As the left bifurcated into black and white segments, branching then into the antiwar movement, student power movement, women's movement, gay movement, and others, music remained an informal part of activism, but with less self-conscious attention to it. Because it made for good sound bites, the mass media both at the time and retrospectively probably exaggerated the role of music in the late 1960s and early 1970s.

Some readers may be surprised at how little this book will say about what they know most about folk music—the commercial folk revival of the 1960s and 1970s. The main reason for this reticence is that the book is about the political *uses* of music. Even though there was overlap between the folk revival and especially the third project, with the likes of Pete Seeger teaching freedom songs to activists and audiences, and even though activists and folkies inspired each other, their equivalence was more a conceit of the mass media than an actual social relationship. Bob Dylan may have appeared at a few movement events, but he was not a part of the movement—one of the more reliable recollections he has shared in recent interviews—and the activists knew it. While the folk revival merits serious sociological study, this is not the book for that.

CHAPTER TWO

Music and Boundaries: Race and Folk

> Sourwood Mountain: This is surely a real folk song; its obvious
> crudity, its simplicity, and above all its swing and go show that.
> A fellow really needs a supply of "white lightening" to sing or
> play it. Its rhythm is irresistible. The words cannot be applied to
> the tune by anybody but a mountaineer.
>
> —*Howard Odum Papers, #3157,*
> *fol. 638, Southern Historical Collection,*
> *University of North Carolina Library, Chapel Hill*

> No one who knows of the vast amount, seemingly unlimited, of
> native material, descriptive of the folk, the life, the regional civi-
> lization of the Negro can fail to regret its neglect. Here are lan-
> guage, literature, and if poetry be the product of feeling and see-
> ing, then poetry of unusual charm and simplicity. They are part
> of the story of the race.
>
> —*Odum 1925: 8*

Though unremarkable to contemporary ears, the claim that "this is surely
a real folk song" would have been esoteric, even academically insolent,
when penned by sociologist Howard Odum in the early twentieth century. The concept of folk music was little known outside elite universities
and antiquarian societies, a European import borrowed by intellectuals
to "discover" the national soul in America's quasi-peasantry. In this quotation can be found the basic contours of a social-musical model that
would be later appropriated by the American political left. Unlike the
polish of classical music and the cultured class who appreciate it, folk
music is considered crude and simple, for crude and simple folk. It is
music that belongs in a social context, presumably where "white lighten-
ing" flows with the music. It is bodily, deriving its musicality from rhythm
more than harmony. And it is "owned" by a group of a particular class
and place, the mountaineer. In the second quotation, Odum makes a similar claim about African Americans, finding the essence of the group in
their folk music. Though granting their culture the ambiguous status of
"regional civilization," like the mountaineer, blacks are affirmed for their
charm and simplicity. Their music is seen as not only a window on their
essence but a means of preserving it. Together these two quotations from

a sociological pioneer document the construction of American folk music and suggest why the left might find it fitting to politically appropriate. In contrast to European folk music, which symbolized purportedly homogeneous national groups, American folk music became a vehicle to contest who was part of the American nation. For activists, the "folk" became the cultural equivalent of "the people" and folk music became "the people's music." Those who first nurtured the concept of folk meant people of English ancestry. But for later generations, including that of Howard Odum, who published about "Negro" folk songs as early as 1911, those of African ancestry were musically, if not socially, as American as anyone.[1] How the music of southern mountaineers and ex-slaves became defined as "folk" and how qualities of music became associated with qualities of people are the questions asked in this chapter. Answering them helps explain why folk music seemed more appropriate than other genres when the left adopted "the people's music" as a project.

The concept and ideology of folk music were constructed in a social and musical context that provided the cultural raw material and set the boundaries of plausibility for the genre's social identity. A genre's social identity—the attributed qualities of people associated with a genre—does not derive simply from its content but, like all cultural phenomena, should be explained at the level of the social, including the social basis of its inventors and purveyors, the institutions through which it is articulated and diffused, and the relationship between those who made the music and those who mediated it to others. Folk music was invented as a concept and developed as an ideology with specifically nationalist ambitions. Inheriting an image of a peasantry set off from the elite by class and time, but embodying the ethnic and national essence of a people, the original American folk project initially celebrated America's closest equivalent to the English peasantry but was unable to restrict the concept of folk to the "pure" Americans of English descent. The social realities of American vernacular music could not be contained. The art world of music was, much more than the rest of society, racially inclusive, providing the raw material for a second, racially inclusive folk project in the hands of politically committed activists.

GENRES

From the sexual associations of rock and roll to the high-status aura of opera to the defiant connotations of rap, the meaning of music lies not only in particular sounds or songs but also in the categories by which people understand music, that is, in genres. When discussing the alignment of cultural boundaries and social boundaries, the cultural boundary most commonly alluded to is genre. Folk music is a genre. To understand how folk music arose, how it developed connotations, how it came to be used by social movements, and how it was consequential for influencing racial boundaries, it is important to consider what a genre is, so to speak, generically. Fabbri (1992) has one of the most complete definitions of genres, specifying them as a set of socially accepted rules including the following:

- Formal and technical rules: musical form, aural characteristics, playing conventions, instruments, rhythm, relationship of words to music. This is the colloquial sense of genre, describing how baroque sounds differ from minimalist or heavy metal from electronica.

- Semiotic rules: rules of communication, how music works as a rhetoric, how meaning is conveyed. Semiotic rules shape how truth or sincerity is indicated musically or how we know what the music is "about." Peterson's description of how authenticity was constructed for country and western music through such devices as clothing, instrumentation, and lyrical themes shows that the sociological analysis can explain how semiotic rules work (1997a).

- Behavioral rules governing performance rituals: not only do classical music, jazz, and heavy metal sound very different from each other, but people are expected to behave very differently at their concerts. Such rules apply not just to audiences and performers onstage but also to behavior in interviews, press photographs, postperformance parties, and so forth.

- Social and ideological rules: different genres invoke different social images of musicians, audiences, and others, regardless of reality. Small, for example, describes the classical music concert as a microcosm of bourgeois respectability (1998). Hebdige uses a similar ethnographic method to show how punks have used their music to defy respectability (1979). It is through social and ideological rules of genre distinctions that racial, ethnic, gender, class, and age identities are mapped onto genres.

- Commercial and juridical rules: different genres are governed by different modes of ownership and financial reward. Much of jazz and classical music has fallen out of copyright and is now in the public domain. Further, there are very different practices for how concerts are organized, how records relate to live events, how performers relate to composers, and so forth.

I would extend the sociological analysis of genres by emphasizing that rules do not float freely but are always expressed and enforced in organizations and institutions. Different genres enmesh different sorts of organizations and institutions, a point often overlooked when focusing only on commercially produced music. Some of the most robust boundaries demarcate genres embedded in different institutional frameworks. DiMaggio, for example, has described how the distinction between high-brow and lowbrow art arose with the adoption of the nonprofit corpora-tion as the organizational basis of art, music, dance, and other fine arts. When cultural expression can be supported by organizations subsidized by major benefactors, it can be lauded as transcending the vitiating pres-sure of the market (DiMaggio 1982a).[2] Conversely, popular music is vali-dated by its broad appeal materialized in the market. Success is signified by gold or platinum records based solely on market success and by the Grammy, bestowed by popularity among intra-genre peers.

The institutional setting of folk music is especially important to the story of this book. Though the ideology around folk music portrays an indigenous social setting, with images of rural folk sitting on front stoops plucking a banjo or strumming a dulcimer, music when labeled folk music has been more typically produced and distributed within academic set-tings, within specialized folk music settings such as festivals or coffee-houses, and by social movements. Except for the commercially successful folk revival of the 1960s, folk music has been embraced as an alternative to commercial music. Like its classical counterpart on the other end of the aesthetic scale, the genre of folk music was embedded in a set of insti-tutions outside the market that substantiated its claim to purity.

By this reasoning, genres are more than means of classification, more than a set of cognitive categories about cultural objects themselves. Rather than categorizing a set of preexisting songs or works, genres also shape composition, production, and reception. The concept of classifica-tion assumes that cultural objects have certain categories that are then ordered according to cognitive schemes. The characteristics of the objects are analytically (and perhaps temporally) prior to the classification. From this perspective, classification is a cognitive map imposed upon reality, as though the reality were there before the classification scheme. Zerubavel, for example, analyzes the logic by which we divide the world, distin-guishing between continuous dimensions, mental gaps, mental quantum leaps, and the like (1991). In contrast, the concept of genres, as a set of rules and practices, assumes that divisions are actively constructed, that the consciousness of the categories informs actions that shape the cul-tural objects themselves. Composers compose, performers perform, and critics interpret according to the reified categories we call genres or aspire to create new rules and practices under the banner of genre labels they are introducing. While some genres are invented to refine the categoriza-tion of existing musical styles and practices, at least as often genres are introduced to validate innovation, not just label. The inventors of rap did not release songs that listeners categorized as rap so much as simultaneously invented the genre and the songs that belong to it. Minimalism, emo, alternative country, and acid jazz refer to new sounds and practices both guided by and constituting new genre labels. Thus genres are projects that people decide to affiliate with and work on behalf of, collectively constructing and/or enforcing standards of practice. A sociology of genres must explain why, how, and with what effects people collectively invent, define, reify, and enforce categorized standards of musical practice. For American folk music, this agenda involves how indigenous southern music in the nineteenth century became crystallized into the styles and practices we call folk. And the social relations of southern culture inevitably involve race.

Music has played a distinctive role in American race relations. The relatively free space of music in slavery, the ambivalent place of blackness in minstrelsy, the use of music by abolitionists to depict slaves' humanity, the remarkable popularity of the black choirs such as the Fisk Jubilee Singers for white audiences, and the dense network of black and white songsters (that would include what we now call street musicians and lounge musicians) add up to an exceptional infusion of black and white society and culture. The syncretic fusion of European and African heritage that emerged as popular music could only happen if blacks and whites interacted more in the world of music than in the rest of society. Even in the nineteenth-century American South, the relationship of race and music was reflexive. Not only did race shape music, but music also helped construct the meaning and operation of race. Southern indigenous music was found in several institutional settings, all of which featured unusually frequent interaction between blacks and whites. This, of course, does not imply that social relations between races were any less oppressive because blacks and whites shared musical experiences. But it does mean that musical influences from both Europe and Africa were blended to create uniquely American styles and character (Levine 1977; McClary 2000; Small 1987; Southern 1983). The syncretism of American popular music has both reinforced and at times destabilized the binary polarization of American race relations. From minstrelsy to spirituals to jazz to rock and rap, racial representation and concrete social interaction have been profound and ambivalent.

Thus, race is the analytic prism through which the genre of American folk music will be examined. From the initial fusion of African and European music under slavery to the reconfiguration of those two lineages in spirituals and minstrelsy to the attempts to purify African influences out of "truly American" music, the history of vernacular music in this country has been pervaded by race.

SLAVERY

During the antebellum period, musical strains from Africa and Europe were fused in several southern institutions. Slave owners used slaves to entertain at dances and parlor socials. Religious events permitted musical interaction. Minstrelsy, despite its often vicious display of racial stereotypes, exposed white audiences to African-influenced music. And socializing among the slaves permitted white musicians to adapt African sounds to European instruments and musical forms.

Just as slave owners used slaves' agrarian and industrial skills, so did they exploit the musical talents the involuntary migrants had brought from home. European observers in Africa had frequently noticed the ubiquity of music and dance. Richard Jobson, an English sea captain, after his exploration of the Gambia River in 1620 wrote, "There is without doubt, no people on the earth more naturally affected to the sound of musicke than these people; which the principall persons do hold as an ornament of their state, so as when we come to see them their musicke will seldome be wanting. . . . Also, if at any time the Kings or principall persons come unto us trading in the River, they will have their musicke playing before them, and will follow in order after their manner, presenting a shew of state" (Southern 1983: 6). Master musicians occupying high status in their societies honed their skills as virtuoso performers sustained by the literature of their people.

In white colonial society, dances were the most popular form of entertainment, held in taverns, meeting halls, and homes. White audiences enjoyed both European-derived and Europeanized African music with slaves playing fiddles and horns as well as banjos and mouth harps. In a society where slaves provided most of the labor and where musicians were considered servants, slaves were trained to provide the music for southern dances. But having learned to play fiddles and horns for the owners, they then would have learned to think musically in diatonic scales and repeated cadences, especially in the generations after removal from Africa, refracting the musical consciousness they imported from home through the new training received in America. Their imported music was further muted by owners fearful of uprising, further fostering the fusion of African and European (Barlow 1989; Krehbiel 1914; Levine 1977; Southern 1983).

Songs played before white audiences also were played in activities of segregated black enclaves such as picnics, barbeques, fish fries, sporting events, holiday parties, and country dances. Especially important were Saturday night social gatherings, a common ritual begun during slavery that continued afterward. Held in homes or outside, and later in "juke joints," they featured singing, dancing, frolicking, discussion, and gambling. The fiddle, the only instrument to span the folk-classical spectrum, was the most popular instrument followed by the banjo, though these became less prominent after the war. Many songs like "Little Lisa Jane," "Chicken in the Birdbath," and "Old Grey Mare" were of Anglo-American origin. As Barlow notes, "The dance music they played syncretized the folk materials and instrumental techniques from both traditions and was played before both black and white audiences" (1989: 30).

Just as the exposure to European dance music facilitated fusion, so did antebellum religious experience. Slaves had relatively little contact with Christianity in the first century of American slavery when whites debated whether they had souls, but the white evangelists of the Great Awakening in the 1740s and 1750s reached out to them. Henceforth African Americans and Euro-Americans often attended the same religious services, learning traditional hymns and adapting them to their own circumstances. In 1819 John F. Watson, a Methodist, wrote with some alarm about the uncomfortable independence shown by slaves in their religious practice: "From this cause I have known in some camp meetings, from 50 to 60 people crowd into one tent, after the public devotions had closed, and there continue the whole night, singing tune after tune (though with occasional episodes of prayer) scarce one of which were in our hymn books" (Small 1987: 89). Not only were they singing songs not in the hymnals, they were influencing how white southerners were sounding spiritual. The qualities that made white gospel music different from traditional European hymns—the greater emphasis on rhythm, the call-and-response structure, the syncopation, and the energy—were all derived from African influence (Levine 1977; Reagon 1975). The fused music sung by slaves eventually became known as spirituals, which used European forms including verse structures, diatonic scales, monophonic harmonies, and measured beats, especially as sung by those aspiring to middle-class respectability such as the Fisk Jubilee Singers.[3]

The Spiritual

Although slaves made music in many social contexts and for many purposes, it is their religious music that became defined in public discourse as the quintessential African American music of the nineteenth century. It was the spiritual that first came to be treated as a separate object (Cruz 1999), the original genre of specifically black music. More important, it was affirmed by both literate African Americans and whites as proof that slaves warranted freedom, as music not just by a race but music of racial distinctiveness. Beginning with Frederick Douglass's celebrated autobiography (1997 [1845]), black religious music expressed the suffering and the humanity of slavery and cried out to the world the desire for freedom. But Douglass notes that it was only freedom that gave him the appreciation of what the music truly meant.

> I did not, when a slave, understand the deep meaning of those rude and apparently incoherent songs. I was myself within the circle; so that I neither saw nor heard as those without might see and hear. They told a tale of woe which was then altogether beyond my feeble comprehension; they were tones loud, long, and deep; they breathed prayer and complaint of souls boiling over with the bitterest anguish. Every tone was a testimony against slavery, and a prayer to God for deliverance from chains. (1997 [1845]: 34)

The book was immensely popular and widely read, its impact as much from its eloquence as its content. That a former slave could be so articulate caused skeptics to question whether a black man had really written it. His own reinterpretation of slave music was mirrored by white abolitionists who came to see that what other whites heard as only noise was in fact an expression of creativity and humanity. Black music became embraced as proof that slaves had the capacity for culture, that most human of traits. In 1849 William Wells Brown, himself a fugitive slave, collected some of the most popular anti-slavery songs in *The Anti-Slavery Harp: A Collection of Songs for Anti-Slavery Meetings*. Most were parodies of well-known songs, predominantly songs from the British Isles, though minstrel songs were not uncommon, for example, "O Susannah," "Old Rosin the Beau," and "Dandy Jim" (Southern 1983). As the abolitionist movement developed, the music was increasingly drawn from the slave community itself, though typically modified for white aural sensibilities. But the effect was still significant. As the lyrics of one of the songs from *Anti-Slavery Harp* made explicit, presaging the more famous words of Sojourner Truth,

> Am I not a man and brother?
> Ought I not, then, to be free?
> Sell me not to one another,
> Take not thus my liberty.[4]

While the activist music of the *Anti-Slavery Harp* was common in political movements of antebellum America, when adherents sought converts and forged solidarity with spirited odes to political candidates and moral campaigns, the abolitionists increasingly fashioned a new purpose for music. Not only could music be used to express one's own spirit, but it could be attributed to people whose humanity had been contested. To make a case for emancipation, abolitionists had to demonstrate that slaves were fully human in order to challenge both bestial popular imagery and scientific classification of species. On the assumption that music is a uniquely human activity, they hoped that by showing that slaves made music (not just sounds), they could authenticate the slaves' humanity. When northern abolitionists brought slave spirituals to the attention of white audiences, slaves were for the first time understood to be fully human, endowed with the quality that sets people apart from other animals—culture.

As abolitionists constructed spirituals to humanize slaves, they unwittingly sowed the seeds to link American folk music to African Americans. Many of the discursive themes around spirituals prefigured later discourse on folk music. Slaves were represented as a folk–people bound to the soil, barricaded from modernity, innocent to the corrosive character of industrial cities and mass culture. For example, Charlotte Forten's personal account of a northern African American teacher who traveled to a liberated region of the South to teach freed slaves was filled with music, from the strains of "John Brown" on her arrival to spirituals when they worshiped and shouts when they worked. Though written for "private perusal," the editor of the *Atlantic Monthly* saw fit to publish it in the midst of war (Forten 1864). More explicit about the racial significance of music was *Slave Songs of the United States*, published by former abolitionists shortly after the Civil War. The authors' introduction employed the language of anthropology to depict themselves as collectors of the cultural artifacts from a threatened tribe. The indigenous informants were described as exotic and innocent, but possessing natural cultural talents beyond the abilities of more civilized races. Their gift of culture came not from civilization but from the archaic savagery of slavery: "The wild, sad strains tell, as the sufferers themselves could, of crushed hopes, keen sorrow, and a dull, daily misery, which covered them as hopelessly as the fog from the rice swamps. On the other hand, the words breathe a trusting faith in rest for the future—in 'Canaan's air and happy land,' to which their eyes seem constantly turned" (Allen, Ware, and Garrison 1971: xix). The imagery is rural ("fog from the rice swamps") and presecular. From the perspective of the mid-nineteenth century, when prevailing images of the future embraced the progress of civilization, only the innocent or ignorant would keep their eyes turned to "Canaan's air and happy land." The overriding image is quaintness, as in this passage: "One of their customs, often alluded to in the songs . . . is that of wandering through the woods and swamps, when under religious excitement, like the ancient bacchantes. To get religion is with them to 'fin' dat ting'" (xii). The simple act of walking through woods and swamps is raised to a custom. The use of dialect, unnecessary for speakers socially close to the writers, heightens the sense of "otherness." The text, then, though written decades before anyone discussed the plausibility of American folk music, discussed whether the songs were written by individuals or grew by accretion, concluding that both processes were common.[5]

Cruz explains how the abolitionists not only influenced the prevailing view of African American culture but changed the way we think about the relationship between groups and their culture: "The juncture at which black culture—or what has come to be known as 'slave culture'—was 'discovered' as culture represents a turning point in the rise of modern cultural interpretation. More specifically, this juncture brought the new cultural inquiry into relationship with the racial and cultural margins within American society" (1999: 5). The spirituals were framed for white audiences not only to elicit sympathy for an oppressed people but to extend to slaves and their descendants a new kind of cultural authority—that of authenticity. Instead of a straightforward correspondence between the stature of a group and the respectability of its culture, cultures can be valorized because they are considered humble or common. Cruz calls this stance toward the culture of a subordinate group "ethnosympathy," by which he means a mode of analysis based on the empathetic understanding of another group's culture. Music is seen as a reflection of other people's inner lives, a way for the dominant group to paternalistically feel a common humanity. Slave songs, especially after the writings of Frederick Douglass, were interpreted differently than music had been previously. As Cruz describes it, "When black and white intellectuals began to embrace the new sense of black subjectivity, they forged links between a humanitarian reformist redemption politics of abolitionism and a quest for cultural authenticity" (1999: 6).[6]

Through the ethnosympathetic stance and application of the concept of authenticity as a standard of aesthetics, urban whites forged a contradictory relationship to black (and rural white) culture, humanizing for whites the image of African Americans but implicitly applying a dual standard for aesthetic worth. While music of European lineage was evaluated in terms of influential composers or performers, music of African Americans prior to the jazz age was framed as the expression of a group. Moreover, at a time when whites compartmentalized religious and secular music, those mediating black music to white audiences valorized only religious music, prefiguring the characterization of black music as soul music. James Miller McKim, a founder of the Anti-Slavery Society and operator of the Underground Railroad, addressed the Port Royal Freedmen's Association in Philadelphia in 1862 regarding his observations of slaves at the South Sea Islands in South Carolina, emphasizing their musical talents. Contributing to the stereotype of African Americans' inherited sense of rhythm, McKim humanized the slaves by describing how musical they were. Furthermore, he explained, they experienced not just any music but religious music, and not just any religious music but doleful music—what later generations would find soulful. It seemed important to McKim that when he asked the slaves where they got the songs, they said that they made them up. In contrast to the prevailing assumption that civilized people capture their culture in enduring literature and art, the slaves were seen as capable only of spontaneous spiritual expression. They had music in lieu of literacy. Though human, they were primitive, with culture coming from the heart, not the mind. McKim's publication of his speech and several slave songs in *Dwight's Journal of Music* (Boston, August 9, 1862) articulated what would become the dominant white image of black music for much of the next century: "They are a musical people. When they work in concert, as in rowing or grinding at the mill, their hands keep time to music" (McKim 1862). The music, he noted, is all written in minor modes, all religious, even when sung in secular settings, expressing sorrow, sadness, and melancholy, the only positive sentiment being hope. Perhaps most important, the music is taken to represent the soul of the black race: "I dwell on these songs not as a matter of entertainment but of instruction. They tell the whole story of these people's life and character. There is no need after hearing them, to inquire into the history of the slave's treatment" (1862: 2).

As African Americans sought to develop the human and cultural capital for fuller participation in modern society, they found that whites continued to imagine black music as spirituals. Shortly after the end of the Civil War, the northern white American Missionary Society founded Fisk University in Nashville, Tennessee. To help raise money, the university sent their choir, the Fisk Jubilee Singers, to northern cities, performing primarily for affluent white audiences. Typical of the nascent black middle class to which most of the students belonged, the choir performed European classical music, inserting a few slave songs arranged along European styles. Like most upwardly mobile groups, students and their teachers shunned the culture of their origins, considering slave music as undignified primitive reminders of servitude. But white audiences responded enthusiastically to the slave songs, embracing them as authentic expressions of a black soul. The Fisk Jubilee Singers became identified with a new genre of American music, the Negro spiritual, bringing them unimagined fame. The construction of the genre crystallized with the explosive popularity of the group. Just four years after the university's founding, a group of nine students, including eight former slaves, toured New York, introduced by the country's most renowned clergyman, Henry Ward Beecher. A year later they sang at the World's Peace Jubilee in Boston, followed by their first European tour, including a performance for Queen Victoria. A host of imitators both on campuses and in the community, the vogue of the term "spiritual," the adoption of aural conventions, the model for ensembles, and the template for performance practices helped popularize the music throughout the country and codify the sound and form we know as the spiritual. Before long spirituals were known more broadly throughout the country than the Anglo-Saxon folk songs studied by Child or Sharp (N. Cohen 1990; Filene 2000; Small 1987; Southern 1983).

In the late nineteenth century, minstrelsy and spirituals presented to white audiences grossly contrasting images of blacks and their music. The Jubilee Singers' popularity and spirituals were complicated by the enduring legacy of minstrelsy—the image explicitly against which they presented themselves, though white commentators continued to liken them. Unlike the risqué buffoonery represented by the Jim Crow of minstrelsy, the Jubilee Singers were models of propriety—neatly dressed, tightly disciplined, and musically elegant. Many whites assumed that they were really white, performing in a new form of blackface. One innkeeper did not realize they were black until they had checked into their rooms, then expelled them all. DuBois felt compelled to explicitly contrast spirituals to the representations of blacks in minstrelsy, positing spirituals as more authentic than minstrel-like "coon songs." Gilroy captures the same theme a century later: "Black people singing slave songs as mass entertainment set new public standards of authenticity for black cultural expression. The legitimacy of these new cultural forms was established precisely through their distance from the racial codes of minstrelsy. The Jubilee Singers' journey out of America was a critical stage in making this possible" (1993: 88). At the time of their first recording in 1909, they were virtually the only black performers in the country whose music was distributed commercially.

For African American intellectuals, the popularity of spirituals presented a dilemma. The soulful and otherworldly symbolism seemed to dampen the urgency of freedom. "Nobody Knows the Trouble I've Seen," "Swing Low, Sweet Chariot," and "There Is a Balm in Gilead" evoked images of salvation more than liberation, redemption more than justice, sorrow more than defiance. But this interpretation was challenged when W.E.B. DuBois, who had been a student at Fisk when the Jubilee Singers were at the height of their fame, in 1903 included a chapter on their activities in *The Souls of Black Folk* (DuBois 1989 [1903]). He argued that spirituals, what he called "sorrow songs," were a central signifier of black culture and a repository of collective memory. Tracing knowledge of the music back to *Slave Songs of the United States* and the Fisk Jubilee Singers, pitting the beauty of the spirituals against the debasement of popular "coon songs," DuBois found the spirit of his people in the music: "And so by fateful chance the Negro folk-song—the rhythmic cry of the slave—stands to-day not simply as the sole American music, but as the most beautiful expression of human experience born this side of the seas. It has been neglected, it has been, and is, half despised, and above all, it has been persistently mistaken and misunderstood; but notwithstanding, it still remains as the singular spiritual heritage of the nation and the greatest gift of the Negro people" (1989 [1903]: 178). DuBois did more than symbolically affirm what the abolitionists had argued—that the humanity of blacks was embodied in their musical creativity. He also bridged the social distance implied in the abolitionists' account by universalizing the music. Spirituals were seen less as the unique expression of the black race than as an expression of *human* experience, a *gift* from their experience (not their nature) to everyone. DuBois's conception of spirituals would later be extremely important to the redefinition of folk music as racially inclusive.[7]

In contrast to the common understandings of minstrelsy, which have overstated the distinction between "phony" commercial music and "authentic" indigenous music, popular conceptions of "Negro spirituals" have exaggerated their racial purity. Much recent scholarship has highlighted the contradictory racial meanings of spirituals, challenging conventional notions that spirituals represented either the essential African American culture or, conversely, that spirituals were only slave renditions of European hymns, or that their main function was to code secret messages of liberation (Courlander 1992; Cruz 1999; Eyerman and Jamison 1998; Filene 2000; Gilroy 1993; Small 1987; Southern 1983).

Spirituals were constructed in a genre and used to make claims about the essence of African American culture, the resilience of European culture, or slaves' deep commitment to liberation, claims that closely paralleled the claims being made about folk music. The white "discovery" of spirituals by northern abolitionists, like the first project of folklorists, shaped a discourse of peoplehood around musical expression. Both abolitionists and folklorists painted sympathetic though alien portraits of people doing the music. While the original shapers of the sympathetic discourse about spirituals were describing the music of groups they did not belong to, a generation later, educated African Americans such as W.E.B. DuBois and the promoters of the Fisk Jubilee Singers were affirming music as the essence of their own groups, just as nationalist folklorists did. Thus it would not be an unreasonable leap to broaden the concept of folk music to include spirituals, an opportunity activists and scholars would undertake in the new century.

Minstrelsy

Though spirituals were widely known to Americans in postbellum America, the genre's social setting was only loosely connected to the market.

Spirituals were typically sung by black college students or local choirs. Performances were more frequently in churches or civic auditoriums than the profit-seeking bars, medicine shows, or music halls where other genres were heard. And though commercial publishers vigorously marketed spirituals to performers, most of those active in the musical world of the spiritual worked through institutions other than business. But the racial dynamics of commercial music adopted very different genres, meanings, and social relations. While spirituals were the genre that contemporaries and subsequent historians have embraced to affirm black respectability, most Americans of the nineteenth century had a very different image of what black music was about, one based in the social setting of commercial music and the genre of minstrelsy.

Unlike dance music and religion, which synthesized African and European music by bringing black and white musicians together, minstrelsy created a fusion based on a white caricature of slave culture. Minstrelsy was *the* mass popular culture in antebellum America, a form of entertainment that reached across class and regional lines, something that most people knew about even if they rarely attended. Traveling troupes of entertainers performed in tents, meeting halls, and lodges, offering an eclectic program of comedy skits, formal oratory, songs, dances, jugglers, acrobats, and dramatic vignettes. They were the conduit of stereotypes and the main source of black cultural images to whites who lacked direct knowledge from interaction. Among the most imitated acts was "Jim Crow," a white (most often Irish) actor painted in blackface, popularized by T. D. Rice in the 1820s. "Jim Crow" was a jolly, happy-go-lucky, feckless plantation slave who implicitly needed a paternalistic master for his own good. Thirty years later, James K. Kennard, Jr. wrote in the *Knickerbocker* magazine, "From the nobility and gentry, down to the lowest chimney-sweep in Great Britain, and from the member of Congress, down to the youngest apprentice or school-boy in America, it was all:

Turn about and wheel about, and do just so,
And every time I turn about I jump Jim Crow."
(1996 [1845]: 52)

Although unabashedly racist, minstrelsy was a site where European- and African-derived cultures influenced each other. The thicket of white attitudes toward black culture included ample ambivalence. While the purveyors of minstrelsy were shamelessly appropriating black culture in support of a vicious slave system, they were attracted to what they were stealing. Lott has eloquently described how white performers and composers exploited, distorted, yet paradoxically affirmed African American culture: "Blackface performance, the first formal public acknowledgment by whites of black culture, was based on small but significant crimes against settled ideas of racial demarcation, which indeed appear to be inevitable when white Americans enter the haunted realm of racial fantasy" (1993: 4). Stephen Foster, the nineteenth century's most popular songwriter, and many of minstrelsy's founders such as T. D. Rice and E. P. Christy reported how they conducted what we would call fieldwork, spending time in black communities, at social functions, and work sites to learn songs and speech mannerisms. Unlike the public accommodations that would be racially segregated under the system later named for the minstrel character Jim Crow, minstrel shows were often shared by the full gamut of class and racial groups. Here is a description of a Boston minstrel in the third decade of the nineteenth century.

> It appeared that the gallery was the resort of the particoloured race of Africans, the descendants of Africans, and the vindicators of the abolition of the slave trade; that the tier of boxes below it in the center was occupied by single gentlewomen who had lodgings to let, and who were equally famous for their delicacy and taciturn disposition. The remainder of the boxes, I was given to understand, were visited by none but the dandies, and people of the first respectability and fashion; while the pit presented a mixed multitude of the lower orders of all sorts, sizes, ages, and deportments. (quoted in Lott 1993: 65)

Not only did minstrelsy bring people of different classes, races, and ethnicities into the same venue, it also provided a locus for groups to sort out their relationships to each other. A harbinger of the multicultural American identity was forged here. While existing cultural forms carried the indelible stamp of distinctively European, African, or Native American sights and sounds, minstrelsy was a new synthesis that mocked all three. W. T. Lhamon Jr. thus describes how blackface was an opportunity for working-class youths of various ethnicities to find a common identity tag. Jim Crow came to represent ethnicity in general: "Precisely because middle-class aspirants disdained the black jitterbug in every region, the black figure appealed all across the Atlantic as an organizational emblem for workers and the unemployed. Hated everywhere, he could be championed everywhere alike" (1998: 44). The frontier rube, the hard-drinking Irish, and the peculiar-sounding German were familiar stereotypes that captured the fancy of audiences, though never as enthusiastically as Jim Crow.

So it is not a coincidence that the cultural meaning of minstrelsy in the first half of the nineteenth century would anticipate folk music in the early twentieth century. Both were contrasted to high culture. Toll (1974) interprets minstrelsy as the origin of the highbrow-lowbrow distinction, a cultural form created in Jacksonian America to demarcate democratic American culture from effete European influence. Folk music is, by definition, *not* high culture. Both were seen as embodying deeply American expressions. All of minstrelsy's stock characters were uniquely American, helping construct the new nation's sense of national character. The ingenious Yankee Doodle, the braggart frontiersman Davy Crockett, and the slaphappy Jim Crow developed as recognizable national types, stock characters in American imagery ever since.

After the Civil War, blacks aspiring to reach large white audiences increasingly took their cues on white tastes from minstrels. Blacks were not only exposed to minstrel shows as audience and performers, they were consumers of the sheet music that circulated minstrel music. For example, African American singer Will Stark sang for Alan Lomax the grossly caricatured song, "Coon, Coon, Coon,"[8] reporting that he had learned it at a show and that it had been very popular among white folks about 1914. But he did not take his cues from white audiences uncritically, telling Lomax that he also learned from that song a more general lesson in race relations, that "Most singers are ignorant and think that anything the boss wants, they ought to do it, that they can't get along without help from him. But white folks don't like a smart nigger, that is, one that knows too much for his own interest or his own race" (Lomax 1942).

Although the invention of folk music was contrasted to crassly commercial popular music, minstrelsy was an important element in the lineage of what became American folk music in the twentieth century. Both the meanings claimed for the music and many of the particular styles and songs were shared. Just as minstrelsy was the cultural expression of a project to define the American nation, folk music was a belated affirmation of the claim that America did indeed have an indigenous culture. J. K. Kennard, Jr. wrote in the New York *Knickerbocker* in 1845,

> The popular song-maker sways the souls of men; the legislator rules only their bodies. The song-maker reigns through love and spiritual affinity; the legislator by brute force. Apply this principle to the American people. Who are our true rulers? The negro poets, to be sure! Do they not set the fashion, and give laws to the public taste? Let one of them, in the swamps of Carolina, compose a new song, and it no sooner reaches the ear of a white amateur, than it is written down, amended, (that is, almost spoilt), printed, and then put upon a course of rapid dissemination, to cease only with the utmost bounds of AngloSaxondom, perhaps of the world. (1996 [1845]: 62)

Folk music apostles a century later would expound no less rhapsodically about blues and spirituals as the true heart of the American spirit: "In representations of black life, audiences sought the wellhead of a native culture; and so, moreover, did a [*sic*] increasingly stylized representation of black culture come to provide the codes for wider representations of American folk culture" (Cantwell 1998: 66–67). Both the exponents of minstrelsy and the later advocates of folk music rooted their authenticity in the dialectic of race. While minstrelsy originally depicted a broad variety of characters, including sympathetic, though hardly equal, black characters, as slavery increasingly polarized the nation and as European immigrant workers found common cause in their whiteness, minstrelsy became more about race (Toll 1974). Just as authenticity symbolically links the identity of audiences to the identity of the performers, minstrelsy helped the white audience find common bonds in who they were not. Similarly, folk music a half century later was defined as authentic by its racial grounding, first as Anglo-American and then more broadly to include racially defined spirituals.

The relationship of minstrelsy to folk was deeper than analogy. Many of the styles and particular songs that became "folk" in the early twentieth century were distinctly colored by minstrelsy, colored both in the general sense of influence of the music and in the specific sense of giving racial meaning. Since popular culture did not distinguish between authentic and commercial forms, vernacular music indiscriminately scrambled songs with ancient roots and songs local singers would learn from minstrels, juke joints, and print.

Because the category of "folk" had not yet reached performers or their audiences, the boundaries between vernacular music and commercial music were virtually nonexistent. The extent to which people made a living through their music ranged from those earning a few dollars occasionally for a performance or lesson to those who identified themselves as professional performers with agents and business managers. People learned music from relatives, coworkers, performers, and sheet music, as well as at dances or minstrels, caring little if a song was ancient or new in origin, if it was composed by an individual or adapted through generations, or if it was performed for profit, fun, leisure, or work. When folklorists began to collect music from rural musicians, many songs that had begun in minstrelsy and had been published as sheet music had been passed along orally and their origins forgotten, then collected as folk music. Well-known tunes that graduated from minstrelsy to folk status include "Old Zip Coon"/"Turkey in the Straw" and "Blue Tail Fly," both of which combined the repetition of short phrases characteristic of African American music with the symmetry of phrase structure more characteristic of European traditions (Lott 1993: 177). The discourse of minstrelsy has emphasized that it was a commercialized, urban, "artificial," and overtly racist form of entertainment, while the discourse of folk music has depicted an indigenous, rural, authentic, and racially innocent past time. But the boundary was much less distinct in lived experience. While minstrelsy was a form of commercial entertainment, it not only was informed by indigenous music but was enjoyed and played by non-professionals in their parlors, at dances, and at juke joints. Rather than facing a wall between commercial and indigenous music, minstrelsy was a loop in the folk process, mediated by professional musicians and theater (Bluestein 1994; Toll 1974).

One of the most enduring legacies of minstrelsy was the set of codes that would later be affirmed as authenticity. The cultural syntax that polarized urban and rural, modern and traditional, sophisticated and simple, commercial and folk, fleeting and grounded gave rise to cultural codes we have inherited from minstrelsy. While the direct lineage of minstrelsy shaped vaudeville, musical theater, Tin Pan Alley, and Hollywood, the critique of superficiality lodged at those heirs was created in the progenitor. "Popular" became a synonym for insincere, contrasting with a more marginal but reputable "authentic." Not only are particular instruments and vocal styles we identify as genuine rooted in minstrelsy, but the notion that performers can appropriate the culture of other groups, representing themselves as faux slaves, frontiersmen, and country bumpkins, distilling for their audiences the alleged "essence" of those cultures, all arose with minstrelsy. And it is the groups that were jeered by the minstrels that are now the measure of authenticity. The blues and country music that now are considered America's most authentic voices are the legacies of racial synthesis refracted through minstrelsy.

SETTING THE STAGE FOR FOLK MUSIC

When the United States abolished slavery, the concept of folk music had not been invented. People made music in many institutional settings with a variety of opinions about the qualities that would eventually be ascribed to folk music. Over the rest of the nineteenth century, the cultural distinctions later crystallized in the concept of folk music emerged from a variety of social settings. The rise of copyright laws and the sheet music industry would heighten consciousness about authorship and anonymity. Urbanization would deepen the distinction between cosmopolitan and parochial cultures, with the defeated South bearing the onus of provinciality. The formation of an urban upper class would engender a cultural elite, increasing the salience of a virtuosity-simplicity antithesis. And aristocratic academics would import from Europe and England an ideology locating the soul of the nation in the preservation of a fleeting past.

By the end of the nineteenth century, minstrelsy was giving way to vaudeville as the most popular form of live vernacular music. Popular music, propelled by the growing music publishing industry, was reaching into the homes of a broad range of Americans, while rural folk were making music at barn dances, juke joints, churches, and hoedowns. High culture was being distinguished from lowbrow, modern from traditional, and urban from rural. But modern urban life elicited a critique that affirmed a nostalgic vision of traditional rural life. The vernacular music of the rural South afforded a cultural project that turned sophisticated, progressive urban life on its head, valorizing the "folk" and their culture as the true embodiment of peoplehood. The folk project began in Europe as a part of a broader nation-building effort and was adapted in America to clarify the American racial dilemma. The concept then became a contested resource for conflicts over who would be defined as American and enjoy the rights and privileges implied thereby, culminating in the twentieth century's greatest conflict over national membership, the civil rights movement.

In the meantime, the music that later became enshrined as "folk" was just music to the people making it. It continued to develop in the same institutions as before the war, where blacks and whites blended the heritage of Africa and Europe into an originally American vernacular music. The people making and enjoying music knew little of the emergent folk music cultural project which claimed that the music was something more than entertainment.

CONCLUSION

The changing relationship between musical genres and social boundaries can be best understood by recognizing the contextual specificity of social boundaries such as race. While fundamental social boundaries pervade all social relations, they operate differently in different contexts such as jobs, the law, media content, intimacy, and cultural production. In some contexts, interaction among people of different races is permissible, though often hierarchical—work, domestic labor, commercial sales, and so forth. In other contexts the boundaries are stronger, though when breached are more egalitarian, as in romance and marriage. In still other situations, there is official equality, though perhaps with a strong undercurrent of informal inequality, as found in sports and music. From this perspective, it is not surprising that racial relations may have been less segregated in music than in other realms of life. Though there is probably no setting immune from race, some contexts are more inclusive than others. To the extent that racial boundaries are contextualized, the variable racial meanings of music can be explained from features of its social context. In the nineteenth century, American vernacular music was made in contexts with more interracial interaction than in many other arenas of society. Such settings were by no means egalitarian, but they were places of interracial contact, not absolute segregation. The vernacular music made in festive occasions, abolitionist organizations, minstrel and medicine shows, spirituals, other religious music, and black middle-class forays into white respectability was the raw material for what would be defined as folk music.

Vernacular American music was threaded through a complex web of social relationships and institutions, bridging and bounding class, race, gender, and region. "The folk" made music in the home, church, dance parlor, minstrel hall, and workplace. Sounds imported from Europe and Africa blended and regenerated to become the music we call American. In a society so infused with the social dynamics of race, it is inevitable that music be given racial meaning and contribute to the functioning of the racial system. But the ways that music has been given racial meaning, the identities that have been built on music, and the effects of the racialization of music have not been inevitable. It was not inevitable that the abolitionist movement would choose to humanize slaves by promoting their music or that postbellum college choirs would crystallize the music into the genre we know as spirituals. It was not inevitable that minstrelsy, the most popular form of vernacular music of the nineteenth century, be built on the ambivalent white appropriation and caricature of slave music. It was the interpretation of these events and relationships by white liberals such as James McKim and black intellectuals such as W.E.B. DuBois that kindled the powerful trope that would later ignite as authenticity. While the humanizing of slaves through music may have had a minuscule effect in ending slavery compared with the carnage of the Civil War, and while the popularity of the Fisk Jubilee Singers in northern cities may not have saved a single black life from the horror of lynching in the late nineteenth century, the social world of music departs from a singular correspondence of cultural difference and structures of domination. In the twentieth century, the status hierarchy of music inverted the broader system of racism. In music, "black" has come to be defined as good, signifying originality, feeling, talent, and that most ineffable but important quality, soul. "White" is an insult for musicians, implying banality, dispassion, even insignificance. The roots of this inversion were planted in the nineteenth century and cultivated in the twentieth. Among the fruits was the opportunity for social movements to influence some of the systems of domination that music by itself could little affect.

Authenticity is especially important in a sociological understanding because it redefines the terms of homology between cultural and social boundaries. Representing an affirmation of culture presumably expressed from the heart, authenticity unsettles the link between social status and respectable culture, justifying elite embrace of indigenous culture, not just their own highbrow culture. Authenticity is an imputed relationship between culture and people, mutually validating a set of qualities about the people and the verisimilitude of the culture. People otherwise deemed uncouth by the dominant group become redefined as pure, and their culture, by its association with the group, shares the purity. Cultural capital gets turned on its head.

CHAPTER THREE

The Original Folk Project

How can a musical project founded to authorize and celebrate a nationality be transformed into a cultural impetus empowering a movement for radical inclusivity? The literary elites who decided to valorize the music sung by rural commoners as the essence of nationhood could scarcely have imagined the genre they invented being used as the anthems of insurgency against the homogeneous national community of their imagination. The theme of this chapter is the early history of the concept "folk," as it developed from an assertion of national identity into a site of contention over who belonged to the nation.

How did interactive practices and discursive practices of doing music help construct race in the period before commercial recording? How did these practices then create social and symbolic resources for social movements to use from the 1920s on as they self-consciously aspired to reconfigure the relations between races? The thesis is that folk music, as both a set of interactive practices and a discourse, was more racially inclusive than the broader American society in general and other genres of music in particular, making its use an appropriate strategy for progressive social movements to undermine entrenched forms of racial domination. The initial project of folk music led by literary scholars created a musical ideology that unwittingly afforded co-optation by a second project led by progressives. By applying the ambiguous label of "folk" to the music they aspired to make quintessentially American, they left the door open for others with a broader conception of who counted as American to use it for a very different political project. When scholars and antiquarians first identified rural music as folk, neither they nor political activists could have anticipated that folk music would ever be adopted as the music of the left.

This chapter will examine the relationship of the folk project to the "folk" and their music. By folk project I mean the activity of academic and amateur folklorists who created and refined the concept of folk music, self-consciously promoting it as a genre with specific social meaning. As they sought to reinforce or undermine existing social boundaries, especially racial, national, ethnic, class, and urban-rural boundaries, people making music had their own ideas and practices, sometimes falling in step with the folklorists and sometimes marching to the tune of a different drummer. One of the most consequential divergences between the early academic portrayal of the folk and the actual practices of people making music was the relationship among races. Actual music-making was not nearly as different in black and white communities as folklorists portrayed. The divergence did not dictate a redefinition of folk music but provided the raw material for a second generation of folklorists and political activists to launch a very different folk project, making the concept of folk music attractive to political radicals looking for "the people's music."

CULTURAL PROJECTS

A cultural project is a coordinated activity by an identifiable group of people to define a category of cultural objects, distinguish it from other cultural objects, make claims about its significance and meaning, promote its adoption by others, and thereby have a social impact. In its ideal-typical form a cultural project is characterized by five kinds of work.

- Definition work. Since the origins of the concept, partisans of folk music have been acutely self-conscious about what folk music is and what it is not. Whether writing for specialists or general audiences, authors tend to begin books and articles about folk music by defining what they mean. There is clearly little consensus. But even the disagreements are important to the project, energizing the attempt to find the true essence of the concept that draws people together and sets them apart from others.

- Significance claims. A project is built around a category of cultural objects, typically a label or genre such as folk music, impressionism, or modern dance. It takes coordinated work to reify the category as a thing, a distinct, identifiable style, distinguished from other cultural objects by putative essential qualities. A project's definitional work, whether consensual or contested, is closely related to the work of making claims about the cultural objects' significance and meaning. Very often claims about what a category *is* are indistinguishable from claims about what it *does*. When music is classified as the music of a nationally defined group "the English people or German people," it is claimed to represent the soul of the nation.

- Boundary work. Defining music by the people who do it rather than its sonic or textual qualities makes a claim about the relationship between social position and culture. Specifying it in national terms claims that nationality is deeply enough cultural that it can mark cultural boundaries. Distinguishing folk music from commercial music implies that some music expresses a natural spirit, not an instrumental aspiration for profit. Thus when a project defines a category and makes claims, it promotes its adoption by others who share the goals espoused in the claims. Nationalist claims about folk music appeal to nationalists; anti-commercial claims about authenticity appeal to those familiar enough with industrial life to seek a refuge from it.

- Cultural innovation. Cultural projects present their cultural objects to the public in terms of innovation, typically a new kind of music, art, or literature. The innovation in the invention of the genre of folk music was not the music itself but the understanding of the music. Instead of treating simple music as crude and unsophisticated, folk advocates "discovered" the eclipsed genius of the nation. Specific songs then were uncovered by the new category of person, the folklorist, doing the new activity of fieldwork.

- Institution building. Concepts like "folk" do not exist in some social ether or spontaneously percolate up from the social soup. A highly formalized academic discipline and myriad interested amateurs in the various folk projects have claimed the term "folk" as their domain, along with the cultural authority to define such terms as "folk," "folk culture," "folk music," and "folklore." Whether defining the folk as Appalachian whites, black and white provincials, workers, or non-elites in general, folk music projects make claims of who belongs and who is marginal. Performers shape their music to sound like what they imagine folk music to sound like. Marketers aim their products at imagined audiences. Coffeehouses and folk venues select some performers and filter others on the basis of whether they conform to the production values of folk music. Museums and archives display the sounds, images, and artifacts of some performers or writers while ignoring others. Among the many categories that guide such practices and decisions, "folk" has been an especially weighty concept, denoting more than entertainment or aesthetic criteria.

A cultural project is not the happenstance work of isolated individuals fortuitously converging toward a common outcome. While it is not necessary that individuals in a cultural project have formal ties, they do tend to know of each other's existence and understand their work in terms of a common goal. It is this common goal and awareness of each other that distinguish a cultural project from a trend.

Unlike many concepts that eventually settle into consensual definitions, discussions of folk music frequently begin by defining the term, and they have been doing so since the concept was introduced. I am less interested in making a case for any of the many specific definitions of "folk music" than examining how others have used the concept—how they have defined it and what implications follow from adopting one definition rather than another. To be serviceable, a definition must distinguish between instances of the object defined and everything else. For "folk" or "folk culture" to be meaningful, we must establish what "non-folk" or "non-folk culture" is. Some definitions of folk music explicitly define it by what it is not. Norm Cohen, a prolific writer about the 1960s folk revival, defines a folk song as "a song that survives without the necessity of commercial media" (1990: 5). In each of the social settings where "folk" is employed to distinguish some music from others—marketing, academic folklore, folk clubs, museums, and archives—there is a sense of what music is not folk music. All the settings share an assumption that most music—classical, rock, jazz, popular music, and all the currently trendy musics—are not "folk." But if one considers "folk music" as the music of the "folk," the distinction becomes murky, contingent on who is included in "the folk." A broad sense of the term "folk" refers to people in general. If folk music is the music of the folk, then "folk music" should refer to the music of the people in general, what some prefer to call vernacular music (Filene 2000; Green 2001a; Small 1987).[1] As the blues singer Big Bill Broonzy once responded when asked if a song he performed was folk music, "I guess all songs is folk songs. I never heard no horse sing 'em" (quoted in "Folk Singing" 1962: 60).

What is at stake are the boundaries of the folk. Who is included in the folk and who is not? What is the relationship between those creating the category "folk" and the folks themselves? Some define the folk in inclusive terms. Most left-wing conceptions of the folk have been inclusive, equating "folk" with "people," excluding only those who oppress (capitalists) or manipulate (mass media). Alan Lomax opened his national radio broadcast on "folk Music of the USA" by characterizing folk music in terms of the people who sing the songs. This show, he said, was about the music recorded from the lips of "cowboys, lumberjacks, convicts, farm hands, housewives, sailors, wandering minstrels and many other folk types . . . the little people who have built and who sustain the U.S.A."[2]

However, the broader the conception of folk, the vaguer the sense of who is not "the folk" or what music would not be "folk music." So the folk of folk music are typically identified by a narrow sense of "folk," some subset of the population—less urban, sophisticated, or cosmopolitan, presumably a remnant of what the more urban cosmopolitan members of the society were like before they were spoiled by civilization. The ambiguity between a broad and a narrow sense of "folk" has bedeviled folk music advocates ever since the term was introduced. To complicate matters even more, the narrowly defined "folk"—the rural, backward, unsophisticated folk—were claimed to embody the cultural essence of a broadly defined folk. "Folk" is never assumed to be a universal term, but the specification of *a* people. What makes the issue contentious is that "the folk" symbolically represents the society, but some people do not count as folk. The selection of the folk that represents the true spirit of the people can exclude large numbers of people, especially minority, immigrant, or marginal populations. Thus while superficially an inclusive concept, "folk" also carries vivid connotations of exclusions.

The issue matters because the discourse of "folk" and "folk music" has been used to do boundary work, forging and reinforcing distinctions not only between musical genres but also between people. Depending on whether "the folk" is equated with "the people," "the nation," "the citizenry," or "society," different groups are either included in folk music or marginalized from it.

The specific boundary most explicitly asserted in folk music's boundary work was national. Anderson (1991) has eloquently described how nation-building projects depict an "imagined community" rooted in a common history, a people that share an ancestry and a common core of myths about national origins, heroes, icons, and heroic events. The concept of nation lies in an imagined primordial people, the ancestors of the modern national members. Just as the members of the modern nation are bounded from other nationalities, the primordial ancestors must be depicted as the origin of primordial peoplehood. One discursive means of creating such boundaries was the "discovery" of a national folk culture, a culture of a national people, different from the folk culture of other nations. Insofar as the folk were rooted in nature, not civilization, the distinctive national culture they offered was validated as national and thus innate. So the English folklorists identified a distinctively English folk culture, just as the French, Germans, and eventually most nations identified their own national folk cultures.

In 1866 Carl Engel, a German émigré in England, published *Introduction to the Study of National Music* and later *The Literature of National Music*, aspiring to create a category of national music. By national music, he meant "any music which, being composed in the peculiar taste of the nation to which it appertains, appeals more powerfully than other music to the feelings of that nation, and is consequently pre-eminently cultivated in a certain country. . . . The peculiar characteristics of the music of the nation are therefore more strongly exhibited in the popular songs and dance—tunes traditionally preserved by the country-people and the lower classes of society, which form the great majority of the nation" (quoted in Harker 1985: 142). Sharp, in one of his books on English folk songs, expresses both the distance between himself and the folk and the shared membership in the imagined national community: "A nation's music, for instance, must, at every stage of its development, be closely related to those spontaneous musical utterances which are the outcome of a purely natural instinct, and which proceed, it will always be found, from those of the community who are least affected by extraneous educational influences—that is, from the folk" (1916). Though Sharp would hardly include himself or those of his class as unaffected by extraneous educational influences, the folk provided for those of Sharp's class a national music that the better sorts could take pride in: "The collection and preservation of our folk music, whatever else it has done, has at least restored the Englishman's confidence in the inherent ability of his nation to produce great music" (1916). Child, too, saw his work as a nationalistic enterprise, as he self-consciously set out to collect a canon of true English music, claiming a national pedigree for the songs he collected, writing that they were composed by the upper class in the Middle Ages and passed down through the folk "in which there is such community of feelings that the whole people form an individual" (quoted in Lomax n.d.: 8).

Origins of the Folk Concept

There is of course nothing necessary or natural in the concept of "folk" culture. Few societies other than modern Western ones make a distinction between the culture of the educated elite and the culture of "the folk." The social roots of the distinction between folk and high culture lie in a nationalist and often aristocratic project to define a people while registering a genteel critique of industrial, urban society. Thomas Percy (1729–1811), generally considered the founding figure in English folk studies, claimed to have found the true heritage of the English people in Elizabethan-era folk music. In his *Reliques of Ancient English Poetry: Consisting of Old Heroic Ballads, Songs and other Pieces of our earlier Poets (Chiefly of the Lyric kind), Together with some few of later Date* (1765), the Anglican bishop collected ballads from published sources, liberally editing them because, according to his nephew, "a scrupulous adherence to their wretched readings would only have exhibited unintelligible nonsense" (Harker 1985: 32). The volume vividly displays the gulf between the folklorist and the "folk." Dedicated to the Right Honourable Elizabeth, Countess of Northumberland, this was an aristocrat writing for other aristocrats. The collector took on the role of mediator between the culture of the folk and the appreciation of the educated audience. Extensive introductions situated them historically, describing different versions, placing them regionally, and summarizing the stories. Such intellectual topology situates the works within the terrain of English national culture, writing for those appreciating folklore from a perch of erudite understanding. It is clear that the "folk" are not the intended audience.

Percy was neither the first nor most important collector in the original folk music project but renowned because of prolonged controversy over the authenticity of his sources, which stimulated others to search for more vernacular songs. Joseph Ritson's *A Select Collection of English Songs* (1783) criticized Percy for sloppy scholarship and asserted that his own work represented the most authentic rendition. Like Percy he argued that the best music came from court society and that much of what minstrels performed for commoners was inferior. But he shared Percy's penchant for boundary work, wherein the search into the past was an attempt to find "pure" English culture unadulterated by foreign influence. William Motherwell furthered the project with his *Minstrelsy Ancient and Modern* (1873 [1827]), packed with three hundred unedited ballads collected from elderly women, and gave us the authoritative definition of a ballad as "a narrative song preserved on the lips of the people" (Lomax n.d.: 4).

In these early works we see the boundary work that would shape the genre of folk music for the next several centuries: folk culture embodies a people; it is contrasted to the polluted culture of civilization; it is rooted in the past; and it is rural. First, an aristocratic class appropriates the culture of a disadvantaged group while maintaining a solid boundary between them. The folk are claimed to represent the essence of a larger group of people, originally a nation, but later a class or ethnic group. So it does not matter if the individual carriers of the culture are lowly, debased, or otherwise unworthy of respect. The American folklorist George L. Kittredge, for example, wrote that folk ballads "belonged, in the first instance, to the whole people, at a time when there were no formal divisions of literate and illiterate; when the intellectual interests of all were substantially identical, from the king to the peasant" (1932 [1904]). Second, this culture is accorded sacred status, in contrast to the polluted culture of larger society. Commercialized popular culture and the opaque complexities of modern high culture are contrasted with the purity and simplicity of folk culture. Third, the folk and their culture are appreciated primarily for their connections to the past; their value to society lies more in their incubation of peoplehood than in their contemporary contribution to society. A recurrent and deeply meaningful theme is the need to preserve the spiritual essence of folk culture being threatened by the advance of civilization. It is implicitly hoped that the gift of the folk's culture will alleviate the rough edges of urban industrial society with little regard for any potential benefits civilization might bring to the folk. Fourth, the folk are generally rural; rural life is considered unchanged, imbued with tradition unsullied by modernity. Thus a social space—the rural countryside—is represented temporally rather than geographically.

As it turned out, the pure, simple, lyrical folk music that the collectors were looking for was only a small part of what the folk were performing and listening to. Beginning in the sixteenth century, printed songs appeared as broadsides (one-sided sheets of varying lengths), chapbooks (cheap books—often single sheets folded twice or more), and small songbooks or garlands, many of them anonymous to avoid official displeasure. It is ironic that the anonymity so celebrated by folk music scholars was just as often a result of contentious politics as origins in a pristine past. Popular in Britain, Holland, France, Italy, Spain, and Germany, and later in America, broadsides were thoroughly mined by folk song collectors who rejected most of them as inappropriate, drivel, or salacious, appropriating for themselves the music that qualified as that of the folk.

Successful cultural projects typically beatify selected cultural objects as a canon, a set of standard works seen to capture the essence of the cultural form and serve as a touchstone against which other works can be compared, not only to measure quality but to determine whether they qualify as the cultural type. The "high" folk tradition was codified in the nineteenth century by Francis James Child. Studying philology in Germany as a young man, he developed an interest in the connection between antiquity and the modern world that dominated the intellectual contribution of his long career as a Harvard professor of rhetoric and English literature. He decided to collect English and Scottish ballads, but after comparing Percy's manuscript to the printed work he decided to base all his collections on manuscript material. His prolific volumes of ballads, romances, and tales from all nations were collected from scholars, antiquaries, and "private gentlemen."

Child's definitive codification of English-language ballads, *The English and Scottish Popular Ballads*, which was revised several times, lastly in 1882, has continued to serve the function for which it was intended, establishing a canon. Child's commentary includes a pedigree for each ballad, verifying ancient origins, both English and European, and elaborating different versions of the story. Previous collections are synthesized, codifying disparate stories into versions of the "same" ballad.[3] But Child did more than codify vernacular culture. He defined what a ballad and, for many, what an authentic folk song was. While his first volume (1857–58) indiscriminately included all ballads that he knew about, he increasingly winnowed out those that did not meet his criteria of what a ballad should be, exercising an authoritative judgment of what was a ballad and what was not, what was original and what was corrupted, which versions were important, and what text was ancient. Rejected was the work of professional ballad makers that filled broadsides and garlands, deemed "products of a low kind of art, and most of them are, from a literary point of view, thoroughly despicable and worthless" (quoted in Harker 1985). Kittredge applauded Child's discriminating sensibility, arguing that he had "a complete understanding of the 'popular' genius, a sympathetic recognition of the traits that characterize oral literature wherever and in whatever degree they exist," a faculty that the folk themselves no longer have (1965 [1882]: xxx). Folklorists, singers, collectors, and scholars still refer to "authentic" ballads by the number he assigned to them. A "Child ballad" continues to be the standard against which authenticity of folk music is measured. For example, Simon and Garfunkel's 1960s hit "Scarborough Fair" is known to folklorists as Child Ballad No. 2.

The first folk project included academics, especially literary scholars, gentlemen collectors, and, in this country, social reformers, primarily women, who shared a romantic vision of premodern purity in rural music. The concept of "folk" is a fundamentally modern concept, much like its ideological cousin, "nation." It is of relatively recent European origin, coming into common usage only in the nineteenth century. While the music of the court or the cathedral may have been distinguished from the music of the minstrel or music hall, not until the late nineteenth century was there a generic term to distinguish the music of the people from that of the elite. More important, the term "folk" is modern in the sense of *modernism*, that frame of mind that has informed European thinking since the Enlightenment. Modernism draws a solid boundary between the modern and the premodern, portraying post-Renaissance Europe as an epochal transformation of human society between two polar types, which prefigures a parallel global watershed. Folk culture is defined as the vestige of premodern culture, a remnant of the primitive within the civilized. Folk culture is traditional culture, in the sense of "tradition" that distinguishes it from modern. Cecil Sharp, one of the first generation of folk song scholars, expresses this point of view especially vividly: "Living only in the memories and on the lips of the singers, its existence has always been conditioned by its popularity, and by the accuracy with which it has reflected the ideals and taste of the common people. Consequently, the folk-songs are stamped with the hall-mark of corporate approbation, and the faithful expression in musical idiom of the qualities and characteristics of the nation to which it owes its origin" (1927 [1908]: n.p.).

One of the characteristics of modernism is a self-critique. Modern art, modern literature, and modern music highlight the anxieties, disquiet, emptiness, and alienation of the modern condition. While the material progress of modernization has produced physical comfort, conquered disease, and enabled global awareness, the psychological and spiritual side has been generally greeted with angst and despair, especially by serious intellectuals. One form of disaffection about the modern world is nostalgia about the loss of the past. The optimism of technological progress has been matched by the remorse over lost innocence, a major theme of nineteenth- and twentieth-century romanticism. The first generation of folk collectors thought they had found, as Marson and Sharp expressed it at the turn of the last century, "the last lingering remnant of the old village life; a survival of the times when the village had a more or less independent existence, built its own church, hanged its rogues, made its own boots, shirts, and wedding rings, and changed its own tunes. All the rest is gone" (quoted in Harker 1985).

The concept of "folk," as it was constructed, shares with mainstream modernism a conceptualization that pits universalism against particularism, and sees universalism as eroding the boundaries between particular groups. But the early folklorists differed from mainstream modernists in their evaluation of the modernizing project. Mainstream modernists endorsed the erosion of nationality, ethnicity, religious segmentation, and aristocratic class. Development was seen as the solvent of the categorical distinctions that constrain individual opportunities and feed animosity. But the folklorists interpreted such change as a threat, boding the loss of premodern innocence and threatening the essence of peoplehood. To be the sovereign individual celebrated by the modernists would render anyone bereft of personhood and identity.

It is in nineteenth-century romanticism that the concept of folk culture and folk music finds its roots. German philosopher Johann Gottfried Herder (1744–1803) is credited with introducing the "folk" concept to the continent and is generally seen as an architect of the romantic critique of modernism. Challenging the notion that European civilization was the apogee of human history, he argued that all societies have value and that the core value of the society was found in its peasantry, the heart of the nation.[4] Thus identity was located temporally, in the imagined community with common historical roots. The "folk's" structural position as rural, poor, often oppressed populations is glossed over in portrayals of "backward," "unchanged," or "primitive." The people who embodied the nation were the ones who had been least changed by modernity, the people who preserved the nation's soul in its inherited culture. Preserving the past, or at least the cultural traditions of the past, then helped ameliorate the universalizing, standardizing, homogenizing force of modernization.

Alarmed that all tradition melts before the searing march of progress, virtually all commentary on folk culture warns of its vulnerability and the need to preserve it, not just for the music itself but for the community and its way of life. The words of folklorist and onetime Cecil Sharp assistant Maud Karpeles are typical: "It is surprising and sad to find how quickly the instinctive culture of the people will seem to disappear when once they have been brought into touch with modern civilization, and how soon they will imitate the manners and become imbued with the tastes of polite Society" (1932 [1904]: xvi). Most late nineteenth-century folk song societies shared the goals of the Folk Song Society founded in London in 1898: "the collection and preservation of Folk Songs, Ballads, and Tunes, and the publication of such of these as may be advisable" (quoted in Harker 1985: 170). But preservation did not necessarily mean preserving the music as performed by the folk. While some of the more antiquarian collectors sought to preserve the music as unadulterated as possible, others were more interested in preserving the spirit.[5] That meant making the tunes, harmonies, and lyrics, as enhanced by folklorists, available for other contexts, including art music. Thus the society's membership included Edward Elgar, Antonín Dvořák, and Edward Grieg.

The mode of preservation, capturing the social spirit of the music more than its actual sounds or language, was justified by claims that the music embodies the collectivity. Henry Krehbiel, a white author writing about black music, described folk songs as "echoes of the heart-beats of the vast folk, and in them are preserved feelings, beliefs and habits of vast antiquity" (1914: 3). Because folk music in this view is the music of the people in general, not of any individual, the collector then must capture the "true essence," not the rendering of any contemporary performer, who necessarily has been tainted by modernity.

The academic claims of the collective spirit found their most explicit articulation in the perspective known as communalism, led by F. B. Gummere in Europe and George L. Kittredge in the United States. Communalism held that folk songs may have been composed by individuals, but the collective process of revision and refinement rendered individual composers irrelevant. Based on specific assumptions about the nature of "primitive" society, music was imagined as communal performance, primarily dance. When civilization struck such simple societies their music would presumably vanish, unless preserved by self-conscious conservancy. Sharp explicitly connected communalism to the national meaning of folk music. His theory of folk music was based on "the assumption that folk-music is generically distinct from ordinary music; that the former is not the composition of an individual and, as such, limited in outlook and appeal, but a communal and racial product, the expression, in musical idiom, of aims and ideals that are primarily national in character" (1927 [1908]: x).

Though the theory was criticized almost immediately, it has continued to influence many interpretations of folk music. Louise Pound, a professor of English at the University of Nebraska, challenged the communal theory, asking whether "primitives" always danced when they sang, sang as a group, or composed communally, as assumed by Gummere and Kittredge. She used studies of contemporary primitives to challenge each point, showing that Kaffirs sat down when they sang, while American Indians often wrote songs individually, and even sold songs to each other (Pound 1917).

The claim that the songs belong to the people rather than the performers and that they are quickly disappearing validates the collector as the most qualified person to render the essential qualities of the culture. In introducing Child's collection of ballad lyrics, which had been criticized by others for his practice of "improving" the literary qualities, Kittredge affirmed the interpretive role of the collector: "Mere learning will not guide an editor through these perplexities. What is needed is, in addition, a complete understanding of the 'popular' genius, a sympathetic recognition of the traits that characterize oral literature wherever and in whatever degree they exist. This faculty, which even the folk has not retained, and which collectors living in ballad-singing tale-telling times have often failed to acquire, was vouchsafed by nature herself to this sedentary scholar" (1965 [1882]: xxx). Thus while the folk might be carriers of the essential qualities of their culture, the leaders of the folk project reserved the cultural authority to render the content in its purest form.

INSTITUTIONAL FOUNDATIONS

Cultural projects work through particular institutions such as the nonprofit corporate entities that sustain classical music or the business of popular music. The first folk project was based in two institutional settings, the university and the settlement school movement, both energized by cultural entrepreneurs. After World War I, they would be joined by the commercial record companies, the organizations of the political left, and the network of folk societies, festivals, and magazines to create the multiple faces of folk music that persist to the present. The universities, settlement schools, and cultural entrepreneurs each contributed their framing of who the folk were, the reasons why a folk–non-folk distinction was important, and a collection of what songs could be considered folk songs. People in each institution defined the relationship between themselves and the "others" that comprise the folk in different ways, ways that reflect the social relationships characteristic of those institutions. University professors often objectify the people they study, framing them in scholarly categories. The "folk" of the university folklorists were primitive, simple, isolated, and easily corrupted—everything the folklorists were not. Their goal was to save the beauty of the folk culture for the race as a whole, with relatively little regard for the fate of common people as people. While those in the university treated the folk as objects, the settlement school workers saw them as clients, though, like the professors, they considered them primitive, simple, isolated, and easily corrupted. Their goal was to help individuals, preserving the best in traditional culture while rising above the retrograde parts. William Frost, president of

Kentucky's Berea College, saw that the challenge of civilization to the mountain folks was to make them "intelligent without making them sophisticated" (quoted in G. Campbell 1999: 160).

The disciplines that provided the intellectual scaffolding for the concept of folk music were English and anthropology. Child and Kittredge were both professors of English at Harvard, the latter one of the nation's leading Chaucer and Shakespeare authorities. From the perspective of academic English, folk songs were a form of literature, the natural literature of a people, or, as folklorists often stated it, of a race. They applied an aesthetic sensibility, taking folk song lyrics from existing texts, codifying them, and creating a canon, much as their colleagues did with elite writers.

Anthropology at the turn of the century helped define modernity, giving substance to the distinction between civilized and primitive peoples. By their portrayal of the primitive, they accentuated both the virtues of civilization—material comfort, rationality, technological progress—and its failures—alienation, standardization, loss of identity, and erosion of the aesthetic. Anthropology spoke to and reinforced a broad cultural fascination with the exotic that projected what was missing from modern life onto people separated in time and space. Those specializing in folklore studies shifted the focus from an "other" place to an "other" time, the distant past where primitive ancestors allegedly forged the spirit of peoplehood, infusing into the nation virtues that modernity could challenge but not extinguish.

This was the spirit in which the American Folk-Lore Society was founded in 1888, sparking the establishment of the *Journal of American Folklore*, edited by Columbia's Franz Boas. The society's members included not only anthropologists but other academics and public figures, including George Kittredge, Oliver Wendell Holmes, Senator Henry Cabot Lodge, Samuel L. Clemens (Mark Twain), historian William F. Allen, Joel Chandler Harris, and historian of the West Hubert H. Bancroft. The agenda outlined in the journal's first issue delineated how they drew the line between modern and primitive. The inaugural issue of the *Journal of American Folklore* justified the need to study folklore in terms of the inaccessibility of the folk mind: "The habits and ideas of primitive races include much that seems to us cruel and immoral, much that it might be thought well to leave unrecorded. But this would be a superficial view. What is needed is not an anthology of customs and beliefs, but a complete representation of the savage mind in its rudeness as well as its intelligence, its licentiousness as well as its fidelity" (1: 6). They proposed to collect the remnants of the fast-vanishing remains of folklore in America, targeting four populations: isolated conveyers of ancient English folklore, African Americans of the South, American Indian tribes, and non-

English-speakers of French Canada and Mexico. For each area they were especially interested in songs and stories having to do with nature, particularly animals, and with lore of superstition and mass beliefs, the parts of culture they felt were most vulnerable to extinction, that is, the beliefs least compatible with modernity. Despite the published agenda, there were few articles on African Americans until the 1920s, when they began to proliferate.[6] Lila W. Edmands published the first Appalachian ballads in the *Journal of American Folklore* in 1893 with little commentary except an introduction noting that most of her informants were too ignorant to read (Edmands 1893). In 1911, Prof. Hubert G. Shearin of Transylvania College published "British Ballads in the Cumberland Mountains" in the *Sewanee Review*, listing the Child ballads he had found. Over the next decade state folklore societies were created in several eastern states both north and south, mostly by English professors.

University professors, most of whom were literary researchers, could easily collect and codify texts, as Child did, but they did not have access to the folk themselves. But another institution, also subsidized by America's upper class, did—rural settlement schools funded by urban elites. Cecil Sharp and the other collectors who actually heard the music were not ethnographers entering inaccessible, alien outposts, despite the common rhetoric about isolation. He was invited by Olive Dame Campbell, wife of John C. Campbell, director of the Southern Highland Division of the Russell Sage Foundation.

Rural settlement schools were modeled after the urban settlement schools, such as Jane Addams's Hull House, and the work of organizations like the American Missionary Association, which was promoting practical education for ex-slaves. After the first settlement house in 1895, they proliferated rapidly, climbing to one hundred in 1900 and doubling each five-year period until there were about four hundred in 1910 (Whisnant 1983). Responding to what they interpreted as a debilitating culture, the settlement house organizers sought to help Appalachians out of poverty through education. Applying what we would now call identity work, they sought to rectify a culture of shame by validating manual skills and indigenous music. Students at the school, both youth and adults, were taught traditional crafts, songs, and dances that would foster a sense of who they were. To raise funds in northern cities, school administrators and their foundation-based supporters disseminated an image of quaint mountaineers minding primitive looms and strumming traditional dulcimers, an image congruent with those promoting a vision of America founded on Anglo bedrock, threatened by non-white and non-Protestant contenders.

The Hindman School illustrates the role of settlement schools in the unfolding folk project. Founded in 1902 in eastern Kentucky by two well-born women, Katherine Pettit and May Stone, with support from the Kentucky Federation of Women's Clubs, the Hindman School encouraged ballad singing, made its own collections, used ballads in promotional literature, and served as headquarters for other ballad collectors. As early as 1907, Pettit submitted a collection of ballads from Hindman to the *Journal of American Folklore* for an article by George Kittredge, "Ballads and Rhymes from Kentucky."

Unlike the academics whose relationship to the people making music could at best be called paternalistic, the settlement movement had a more complex and ambivalent relationship. Motivated by genuine concern for the people, urban reformers ignored the economic and political forces that were shaping the region, trying to preserve what they felt was admirable in traditional culture and resisting successful transition to a modern way of life. Though most of the settlement students came from worker or farmer families, they were taught traditional handicraft to sell as quaint artifacts. No heed was given to the colonization by northern capital into the region. While many of the very talented musicians were listening to music on the radio and buying banjos from mail order catalogs, they were being taught the dulcimer, an instrument with little local history, and sword dances, which had disappeared centuries earlier. At the same time, the ballad collectors did preserve and reinvigorate a vital musical tradition, helping affirm a culture that the larger society had discarded as primitive. This selective attitude toward the local culture is captured in a 1939 fund-raising letter: "A child with a genuine love for music expressing itself in raucous singing of so-called [commercial] 'hill-billy' songs, learns at our Saturday night gatherings beautiful lasting melodies, and the true mountain ballads that are a heritage from English forbears" (quoted in Whisnant 1983: 57–58).

The settlement schools were one of the main links between the ballad collectors who gave form to the concept of American folk music and the people who made the music. When Olive Dame Campbell came to the South for the Russell Sage Foundation, hearing ballads at the Hindman School inspired her to become one of the first collectors. After traveling to Scandinavia to study the folk high school movement, she founded the John C. Campbell Folk School, named after her late husband, and directed it for twenty-five years. Through mutual friends in the Russell Sage Foundation, she met Cecil Sharp and, with a decade of song collecting behind her, guided his endeavors to track down Elizabethan ballads in the mountains. To his delight he found what he considered the genuine English folk that no longer resided in his native England. Campbell's orientation was connected to the people, aspiring to affirm what was still very much alive, even if she shunned the culture that many of the folk may have fancied. As she explained in a 1916 letter to him, "[The] folk movement in the mountains . . . seeks the recognition and preservation of all that is native and fine. . . . We would like to have the people recognize the worth and beauty of their songs; we would like to have the singing of these songs encouraged in all the mountain schools and centers; we would like to have them displace the inferior music that is now being sung there. . . . The people have already begun to be somewhat ashamed of their songs; they need to have them appreciated by outsiders" (quoted in Whisnant 1983: 103). Sharp began collecting in 1916 and spent forty-eight weeks there over three years, collecting 1,612 tunes from 281 singers.

Despite the distorted images of mountain folk projected to the rest of the country, the ballad collectors were very successful at creating a bounded genre of music and appropriating the mantle of *the* American folk music to Anglo-American heritage. Francis Child, like most American folklorists of his era, believed that America had no folk tradition because America lacked an ancient past and a peasant class. It would take an Englishman, Cecil Sharp, to convince respectable scholars and folklorists that such a notion was wrong, though it was specifically English music that was identified. Their collaboration resulted in *English Songs of the Southern Appalachians*, the canon of ancient English music in the new world. As fruitful as their collaboration was, it was based on a different relationship with the folk. Sharp's was distant and romanticized, seeking a world that no longer existed.

Cecil Sharp was probably the most influential cultural entrepreneur of the first American folk project. This son of a London slate merchant was never very successful at anything until, in mid-life, he discovered folk music and folk dancing, which he embraced with the zeal of a convert. His original goal was nationalistic—to forge a British national culture, to help the young Englishman "know and understand his country and his countrymen far better than he does at present; and knowing and understanding them he will love them the more, realize that he is united to them by the subtle bond of blood and kinship, and become, in the highest sense of the word, a better citizen, and a truer patriot" (quoted in Filene 2000: 22). After despairing that the English people had been polluted by civilization, preferring the music they found in pubs, he found in America the British past he thought had been lost in England, a peasant culture in full operation, "a case of arrested degeneration" (Filene 2000: 24). The people of Appalachia were said to be removed from civilization by the hills, an isolated outpost where people frozen in time and removed in space still spoke Elizabethan English. The contaminating corrosion of civilization had not yet reached them, isolated in the southern mountains, a time-warped society of simplicity and innocence, purportedly everything the common people of England were not.

Sharp would not have ascribed to just any isolated group the cultural richness he celebrated in the people of Appalachia. In his mind, though uneducated, coarse, and backward, they still had the inherent genius of their race. The mountaineers' "language, wisdom, manners, and the many graces of life that are theirs, are merely racial attributes which have been gradually handed down generation by generation" (quoted in Filene 2000: 25). To cap it off, he found that they knew and sang many of the ballads that the American Child had codified from English sources. It was as if he had found the lost tribes. The fact that these musically adept people knew a lot of other music, including popular commercial music, did not dilute his enthusiasm or deter him from collecting and publishing the ballads as genuine folk music. Here was proof that America really did have folk music, the "real" folk music that Child had consecrated while he lamented that America had no folk music. The music of these people would be Sharp's gift to future generations: "remembering that the primary purpose of education is to place the children of the present generation in possession of the cultural achievements of the past, so that they may as quickly as possible enter into their racial inheritance, what better form of music or of literature can we give them than the folk-songs and folk-ballads of the race to which they belong, or of the nation whose language they speak?" (Sharp 1932: xxxvi). But what could be the affirmation of one social group, in a context where identities are contested, can signal an invidious distinction to those omitted.

CULTURE AND THE FOLK

Contemporary social science distinguishes between two meanings of the word *culture*—the aesthetic domain of music, art, literature, and mass media versus the common understandings, meanings, and values of a society. Before the invention of the folk concept, the word was used only in the sense of aesthetic activity and assumed to be possessed only by the refined members of society. The first generation of folklorists challenged the conventional definition of culture, which had restricted the domain of culture to high art, literature, and music. In contrast to the widespread distinction between "cultured" and "uncultured" people, the concept of folk culture rested on an overt claim that all people had culture. But this potentially egalitarian claim was undermined by a new distinction between popular (unmarked) culture and "folk" culture. The folklorists snuck the distinction between high culture and low culture in the back door by staking out a new domain of scholarly study in which they would exercise scholarly authority. While rebutting the notion that the art, music, and stories of people outside conventional circles of literate discourse did not deserve the designation of culture, they reinforced the assumption that such culture was fundamentally different from high culture, so different that it warranted a distinct scholarly discipline. Whereas conventional art, music, and literature were seen as products of profoundly talented individuals, folk culture was the product of a collective effervescence, long bubbling up from ancient roots, passed from generation to generation. Whereas conventional art, music, and literature was seen as complex, refined, and elaborated, folk culture was distinguished by its simplicity. Whereas traditional culture was considered great when it innovated and prefigured later work, folk culture was most revered when it preserved the past and resisted change.

The problem was that the boundary between folk and civilized culture was recognized only by those deemed civilized. As "the folk" made music, decorated artifacts, and told stories, they were aware neither of the purported boundaries separating their activities from those of other people nor of the alleged qualities that made their culture pure. Sharp's characterization of his Appalachian informants could never be written about one's own group: "Although uneducated, in the sense in which that term is usually understood, they possess that elemental wisdom, abundant knowledge, and intuitive understanding which only those who live in constant touch with Nature and face to face with reality seem to be able to acquire" (1932: xxiii). John and Alan Lomax exemplify a more subtle characterization of the "other": "We offer a composite photograph of what we and others, in field and forest, on mountain and plain, by the roadside and in the cabin, on big cane or cotton plantations and in prison camp, have set down of the songs of the people—isolated groups, interested only in an art which they could immediately enjoy, and thus an art that reflected and made interesting their own customs, dramas, and dreams" (1934: xxviii). The construction of the "other" here is less an explicit boundary claim than an intersubjective bond with an urban, sophisticated, and cultured readership. People only take note of that which they rarely take for granted, that which is different from what they are surrounded by. Just as fish are oblivious to water and landed creatures to earth, people are rarely enchanted by their own "customs, dramas, and dreams." The perspective here is from the urban, industrial segment of society, defining itself by what it is not. Such a characterization not only describes the personal perspective of folklorists but also reflects their understanding of the audience reading their text. The folk project assumed urban, educated audiences. To make the music appealing as folk music, the folklorists had to make the folk appealing as interesting, picturesque, and different.

As benevolent as the folklorists might have felt toward the people they identified as folk and as sincerely as they may have hoped for their best interests, it is clear that they themselves were not folk. While folklorists may romanticize the folk's innocence, simplicity, and collective creativity, they do not offer to surrender the pressures of modern society for the quaint life of the folk. If the essence of folk culture is found in the collectivity more than the individuals, and if the cultural authority for rendering that collective culture is accorded to the individual scholars, the figurative construction of the "folk" affirms the boundary between modern people and premodern people. While the concept of folk culture was a critique of modern society, it embraced the central worldview of modernism, the juxtaposition of tradition and modernity, inverting the aesthetic hierarchy, treating as negative many of the features that modernism endorsed. Few proclamations are more colorful than that of Prof. Hubert G. Shearin, who wrote in his "British Ballads in the Cumberland Mountains": "The clank of the colliery, the rattle of the locomotive, the roar of the furnace, the shriek of the factory whistle and, alas even the music of the school bell, are already overwhelming the thin tones of the dulcimore [sic] and the quavering voice of the Last Minstrel of the Cumberlands, who can find scant heart to sing again the days of olden years across the seas" (quoted in Filene 2000: 17).

The attempt of academic and antiquarian elites to control the boundary between "folk" culture and both high culture and popular culture can be seen in the incessant and contentious debates over what is truly "folk." From the first use of the term by scholars like Percy and Herder, through the institutionalization of folklore societies, continuing up to contemporary discussions, the term has been constantly debated. Virtually all scholars on folk music, folk art, folklore, and other folk activities stake out the boundaries of their topic by giving their definition of "folk." Even authors who adopt a rudimentary definition feel required to explain what they are doing. Can music by identifiable composers be considered folk music? Can music learned by any means other than word of mouth be considered folk? Must folk music be simple in form? Must folk music be of ancient origin? When I have interviewed scholars and performers of folk music, their first question to me is often, "What do you mean by folk?" denoting both the ambiguity and the salience of the term. Rarely do they stop to consider why consensus on a definition is so elusive.

The social boundaries designated by "folk" are most commonly ethnic, national, or racial groups. Sharp was among the most nationalist of the founding folklorists, declaring that national culture was "always to be found in its purest, as well as in its most stable and permanent form, in the folk-arts of a nation" (1932: xxxv). Herder specified what the boundaries among different folk were, insisting that folk groups were distinguished along language or ethnic lines, not bloodlines. While the architects of the folk concept constructed a cultural wall between themselves and the folk, they did share rational, ethnic, or racial identity.[7]

A Blinkered View of Folk

The first folk project neglected two kinds of music that were central to later folk projects: African American music and protest music. With an open-minded reading of most definitions of folk music, both should have been included, but both challenged the prevailing Anglo-Saxon nationalist goals of the project. Yet effective voices were making a case that would later be successfully adopted by the second project.

With shallow historical roots, Americans have had a particularly difficult time finding their folk heritage. A former colonial society, claiming no lineage from its indigenous population, offers no raw material for a distinctly American folk culture if folk culture is defined in terms of premodern remnant. Many early folklorists insisted that the United States had no genuine "American" folk culture.[8] Since they considered Anglo-Saxon culture to be the core of American culture, American folk culture would be found in the remnants of Anglo-Saxon culture. This is why Cecil Sharp searched for English ballads in the remote mountains of Appalachia. Half a century later the imagery was still prevalent. In a typical news story about folk singer John Jacob Niles in Santa Barbara, California, a local reporter warbled, "Here is the authentic ministrel [sic], not of the courts and palaces, but of the people in the villages, the countryside, the isolated mountain hamlets." Niles's concert included "the tall tales, the romantic conceits, the Biblical narratives and nursery rhymes that somehow were born and circulated throughout England, Ireland and Scotland centuries ago, and were brought to the hill country of Kentucky some 200 or more years ago, to take root there in the hearts and memories of self-taught musicians and singers" (Scofield 1953). The writer was careful to indicate that the cultural boundary demarcated white, not just Anglo-Saxon, that the music included Scandinavian, Slavic, and Mediterranean influences. Even though Niles also performed black spirituals, African Americans apparently did not inhabit this reporter's mythical villages.

The rhetoric of purity linked the concept of folk to racism in early twentieth-century America, banishing African Americans from the folk. Gavin James Campbell has described how early twentieth-century fiddle contests in Atlanta contributed to the construction of the Jim Crow consciousness: "The Anglo-Saxon mountaineer appealed not only to old-stock Northerners, but also to white Atlantans, who turned the mountain fiddler into a foot-soldier for segregation. They saw the fiddlers and their music as sturdy vestiges of an uncompromised white folk culture. The music hearkened back, not to the racially-entangled world of the plantation South, but to a racially-pure mountain South in which blacks simply vanished" (1999: 133–34). In the discourse around the very popular Atlanta fiddle contests, mountain people were depicted as a cohesive people who knew nothing of cities or industries and had no contact with blacks or immigrants. Despite the fact that many southern blacks were highly accomplished fiddlers, the fiddle contests mirrored the imagined pure white society of Appalachia. The "folk" in fiddle contests were white.

The attempts to evoke Anglo-Saxon purity on behalf of whiteness were not restricted to the South. As part of a broad social movement to reassert white power, Henry Ford spearheaded a movement to preserve and propagate pure Anglo-American musical forms. He contrasted the "unnatural," "twisted," "cooped up" city with the "wholesome" "independence" and the "sterling honesty" of agrarian life (Peterson 1997a: 59). Oblivious to how industrialization might have changed society, he blamed alcohol, tobacco, and sexual license, all fostered, he thought, by jazz dancing, foisted on society by blacks, foreigners, and "the international Jew" (Peterson 1997a: 60). Only the old agrarian ways could recapture the innocent world he sought. So in 1925 he began a crusade to bring back old-fashioned dances to replace close dancing, bringing musicians and square dance instructors to Michigan and enlisting Ford dealers across the country to sponsor fiddle contests.

As pervasive as the imagery of the Anglo-Saxon roots of the American nation was, a forceful dissenting voice asserted that from the beginning of organized folklore in America the most distinctively American culture came from slaves and ex-slaves, who had synthesized European and African cultural forms into a novel creolized culture. The essence of America lay, they proclaimed, not in its "pure" roots but in its rich blend of old world and new world strains. Robert Winslow Gordon, after he was appointed as head of the Archive of Folk Culture in the Library of Congress, wrote the chief of the Music Division that "What the negro has to-day is a combination of many different things. He has adopted, and he has assimilated, and he has created. I grant him all that is due."[9]

As the closest thing America had to a peasantry, a simple "primitive" population without a literate culture, African Americans should have qualified as folk. But insofar as the folk represented the soul of a nation, and to the extent that the American nation was Anglo-Saxon, blacks could not be accorded status as "folk." So debates among folklorists over whether African American music qualified as folk music were also debates about whether blacks belonged in the American nation. The question of whether blacks belonged to the "folk" of folk music was reflected in divergent views of which music most faithfully represented the black race—minstrelsy or spirituals. For the most part, spirituals, the music flowering from the anguish of suffering, were more commonly seen as folk music than minstrelsy, the mocking caricature of a supposedly inept but cheerful "Sambo." Spirituals were claimed by both black intellectuals and progressive whites as the black voicing of their experience in America. In contrast, the prevalent label of blackface minstrelsy as "Ethiopian" captured both senses of the term "exotic," the original definition of a foreign species from the outside, but also its more popular definition as excitingly strange. An anonymous writer in the *New York Tribune* in 1855 asked,

> Why may not the banjoism of a Congo, an Ethiopian or a George Christy [one of the most famous blackface performers of the 1840s and 1850s], aspire to an equality with the musical and poetical delineators of all nationalities? . . . Absurd as may seem negro minstrelsy to the refined musician, it is nevertheless beyond doubt that it expresses the peculiar characteristics of the negro as truly as the great masters of Italy represent their more spiritual and profound nationality. . . . [And] has there been no change in the feelings of the true originators of this music—the negroes themselves? . . . Plaintive and slow, the sad soul of the slave throws into his music all that gushing anguish of spirit which he dare not otherwise express. (quoted in Lott 1993: 15–16)

Shortly after the Civil War, *The Nation*'s reviewer of *Slave Songs of the South* associated spirituals and minstrels to assert the Americanness of African Americans: "We utter no new truth when we affirm that whatever of nationality there is in the music of America she owes to her dusky children. Negro minstrelsy sprang from them, and from negro minstrelsy our truly national airs" (quoted in Laubenstein 1930: 378). But according to scholarly definitions of folk music that emphasized anonymous origins, ancient roots, and noncommercial production, minstrel music clearly did not qualify as folk music.

While minstrelsy was generally rejected as folk music, spirituals, though also falling short of most scholarly definitions, were accepted by some of the folklorists of the first folk project. While some spirituals were of anonymous origins with ancient roots, many were not. "Deep River," one of the most beloved and often performed spirituals, was composed by H. T. Burleigh, an African American student of Antonín Dvořák. It was Dvořák who popularized the use of spirituals in European classical music. Teaching at the National Conservatory of Music in New York City in 1892, he learned many songs from Burleigh, several of which he used in the *New World Symphony* (1893). He was quite explicit that he considered the songs he learned folk music in the European sense of music that rises from an agrarian people: "These beautiful and varied themes are the product of the soil. They are American. They are the folksongs of America, and your composers must turn to them. In the Negro melodies of America I discover all that is needed for a great and noble school of music" (quoted in Southern 1983: 265). A similar argument was made by the Harlem Renaissance critic Alain Locke, making explicit the association of folk music, authenticity, and the boundaries of the nation.

> The spirituals are really the most characteristic product of the race genius as yet in America. But the very elements which make them uniquely expressive of the Negro make them at the same time deeply representative of the soil that produced them. Thus, as unique spiritual products of American life, they become nationally as well as racially characteristic. It may not be readily conceded now that the song of the negro is America's folk song; but if the spirituals are what we think them to be, a classic folk expression, then this is their ultimate destiny. Already they give evidence of this classic quality. The universality of the spirituals looms more and more as they stand the test of time. (quoted in Gilroy 1993: 91)

Because the academic folklorists insisted that folk music be anonymous, rural, and ancient, they entirely ignored one of the most vibrant forms of the folk process in America around the turn of the twentieth century. Just as early English folklorists had shunned English broadsides, American folklorists rejected music with contemporary relevance, especially overt political relevance.

TOPICAL SONGS AND WORK SONGS

Ordinary Americans, of course, participated in much more music than what scholars and antiquarians would call folk songs. Besides the Anglo-Saxon ballads and reels that were analyzed in the *Journal of American Folklore* and the African American spirituals, two streams of music would spill into the musical project of the twentieth-century left wing: work songs and topical songs. Work songs included the musicking found in many occupations that involved clusters of workers engaged in repetitive and tedious activities, most notably sea men, loggers, miners, field hands, railroad workers, and cowboys. Sea shanties such as "Blow the Man Down," "Shenandoah," and "Santa Anna" helped synchronize the collective effort of raising and lowering sails. Loggers cut trees, dragged them through the forests, and spent spare time to the accompaniment of "The Farmer and the Shanty Boy" or "Bold Jack Donahue." And railroaders laid the iron ribbons that knitted together the nation to the rhythms of "Take This Hammer" and "Drill, Ye Tarriers, Drill." Philip

Foner's authoritative collection of American labor songs notes that even though most folk song scholars have deemed them unworthy for collection, toward the end of the nineteenth century and into the early decades of the twentieth century a broad range of union organizations, independent collectors, and others began to gather them into songbooks and collections (Foner 1975; Gioia 2006). Some were passed on to other workers and some, such as John Lomax's book of cowboy songs, were attempting to broaden the academic span of folk music. But the twentieth-century left was apparently ambivalent about these songs. On one hand many work songs functioned more to increase the efficiency of work, to make it more tolerable, and to reduce the boredom. Hence sea captains, lumber companies, and mine operators often hired shanties or song leaders, just as employers today pipe Muzak into offices. On the other hand, many work songs protested working conditions, low pay, and the wickedness or cruelty of their bosses. So unions often embraced songs that voiced grievances and rallied for solidarity. Thus did the Massachusetts *Voice of Industry* declare that "if anything can arouse the masses in our country from the fearful state of apathy into which they are sunk, the thrilling tones of the songs of labor must do it. And they will do it, for greater than the Philosopher or the Legislator, is the Child of Song" (quoted in Foner 1975: xv).

Music had long been an important part of American politics across the political spectrum. Before the mass media existed to broadcast political ads, parties and movements of all sorts reached out to new members and braced the solidarity of old ones with music. Revolutionary patriots, Federalists, Whigs, Republicans, Abolitionists, Prohibitionists, and Populists had all expressed their political commitments in song. Before the twentieth century, rare was a political rally that lacked music. From "Yankee Doodle" to "Yankee Doodle Dandy," Americans had linked arms and at times borne arms to the strains of "The Liberty Song," "Jefferson and Liberty," "Peg and Awl," "O Freedom," "John Brown's Body," "Johnny I Hardly Knew Ye," "The Preacher and the Slave," "The Women's Rights Polka," and "Bread and Roses." The nineteenth century and the years leading up to World War I were the golden era of topical song.

Organizers associated with the Industrial Workers of the World (IWW, or Wobblies) adapted popular songs, hymns, and ditties as propaganda pieces. Goaded by the Salvation Army bands that were drowning out their soapbox oratory in Spokane, Washington, they began by parodying the evangelical songs that promised a better life in the hereafter. Their most famous song-maker—actually the most famous Wobbly of all—Joe Hill, mocked the well-known hymn "Sweet Bye and Bye" in "The Preacher and the Slave": "You will live, bye and bye / In that glorious land above the sky / Work and pray, live on hay / You'll get pie in the sky when you die." Their frequently revised *Little Red Songbook* is one of the most famous and widely distributed sources of radical songs in American history. Richard Brazier, a member of the elected committee that put out the first version in 1909, recalled that the ten thousand copies of the first edition were bought up within its first month (Brazier 1968). While some IWW members were skeptical of the book's value, others were persuaded by the opportunity for name recognition, in retrospect a farsighted insight, indeed.

Topical song takes its political meaning from its lyrics, though occasionally a genre or particular melody adds meaning by its juxtaposition to lyrics. Any song known to audiences can be fair game. Minstrel songs such as "Old Dan Tucker," traditional ballads, marching songs ("Marching through Georgia"), and religious hymns ("Sweet Bye and Bye") have all been grist for the topical singer's mill. Some tunes have been selected to emphasize the boundary between singer and target, as when the Wobblies satirized hymns to mock the otherworldly palliatives that evangelists were offering disaffected workers. A rousing song like "The Preacher and the Slave" ("Pie in the Sky Bye and Bye)" not only propagated an ideological message but also enfeebled the genre of evangelical hymns for the preachers. By appropriating the genre itself, the Wobblies reinforced the boundaries between the radicals and evangelists on their own terms.

For other topical songs, the genre of the music was relatively unimportant, merely a vehicle for the messages in the lyrics, chosen more because the tune was familiar than because of any connotation in the melody. The popular "Soup Song" that livened up picket lines and sit-down strikes in the 1930s and 1940s was based on "My Bonnie Lies over the Ocean." While the tune may have been known to more whites than blacks, it did not signify a social boundary in itself. Groups of people would not have embraced it as "their" music to the exclusion of others in the same way that Christians would have embraced "In the Sweet Bye and Bye," taking offense when the Wobblies sang "Pie in the Sky."

The distinction between folk music and topical music was enforced by folklorists more than activists. Those who wrote broadsides or made little red books took any song their audiences would know, making no distinction between anonymous or known composers, ancient or modern, oral or written. Several features of topical songs conform to academic definitions of folk songs in the first folk project. Many were of unknown origin and refined by communal usage. And many canonical folk songs started as topical songs, commenting on political affairs. By insisting that the only popular music worthy of refined appreciation be anonymous, ancient, and oral, folklorists of the first folk song project excluded topical music, even when adapted by ordinary people and based on the music sung by the folk. Implicit in this distinction was the traditional-modern dichotomy, at that point using the language of primitive-modern. Folk music was supposed to be traditional—pre-rational, organic, emotional. It sprang from the soul of the folk, not from their ability to reason. The most commonly cited reason for collecting folklore was to preserve it from the taint of modernity, to save the primitive from civilization. According to prevalent understandings of the time, political reasoning was a higher mental faculty, foreign to the primitive mind. By expressing overt political opinions, topical music was a modern, civilized activity, and not folk. Real "folk" were not political because they had not reached that stage of civilization.

However, all music is political. If one is interested in the political meaning or consequence of music, the agenda is less a matter of deciding which music is political and which is not than probing how music and its social contexts affects who gets what, when, and how—as Lasswell famously described the meaning of politics (1936). The distinction between folk and topical music is political in at least two ways. First, to identify some music as political and other music as non-political obfuscates the implication that music holds for the distribution of power and the political dimensions of its context. Whether lyrics use political language or not, they express assumptions, preferences, and values about how society is organized and how people can improve or cope with their lot in life. Second, the folklorists were engaged in a nationalist project, building an imagined community. Though the political claims of national identity are adamantly implicit—posturing above the competition for position and policy—nations systematically relate to that most political of all entities: the state. It is the dubious claim that nationality rises above politics that required that the first folk music project distinguish topical songs from folk music. Only after a second folk music project, discussed in the next chapter, captured the genre from the scholars and antiquarians did it make sense for folk singers to link Child ballads like "Barbara Allen" and topical songs like "Soup Song."

CONCLUSION

The university professors, settlement house reformers, and cultural entrepreneurs had little aspiration to reach broad audiences. They were more interested in preserving an isolated culture than in propagating it to people already sullied by civilization. Yet the first folk project succeeded on its own terms, achieving several important goals.

- It created a set of interlocked distinctions that entered into the broader culture—folk versus commercial, authentic versus pop, quaint versus sophisticated. These particular binary oppositions continue to inform how Americans think about creative endeavors, especially music.

- It contrasted the interpreters/proponents of some forms of music to the people who make the music. The category of "folk music" was constructed as "someone else's" music. Thus "the folk" were denied a voice in defining the boundaries between "folk" and "non-folk." Who counted as "folk" and who did not was defined not by the people who made "folk music" but by the interpreters/proponents who promoted "folk" as a meaningful category.

- It defined a kind of music in terms of a group, "the folk" (in contrast to its musical qualities or uses, as in genres such as jazz, rock, polka, or ballet), and by doing so the imputed music qualities were equated with imputed qualities of the people—simplicity, authenticity, durability, purity, and tradition. While most other genres are defined on aesthetic or marketing bases, folk music is defined in terms of a putatively universal designation—in principle everyone is folk—but manifested in exclusive terms—in practice, only some can be "real" folk. For the first folk project, the qualities that defined "folk" were national and racial. By defining "folk" along national and racial lines, folk music became a target for those who wanted to enlarge the meaning of American to include all those born here or moving here. Thus was folk music afforded a political potency that became manifested in later decades.

- It organized a template that could serve as a model and launching pad for a second folk project that redefined the meaning of American folk music and actualized the latent political potential created by the first project. The coalescence of scholars, moral entrepreneurs, and associations created in the first folk project was taken up by political activists and professional musicians in the second project and later. Except for the commercial folk revival of the 1950s and 1960s, folk music has remained alive by organizational forms primarily outside the market.

Several variables shape the kinds of social impacts that cultural projects have, including the social basis of the cultural entrepreneurs, the social basis of the boundaries in their definition of cultural distinctions, the social implications of the claims made on behalf of their promoted categories, the relationship of project entrepreneurs and claims makers to those doing the culture, cultural entrepreneurs' relationship to the target audience, and the social setting in which the culture is done.

Cultural entrepreneurs can be business people, performers, composers, scholars, journalists, activists, or unaffiliated individuals. The social situation of cultural entrepreneurs will affect the kinds of categories created. The scholars and antiquarians who constructed the category of folk music defined music explicitly in terms of the kind of people who made it, the process by which it was composed, and the simplicity of its content. In contrast, business people are more likely to create genres along the lines of marketing categories than on the basis of formal qualities of music. The racial categorization in the genres of race records and hillbilly music, which evolved into R&B and country and western, were created more by marketing categories than by any musically meaningful differences (Roy 2004). Performers can be expected to create genres on the basis of musical features such as rhythm, harmony, or timbre, including categories such as heavy metal, electronica, or calypso.

The social basis of boundaries, that is, the kind of social boundaries highlighted in the discourse around music, depends on and reinforces race, ethnicity, gender, class, and generation. Virtually all social categories imply a social basis of the boundaries distinguishing them from other cultural objects. A cultural project defines what those social boundaries are in formulating a category, though subsequent projects or cultural drift can redefine them. The original folk music project defined folk music as the music of national groups and, in doing so, also defined who belonged to the nation. This was particularly important where national membership was contested, as it was in the United States. Subsequently folk music has been a site of contention over who belongs to the nation. From the original definition of American folk music as the exclusive domain of Anglo-American southerners to its broadening to include African American spirituals to the more recent "discovery" of non-English-language indigenous music, "our" music has defined who we are.

The impact of a cultural project depends not only on the social position of the project's promoters and the content of the boundaries claimed in promotion but also on the relationship of the promoters to the people actually doing the culture. Sometimes these will be the same people. Musicians often engage in cultural projects, typically inventing a new genre by pushing an existing genre to the next step, as in the movement from bebop to cool jazz, or recombining diverse genres in a bricolage, as rock and roll combined country and western and R&B. Or they can revive or preserve an older form, as in the folk revival and shape note movement. If musicians are engaged in a cultural project only as musicians, making claims about the music they perform, the impact of the cultural project is likely to be limited. The proliferation of commercial music genres in the last few decades has been based mostly on musicians seeking distinctive sounds and "brand name" labeling for a genre they can be identified with. Most are fleeting with little permanent effect on the music or the social relationships within which it is done.

At the other extreme, a cultural project can be built on a deep division of labor between the promoters and the musicians, as is found in folk music, especially in its origins as a genre.[10] It is a category that is almost always about someone else's music; those who invented the genre and those who performed were distinctively different groups. The scholars and antiquarians who invented and propounded the concept occupied distinctly different social worlds and interacted with the folk only occasionally when fieldworkers listened clinically to informants. "The folk" did not think of themselves as folk and did not consider their music folk music. Informants singing for field sessions captured on Library of Congress tapes made little distinction between the songs learned from their parents, songs on the radio, or songs learned from sheet music.[11] "Folk" was not a relevant category even when the collectors treated them as folk singers. Yet it was this new relationship between cultural entrepreneurs and performers that helps account for the impact of the claims being made about the cultural category. The claims about the social importance of the music were made by discursive specialists—scholars, activists, and journalists—using rhetorical skills buttressed by their social standing.

With folk music, the impact of the project was further influenced by another important variable: the relationship of the claims makers to the target audience. The invention of the category folk music was pitched to other academics and intellectuals with little personal experience with "the folk" but a hungry appetite for romantic accounts of innocent life unsullied by modernity. The fact that folk music is always mediated between the rural "folk" and urban audiences is a central feature of folk music that gives the mediators unusual influence in making claims about the music.

Finally, the social setting of the project has an impact on the effect of cultural projects. Cultural projects situated within commercial musicking, political movements, scholarly discourse, nonprofit cultural institutions, organized religion, and informal networks have different impacts on different parts of society. When folk music was a project within scholarly and antiquarian communities, its impact was confined, though it left vivid footprints in the historical record, tempting subsequent scholars to exaggerate its more general influence. It was activists in the 1930s and 1940s who introduced the concept of folk music to the general public, working in partnership with the federal government, aspiring to mobilize the union movement, and making inroads at the margins of commercial music. The folk revival of the 1960s was centered in three social settings: the civil rights movement, which was the least self-conscious about making musical claims, the commercial fad based on transparently ersatz claims of authenticity, and the folk purists promoted by mediators based in an informal network of festivals, coffeehouses, magazines, and inde-

CHAPTER FOUR

White and Black Reds: Building an Infrastructure

As America entered the age of commercial recording, few people other than scholars and antiquarians would have recognized folk music as a meaningful category in the cultural landscape. The establishment of classical symphonies in large cities around the turn of the century solidified the nascent boundary between highbrow and lowbrow music (DiMaggio 1982a, 1982b; Levine 1988). Minstrelsy had given way to vaudeville as the most popular form of live entertainment. And the business of music revolved around the publication of sheet music as middle-class families in every region displayed respectability with a piano in the parlor. And while many Americans knew "Barbara Allen," "Old Dan Tucker," or "Swing Low, Sweet Chariot," they would not have thought of them as folk music.

By mid-century folk music had broken into popular culture as children sang folk songs in school and *Billboard* included it as a genre of top hits along with popular, jazz, R&B, and country. *Time, Life, Look,* and daily newspapers carried articles on Woody Guthrie, Leadbelly, and the Weavers. But unlike folk music in European countries, folk music in the United States had acquired a left-wing connotation, strong enough that it became a target of the anti-communist witch hunt. Within a decade it would fortify one of the most consequential social movements in American history. The explanation for the political meaning of folk music lies not in the music itself, not in the politics of "the folk" who originated the styles, and not in any audiences demanding it, but in a second folk project associated with the left wing of American politics, especially the American Communist Party. Just as the institutional and social context of the first folk project helps account for the specific meanings attributed to folk music and its use early in the century, the political roots of the second project, led by eastern elites and recent immigrants, help explain how it took on a political connotation but failed to bridge the social boundaries its sponsors intended, especially in terms of racial inclusiveness. Both projects succeeded in creating an audience beyond the folk themselves, but both sustained a gap between the promoters and the folk. Folk music remained "someone else's" music.

The American left adopted folk music as their music not only because of its populist connotations but also because it could be racially inclusive politically. Other genres might have well served as "the people's music" in the 1930s and 1940s when folk music was taken on as a project. Country and western, R&B, ethnic tunes, and even mainstream Tin Pan Alley, which probably had more listeners than all the others, would have served. But folk music was singled out.

The Communist Party's national leadership emphasized racial justice for several reasons. Ideologically, because the Soviet Comintern in the 1920s was emphasizing the "Nationality Question," leaders in the American party identified blacks as the most oppressed segment of society, thus meriting vanguard status. Partly at the urging of American representatives, the Fourth Congress of the Communist International initiated a Negro Commission. The *Daily Worker*'s account compared the situation of African Americans with oppressed black people around the world, framing race in terms of imperialism and recommending that African Americans be educated to understand their plight as a condition of capitalism and imperialism (*Daily Worker*, March 10, 1923). As Otto Huiswood, the most prominent black leader in the young party, wrote in the 1923 *Daily Worker*, "The Negro Problem is one of the most important problems facing the Workers Party. Fundamentally an economic problem but intensified by racial antagonism it demands our special attention and careful study. . . . It is your duty to rally the Negro workers under the revolutionary banner of the Working Class Movement. Comrades, go to the Negro Masses" ("Lenin Meetings Hear New Songs and Fine Pageant" 1923). Yet the party's commitment to racial inclusiveness was more than their adherence to Moscow's line. Strategically, they needed to mobilize black workers to prevent employers from weakening the union movement by exploiting racial divisions. Party literature frequently rallied workers to unite across the chasm of racial hostility, lest capitalists pit blacks and whites against each other to the detriment of all. Beyond international directives or strategic considerations, many white party leaders and members genuinely believed that racial domination was morally wrong, that a more just America would be racially equal. Although factional disputes festered over whether racial issues should be subordinated to the class struggle, many of the party's black leaders were able to build the American Negro Labor Congress. But by the early 1930s, the party made race a priority, especially in local organizing projects (Solomon 1998). Southern communists especially explicitly organized around racial issues (Kelley 1990). The *Southern Worker* in the early 1930s was filled with articles about lynching, which figured as prominently in its pages as unions or wages.

THE AMERICAN LEFT AND CULTURE

The prevailing image of the American Communist Party, both in the popular press and in scholarly accounts, is that of a heavy-handed, soulless revolutionary party ideologically committed to narrowly conceived class struggle. Its cultural expression is commonly viewed as clunky ideological expression, its aesthetic sensitivity curbed by Marxist-Leninist political economy, like a Soviet automobile compared to a 1957 Corvette. There has certainly been enough Communist Party–supported art, music, and literature to bolster such a generalization. However, recent scholarship has begun to explore the rich cultural life that permeated radical politics in the 1930s and 1940s. As early as the 1920s, the *Daily Worker* gave coverage to all aspects of life found in the mass media—cultural criticism, sports, advice columns, and leisure activities. Michael Denning's *The Cultural Front* vividly recounts the enormous cultural effervescence of the late depression years. Robbie Lieberman's pathbreaking analysis of the party's use of music begins with an autobiographical glimpse of growing up in a pervasive communist subculture filled with literature, music, theater, and art. Among these cultural initiatives was a second folk music project that redefined the meaning of the genre itself.

The left-wing movements of the 1930s and 1940s more than any social movements before or since erected an organizational infrastructure, a coherent art world to control the production, distribution, and to some extent the consumption of culture. As the mass media achieved near hegemony in the world of popular entertainment, especially music, only self-consciously political organizations, unbeholden to the market, could sustain a genuinely insurgent cultural presence.[1] This is what Howard Becker has described as an art world—the interaction of all the people whose collective activities make possible a cultural object. Art (used broadly to include all the arts) requires not only the creativity and inspiration of those we deem artists but also the cooperation and effort of those who create the physical forms, the materials, the support, the responses, the rationales, and the institutional infrastructure within which art transpires. Creative expression is a bundle of tasks, not a solitary act of genius (or would-be genius). Thus to explain why art happens, it is necessary to examine the full range of individuals, organizations, and institutions that underlie the art world (Becker 1982). For music, the art world includes composers, performers, record companies, acoustical scientists, music publishers, instrument makers, critics, record store owners, radio and phonograph manufacturers, and listeners (Lopes 2002). In addition to content creators and consumers, culture requires an organizational infrastructure. By infrastructure, I mean the organizational and material activities and resources through which content is expressed, but which themselves are content-neutral. Transportation and communication facilities are part of the social and economic infrastructure. A highway can be used to take a vacation, haul food, or escape the law. A telephone can be used to make a date, place a business order, or fight with a sibling.[2] A record can play opera, hillbilly music, religious sermons, or birdcalls. Musical infrastructure includes record companies, music publishers, instrument makers, radio facilities, buildings and managers, agents, professional associations, and so forth.

For social movements, infrastructure is necessary for the mobilization of cultural as well as material resources. Tilly (1978, 2000) defines mobilization as the process by which contenders gain the collective control of useful resources. Just as a professionally staffed office facilitates recruitment and coordination, access to a theater enables drama and a record company enables music. A movement's cultural activities require material resources no less than its other activities. If the movement does not mobilize cultural activities within its own organizations, it cannot control the culture and is dependent on others and vulnerable to co-optation of content and degeneration of form. By developing its own infrastructure a movement can shape the content to serve its causes and set culture within social forms that reinforce rather than distract from its goals. Thus the dilemma faced by social movements in a media-saturated environment is that the infrastructure with the greatest reach—commercial mass media—is likely to co-opt and corrupt any insurgent content. Fortunately for the left, they were able to develop an infrastructure when society was much less media-saturated than it is today.

The American Old Left and Culture

In the early decades of the twentieth century, the organized left simmered down from a peak of intensity. Labor militancy translated its success into trade unionism while populism gave way to progressivism and corporate liberalism. Socialists focused their energy on electoral politics, winning mayoral races in several major cities and an occasional legislative race (Weinstein 1975). Under AFL leadership, unions increasingly defined their goals and tactics around business unionism, which elevated collective bargaining over organizing, leaving little room for music or other expressive activity. Nascent organizations for racial equality such as the NAACP turned to the legal system to dismantle the still-formidable walls of legal segregation. Only the anarcho-syndicalist Industrial Workers of the World (Wobblies) made serious use of music. And it is mostly for their music, especially their *Little Red Songbook*, that they are remembered today.

Unlike the socialists and the leadership of the AFL, the early communists were mostly immigrants, many of them highly cultured. The cultural milieu was strongly flavored by European Jewish roots that put a premium on education, refinement, and aesthetics. Many artists, musicians, and writers with progressive sympathies gravitated toward the growing Communist Party (CP) as it increasingly fostered cultural expression.

Moreover, the CP not only provided an outlet for culture that expressed political overtones but also sought to organize cultural practitioners as workers and constituents. It is within the context of a highly mobilized art world that the Old Left did music.

The Communist Party from its earliest days self-consciously used culture as a weapon in the class struggle, creating art, literature, and music for, about, and sometimes by the working class. In doing so, its creative practitioners also created culture by and for themselves, many of whom were not working class. Beginning in the 1920s, they were especially active in literature, reflecting the high-culture orientation of many participants. "John Reed Clubs," named after the renowned communist journalist who emigrated to the Soviet Union, were created in many cities. With no official relationship to the party, and few party members except in the leadership, they hardly fit the stereotype of a disciplined cadre of stalwarts. A 1932 party document complained that the John Reed Clubs were filled with members who were not intellectuals, workers, or revolutionaries but bohemians, an insult not far from "bourgeois" (Hemingway 2002). The various clubs in major cities across the country sponsored activities in a variety of arts, including music. The Chicago club, for example, had an international orchestra.

The John Reed Clubs reflected the party's policy that literature was the queen of the arts. Not only did party officials tend to identify as intelligentsia, they felt that literature was the most accessible art form for the proletariat. Moreover, literature among the arts had the closest affinity with ideology. Insofar as arts were seen as a form of agit-prop (agitation-propaganda), literature could directly communicate and proselytize workers to the party's political message. And literature was the medium in which the proletariat could most easily participate, whether in a union newsletter or *New Masses*. The prospects of a proletarian literature seemed more realistic than worker art, worker music, or worker drama (Denning 1996; Lieberman 1995). Still, the New York John Reed Club did manage to create a music committee, which they announced in *New Masses* ("Workers Music" 1931).

In 1935, a group of left-wing writers founded the League of American Writers, which included left-wing writers of the caliber of Malcolm Cowley, Erskine Caldwell, Archibald MacLeish, Upton Sinclair, Langston Hughes, Carl Sandburg, Carl Van Doren, John Dos Passos, Lillian Hellman, and Dashiell Hammett. Although begun by members of the cultural wing of the party, it broadened to include a range of politically engaged writers, with about eight hundred members and chapters in several major cities. Among its activities were writing schools that included over three thousand young writers.

Literature shared some of the contradictions that bedeviled music later on. The implicit model of action in the communist strategy was a "hearts and minds" orientation—individuals would first develop consciousness, then commitment, then action, a paradoxically voluntarist model to propagate a materialist ideology. We will see later that the civil rights movement, in contrast, mobilized by getting people into action, *then* letting the experience of engagement operate through praxis to solidify commitment. For the communists, since developing consciousness was the first priority, the propaganda of culture overrode its ability to build solidarity. The content more than the social form was primary. The party had the truth to impart to the naive, primarily through words (and indirectly through images). When true consciousness was propagated to the masses, they would eventually rise up to overthrow the system, just like in Russia. Sohrabi (2005) has described the revolutionary template that Lenin formulated: in contrast to the constitutionalist model based on the French experience in which revolutionaries demanded constitutional transformation through sovereign assemblies, the Leninist model anticipated a sudden overthrow with no diversion of struggle through legal frameworks. This implies that the role of the party is to inculcate the masses with a revolutionary fervor more than to develop institutions to change the system before the revolution or anticipation of the post-revolutionary society. The organizational apparatus is more an instrument to build the party than to directly embody change.

While most participants in party-sponsored cultural activities were not revolutionaries, their cultural model was similarly oriented toward hearts and minds. As what Marxists might call bourgeois intellectuals—in the sense of people who work as creative individuals—their social world was built on the experience of individual thinkers speaking *to* audiences. Political culture meant the ideas that would heighten consciousness.

The party not only brought writers together, it also created an infrastructure for them, establishing outlets both popular and serious. Some were short-lived, such as *Photo-History*, an unsuccessful picture magazine. More enduring was *Direction*, a glossy arts monthly lasting from 1937 to 1944. With the active support of well-known writers such as Theodore Dreiser, it reviewed most of the lively arts and presented reproductions of leftist artists. With advisors and contributors that included Richard Wright, Kenneth Burke, Jay Leyda, John Gassner, and Catherine Littlefield, "Perhaps more than any other magazine, *Direction* embodied the alliance of the moderns, the plebeians, and the émigrés" (Denning 1996: 93). Not confined to American contributors, the magazine also published pieces by Thomas Mann, Bertolt Brecht, and Ernst Bloch. Other magazines on the left included *Ken*, an attempt to compete with the glossy *Life*, *Friday*, staffed by left-wing *New Yorker* writers, and *PM*, a tabloid that lasted until 1949 (Denning 1996).

Like music, left-wing theater in the 1920s tended to be ethnic and European, growing out of the immigrant working class. The Yiddish-language Artef Theater was part of a larger movement of Yiddish theater in the United States. Trying to bring Tin Pan Alley musical sensibilities to musical theater, several young radicals helped transform vaudeville into the modern Broadway musical, with such popular hits as Marc Blitzstein's *The Cradle Will Rock*, Harold Rome's *Pins and Needles* (produced with the International Ladies' Garment Workers' Union [ILGWU]), and Duke Ellington's *Jump for Joy*. In conjunction with the theater activities, activists created the *Workers' Theatre* magazine, which discussed how to reach the working class with a political message linking theater to other arts (Denning 1996; Lieberman 1995; Reuss 1971; Trumbull 1991).

The Theatre Arts Committee (TAC), a Popular Front organization of film, theater, and radio entertainers, published a monthly magazine, issued recordings, and broadcast radio programs. Its weekly cabaret, *Cabaret TAC*, featured skits, dances, and topical songs. Participants included Marc Blitzstein, Earl Robinson, Howard Da Silva, and Miss "God Bless America," Kate Smith.

Connected to the theater organization through writers and performers, radicals created other political cabarets, at least in New York City. The first was Le Ruban Bleu, which opened in 1937, modeled after European political cafés and often presenting European art. Perhaps the most important was Café Society, which provided a venue for such notable comedians as Jack Gilford, Carol Channing, and Zero Mostel, and such celebrated singers as Billie Holiday, Lena Horne, and Hazel Scott. In such a setting entertainers, activists, and the general public could forge a politically aware culture linking the African American, immigrant, and intellectual communities. According to founder Barney Josephson, the son of Latvian garment worker immigrants, "I wanted a club where blacks and whites worked together behind the footlights and sat together out front" (quoted in Denning 1996: 325).

One infrastructural form that showed early promise as a medium of insurgent culture but failed to develop was radio. Before the Communications Act of 1934 institutionalized the dominance of commercial broadcast, early radio was owned and operated by a variety of organizations, especially educational, religious, and retail marketing, most notably furniture stores. Roscigno and Danaher (2004) vividly portray how the indigenous music and protest songs of textile workers helped galvanize the most militant labor insurgency in southern history during strikes from 1929 to 1934. Radio in that region also helped talented textile workers earn a living, fostering the development of a musical world of working-class professional musicians who could lend their voices to the mobilization. Broadcast licenses were granted to the UAW-CIO in Detroit, the

Amalgamated Clothing Workers in Rochester, and the ILGWU in Chattanooga. Several New York unions, workers' fraternities, and church and civic groups established the People's Radio Foundation in the late 1940s to establish a progressive radio outlet for which People's Songs, Inc. had promised to provide some programming. But the venture never broadcast a word. There would have been the talent to program and perform content, but by the late 1940s radio had been regulated into a few organizational forms accessible only to commercial broadcasting, educational institutions, and religious groups.[3]

Knitting the different arts together and offering a forum where culture could be discussed, debated, and evaluated were general cultural magazines, especially *New Masses*. Created by Hugo Gellert and Michael Gold in 1926, it emerged to be one of the premier American outlets for literate arts during the 1930s and 1940s. Only a few of the fifty-six founders were members of the party, though three of six original editors (Joseph Freeman, Michael Gold, and Hugo Gellert) were party members. The staff wanted it to be first and foremost artistic and literary, not political in the narrow sense, to develop an aesthetic appropriate for "contemporary existence" (Hemingway 2002: 9). Its roster of authors read like a "Who's Who" of cultural writing in those decades, even including writers hostile to communism such as Ezra Pound and Allen Tate. With poetry by the likes of Kenneth Patchen, Richard Wright, James Agee, and Federico García Lorca and short stories by Langston Hughes, William Saroyan, and Albert Maltz, it had formidable literary stature. In its reportage could be found Richard Wright on Joe Louis's knockout of Max Baer, Albert Maltz on a strike in Flint, Michigan, Dorothy Parker on a visit to Madrid during the Spanish Civil War, and Ernest Hemingway on the veterans killed in a Florida hurricane. Essays and commentary ranged from Michael Gold on John Reed and Theodore Dreiser on the Great War to S. J. Perelman on campus-based anti-communism and Vincent Sheean on Furtwangler versus Toscanini. As literary critic Maxwell Geismar summarized in his introduction to a collection of *New Masses* articles, "there is no question the *New Masses* was *the* magazine of the period" (Geismar and North 1969: 6). In addition to serving as the voice of the literary left, the people associated with the magazine wanted to be the center of a social milieu and alternative intelligentsia. Dances and balls in the late 1920s included a Workers' and Peasants' Costume Ball, an Anti-Obscenity Ball, and a Russian Anniversary Ball. Its *New Masses* Costume Ball boasted music by "the best, most mournful Jazz Band in Harlem" (Hemingway 2002: 13).

During the Popular Front period of the 1930s, the emphasis shifted from fine art and high culture to indigenous art and popular taste, from the literati's selection of what the proletariat should appreciate to vernacular "people's culture" (Reuss 1971). Denning describes the Popular Front as being a cultural trend deeper than a strategic phase of the Communist Party—a structure of feeling that pervaded the entire culture, "a moment of transition between the Fordist modernism that reigned before the crash, and the postmodernism of the American Century that emerged from the ruins of Hiroshima" (Denning 1996: 37). On one hand, those with left-wing persuasions, most of whose tastes tended toward high culture, reached out to embrace what they considered the culture of the people. On the other, many of them aspired to raise the aesthetic standards of common folk. As Charles Seeger put it, "The main question . . . should not be 'is it good music?' but 'what is the music good for?'" adding that if it inspires people it will probably be aesthetic (quoted in Lieberman 1995: 39). Seeger's stature in the movement validates his words as not only a description of the change but also a formidable force in promoting it. Angel Flores, reviewing a Latin American Folk Festival in the *Daily World*, expresses a similar sentiment, distancing himself from the high-culture aesthetic of the earlier period, embracing a bond of sympathy between audience and performers "because of the spontaneity of the art, the art of the people, of the masses, devoid of trappings and silly sophistication" (1935: 5).

As another bond of sympathy, left-wing authors and literary critics reversed their earlier interpretation of regionalism. Instead of associating regional literature with reactionary sentimentality, they embraced it as the seeds of revolution. Grace Rourke, for example, endorsed the "humble influences of place and kinship and common emotion that accumulate through generations to shape and condition a distinctive native consciousness" (quoted in Denning 1996: 134). Radical artists softened the socialist realism of the 1920s and embraced a more naturalistic style representing the American scene, though much of the content continued to depict labor and oppression. They wanted to reach out more to the middle class and in coalition with rather than competition against other progressive forces (Hemingway 2002).

In those instances when leftist artists continued to use the forms of high culture, they typically reached out further than they had earlier to meet the tastes of common people. Marc Blitzstein had originally aspired to "carry on the best musical traditions of the past," which excluded musical theater (Denning 1996: 288). But when this onetime student of Arnold Schoenberg met Paul Hindemith, Kurt Weill, and Hanns Eisler, he saw the potential for reaching broad audiences by using that format with a strong component of vernacular speech and popular music. His "proletarian opera" *The Cradle Will Rock* about a strike at a steel plant was originally part of Orson Welles's Federal Theatre Project but was canceled by the Works Progress Administration (WPA) days before opening.

Moving it to another theater where union rules prohibited the actors from appearing onstage compelled them to deliver their lines from the audience. After its New York run, a stripped-down agit-prop version was taken to the industrial regions of Pennsylvania and Ohio for steelworkers themselves. Similarly, the literature of the left shifted from the heroic proletarian avant-garde of the 1920s and early 1930s to a more popular and influential genre, the ghetto or tenement pastoral. Henry Roth's *Call It Sleep*, Tillie Olsen's *Yonnonidio*, and Richard Wright's *Native Son* are just a few of the best-known representatives of a generation of politically inspired fiction that captured and spoke to the lived experience of ethnic America.

While the party-inspired cultural activity embraced the culture of the people, the social forms of doing culture were decidedly hierarchical. Although the Popular Front was a coalition of the party and the broader left, the party regarded itself as the vanguard and sought to pilot the movement as a whole. Party members were very often the most committed and organizationally the most savvy. Even if the movement was too broad and heterogeneous to dictate from the top, the party served as the organizational model most commonly adopted by activists. Adopting an implicit vertical image of cultural creativity and criticism, a political and aesthetic hierarchy sorted cultural objects, creators of culture, and performers. The prevailing discourse of culture was criticism, in which the anointed few claim the mantle of taste for the masses, even if interpreting in the name of the masses. The writers, dramatists, actors, and musicians aspired to the pinnacle of their professions. Such hierarchy was not necessarily elitist or hypocritical but, except for the commercial mass media, the only model available.

The Party and Music before Folk Music

The Old Left's musical infrastructure gave them the autonomy to recast the political connotation of folk music from conservative to insurgent and, more important, from racially exclusive to potentially inclusive. That they did not succeed in making it fully inclusive is due to their failure to transform the performer-audience relation. Still, no other American political movement has mobilized a music infrastructure as formidable. Unfortunately, the red scare of the cold war not only extinguished most of the organizations in the infrastructure but muzzled their collective memory. The extensive range of clubs, cabarets, composers' collectives, musicians' leagues, periodicals, concerts, and performers created a coherent music world in the sense that Becker has described art worlds (1982). But for the most part only the actors anointed by the mass media remain in the public memory—the Lomaxes, the Seegers, Guthrie, Lead-belly, and Robeson. As pivotal as these individuals were, their flowering was rooted in the left's infrastructure. Thus analyzing the construction of the infrastructure requires attention to the party's formal organization, the auxiliary organizations built by activists, and the actions of some extraordinary cultural entrepreneurs.

During the 1930s the Communist Party was divided into an industrial section and a community section with most of the cultural activities in the industrial section because people in the arts were organized as work-ers. Writers, musicians, actors, and technical workers in each of the arts were divided into separate divisions, with greater emphasis on their work-ing conditions and occupational interests than on the content of their artistic output.

The party's cultural division had about 1,000–1,500 members, orga-nized by craft—music, writing, theater, art, even advertising. Each section was divided into clubs, with an executive committee, a president, an or-ganizational secretary, and an educational director. The executives fit into a chain of command. On paper, it looked like a hierarchical chain of com-mand from the central committee through the cultural division to the activists engaged in cultural politics. But in fact, the party leadership was indifferent to what the cultural arms were doing (Lieberman 1995; Silber and Dane 2001). Earl Browder, even though he played in the Kansas City Philharmonic Orchestra as a youth, later recalled that he had neither knowledge nor interest in folk music, though he knew a few Wobbly songs. Activity of that sort, he said, would have been handled at the divi-sion level (Browder 1968).

As the CP shifted from its combative and self-isolating "Third Period" in the 1920s to the compromising and coalition-based Popular Front of the 1930s, the party and its cultural infrastructure became the hub for a broad, culturally rich, left-wing movement. Focusing on both the organi-zation of cultural workers as workers and creative artists as artists, the party-supported movement profoundly influenced the operation and content of American culture during the 1930s and 1940s (Denning 1996). It was within this context that the left adopted folk music as the people's music and mounted a cultural project that would transform the meaning of radical music.

In the 1920s, the party's musical activities centered on its two major overlapping constituencies: New York intellectuals and recent European immigrants. Immigrants, many of them eastern Europeans, brought from home the concept of the revolutionary chorus. Nearly every language group had its own chorus, the best-known being the Jewish Freiheit Ge-bang Ferein, or "Freedom Singers' Society," formed in 1923. Though gaining little attention outside communist or immigrant communities, they were an important part of the culture and strongly influenced later musical thinking. Lyrics were typically bombastic and highly doctrinaire (Reuss 1971). In the late 1920s, the party decided to Americanize and discouraged foreign-language choruses, though no English-language chorus was created until 1933.

While the styles sometimes grated on the ears of non-immigrant Americans, the sonorities reflected members' home cultures. The Yiddish-language Freiheit Gebang Ferein and other foreign-language choruses met people halfway between their home culture and mainstream American culture. Thus, though nominally preserving their homeland culture, the choruses helped assimilate members into American culture. Moreover, since the music was fundamentally collective, it instilled a deep feeling of membership in a larger left-wing culture.

However, the organizational model of the choruses compromised the flowering of solidarity. Organized hierarchically, the conductor operated like a party leader defining what was appropriate for the masses, deciding the correct musical "line." Party strategists felt that demanding music and painstaking rehearsal helped instill commitment, much like soldiers' marching drills. Even when they discussed how choruses contributed to the movement, the image was the aggregation of individual sentiments. Robert Kent, writing in the *Daily Worker*, made the evangelical analogy explicit: "The chorus is one of the most popular mediums for reaching the masses. The capitalist class, through the churches and so-called people's choruses use this medium for lulling the workers. The revolutionary movement uses it for rousing the workers against the oppressors" (Kent 1934: 5). Music could lull or rouse, depending on its content.

The most influential and best-known musical club was the Pierre Degeyter Club, named after the writer of the *Internationale*. The Degeyter Club was composed mostly of musical professionals, especially composers, writers, and performers. They set about creating a music for the proletariat, most of it avant-garde or politically orthodox. Songs included L. E. Swift's (Elie Siegmeister) "The Scottsboro Boys Shall Not Die," Lan Adomian's[4] "Stand Guard," and Hanns Eisler's "The Comintern." After Charles Seeger criticized Swift's material as unsingable by amateur choruses, Swift (Siegmeister) conceded that the material was too difficult and "quite stilted, un-American, old-fashioned, difficult to sing, politically vague" (Denisoff 1971: 43). The club founded the Composers' Collective in 1932, with about two dozen composers, including Henry Cowell, Charles Seeger, Lan Adomian, Elie Siegmeister, Marc Blitzstein, Max Margulis, Herbert Haufrecht, and, on the periphery, Aaron Copland. Few were full members of the CP, though the party paid rent for the collective's office and maintained a liaison. Setting about "the task of writing music of all sorts to meet the needs of the growing mass work class movement" ("Composers Collective" 1936), most of the early products were crude and heavy-handed, quite explicitly art as propaganda.

The Workers Music League (WML) was formed by the party in 1931 to consolidate the efforts for proletarian music. With eighteen to twenty affiliated organizations in Boston, Philadelphia, Chicago, and New York, most early members had belonged to the revolutionary choruses, and leadership came from the Pierre Degeyter Club in New York. Fully aware that their efforts were crude, faith assured them that when socialism triumphed, working-class musicians could blossom into mature composers and performers. Charles Seeger, writing as Carl Sands, explained that "The special task of the Workers Music League is the development of music as a weapon in the class struggle" (quoted in Reuss 1971: 58). They strove to create a non-bourgeois musical form that would be unequivocally associated with the working class. Initially this was defined in terms of high culture, bringing the masses up to the level of cultural appreciation and imparting class consciousness through music. In 1934, the WML issued the *New Workers Song Book*, compiled by Adomian and Sand (Charles Seeger), which included compositions with classical structures and proletarian lyrics designed for trained choruses. About the same time, they published the *International Collection of Revolutionary Songs*, offering people an alternative to national patriotic songs. Its thirteen songs originated in eight countries and were translated into three languages: English, German, and Russian.

The WML's guiding theory was drawn from Hanns Eisler, a pupil of Arnold Schoenberg. In his native Germany, Eisler had created music for the masses, much of it ultra-modern, including twelve-tone scale compositions such as "Comintern" and "In Praise of Learning," which were very popular in European political circles. Fleeing Hitler in 1933, he came to the United States and became the hero of leftist musicians. Like many of the participants in party-sponsored musical activities, few qualms hindered emphatic advice for the working class about what they should listen to or perform. At a 1938 speech to the Choir of the International Ladies' Garment Workers' Union, he reproached them with, "What is being offered to the people as musical fare? Songs like, *Bei mir bist du scon*, *Ti-pi-tin*, and similar stupidities. And I shudder to think of the thousands of sentimental love songs produced by Broadway and Hollywood. Some of you will say, that's harmless, that's just entertainment, don't worry. But as a musician I do worry, for I know all is poison, opium for the people. But what is the solution? Should the working people grow long beards and with great dignity attend only concerts of serious music? That is ridiculous and impossible" (Eisler 1938). To escape their stupid music and ensure music be interesting to performers and audience, they were instructed to choose progressive composers, including class-conscious compositions from the Soviet Union. Not surprisingly such admonitions won few converts among the rank and file. A typical Eisler lyric: "We are the builders, we build the future. / The future world is in our hands. / We swing our hammers, we use our weapons / Against our foes in many lands." An excerpt from an item about the Pierre Degeyter Club in the *Daily Worker* gives the flavor of the party's musical direction during this period: "This new chorus, which will be under the direction of Jacob Schaefer, proletarian composer and director of the *Freiheit Gesang Ferein*, is to co-ordinate its work with other divisions of the Pierre Degeyter Club. Plans are being made for the performance of operas by members of the Composers' Collective of the club, with the use of the club orchestra. New Soviet works as well as other important choral works are to be given. Several scenes from a Davidenko opera are to be performed some time in February for the benefit of the John Reed Club and the Pierre Degeyter Club" (November 15, 1933: 5).

Despite the bombast, Eisler exercised considerable influence among professional musicians in the Workers Music League and the Composers' Collective, confident that their music was not stupid. These classical musicians, trained at the top conservatories, were dedicated to bringing "good music" to the masses. Excluded from "good music" was folk music, which grated on their refined music sensibilities. It was during this period that Charles Seeger wrote, "Many folksongs are complacent, melancholy, defeatist, intended to make slaves endure their lot—pretty but not the stuff for a militant proletariat to feed upon" (Lieberman 1995: 30).[5] The *Worker Musician*, a publication of the Workers Music League, criticized the few folk songs, mainly Kentucky mining songs, included in its own 1932 *Red Song Book*, as immature and reflecting "arrested development." Prior to the Popular Front era, party print media had only scattered interest in folk music. For example, in 1928, the *Daily World* reviewed Carl Sandburg's *American Songbag*. It is curious why they would review this. Sandburg was not a CP person, and this was not a political book. Nor did the reviewer expect the book's music to have much impact, writing, "The United States is not a singing nation in the sense in which the European and African nations are" ("Folk-Lore Collected" 1928: 6).

But change was on the horizon. As the Soviet Union began to feel threatened by Nazi Germany in the mid-1930s, the Communist International changed its strategy from the immediate overthrow of capitalism to an alliance with all progressives against fascism. The American Communist Party's national leadership responded by opening up the party both politically and culturally, adopting a "Popular Front" strategy that replaced the goal of immediate revolution with defense against fascism, supplanting their hard-line intolerance of "deviationism" with a more inclusive attitude toward diverse leftist activists. At the same time, rigid economism was succeeded by greater political latitude, including arts and music for their own sake, not just as a vessel of party doctrine. This change in party strategy made it possible for activists close to the party to spark an effervescent and influential movement that shaped American politics and culture for a decade or more. Though it was initiated at the top, the leadership did not so much direct the cultural flowering as provide a stage for artists, writers, and musicians to interact with and facilitate each other. Though not immediate, the movement drifted toward folk music.

Between 1934 and 1936, the WML conducted a self-review that addressed its failure to reach workers, suggesting that simpler and more familiar tunes would have more immediate appeal. The second edition of the songbook in 1935 contained about half labor-radical songs, reflecting the new emphasis on simplicity. But they still composed complicated music and equated singing masses with the choruses. Another important change was a break with their intellectual leader, Hanns Eisler, who was criticized for ignoring aesthetic qualities in his quest for ideological correctness. In the mid-1930s, party organs began to include more positive references to folk music. George Maynard wrote in the *Daily Worker*: "Since time began the masses of the people have been the truest creators of music. Love, fear, worship and bondage have been some of the themes which have given birth to folk music. The theme of revolt has been rarer, but strong and compelling when it appeared" (January 23, 1934, quoted in Reuss 1971: 83). He cites Negro and hillbilly music as proof of the people's creativity. Lan Adomian proposed in the *Daily Worker* that workers' choruses should include "Negro songs of protest, work songs, railroad songs, [and] cowboy songs. . . . Such an approach would carry us a long way toward rooting our work in the tradition of American music. It would give the lie to those who insist that our music is nothing but an importation from the outside" (quoted in Reuss 1971: 83).

Though not making explicit reference to folk music per se, the quotation captures what the party's musical leaders were seeking—a type of music that represented all the people. As a group the Composers' Collective never singled out folk music for attention, though many of its members increasingly moved in that direction (Dunaway 1980).

While progressive political movements had long expressed themselves musically, it was not until activists associated with the American Communist Party entered the picture that a particular genre of music became represented in political terms. Earlier movements had used any music that their members knew or that was close at hand—minstrel music, religious music, military music, popular music, bar songs, bawdy songs, and occasionally classical music. Though the songs expressed political meaning in the lyrics, the only quality that made music "of the people" was popularity and use on behalf of the people.

"Discovering" Folk Music

During the Popular Front era, a small group of middle-class, formally trained musicians began to coalesce around a vision of folk music as the embodiment of the people's music. Charles Seeger, Alan Lomax, Elie Siegmeister, and Earl Robinson built on each other and influenced the course of American musical history. Their quest for the people's music was partly an attempt to reach down to the people and partly a "discovery" (in the sense of Columbus "discovering" America) that ordinary folks were already using music for insurgency in an unlikely place—southern unions.

The party's adoption of folk music as a project did not come only from a change of heart by its cultural leaders. The roots were also genuinely indigenous. Labor insurgence in that most politically inhospitable of regions, the South, was visibly energized by local music, as workers used old and adapted songs to solidify the movement. The 1929 Gastonia, North Carolina, strike made an especially indelible impression on the national party. In April of that year 1,800 workers, led by the communist National Textiles Union, struck against the Loray Mill, sparking other strikes throughout the South. Though eventually defeated by such repressive measures as the eviction of workers and the heavy hand of military power, the nearly six-month standoff inspired later generations of southern unionists and leftists. Among the casualties was a twenty-nine-year-old, musically talented worker who supported small children and an invalid husband on the mill's meager wages. Ella May Wiggins had galvanized other workers with her example, speeches, and songs, most famously "Mill Mother's Lament." As one participant later recalled,

> They [nightly meetings] were interspersed with songs, reports from other strike areas, and tales of local incidents between strikers and the bossmen. No evening passed without getting a new song from our Ella May, the minstrel of our strike. . . . The crowd would join in with an old refrain and Ella May would add verse after verse to her song. From these singers would drift into spirituals or hymns and many a "praise the Lord" would resound through the quiet night. (quoted in Roscigno and Danaher 2004: 84–85)

Though most historical accounts emphasize her martyrdom, the northern left-wing press had taken full notice of music's role in the Gastonia events even before her death. In August 1929 New Masses printed a song by an eleven-year-old Gastonia striker and "poet laureate" of the strike, Odell Corey. After Wiggins's death, the party organs quickly moved to construct a musical martyr. The Daily World described her musicking.

These songs spread over the countryside faster than literature or leaf-lets. Listless and half-illiterate mill workers glowed to life as they heard them, grinned at the novel idea that instead of standing their condi-tions they could get together and change them. They grinned and agreed, and the word grew in power. . . . Now Ella May is dead. The unquenchable has been quenched—by a bullet in the heart. But even this ruthless murder has failed to stop her words. Wherever her songs go—and they will go far in the newly awakened South—she will go, too. (September 20, 1929: 1)

Wiggins and Gastonia would continue as icons of indigenous, insurgent music—evidence of the power of music to fortify collective action under the most adverse circumstances.

As inspired as the New York leftists may have been by the strikers' use of music to fortify their efforts, there were social facts that could not be easily appropriated. Roscigno and Danaher have insightfully analyzed the social basis of the textile workers' music. Many of the musicians were ex–mill workers who included their mill experiences in the songs. The music was transmitted through numerous local radio stations that pro-grammed vernacular culture. And much of the musicking was done by union organizers who made little separation between organizing and singing. Though the lyrics were certainly propagandistic, the function of the music was less to persuade than to build solidarity among those whose lives were already in the factory (Roscigno and Danaher 2004).

The activists who hallowed Ella May Wiggins were more interested in the political content than in the musical form, with little ambition for a broader musical movement.[6] One of the few voices for folk music before the era of the Popular Front, and one of the people who most actively publicized the life and death of Ella May Wiggins in both leftist and mainstream circles, was Margaret Larkin. A native of New Mexico, she was primarily a scholar of cowboy, Mexican, and Indian subcultures of the Southwest, notably in her 1931 volume, *The Singing Cowboy*. Hav-ing moved to New York in the 1920s, she gravitated to left-wing circles, writing plays and the screenplay for *The Passaic Textile Strike*, seen from the workers' perspective. Her reputation grew from such activities as be-coming the founding secretary of the Marxist-oriented Theater Union and her frequent appearances at radical gatherings singing cowboy songs, protest songs, and topical songs (Wald 2007). Though at first regarded as no more than a pleasant entertainer, she began in the 1930s to under-stand her music in more political terms, partly from journalistic assign-ments covering strikes, including that in Harlan County, Kentucky. As her interest in folk music and her politics moved closer together, she criticized the Workers Music League for its shallow treatment of folk music, contending in *New Masses* that folk-rooted strike songs were "a direct and vigorous expression of large numbers of American workers" (quoted in Reuss 1971: 87). According to Archie Green, "To my knowledge, Larkin was the first musician in the communist orbit to deflate the polemics of Marxist critics who had called American folk melodies 'arrested' or 'immature'—debased by capitalist exploitation" (1993: 316). The main contours of the Old Left's approach to folk music can be seen in Larkin's 1929 eulogy for Ella May Wiggins in *The Nation*. Wiggins was portrayed as not only a heroic individual—a worker who stood up to the bosses—but also an embodiment of the people—"mountain people, with the habits of peasants . . . suddenly confronted with modern industrialism" (Larkin 1929: 383), a juxtaposition echoing the first folk project's characterization of folk a generation earlier. With a native intelligence that belied her lack of schooling, Wiggins was described as bringing the old mountain ballads to the factory in her untaught but beautiful voice, "bare of all ornament, full of earnest and feeling" (Larkin 1929: 383). Though Larkin fully appreciated the importance of the folk process to the people's music, she found the political significance in the lyrics. Wiggins sang of the union, the bosses, the martyrs, and the International Labor Defense (ILD), the CP-affiliated legal team assisting the strike. Wiggins's songs express "her faith in the union as the only power she ever met that promised her a better life" (Larkin 1929: 382). Thus about half of the article reprints lyrics that "are destined to be the battle songs of the coming industrial struggle" (Larkin 1929: 383).[7]

Another early communist voice for folk music was Mike Gold, a cultural critic for *New Masses* and the *Daily Worker* who wrote on cultural matters in the leftist press for most of the first half of the 1920s. Growing up steeped in Yiddish folk music, he had a genuine appreciation of working-class culture and as a youth learned many of the IWW parodies. In the *Daily Worker* he wrote that "the nearest thing we've had to Joe Hill's kind of folk balladry has been from such southern mountaineer Communists as Aunt Molly Jackson and the martyred textile weaver, Ella May Wiggins" (April 21, 1934). Looking for a proletarian writer-poet, a "Shakespeare in overalls," he liked Ella May Wiggins, Jim Garland, Molly Jackson, Sarah Ogan, and Florence Reece, but considered them oddities more than true artists. Eventually he found Woody Guthrie, whom he soon anointed as the genuine voice of the people.

If the left wing had stayed on this cultural trajectory, it is unlikely they would have taken on folk music as a project or that they would have found a genre with genuine multiracial possibilities. Although the Gastonia events were remarkably integrated for that region and period (Solomon 1998), the music, both in the events themselves and in discourse on the strikes, was white country and western music. The musical template was Joe Hill, an eclectic musician without a specific genre, distinguishable from other kinds of music more by the political content of lyrics than by the social connotations of the music itself.

About the time that the national party was moving into its Popular Front period, Ray and Lida Auville, a West Virginia couple who had settled in Cleveland, published *Songs of the American Worker*, a collection of twelve songs filled with militant rhetoric set to folk-style tunes. When Carl Sand (Charles Seeger) rejected the Auvilles as "a hybrid mixture of jazz and balladry," Michael Gold admonished the Workers Music League for being sectarian.

> Would you judge workers' correspondence by the standard of James Joyce or Walter Pater? No, a folk art rarely comes from the studios; it makes its own style, and has its own inner laws of growth. It may shock you, but I think the Composers' Collective has something to learn from Ray and Lida Auville. . . . They write catchy tunes that any American worker can sing and like, and the words of their songs make the revolution as intimate and simple as "Old Black Joe." Is this so little? (quoted in Denisoff 1971: 48)

Richard Reuss calls this interchange "in retrospect . . . the single most identifiable watershed in the American Left's acceptance of traditional songs and lyrics composed in the folk idiom" (Reuss and Reuss 2000: 74). The caveat at the beginning of the quotation is important. The event was not an epiphany, either individually or collectively, but looking back we can see an important change from a stance of overt elitism in which the party aspired to bring the working class up to its level to a more compromising attitude in which, artistically at least, they would meet the people halfway. Gold is still writing from the critic's perch, still arbitrating taste, still attending to content rather than what people were doing. Few would have predicted in 1936 that "the people's music" would come to be defined as folk music, but some of the pieces were beginning to fall into place. Not long after Gold's attack on the Workers Music League, they disbanded and were replaced by the American Music League, which pledged to "encourage the study, collection and popularization of American folk music" (M. M. 1936).

Conclusion

Social infrastructure is the organizational apparatus that makes activity possible, the form through which content flows. Just as public transportation or highways constrain the places people can go and what they can do along the way, cultural infrastructure constrains not only the kinds of meanings that can be communicated but, more important, the kinds of social relations that can be realized. By using institutionalized cultural structures as the template for creating cultural organizations, the social relations by which they did culture tended to reproduce those of the dominant society, despite the best intentions of many of the participants. The Composers' Collective, by definition, reinforced the division of labor between composer and performer. Similarly, CP-led art, drama, journalism, and literature adopted conventional organizational models, all of them embodying the party's strategy of a vanguard-led movement. Given the pervasiveness of racial inequality in American society, it followed that such an infrastructure would thwart the party's efforts to create a racially inclusive cultural presence. Adopting what they considered a racially inclusive genre of music, folk music, was not sufficient to overcome the structural impediments to equality.

The more organizationally autonomous the actors in an art world are, the more autonomous the cultural production. A political movement (or avant-garde organization, religion, counterculture, etc.) that aspires to create a new art form or give new content to existing forms must either create its own art world or depend on others for sustenance and infrastructural support. Conversely, the more interdependent an art world is with other parts of society, the less autonomous the cultural products. When political movements work within art worlds they do not control, they are constrained by at least three factors.

First, they must work within selection mechanisms that may conflict with their values. Commercial music is based on a star system that glorifies a handful of anointed individuals. Performers and performances that reach the broadest possible audience (lowest common denominator) trump those that speak deeply to limited audiences. Thus even when singers might offer alternative messages through their lyrics, they can reach audiences only when they attain star status, as Pete Seeger, Joan Baez, and, recently, Ani DiFranco have done. The selective mechanisms (chiefly the market) that gave them access to the public are impervious to political organizations that might benefit from any lyrical message the musicians offer. Political movements that seek diverse musical voices for multiple audiences are thus virtually excluded from the system.

Second, the aesthetic and commercial standards are dictated by those who control the art world, including the A&R people of record companies, critics, and, to some extent, customers. There are genuine differences of opinion about whether politically meaningful content inherently debases aesthetic quality, but those who control the art world get to decide which standard is applied. Taste makers in the commercial realm decide not only which political message might appear in lyrics but also whether political messages disqualify music for play. The cultural division of the CP, *New Masses*, and the Workers Music League helped constitute an alternative art world that offered an alternative aesthetic. The literature, drama, art, and some of the music created in this art world left a permanent stamp on American culture (Denning 1996).

Finally, and perhaps most important, dependence on the art world controlled by others limits political movements to the social forms of those art worlds. Commodification itself is a social relationship in which relationships among those in an art world take the form of buying and selling. Unless a political movement has an organizational base in its own art world, it cannot reconfigure the relationship between the composer, performer, and audience, the setting within which music is created and heard, the boundaries between music and other art forms, the selection of who learns musical skills, or the means by which skills are imparted. Insofar as a political movement aspires to embody alternative social relations for doing culture, it must construct its own cultural infrastructure.

The control of the art world affects not only the content of the art but also the practical consequences of art as a social activity and the social relationships within which art is done. The effect of music on racial boundaries depends less on whether the content of music advocates equality or prejudice than the racial practices of the music world. Thus a political movement that strives to reshape racial boundaries through music needs to create its own music world. And though the left's success in achieving racial unity was modest, the success they did sustain was a consequence of their organizational independence. In a period when the world of commercial music was highly racialized, only an autonomous organizational base could have had any progressive impact on the racial meaning of music.[8]

As the left grappled to define and establish a "people's music," it experimented with organizational forms outside the nexus of the composer-performer-audience relationship and beyond the media of commodified products. Some of the veterans of the CP-led apparatus searched for new allies and a new generation of activists joined the effort, eventually erecting a full-blown second folk project.

CHAPTER FIVE

Movement Entrepreneurs and Activists

Structures, social or otherwise, do not do things. Agents do. The infrastructure developed in the last chapter did not transform folk music or give it a political connotation. This chapter focuses on the cultural entrepreneurs who used and altered structures to metamorphose folk music from an esoteric concern of academics and antiquarians into a politically charged expression of "the people." The sociological literature on social movements often reads as though social movements were autonomous entities acting within a context of opportunities and constraints and occasionally entering into coalitions with like-minded political actors. But rarely are social movements political actors sui generis reacting only to environments. Understanding their origins requires attention to the organizational kaleidoscope of individual and corporate actors, churning with and reflecting off of each other. Social movement organizations are spun off of, interact with, and evolve into explicitly political organizations such as organized lobbyists, artistic clusters, invisible colleges of intellectuals, profit-seeking entrepreneurs, religious organizations, student groups, media outlets, government agencies, and friendship networks. These networks are too dense and too reflexive to characterize merely as actor and environment. What social movements become and what they do is shaped by the interaction between the movements and other types of actors. The adoption of folk music as "the people's music" is a clear case in point, an interaction among several types of actors, mutually constituting and shaping each other so thoroughly that it is sometimes difficult to find the boundaries.

Although the Communist Party was one of the most hierarchical social movements in American history, it was cultural entrepreneurship that propelled the folk music project with which the party has become associated. Its leaders achieved the transformation of a musical genre less through exercise of authority in institutional incumbency or through celebrity status in the public sphere than through ceaseless effort to bring people together, germinate organizations, publicize activity, and articulate a distinct vision of the relationship between music and society. Groups connected to the party helped transform folk music, but it was also a project of New Deal government groups and performers acting collectively and individually, coordinated by an extraordinary pair of families engaged in a whirlwind of cultural entrepreneurship. Without the Lomaxes and Seegers, it is likely that American folk music would still have the quaint nationalist connotations of English folk music, if it had any connotation at all.

Cultural Entrepreneurs, Social Movements, and Bureaucratic Structures

The conventional image of cultural entrepreneurs and social movements is that cultural entrepreneurs actively bring people together to form social movements that then make claims on authorities to change the people in power or change policies to the benefit of the activists. Certainly many situations fit that model from the abolitionists to the suffragettes to the civil rights movement. William Lloyd Garrison, Frederick Douglass, Elizabeth Cady Stanton, Susan B. Anthony, Martin Luther King, and Huey Newton were all as entrepreneurial as they were charismatic. The organizations they led eventually made major concessions of personnel and policy in response to the mobilization they sparked.

Similarly, the success of entrepreneurs for social movement organizations is typically measured in terms of taking over the formal organization. The takeover of civil rights organizations by Black Power advocates described in a later chapter is an archetypical case of this process. The social movement organization becomes the site of power struggle analogous to a government coup or revolution with a new regime and altered policy.

Yet there are different kinds of relationships between cultural entrepreneurs and organizations, whether governmental or social movement. The second folk project sought neither displacement nor major policy changes in their mobilization toward the government and the Communist Party. Rather, they were bottom-up activists gaining a beachhead within each, which they used as a structure to promote cultural activity, reaching to new audiences, solidifying links with other activists, codifying musical conventions, and permeating other institutions. When the party was stifled and government ended its cultural support, suppressing the left into a period of abeyance, the activists turned to other forums for sustenance such as left-wing summer camps, college performances, marginal cultural media, and exile. The main lesson from the successes of the cultural entrepreneurs who constituted the second folk project is that footholds or beachheads in top-down organizations such as the Communist Party or the government can be an alternative strategy for promoting a cultural form. Responses that might normally be interpreted as co-optation—creating organizational niches at the margins of bureaucracies—can be effectively used to further a cultural project. Black and ethnic studies departments in universities are a case in point. Though they have sapped some of the militancy out of some of the most talented young activists, on many campuses they are a free space in which activists gather and work together to keep social movements alive and active. Both the government and the Communist Party shaped folk music into their form, but in both folk music was used in unintended ways. One of the legacies of these two sites for folk music has been the continued tension between the "pure" folk music preserved and promoted by the government and the "modern" folk music promoted by the party. In the short term, the party's image prevailed. Until the 1970s folk music was virtually equivalent with left-wing music. Even politically conscious contemporary singer-songwriters like Phil Ochs were known as folk singers. But in the long run, the genre has been bleached of the political connotations to the point where folk music is a style or sound with a vague liberal connotation reinforced by occasional musicians such as Ani DiFranco.

Collective action cultural projects thus force us to temper the dichotomy between activists and authorities. Cultural projects often mobilize to infiltrate social movement organizations, especially hierarchical organizations like the Communist Party, as well as government organizations. Instead, we need to attend to other sources of variations in cultural projects. Cultural entrepreneurs can play a variety of roles in cultural projects, acting as charismatic leaders, organization builders, networkers, canon-builders, standardizers, or public spokespeople. They can be talented performers or behind-the-scenes coordinators. Cultural projects can take a variety of organizational forms from entrepreneurial networks to centralized, formal organizations, with various combinations of organizational types. The participants can have a variety of social roots, especially class, race, gender, ethnicity, immigration status, and urbanity. And there can be a variety of social relations within which the cultural expression is done from participatory to star-based.

In the Lomaxes and Seegers we have two pioneering fathers, two extraordinary sons, and two remarkable families. Throughout the history of American folk music, they are ubiquitous from the first generation of song collectors to the living legacy of the genre today. John Lomax and Charles Seeger expanded folk music beyond the Appalachians and the dominion of Anglophile academics. Their sons Alan Lomax and Pete Seeger made it a popular form. And their other children, including Bess Lomax Hawes, Peggy Seeger, and Mike Seeger, have been celebrated performers and thoughtful interpreters of folk music. When a sociologist considers agency in the story of American folk music, the Lomaxes and Seegers loom as giants.

The Lomax and Seeger families mattered not just because they had individuals of prodigious talent, exceptional vision, and limitless energy. Many individuals have the personal qualities to make a difference but do not find themselves in a structural position to succeed. What made the Seegers and Lomaxes distinctive was that the most pivotal of them never achieved long-lasting positions of authority within any major institution. Instead they bridged institutions, playing an entrepreneurial role in the Schumpeterian sense—cobbling programs, building organizations, recombining various elements into new forms, and using a broad range of social and professional contacts to mold American folk music as not only a style or sound but a musical world that itself bridged institutions. The social world of American folk music has representation within and links together universities, commercial media, government agencies, professional associations, political movements, and its own organizational base, mirroring the affiliations and linkages forged by the members of these two families.

These structural relationships helped sustain folk music as a form and mode of musicking. But the attempt to bridge racial boundaries was less structural than a matter of agency. The four most influential individuals in these two families—John and Alan Lomax, Charles and Pete Seeger— were each strongly committed to racial inclusion in the music, though as we shall see, not necessarily racial equality in society. They had ample precedent in the social world of folk music to restrict folk music to white music, but each self-consciously and consistently included black and white music as well as black and white musicians in their musical activities. But because the choice of racial inclusion was more voluntary than structurally mandated or structurally institutionalized, racial inclusion was a fragile achievement, easy to abandon by those with a weak commitment.

THE LOMAXES: FATHER AND SON

John A. Lomax (1867–1948), father of John Jr., Shirley, Alan, and Bess, is usually given credit for expanding the meaning of American folk song beyond the Elizabethan ballads sung by Appalachian highlanders (Porterfield 1996).[1] A relentless collector, promoter, networker, and publicist, he helped bring a more inclusive and truly American folk music to the general public. Like many entrepreneurs, his marginal status, at least relative to the academic establishment, channeled his energies to new kinds of activities and helped him reach new kinds of audiences. And though he was hostile to the left in general and communists in particular, his achievements helped make folk music inclusive enough to qualify as "the people's music," as packaged by his son Alan. Thus, more than any other single figure, he bridged the first and second folk projects, even though he was a major figure in neither.

John Lomax's *Cowboy Songs and Other Frontier Ballads* (1910) was one of the first collections of truly indigenous American music. One of ten children born to a middling farming family, he aspired to better himself through education. After trying his hand at teaching, he enrolled at the University of Texas where he became enamored of folklore and the romance of the cowboy, even publishing a piece in the *University of Texas Magazine* titled "The Minstrelsy of the Mexican Border." After following the model of English folklorists to collect some vernacular songs, he took a pile of cowboy songs to an English professor who declared them "tawdry, cheap, and unworthy," so he burned them. But he found a pair of mentors and lifelong patrons at Harvard in two giants of American folklore, Barrett Wendell and George L. Kittredge (N. Cohen 1990). Although *Cowboy Songs* was casual in its attention to musical provenance and transcription, with many of the songs contributed by readers of newspaper ads, it was a major contribution to awakening academic and public interest in folk music.[2] The book was the vehicle that introduced to the American public such characteristically American songs as "Whoopee Ti Yi Yo," "Git Along Little Dogies," "Sweet Betsy from Pike," and the archetypical cowboy song, "Home on the Range." Yet the book's success was not sufficient to secure Lomax an academic position. Although a founder of the Texas Folklore Society and twice president of the American Folklore Society, he never won scholarly respectability. After a short stint on the faculty at Texas A&M, the bulk of his career was spent in administrative positions and working in finance. Throughout those decades he frequently combined song-catching expeditions with lecture tours, speaking at universities, ladies' clubs, public lectures, churches, and folklore societies. A post-retirement second wind energized some of the canonical collections of American folk music, including *American Ballads and Folk Songs* (with Alan Lomax) (Lomax and Lomax 1934) and *Our Singing Country* (J. Lomax et al. 1941).

Besides the obvious contribution of his books, his relationships with universities were informal and fleeting. Especially when his career was starting out, before the age of electronic media, public lectures were an important part of academic and civic life. Lomax regularly organized tours that took months and covered hundreds and at times thousands of miles, speaking at colleges and universities from coast to coast. He delighted in the limelight, chumminess, and opportunity to introduce folk music to new audiences. The tours also broadened his network of song collecting for both those who knew music and those who knew about it.

By his reckoning, over the course of his lifetime he delivered five hundred lectures at over two hundred colleges and universities.

Participation with professional associations was also high in networking and ambivalent in content. Except during his years as a banker, he regularly attended and presented papers at the American Folklore Society and Modern Language Association, the two organizations with academic jurisdiction over folk music. The American Folklore Society, despite his service as president, twice expelled him for lacking a doctorate. He laconically responded, "Perhaps the collector must go out among the people dressed in cap and gown" (Porterfield 1996: 407). His relationship with the Modern Language Association was more agreeable. An appearance at a nationally noted presentation at the 1909 convention primed the market for his *Cowboys* book. Nearly a half century later, he introduced Huddie Ledbetter (Leadbelly) as a primordial treasure of pristine American culture.

Government, especially the parts that fostered folk music and helped institutionalize its preservation and dissemination, was alternately supportive and indifferent, offering legitimacy more than employment and a site for institution building. But like his academic involvement, his role was historically consequential and organizationally peripheral, all the better to bridge with other institutions. The lofty title Honorary Consultant and Curator of the Archive of American Folk Song at the Library of Congress lacked salary but legitimated his various endeavors (and gave the Library of Congress the rights to music under their auspices). The level of compensation reflected his equivocal relationship with the archive. Its founding director, Robert W. Gordon, feared, perhaps with some justification, that Lomax wanted his job. Typically unable to supply the recording equipment and supplies Lomax pestered it for, the library's main benefit for Lomax was an institutional setting for the collection, storage, reproduction, and dissemination of music collected in the field. The benefit for society was a repository of music outside the commercial music industry. When he solicited contributions, recruited informants, approached foundations, and played music for audiences, it was not just as an individual or even as an affiliate of the University of Texas but on behalf of the nation's premier cultural archive. Although he at times hoped that his position would become a source of income, it was Alan who eventually became the first salaried employee of the archive.

Lomax did use his political connections in Texas to secure a paying job as part-time advisor on folklore to the Historical Records Survey, part of the Works Progress Administration, a job used to support collecting activity. This led to another New Deal position, working with the Federal Writers' Project helping develop a set of guidelines for the collection of invaluable information on everyday life among common people, including the highly celebrated slave narratives.

The final node in the network that Lomax cobbled together in his folk music project was the world of foundations. In conjunction with the Library of Congress and as an individual he sought and occasionally received financial and institutional support from some of the country's best-known foundations, including the Carnegie Corporation and Rockefeller Foundation. With the intervention of Theodore Roosevelt, the Carnegie Corporation provided a grant of $3,000, a munificent amount for the Depression era. About the same time, the Rockefeller Foundation was providing and occasionally offered other modest sums, though Lomax had hoped for a multiyear contribution.[3]

Lomax's historical reputation is debated between those who recognize his contribution to the spread of folk music and those who condemn his racism. Oscar Brand expresses one view, admitting some of his foibles, but honoring him nonetheless: "John Lomax was the great pioneer. Folklorists say that he should have listed his sources more carefully. It is said that there is evidence that he borrowed some copyrighted songs from other collections without credit. But it was Lomax who introduced most of our experts to folk music—the living art. And it is doubtful whether we would have had our current 'revival' without his work" (1962: 67). Cantwell, acknowledging his contribution, also highlights his racism: "As a man of his time John Lomax could only enact the role of Mr. Interlocutor in the minstrel show; his message was superiority, mastery, command . . . he could represent but not contemplate, and certainly not assimilate, the black Other" (1998: 75).

Still, Lomax's vision of American folk music helped move it not only from the Appalachian Mountains to the cattle ranges of Texas but beyond the Anglo-Saxons cherished by Sharp and Kittredge to a multiracial mix of America's South and West. Although he was racist even by the bigoted standard of his era, he worked tirelessly to introduce and make respectable the music of rural African Americans to white audiences.[4] While he never entertained the possibility that blacks could be politically or economically equal to whites and his attitude toward black music was at best patronizing, he did reach across racial boundaries (or as he would have seen it, down) to incorporate black music into America's cultural heritage.[5] Lomax saw in the former slaves and their descendants America's peasantry, the agrarian primitives who, unsullied by civilization, embodied a folk culture worthy of preservation. When they individually or collectively, socially or musically, failed to fit his preconceptions of benightedness, he ignored them or renounced them. He especially loathed jazz as too commercial, too urban. His mission was given special urgency by the desire to capture black music in its pure form before the race was tainted by the seduction of the bastardized new genre. This appreciation of rural black music set him apart from both the earlier ballad collectors, who saw purity only in the music of rural whites, and mainstream promoters of black music in jazz, spirituals, and vaudeville, who were perfectly comfortable with the synthesis of African and European influences. In this sense, Lomax was a forerunner of later interpreters of folk and non-folk music who defined authenticity in terms of blackness. His collections, writings, and promotional activities helped set the terms of racial authenticity that survive to this day.

Lomax's contradictory role in bridging and reinforcing black-white boundaries can be seen in two examples: his famous or infamous relationship with Huddie Ledbetter (Leadbelly) and a paper he delivered on "Negro" music.

John Lomax's complicated and stormy relationship with Huddie Ledbetter is a major staple of the lore about American folk and popular music. Leadbelly is now an American icon whose records continue to sell, the object of Hollywood biopics and a substantial academic literature. He has even been inducted into the Rock 'n' Roll Hall of Fame, the Blues Hall of Fame, and the Nashville Songwriters' Association International Hall of Fame (Filene 1991). The story, actively circulated while Lomax managed his career and now central to the Leadbelly myth, recounts how John Lomax "discovered" Ledbetter as a convict at the Angola State Penitentiary in Louisiana and was so moved by his musical talents and vast storehouse of songs that, after release, Lomax took him under his wing and introduced him to the music world, creating a legend of American culture. Both men helped propagate a tale, now known to be false, about how the Texas gentleman used the prisoner's music to secure a pardon from the governor. Parroted by newspapers, national news magazines, concert promotions, and a movie theater newsreel, the powerful fable of a murderer redeemed by music had great appeal for the generally white, urban sophisticates that Lomax cultivated (Wolfe and Lornell 1992).

Different accounts of their relationship interpret it as variously benevolent or exploitative. Some attribute Ledbetter's success to the Lomaxes. Lawless, for example, notes that after meeting them, "Leadbelly experienced a degree of success, at least musical if not financial, that few would have thought possible" (1960: 139). Yet others characterize the relationship as primarily exploitative: "one of the most amazing cultural swindles in American history," in the words of Richard Wright (quoted in Wolfe and Lornell 1992: 201). For the purposes of this discussion, the question of how exploitative their relationship was matters less than what it shows about the racial dynamics of American music, especially in the construction of folk music.

Lomax had scoured the South looking for "the folk songs of the Negro," which, he said, "in musical phrasing and in poetic content, are most unlike those of the white race" (Porterfield 1996: 298). This phrasing situates black folk music both racially and along the axis of modernity. The black authenticity he sought could not be contaminated by urban commercial music. Frustrated that so many of the informants he located in towns and plantations were oblivious to the musical boundaries he wanted to construct between folk and popular music, he cast about for places where African Americans were most isolated from whites or modern life. Southern prisons seemed to be the answer. As Lomax explained it, not only could he find individuals long removed from the modern world, but prison supported a musical culture, with songs passed from generation to generation, creating in a microcosm the folk process. At the Angola State Penitentiary near Baton Rouge, Louisiana, he found Huddie Ledbetter, who impressed him so much that he deliberately sought his release. A year later, after discharge, the ex-convict followed up on Lomax's invitation to travel with him.

Ledbetter had been born near the Texas-Louisiana border in 1888 and grew up in relatively comfortable circumstances. Taking up guitar as a teenager, his talent quickly showed itself, but whiskey, women, and his temper soon got him in trouble. After being convicted in 1917 for murder and assault, in prison he developed a reputation as a singer. Once free, he again found himself in trouble for attacking a white man with a knife and was imprisoned in Louisiana, where Lomax found him. By that time, in his mid-forties, he was an accomplished performer commanding a broad range of styles (Wolfe and Lornell 1992).

In 1934 they began to travel together for Lomax's fieldwork in southern prisons and towns. Ledbetter served as a chauffeur, cook, source of songs, and entrée into haunts rarely frequented by whites, while priming the musical pump of wary informants reluctant to be recorded by a white southerner. Using Texan political connections to gain official endorsement from southern governors, Lomax was warmly greeted by prison wardens, but needed Ledbetter to break the ice and elicit songs from the prisoners. Lomax also managed Ledbetter the performer, setting up the tours and handling the finances. Despite Ledbetter's wish to perform in his best clothes, as respectable musicians were wont to do, Lomax dressed him in prison garb, often seated on a bale of straw. Rather than perform the vast range of music in his personal repertory, he was confined to "genuine" folk songs. Performances were arranged for scholarly groups, political figures, benefit concerts, and the general public. They even appeared together at the Modern Language Association, where Lomax presented a paper, "Comments on Negro Folksongs." Lomax discouraged and at times prohibited the singer from performing for African American audiences, preferring audiences that could "appreciate" the cultural significance of authentic American folk music.

The height of their notoriety came not in the shanties of the South, the halls of academia, or the isolation of the prison camps but on the concert stage of New York. Porterfield places Ledbetter's 1935 arrival in New York in cultural context, noting that another cultural phenomenon had just swept through the city: the black ape–white woman fable, *King Kong*. The parallels were not lost on the public: "A savage being, primitive and violent, is discovered by a white man, put in bondage, transported to Manhattan, and placed on public display" (Porterfield 1996: 347). Not only did the arrival of Lomax and Ledbetter (treated as a pair) make headlines in the local papers, but *Time* magazine carried a story about the folk collector and his "Murderous Minstrel." Not long after arriving, they appeared in numerous performances, interviewed for local and national publications, recorded scores of sides for the American Record Company, and signed a contract with Macmillan for a book to be written by Lomax about Ledbetter. The two men also signed a contract making Lomax exclusive agent, splitting the income half each, soon modified to include Alan with equal thirds going to each party. The inequity not only caused hardship but also wounded the singer's pride. With Ledbetter becoming a media star, Lomax felt he was at last earning "a permanent and honorable place in the history of American literature" (Porterfield 1996: 351). At the same time, Ledbetter continued to do laundry, shine Lomax's shoes, and drive his car (Porterfield 1996; Wolfe and Lornell 1992).

Such were the terms of the relationship. Lomax was the bridge between the chain gangs, juke joints, and house parties. Ledbetter was the ticket that Lomax needed to the big show in New York. In their codependent relationship it was Lomax with the cultural and social capital who set the terms. His network connections to the academy, southern music world, and the mass-mediated public, within the context of American race relations, made it possible to manage the Leadbelly phenomenon, culminating in a Carnegie Hall concert and a national tour. But to sustain the success, Lomax had to ensure that Ledbetter remained authentic. The two men's priorities and aspirations were clearly at cross-purposes. The Texan's personal goal was the affirmation of American folk music, legitimized within the academy. He craved respectability in the eastern intelligentsia and worked diligently to find appreciative audiences on campuses, at conferences, and in elite private homes. He opportunistically embraced the limelight when it seemed possible, but was not willing to compromise on what he considered authentic (Porterfield 1996). Ledbetter unabashedly hungered for fame and fortune. He was an entertainer who basked in the public veneration (Wolfe and Lornell 1992). Each aspired to more than what their race, class, and region offered, and each needed the other.

Insofar as social structure determines the consequence of agency, the social structures of class and race in the 1930s rewarded blacks when they acted like "the folk" and blocked their way when they did not. Social structures shape options, and for a talented and ambitious individual like Ledbetter, John Lomax offered the opportunity to escape the hand-to-mouth life of the songster and the possibility of major success—but only if he played the role that Lomax and the audiences he mobilized expected the singer to play. In playing his role so well, he helped construct a new musical world of urban folk music.

As Ledbetter became increasingly disenchanted with the arrangement, Lomax felt that he was getting "uppity." When a squabble over money ended with the singer waving a knife, the manager decided that his attempts at civilizing had failed and the relationship crumbled (Porterfield 1996). For Lomax the terms of the relationship demanded servility, something Ledbetter could only temporarily tolerate. Ledbetter returned to the South, struggled to find singing work, and cobbled together a living with whatever work he could find. He never again found the same renown as when Lomax managed his career, and despite some notoriety in the flowering of the folk music scene in the late 1930s, his legendary stature followed his death. After the split, Lomax briefly scoured the southern prisons for "another Leadbelly," then sought other pursuits. Ledbetter kept an active correspondence with Alan, reporting details of his performing life, his relationships with other folk singers in New York, and seeking advice.[6]

The relationship between John Lomax and Ledbetter was an emblematic instance of folk music as other people's music. While Lomax was no doubt sincere in his belief that black American music fathomed the essence of the American experience and touched on universal truth, it was to be discovered, packaged, and presented entirely on the terms of the beneficent white man. What was to be cherished and preserved was the idyllic fantasy of the untarnished other—the primitive in contrast to the civilized, the natural as opposed to the artificial, and the past rather than the present. The most advanced audio and visual technology captured and froze the sounds and sights of the raw authenticity that industrialization was threatening to extinguish. The institutional structures of the academy, state, and mass media reinforced the images of the uncontaminated, validating conformity to the traditional and handicapping movement to the modern. But unlike the earlier folklorists who collected music from white Appalachians, the relationship of Lomax and Ledbetter revolved around the nexus of race.

John Lomax's conception of black as folk was elaborated in a 1934 article published in the *Musical Quarterly*, "'Sinful Songs' of the Southern Negro" (1934). The opening lines vividly capture the white gaze: "I first saw Iron Head as he peered through the bars of the operating room of the hospital for Negroes on the convict farm" (177). He then elaborated what he meant by "songs of the black man": "rhythmic, surging songs of labor; of the jailbird; of the 'bleed hounds' tracking the fleeing Negro through river bottoms; of the bull whip ('Black Betty') and cowhide in the hands of an angry 'Cap'n'; of the loneliness and dismal monotony of life in the penitentiary; of pathetic longing for his 'doney'; of the bold black desperado with his trusty 'forty-fo' in his hand and with his enemy lying dead in the smoke pouring from its blue barrel; of his woman 'dressed in green, lavender and red,' who waited hopefully outside the prison walls for his long deferred coming" (177).

The imagery fuses work, prison, prey, torture, love, crime, and fidelity. When describing Africans, Lomax made no distinction between criminal and law-abiding, upper and lower class, urban and rural, or folk and sophisticated. The man identified only by his prison moniker represented the black race: dangerous, carnal, and musical. "Here was no studied art. The words, the music, the peculiar rhythm, were simple, the natural emotional outpouring of the black man in confinement. The listener found himself swept along with the emotions aroused by this appeal to primitive instinct" (J. Lomax 1934: 177). The gaze gives way to listening, portraying the convict's "natural" emotional outpouring. Comparison to Homer and Rome displays the writer's appreciation for both folk and classic culture, an allusion that presumably the reader but not the subject of the comparison would appreciate. "Iron Head" Baker's humanity is revealed by his love for his woman, expressed in the lyrics of a sorrowful song and the sobs that followed, an emotional outburst Lomax tried to comfort.

The article identifies the prison's star musician, Oliver Platt, only by his prison sobriquet "Clear Rock," whom Lomax quotes in dialect boasting, "I'se de out-singingest nigger on dis here plantation" (J. Lomax 1934: 178).[7] What makes Platt notable for Lomax is not only his "capacious memory" but his knowledge of old English ballads traditionally framed in terms of Anglo-Saxon identity. In passages that would have evoked for readers of the *Musical Quarterly* echoes of Cecil Sharp or Francis Child, Lomax described the different versions of "Barbara Allen" mixed with "Sir Patrick Spens." Platt's new version of "The Old Chuzzum Trail" was quoted at length. But what made these songs interesting to Lomax was their primitive, specifically African American, rendering.

Relative to the academic discourse of the day, this article simultaneously reinforced and bridged racial boundaries. The broader racial boundary was reinforced, as African Americans were stereotyped as ignorant, dangerous, carnal, exotic, and naturally musical. But the conventional racial boundaries of folk music were breached. Not only were blacks endowed with folk music—an authentic *American* folk music—they were also described as sharing the folk music previously considered an expression of whiteness. The readers of these pages would have equated African American music with spirituals. Lomax distinguished the sacred music from "sinful songs" (which he always put in quotation marks). The former was otherworldly, the latter mundane—"his hates, his loves, his earthly trials and privations (including the injustice of the whites), hunger, thirst, cold, heat, his physical well-being, his elementary reactions" (J. Lomax 1934: 183). The music he found in prisons was more truly authentic than the spiritual, which was the music of the more enlightened African Americans, tainted by European influence. The secular songs were "practically pure Negro creations, both in words and music" (182). To this folklorist, black music was salient only insofar as it had not been "contaminated by white influence or by the modern Negro jazz" (181). As his relationship with Huddie Ledbetter showed, he was willing to quarantine blacks from whites, even in segregated prison camps, to preserve their picturesque ethos. He thus wanted to enlarge the vision of American folk music to include African Americans, though he took it for granted that it was on the terms of educated white elites. His efforts helped make the meaning of "folk" available as an inclusive category, capable of a more egalitarian representation, a potential his son Alan would help realize.

While John Lomax contributed to a broader understanding of American folk music than did the Anglo-Saxon ballads that defined the genre in the early decades of the century, his son Alan (1915–2002) was central to the project that defined folk music as the music of the left. Though rarely identified with any political organization and always highlighting the musical more than the political, he shaped the social meaning of folk music and embedded social settings that effectively complemented the more explicitly political activists like the Seegers. Like his father, never holding a secure, prestigious institutional position, despite sojourns at the Library of Congress, Columbia University, and Hunter College, he was mainly a collector, writer, and behind-the-scenes facilitator. More than any other individual, his entrepreneurship built a mode of music that could help bridge racial boundaries in an era in which the organized left was one of the few agents contributing to racial progress.

Two contrasts with his father are especially salient. First, the son's political sentiments were firmly tilted left, and, consistent with his politics, he defined the realm of folk music as universal rather than nationalistic. As early as the mid-1930s, he was conducting fieldwork in Haiti with his wife, Elizabeth Lyttleton Harold, after which he did graduate course work in anthropology at Columbia (Kahn and Cohen 2003). Second, Alan's vision of folk music was much more oriented to the broad public than was that of John, who preferred academic and refined audiences, even as he pursued fame.[8] The younger Lomax was a promoter who hosted radio programs that introduced to national audiences Huddie Ledbetter, Woody Guthrie, Josh White, Burl Ives, and Pete Seeger. He prepared collections for broad audiences, organized concerts in venues large and small, wrote for both academic and popular publications, and worked for record companies.

From the 1940s through the rest of the century, Alan Lomax was in the thick of virtually all important folk music activity. The authoritative account of music and the Old Left by Richard Reuss accords him perhaps the greatest accolade a scholar can: the labeling of a historical era. His label for the activist folk singers of the Popular Front era is the "Lomax Singers." His reasoning is that Alan Lomax "more than any other scholar or performer of the 1930s shaped the popular outlook on folksong, particularly in left-wing circles. His collections of indigenous American music and his recordings of heretofore obscure traditional musicians influenced an entire generation of urban folksingers long after the Old Left had collapsed" (Reuss and Reuss 2000: 122). Labor activist and folklorist Archie Green, though disagreeing with some of Alan Lomax's politics and critical of some of his methods, acknowledged him as doing "more in his lifetime than any cultural critic" (2001a). Even *Newsweek* acknowledged him as "Dean of American Folklorists" (Gates 1990: 60).[9]

Institutional sociologists have identified bricolage as one of the mechanisms by which institutions are built and altered (J. Campbell 2004). Existing institutions offer principles, models, resources, and organizational templates that can be recombined to form new institutions that resemble their predecessors while creating novelty. Alan Lomax pooled together myriad programs and initiatives from an assortment of organizations, individuals, and networks that added up to a second folk project under the aegis of the political left. Starting as head of the Archive of American Folksong at the Library of Congress just a year after graduation from college, he cajoled, pleaded with, sponsored, and bridged academics, political activists, government officials, foundations, performers, and media outlets to construct, bit by bit, what we know as American folk music. His formal position offered little authority and virtually no resources, but it endowed a certain legitimacy in dealing with both the public and, in the context of the New Deal, the people from whom he collected songs and stories. His energy was prodigious: he scoured the country for music, published collections, promoted musicians, prodded record companies to include folk music, produced and presented radio programs, worked with educators, goaded unions to sing more, and wrote for anyone who would publish him, even the likes of *House Beautiful*. Later in his career, after McCarthyism prompted an exile in Britain, he took a position at Columbia University, which gave him an opportunity to theorize and systematize the relationship between music and society (A. Lomax 1959, 1962, 2003a; Lomax and Rudd 1976).

For the younger Lomax, personality and social circumstance reinforced the entrepreneurial style. Joe Klein, in his authoritative biography of Woody Guthrie, described Lomax as "a precocious, arrogant, bearlike young man, of great appetites and greater enthusiasms. He was an idealist, inordinately protective of the music he loved, scornful of those who attempted to dilute or fancify it, and utterly contemptuous of the music executives who peddled garbage and refused to acknowledge the treasures in his storehouse" (1980: 153). His personal correspondence shows him a man capable of almost any idiom—folksy with his informants, erudite with academics, formal with bureaucrats, and strategic with the radicals. He could be solicitous at the same time as he was demanding, always finding a way his correspondent could contribute to the spread of folk music. Among his most important skills were his ability to produce music, to identify talent, to bring people together, to convince them to participate in activities, to mobilize audiences, and to endow events with meaning. As Anthony Seeger has described, he was the consummate producer, both in the sense of a recording engineer and in the sense of selling the concept.[10]

Assisting and extending his father's project to broaden folk music beyond Anglo ballads of Appalachia, Alan Lomax's main contribution to the second folk project was threefold: helping broaden folk music from a characteristic of songs to a style of music; broadening and solidifying a folk song canon; and spearheading the folk music side of the partnership between folk music and the political left. All three made folk music more racially inclusive.

As discussed in earlier chapters, the first folk music project, though never reaching consensus on a workable definition of folk music, tended to treat folk music as a type of song. Though debating whether folk *songs* had to be anonymous or not, whether they had to be passed on orally, or whether they had to be ancient, it was clear that city dwellers could borrow folk songs, perhaps performing them as art music, but they could not write new folk songs. While the first folk project located the essence of folk songs in the text, as Child and Kittredge had, or transcribable qualities such as melodies and harmonies, the second folk project broadened the meaning of folk music to include the style of music—the vocal qualities, instruments, demeanor of presentation, and lyrical themes. Alan's sister, Bess Lomax Hawes, herself a respected scholar, feels that his most profound contribution was to advance the idea introduced by others that the social effect of music comes from its function, not just its content (Hawes 2001). Lomax broadened the definition of folk music to fit a *style* of song (Rosenberg 1993). Though he probably never intended to reduce folk music to a style that merely mimicked "real" folk songs, his detailed attention to style opened the door. His focus on style derived from his understanding of the social roots of music. As early as 1932, he proposed to his father that there was a strong correlation between the style of music and the structure of society (Reuss 1971). For example, he proposed that high-pitched, squeezed, narrow vocal delivery is characteristic of societies with strict sexual mores (A. Lomax 1968). Thus the exemplary social qualities of the folk would be reflected in their music—their simplicity, authenticity, and naiveté, and at times their coarseness. As he asserted in the preface to *The Folk Songs of North America*, "The first function of music, especially of folk music, is to produce a feeling of security for the listener by voicing the particular quality of a land and the life of its people" (A. Lomax 1960: xv). Earlier conceptions of folk music had assumed that urbane devotees would incorporate only the musical essence of folk music into their own musicking, composing around folk tropes, as did Dvořák, Sibelius, and Bartók, or arrange and perform folk songs in classical style as did John Jacob Niles, Paul Robeson, and the Fisk Jubilee Singers. Though Lomax continued to rhapsodize about the qualities of the people who made folk music, grounding authenticity in the person of the musician, by articulating the qualities of style he opened the door for what would have been inconceivable under earlier thinking: the urban folk singer. Though Lomax himself frequently performed to illustrate what he meant by folk songs, usually in small-scale settings, his close friend Pete Seeger became the pioneer and prototype for the urban singer for the rest of the century, insisting that he be called a singer of folk songs to distinguish himself from the true folk.

While the canon of the first folk project was defined by Francis Child, it was the Lomaxes who shaped the canon of the second folk project. They were not the first to publish a relatively broad collection of folk songs, nor were they the first to reach beyond academic and antiquarian audiences to the general public. Carl Sandburg's *American Songbag* (1927) did both. Generations of Americans learned to play and sing such songs as "Careless Love" and "Midnight Special" from this book. But it was the four volumes compiled by the two Lomaxes—*American Ballads and Folk Songs* (Lomax and Lomax 1934), *Our Singing Country* (Lomax et al. 1941), *Best Loved American Folk Songs (Folk song: U. S. A.)* (Lomax and Lomax 1947), and *The Folk Songs of North America* (A. Lomax 1960)—that really defined the folk canon. Thus Pete Seeger's five albums recorded for Folkways Records, which both reflected and solidified the canon, were drawn heavily from these volumes, the source of more than half the songs (Filene 2000).

By expanding the essence of folk to include folk styles, it became more thinkable for blacks and whites to sing each other's music. If the discursive authenticity of music is in the singer's social origin—whether rural, peasant, black, or worker—urban, middle-class whites can only borrow a refracted abstraction. Whites can only perform bleached versions of black music, as when the Charleston Society for the Preservation of Spirituals dressed in plantation garb for recitals during the 1920s (G. Campbell 1999). In contrast, during the second folk project, groups like the Almanacs could sing in a folk style songs from all racial groups (and other nations). Thus Bess Hawes explained that Pete Seeger prepared to sing with the Almanacs by deciding he was going to learn to play the five-string banjo like Lilly Mae Ledford, and he got her 78 rpm records and slowed them down by putting his finger on the edge of them until he learned every note (Hawes 2001).

Lomax not only facilitated the emergence of the urban singer of folk songs and provided a core canon, he inspired individual singers to learn folk songs, helped them hone style and repertoire, organized performance venues, linked them to record companies, gave them exposure on his radio shows, and championed them in print. Even if Reuss is exaggerating in calling them "Lomax Singers" (Reuss and Reuss 2000), Pete Seeger, Aunt Molly Jackson, Huddie Ledbetter (Leadbelly), Burl Ives, Josh White, Woody Guthrie, and Paul Robeson would probably not have become as big as they did without Lomax.

Lomax described himself as a mediator between the folk and the larger culture, explaining that he had realized that "the folklorist's job was to link the people who were voiceless and who had no way to tell their story, with the big mainstream of world culture" (A. Lomax 2003b: 93). While this quotation captures his relationship to the music—an outsider assuming responsibility for other people's culture—it does not depict the social reality of what he did. His actions constructed the entrepreneurial mission of facilitating interaction among all the components of the second folk project. The musical informants from whom he collected songs, the performers he promoted and influenced, the government agencies that legitimated and occasionally coordinated the project, the academics who resented but benefited from his energies, the political activists whom he inspired, the recording industry that he courted, and the mass media that found in him a sentimental story about modernizing America all added up to a bricolage of a cultural form.

THE SEEGERS—FATHER AND SON

While the father and son Lomaxes approached folk music from folklore, rooted in Child's, Sharp's, and Kittredge's literary background, the father and son Seegers came to folk music from music and politics.[11] Charles not only has been credited as a founding figure of ethnomusicology, he also provided the Communist Party with the justification for adopting folk music as the music of the people. His son Pete, like Alan Lomax, was ubiquitous in left-wing music-making for the better part of a century as performer, inspirer, organizer, codifier, and proselytizer.

John Lomax found the music to make folk music more than the music of white Anglo-Americans; Charles Seeger sold the idea of racially inclusive folk music to the American left. A member of an old New England Unitarian family, he was born in 1886 in Mexico City, where he spent his formative years. After graduating from Harvard with a degree in music, he spent time in Europe to master contemporary music at a level unavailable in the States and then served as chair of the music department at the University of California until his pacifist politics in World War I hastened his departure. An original member of the Pierre Degeyter Club, Seeger had earlier embraced the party's definition of proletarian music. Seeger's conversion was motivated by the realization that his previous stance distanced himself from the people he was acting for. In a 1934 article ("On Proletarian Music"), he adopted an openly orthodox view of music as an element of class struggle. The proletariat, though presently a backward (dehumanized) element of society, needed to be cultivated by creative minds in the vanguard. While the analysis was, on one level, crudely reductionist, the article revealed a search for the relationship between music and society. Music was described as a weapon of propaganda, but propaganda meant something other than ideological content. Rather, music could be propaganda for a better way of life. The proletariat by their structural position could better appreciate music for its content, not just the idle fixation on technique. Though the article is patronizing in its attitude toward common folks, the seeds for an appreciation of folk music can be seen in his advocacy that music should be *of* the proletariat, not *for* them (C. Seeger 1934). Because the Composers' Collective was failing, he turned to music that people wanted to make, the music they valued. Initially exposed to folk music by artist Thomas Hart Benson, who performed folk music in the early 1930s, by Appalachian activist and singer Aunt Molly Jackson, and by George Pullen Jackson's book *White Spirituals in the Southern Uplands*, he was also influenced by John and Alan Lomax.

In 1935 Charles Seeger moved to Washington, D.C., where he would live for the next two decades, doing what he described as applied musicology. Beginning as a technical adviser to the Special Skills Division of the Resettlement Administration, he joined the New Deal's effort to revitalize and democratize American culture while providing employment for needy artists, writers, and musicians. So Seeger was put in a position of overseeing song collection. The government had created resettlement communities in rural areas, taking seriously the challenge of cultural and social as well as economic needs. The bureau's job of gathering the musical culture of the residents and facilitating its incorporation into the community faltered under the inability of professional musicians to integrate into their communities, probably achieving more to bring folk music activists together than to benefit the folk. He considered his next job as assistant director of the Federal Music Project no more successful, chafing under the management of a European director who wanted to enlighten benighted Americans with "good" music. During that time he was also involved with the Folk Arts Committee, which organized a relatively successful field trip through the South collecting songs, stories, games, and so forth. Over his career, he shows prodigious organizational abilities, helping found the American Musicological Society and the Society for Ethnomusicology, as well as the International Music Council (Pescatello 1992). The endeavor of that period that gave him the most pride emerged from his relationship with the First Lady, Eleanor Roosevelt, who asked him to develop a program of American folk music for the visiting king and queen of England, a widely publicized occasion that exposed the concept of folk music to perhaps its biggest audience to date. The *New York Times*, for example, headlined its story about the visiting royalty with "American Songs Are Played and Sung for King and Queen" ("American Songs Are Played and Sung for King and Queen" 1939). The program included "folk songs" by the "Coon Creek Girls" of Kentucky, spirituals sung by the North Carolina Spiritual Singers, cowboy ballads sung by the peripatetic Alan Lomax, and classical music sung by an African American, Marian Anderson, and a white, Lawrence Tibbet. Popular music was represented by Kate Smith. The concert and its news coverage were notable for their racial inclusiveness. The program, printed in the *New York Times*, explained to the royal couple and the rest of the audience that the North Carolina Spiritual Singers was a community activity under the direction of the North Carolina Federal Music Project and represented a "cross-section of Negro life" including workers from the tobacco plants, clerks, a doctor, school teachers, the proprietor of a beauty shop, and housewives.

By now, Seeger had thoroughly abandoned his earlier fears that folk music would enfeeble ordinary people. A 1938 essay titled "Music in America" articulated what has become a customary categorization of American music, distinguishing between academic (or classical), folk, and popular music (Eyerman and Jamison 1998; Filene 2000; Frith 1996).[12] More than three kinds of music, these were three relationships between music and society. Classical music is the culture of the elite, and is necessarily exclusive, requiring special knowledge to fathom. Both classical and popular music were individualistic and sophisticated. Folk music reflected a shared experience and common spirit, drawing on cultural diversity and a constant integrative drive (Pescatello 1992). Conceptually it put folk music aesthetically on a par with classical and popular music but folk music was socially egalitarian. And in contrast to the first folk project, the second folk project identified it unequivocally as music, not a type of literature that happens to be set to tunes.

Seeger's advocacy of folk music was politically progressive but racially equivocal. Arguing that there was no such thing as a revolutionary music, only the music of one class or another, Seeger, more than many of his contemporaries, shifted the social orientation from race to class, distinguishing between elite and people's music more than between white and black music. While sincerely appreciating the music of all Americans and no doubt personally sensitive to the contributions of African Americans to American music, Seeger's social position exposed him to a white world. When he recalled the influences that swayed his conversion to folk music—Thomas Hart Benson, George Pullen Jackson, the Lomaxes, and Aunt Molly Jackson—all were white. I am not implying racism, even subtle racism—there is no reason to believe that his commitment to "the people" omitted anyone. But his experience suggests that the commitment to racial justice in the development of people's music was more elective than mandatory. Without a specific commitment to black music, as Alan Lomax made, folk music too often meant white music. Unlike workers vulnerable to the use of black scabs in strikes, the privileged architects of the communist folk revival had the choice to include race in their folk music project or ignore it. The fact that only some did testifies to their compassionate commitments but exposes the vulnerability of the project. When folk music is the music of the "other," the agents have discretion about who is included in the "folk."

Today Charles's son, Pete, is known primarily as a politically engaged folk singer, a celebrity as taciturn about fame as he is exuberant with audiences. His many fans are divided between those who admire him because of his politics and those who revere him despite his politics. But stardom came relatively late in his long career. Sociologically, he is more important, especially in the second folk project being examined here, for his organizational skills, his entrepreneurial energies, and his political movement-building offstage rather than onstage. To analyze his role in the second folk project we must resist the temptation to project his recent fame back to a time when only activists were aware of his prodigious talents.

It is customary to treat Pete Seeger as a singular persona, encapsulating his career into the qualities of the person. Thus does Filene, in contrasting Seeger to Bob Dylan, write, "Pete Seeger was the archetypal folk stylist, moving from a privileged background to become the personification of folk music to millions of Americans, an identification he reinforced in thousands of concerts, well over a hundred albums, and scores of books and articles" (2000: 187). Cantwell, similarly in his chapter on Seeger, crystallizes his character as "a system of paradoxes: masculine and feminine, patrician and proletarian, cosmopolitan and provincial, cultivated and uncultivated, educated and anti-intellectual" (1998: 262). Thus when reviewing the second folk project, it is difficult to avoid treating Peter Seeger, the young, well-connected, but politically naive activist and singer as "Pete Seeger," the giant of twentieth-century folk music.

But a brief look at Seeger's coverage in the *New York Times* documents his slow rise to popularity.[13] Standard biographies of Pete Seeger typically review his musical unfolding by recounting his participation in two pioneering groups, the Almanacs and the Weavers (Cantwell 1998; Dunaway 1990; Filene 2000). Even though Seeger often sang lead and emceed many appearances, their popularity was collective. When the group got any coverage in the *New York Times*, Seeger was not featured, as their collective ethos preferred. The person Pete Seeger does not appear in the *New York Times* until 1945, when an article titled "Miss Bettis Guest with Dance Group" ended with "The evening closed with 'Folksay,' with Tony Draber and Pete Seeger as the wise-cracking, folk-singing chorus that sits on the sidelines with guitar and banjo" (December 29). He rarely appeared in the newspaper pages until 1948, when his participation in the Henry Wallace presidential campaign was often noted. In each of 1951 and 1952, his name appeared only once. Until the HUAC hearings in 1955, his name appeared more frequently in display ads than in stories, when he appeared twenty-two times. The Weavers had been famous enough that his defiance propelled his fame, though news accounts still had to remind the reader who he was. His first appearance before the committee was covered by the *New York Times* but only in the continuation of a story about individuals associated with a Broadway show (August 19, 1955). The first time his name appeared in a headline was April 13, 1956, in a short piece titled "Folk Singer Opposed: Cashmore Lauds Veterans' Protest on Seeger." If the *New York Times* is any indication, he was little known outside progressive circles until he refused to answer questions before the HUAC hearings.

His performances were still getting little notice until Robert Shelton began to write regularly on folk music in 1958, when, in typical journalistic fashion, he anointed some individuals as stars, including Seeger. This slow trajectory to public recognition says less about Seeger than about the gap between celebrity and contribution. By the time Seeger's solo music became known to large numbers of people, he had been steadily promoting politically engaged music-making for more than two decades. Ironically, or perhaps tragically, his musical fame rode the crest of a wave that faintly echoed the political significance of folk music he had helped create. Even then his continued political work, though getting journalistic coverage, was as much below the radar as above it.[14]

Still, during the eclipse of folk music between the banishment of the Weavers and the commercial folk revival, Seeger's renown was growing beyond his base in the cultural left, as he frequented college campuses, recorded frequently for Folkways, and captured the notice of the entertainment industry. In 1956, *Downbeat* announced to the entertainment industry that "If this nation has seen a restoration of the glories of the American folk song, a good deal of it has been accomplished through the itinerant, indefatigable banjo and infectiously happy voice of Pete Seeger" (Little 1956: 16).[15]

The point is not at all to belittle Pete Seeger or his renown but to emphasize that the second folk project was a collective more than an individual project. While it included exceptionally talented, organizationally savvy, politically astute, and deeply committed individuals, for the most part the individuals that made the most difference achieved what they did by working together on a common project. If any skill stands out in this effort, it is entrepreneurship, not just for those remembered as operators and organizers like Alan Lomax or Irwin Silber, but also someone like Pete Seeger who is now most visible as a performer.

Before Peter Seeger, the person, became "Pete Seeger," the icon, he played a central role in the construction of the second folk project as organizer, enabler, and inspirer. Like his father and the Lomaxes he rarely occupied important or prominent formal positions, but seemed to be everywhere bringing people together, forging a vision of a singing movement, and gradually eking out the template for the activist musician. Unlike the Lomaxes, he never had a unified vision of how to connect music and society. His career more or less muddled along, responding to opportunities and adapting to circumstances. Though the child of two musicians, he did not initially gravitate toward that world. Enrolling at Harvard with the intention of becoming a journalist, he soon dropped out, in part because of disillusionment with sociology, though not before joining the Young Communist League. He then tried his hand at journalism and art, at times traveling around painting pictures of farmhouses in exchange for room and board. He spent a summer playing banjo for a traveling puppet show and worked at the 1939 New York World's Fair sweeping cigarette butts. Though he was thoroughly familiar with folk music from his father's and his mother's experience transcribing folk songs for Carl

Sandburg, he gives credit to Alan Lomax for inspiring him to think about folk music in career terms. After Seeger dropped out of Harvard, Lomax offered him a job working with him at the Library of Congress, though he was soon back in New York, where he began to hang around and soak up Woody Guthrie, Huddie Ledbetter, and Aunt Molly Jackson. Guthrie was his model for authenticity and Ledbetter a musical inspiration. Instead of following the Grand Tour of Europe as young people of his age and station often did, he took off with Guthrie to hitchhike and ride the rails across America. When he returned to New York, Lomax introduced him to a southern singer named Lee Hays and with Pete Hawes and Alan Lomax's sister, Bess, they formed the Almanac Singers. The goal was not to get famous but to use music to promote the movement, as elaborated in chapter 6. When he was drafted into the army, his father's Washington contacts got him transferred from his initial assignment as a mechanic to the special services as a performer. While overseas in Saipan, he met Boots Cassetta, who joined him in organizing a singing group. When the war ended, the two of them called a meeting to organize People's Songs, Inc. (PSI). When he was asked about his life's purpose in 1946, he said it was to "Make a singing labor movement. Period. . . . I was hoping to have hundreds, thousands, tens of thousands of union choruses. Just as every church has a choir, why not every union?" (Dunaway 1990: 117). Performance in PSI was secondary to facilitating other people to sing, providing music for picket lines, publicity, or meetings, making music a way to bridge boundaries. Pete headed PSI and edited their *Bulletin*, but as only one of his many activities. While still largely unknown as a performer outside leftist circles, he partnered with Woody Guthrie to compile *Hard Hitting Songs*, a collection of music discovered by Alan Lomax, which was completed in 1941, though not published until 1967. He traveled with Henry Wallace's presidential campaign in 1948, singing on the stump and compiling a songbook. He wrote a manual titled "How to Play the Five String Banjo," which eventually sold eighty thousand copies. After PSI succumbed to financial woes, he spearheaded the creation of *Sing Out!*, which still continues as the major magazine of folk music. Except for the Wallace campaign, these activities were based less on his talent as a performer than on his entrepreneurial and organizational skills.

Although the media have dubbed him a star, he has not had a star's career or lived a star's life. He has been as active behind the stage as on it, organizing hootenannies, founding and running organizations such as People's Songs, Inc. and People's Artists, promoting and planning folk festivals, most notably at Newport, helping found *Sing Out!* and for more than half a century writing a regular column in it, then helping Sis Cunningham found *Broadside Magazine* as an outlet for topical songwriters. As a performer, he always insisted that other people get equal billing and that his name be no larger than others' in promotional material. Thus the politics of the music was always as much in the social relations in doing it as in the content of the lyrics.

CONCLUSION

Cultural entrepreneurs build bridges that link parts of society in new ways or around new activities. Poor rural people who sing old songs in their daily life come to the attention of universities, government agencies, union organizers, and eventually the urban middle class. "Folk" mutated from a concept cherished by English professors and dilettantes to one that could be found in newspapers, radio shows, and record stores. Cultural entrepreneurs leave a legacy through three kinds of impacts. They knit webs of cooperation and shared activity. They build new structures with the capacity to sustain activities. And they inspire cultural effervescence that later individuals and organizations can reactivate. Just how enduring a legacy they leave depends on how effectively they succeed at each of these dimensions.

Entrepreneurs often bring together people and organizations from different social domains that mutually benefit from the newly formed bridge between them. Whether linking buyers to sellers, producers to suppliers, or organizations across sectors, entrepreneurs help people find others with shared interests. Thus could John Lomax bridge the American Folklore Association and the Library of Congress as it developed what became the American Folklife Center. His entrepreneurship helped move "folk music" beyond the music of Anglo-Saxon ballads to cowboy songs, southern black prison music, and Texas border music, finding threads of unity in what had been seen as distinct cultures. Similarly Charles Seeger could bring together the European-oriented high-culture activists in the organized left, the New Deal progressives of the federal government, and the fledging discipline of ethnomusicology that he helped create. Neither of them settled into any institutional setting, sojourning from job to job in government, universities, nonprofit organizations, and the lecture stage. Their most famous children would add musical performance, though only marginally so for Alan.

The webs of cooperation that are knitted by entrepreneurs can endure or evaporate. Their permanence in part depends on whether the bridged organizations follow through, whether successor bridging agents keep the links active, and whether the organizations themselves survive, factors beyond the control of the original entrepreneurs. It is doubtful that the music of southern prisons has been often heard in the Modern Language Association since John Lomax's day. But entrepreneurs can help sustain the webs of cooperation by erecting a cultural framework that makes the linkages seem intuitive. The concept of folk music creates a "natural" overlap in the activities of the Library of Congress, the Modern Language Association, departments of musicology and ethnomusicology (but no longer English), commercial music producers, and left-wing activists. Representatives in each may quarrel with some of the others, but even the disagreement is a relationship that might not have existed without the energetic persistence of cultural entrepreneurs.

In addition to the webs of cooperation among different sectors, entrepreneurs also help build new structures. The second generation of Lomaxes and Seegers, especially Alan and Pete, focused much of their energy here. The new structures included organizational forms such as the urban folk group pioneered by the Almanacs and particular organizations such as People's Songs, Inc. and *Sing Out!* magazine, which are discussed in more detail in the next chapter. Some of these organizations did not endure, dying in the toxic rain of McCarthyism that fell on the entire organized left in the middle of the century. Others, such as the American Folklife Center at the Library of Congress, found protection under stable organizational shelters. Altogether folk music has survived as a distinct "art world" (Becker 1982)—the producers, consumers, mediators, and interpreters that make cultural activity possible. For folk music, the art world includes the performers, fans, record companies, magazines, instrument makers, guitar shops, annual festivals, and academics who keep folk music alive, many of them engaging each other in distinctively entrepreneurial activities.

Finally, entrepreneurs can make an enduring contribution by arousing a cultural effervescence that can inspire later activists to renew the fires of activism. Eyerman and Jamison (1998) see this as one of the most important legacies of left-wing movements in the 1930s and 1960s, arguing that the mobilization of tradition is an enduring project of social movements that outlives the original organizations. Thus Pete Seeger, whose charismatic career spanned nearly the whole history of left-wing folk music, appeared at President Obama's Inaugural Celebration Concert with Bruce Springsteen, singing Woody Guthrie's "This Land Is My Land," including the often omitted critique of private property.[16] How successfully later activists can rekindle the fire of earlier cultural movements depends on the quality of the culture being passed on, the talent of the later bearers of the culture, and the ability of the later movement to harness the energy of culture into action. Songs like "This Land Is My Land" or "We Shall Overcome" have shown an impressive persistence. Having the likes of Bernice Johnson Reagon, Ani DiFranco, and Bruce Springsteen keep the music of the 1930s and 1960s before the public has certainly continued to keep it alive. But as inspiring as it was for many to see Seeger and Springsteen sing the music of Woody Guthrie to celebrate the inauguration of the first African American president, it is not clear how much grassroots activism was sparked.

If the inauguration of Barack Obama can be seen as denoting the success of the long struggle for racial justice, the success of the Lomax and Seeger entrepreneurship, especially the first generation, must also be seen in historical perspective. For John Lomax and Charles Seeger, especially, were bridging racially inequitable structures, limiting what could be achieved. (John Lomax, of course, had no intention of dismantling the system of racial domination, though he did help end the racial exclusivity of folk music by including black music in it.) Seeger, as part of one of the major adversarial movements against racial injustice, contributed to pre–civil rights racial progress. But he, and the project of which he was a member, was limited by the sectors being brought together. The government, mainstream foundations, major universities, and even the Communist Party were basically white organizations, though each had individuals committed to racial justice. Thus the entrepreneurial activities had a broad impact on popular culture but a limited impact on race.

CHAPTER SIX

Organizing Music: The Fruits of Entrepreneurship

The vibrant energy, ceaseless networking, and long-term vision of the Lomaxes and Seegers, refracted through the methodical discipline of the party and the creative spirit of other leaders and artists, gave rise to new organizational forms of music in the service of activism. Though part of a social movement, they were not social movements as ordinarily conceptualized—groups of activists making claims, recruiting new members, and raising consciousness. Rather they facilitated music-making.

The musical activists of the Old Left pioneered in the creation of four new kinds of creative organizations. The Almanacs invented a form that fully blossomed in the commercial folk music revival of the 1960s—the urban folk group. The group's direct heir, the Weavers, introduced the form to the broader public and showed that folk music could be commercially successful. People's Songs, Inc. (PSI) was a musical incubator, a small-time, staffed office that inspired, facilitated, and nourished individuals and groups around the country. As an organizational form, the musical incubator has not thrived in the period since the 1940s, though efforts such as *Broadside* magazine were similar. PSI's organizational spin-off was another organizational form that has not caught on, the political music agent, in which business-minded activists perform the practical jobs of securing and promoting gigs for politically committed performers. The second folk music project was also an early adopter of a now pervasive organizational form, the genre magazine, a periodical that links performers, record companies, suppliers, and fans. Initially intended as a successor to the *People's Songs Bulletin, Sing Out!* continues today as the discursive forum of the folk music art world. Ebullient articles on new trends, rising stars, mature practitioners, and events interleave ads selling instruments, music, and albums.

These organizations and the shape they took helps explain why the second folk project was much more successful making folk music accessible to ordinary Americans via the medium through which twentieth-century Americans best knew music—the mass media—than at infusing radical activism with music, a goal they aspired to but never fully achieved. The Weavers and the other musical activists wanted to reach American workers, but they reached more of them through their violin-accompanied Decca recording of "On Top of Old Smokey" than in the union halls where they occasionally performed. Explaining the difference between their success in popularizing folk music in the mass media and their failure to reach working-class audiences through the movement requires that we examine the organizations of the second folk project.

THE ALMANACS

Alan Lomax's hope for a group that would combine folk and topical songs came to fruition in the Almanac Singers. He introduced Pete Seeger and Woody Guthrie to Lee Hays because they were all working on books of labor songs. Hays, the son of a southern minister and an alumnus of the Commonwealth School, had been performing by himself, mostly at progressive events, getting people to sing. Seeing a kindred spirit, he suggested that he and Seeger do some gigs together. Woody Guthrie, who had a knack for down-home lyrics, and writer Millard Lampell joined them. The name "Almanac" came from Woody's writings, because country people have two books in their houses: the Bible to get them through the hereafter and the almanac to get them through the here and now. The chemistry was magical. Guthrie brought his musical genius and credentials of authenticity. Hays was the experienced group singer, capable of rousing crowds to enthusiastic participation—a skill that Seeger acknowledges as his model for group leadership. Lampell was the facile word master, like Guthrie able to spin lyrics for any occasion but with more urbane tastes. Partly because times were hard and partly because they shared a collectivist ideology, they soon shared a New York apartment, which became the hub of activities for a burgeoning interest in folk music. Resolute to resist commercial glitz, they embraced spontaneity, including casual participation and minimal rehearsal.

Their anti-commercial stance derived from their feeling that because capitalists controlled the mass media and allowed only watered-down kinds of protest, people's culture had to be found outside that realm. Capitalism could be fought through the form, not just the content, of the music, implying a double role—to create working-class culture and to facilitate those workers' development of their own culture. So instead of pursuing mass audiences, they focused on union and progressive organizations. "People" and "workers" became synonymous. But they never claimed that singing would be an adequate substitute for organizing (Reuss 1971; Reuss and Reuss 2000). That does not mean that they shunned broader audiences. Music was still a propaganda weapon as well as an organizing tool. Reaching the people required both personal appearances at union and party functions as well as a presence in the mass media. Though generally recording with small, politically connected record companies, they accepted opportunities to perform on radio, including the national CBS radio programs *We the People* and *This Is War*.[1]

In reaching broad audiences they invented what is perhaps their biggest contribution to American culture: the urban folk performer. Earlier performers of indigenous American music had either been singers from rural America who merely sang the songs they grew up with, overtly urban, educated collectors like Carl Sandburg or Alan Lomax, who freely affirmed that they were singing someone else's music, or classically trained interpreters who used folk-based themes. The Almanacs became ersatz folk, adopting rural dress, speech, and mannerisms. Guthrie was the bridge, the man from Oklahoma who reveled in his authenticity and frequently used it to assert his will on the group. As Seeger has often said, Woody was their hero, the real McCoy, a genuine Okie with politics not to mention a profound musical and literary gift. So they dressed like Woody and talked like Woody, though they rarely caroused like Woody. Audiences, even radical audiences, did not always appreciate their proletarian romanticism. Some of the group were surprised to learn that Detroit workers shed their overalls after work and dressed in nice clothes when they went out in public.

The Almanacs' musical repertoire fell into three general types. First, there were union songs, such as their album *Talking Union & Other Union Songs*, which included "Talking Union," "The Union Maid," "Get Thee behind Me," "The Union Train," "Which Side Are You On?" and others. In May 1941 the group performed for twenty thousand striking transport workers at Madison Square Garden. Second were political songs, especially about the president, peace, and war. On their first album, released in mid-1941, *Songs for John Doe*, songs such as "C for Conscription" and "Washington Breakdown" denounced America's growing militarism and opposed any move toward war. The highly successful album brought them much notoriety in and out of the movement. Theodore Dreiser, at a meeting of the League of American Writers, kissed Lee Hays on the cheek and said, "If we had six more teams like these boys, we could save America!" (Reuss and Reuss 2000: 152). But after the United States and the Soviet Union entered war, they enthusiastically embraced the war effort and splintered when Seeger and Lampell enlisted in the army while Hays and Guthrie joined the merchant marine.[2] The third category was traditional non-topical folk music, songs such as "Blow Ye Winds, Heigh Ho," "House of the Rising Sun," and "I Ride an Old Paint."

Missing from the Almanacs' strategy is any systematic attention to race or African Americans. Although participants in the group widely acknowledged Woody Guthrie and Leadbelly as the primary musical influences, both in terms of songs and style, Guthrie's imprint is much more evident than Leadbelly's. Both knew hundreds of songs, but Guthrie was a much more prolific composer, able to conjure new songs for any occasion. While both were frequent visitors at the Almanac House, Guthrie was much more of a fixture. And while Leadbelly occasionally performed with the Almanacs, he was never a regular, as was Guthrie.

The Almanac singers wanted to reach audiences through concerts and movement organizations, especially unions. It is not surprising that concerts reached more whites than blacks, since few blacks attended concerts of any type. It is unfortunate that the organizational sites in which the Almanacs were most involved were also very white—unions. While the CIO unions that the Almanacs sung to were more racially integrated than AFL unions of the period, they were still predominantly white. So it is not surprising that their *Talking Union & Other Union Songs* album had a very white feel, with no songs that the casual observer would recognize as black.

PEOPLE'S SONGS, INC.

The communist movement emerged from World War II with contradictory prospects. On one hand, involvement with the CIO unions and poor people's organizations during the Depression years gave them legitimacy among progressives as the standard-bearers of the left. America's alliance with the Soviet Union against Nazism during the war had muted some of the fear of the party's Bolshevik loyalty. The cultural activism of the Popular Front policy had built complex networks between the party and non-party organizations. On the other hand, a right-wing backlash in the early cold war and the party leadership's reversion to ideological rigidity reinforced each other in the late 1940s, leading to political repression and the party's retreat into sectarianism. For folk music, this period saw a brief flash of activism, reaching a high point of public enthusiasm followed by a dismal eclipse and organizational collapse until the commercial folk revival at the end of the 1950s and the renaissance of insurgent music in the civil rights movement.

The second folk project reached its peak after World War II, when the organizational infrastructure blossomed and folk singers, most notably the Weavers, hit the top of the popular music charts. Although the Communist Party was coming under assault from McCarthyism, in the form of expulsions from labor unions, and with the rise of the cold war, People's Songs, Inc. (PSI) briefly but consequentially drew together progressive musicians from the party fringes, New Deal activists, unions, and college campuses. By publishing books and magazines, sponsoring events, creating forums for interaction, and linking to other producers and distributors of left-wing music, they gave folk music a greater presence both in the media and in the movement at large. At no point before or since has the organized left had such a significant presence in the musical culture of the nation, especially in its production. While American folk music had been given a radical tinge during the era of the Popular Front and the Almanacs, it was indelibly stamped as pink in the PSI era. Its musicians included many who are now considered folk legends—its inspirational leader, Pete Seeger, its icon of African American heritage, Huddie Ledbetter, its conscience of authenticity, Woody Guthrie, and its storehouse of talent including Josh White, Brownie McGhee, Burl Ives, Tom Glazer, and Oscar Brand.[3]

Richard Reuss (Reuss 1971; Reuss and Reuss 2000) and Robbie Lieberman (1995) have offered solid accounts of the history of People's Songs, Inc. In many ways it was an extension of the Almanac project in leadership and concept. A cohesive network of performers, managers, and activists embedded within the New York musical and political scenes decided to construct a national movement dedicated to the political use of American folk music. After the Almanacs drifted apart during the war, with Pete Seeger joining the army, Woody Guthrie enlisting in the merchant marines, and others finding new opportunities, other groups stepped in to offer folk music. A group led by Tom Glazer, the Priority Ramblers, worked out of Washington, D.C., recording the now-cherished inflation song "A Dollar Ain't a Dollar Anymore" in 1943. Some of the former Almanacs were involved in an ad hoc group called the Union Boys, which did an album of war songs, *Songs for Victory*. The wartime alliance with the Soviet Union sparked such songs as the Golden Gate Quartet's "Stalin Wasn't Stallin' Any More," and Josh White offered lines such as "While the Soviet Union goes rolling along." Thus, while the war time is often seen as a lull between the Almanacs and PSI, there was plenty happening. Behind the scenes, Alan Lomax was actively promoting folk music. Working in the Office of War Information, along with his sister Bess, he enlisted Pete Seeger, Burl Ives, Woody Guthrie, and others to record hundreds of hours of anti-fascist folk songs for the government and helped produce *Freedom Songs of the United Nations*, a compendium of progressive war songs of the Allied nations.

Also created during the war was an organization called Folksay, which was affiliated with the American Youth for Democracy, the successor to the Young Communist League. Under the slogan "Folk Culture—A Weapon for Victory," they sponsored square dances featuring politically themed calls and folk plays, including Irwin Silber's "Circle Left" (later renamed "Hallelujah Chorus"), and engaged in various other movement activities. Folksay would continue into the PSI era, with Irwin Silber taking active roles in both.

The specific origins of PSI came from conversations in the South Pacific where Pete Seeger, on duty with the army, met with USO performers Betty

Sanders, Mario "Boots" Cassetta, and Felix Landau. Following the war's conclusion, a meeting of about thirty people at Seeger's New York apartment decided to continue the Almanac project with a formal organization. As the inaugural newsletter stated their mission, "There are thousands of unions, people's organizations, singers, and choruses who would gladly use more songs. There are many songwriters, amateur and professional, who are writing these songs. It is clear that there must be an organization to make and send songs of labor and the American people through the land. To do this job, we have formed PEOPLE'S SONGS, INC. We invite you to join us" ("People's Songs" 1946). With Seeger acting as guiding spirit, they recruited an advisory committee that included almost everyone the small folk music public would recognize as an urban folk singer. Their *Bulletin* listed thirty-three people including Oscar Brand, Agnes Cunningham, Tom Glazer, Michael Gold, Woody Guthrie, Burl Ives, Millard Lampell, Bess Lomax, Walter Lowenfels, Earl Robinson, Betty Sanders, and Josh White. The advisory board was their link to the music world, and included performers, composers, and party-affiliated intellectuals (Gold and Lowenfels), the New York–based network that had coalesced before the war. But omissions also reveal the group's social location. Only Woody Guthrie, Josh White, and possibly Agnes Cunningham would be considered genuine "folk," that is, growing up outside the urban Northeast (though all resided in New York at the time). Leadbelly, Brownie McGhee, Aunt Molly Jackson, Jim Garland, Bill Broonzy, and other more "authentic" musicians were not on the masthead, even though they performed at PSI events and contributed songs to its *Bulletin*. There were no union people, even though CIO representatives participated in the meetings leading up to the organization's founding (Dunaway 1990). Though several CIO unions had cultural directors, none had any official affiliation with PSI. Another curious omission was Alan Lomax, though he wrote a letter to potential sponsors expressing that "the whole American folk tradition is a progressive people's tradition" (Reuss and Reuss 2000: 187). As usual, he played the role of movement entrepreneur connecting people and organizations together. While the board of advisors played an active role in decision making, a board of sponsors offered legitimacy in the eyes of the larger public, including such luminaries as Aaron Copland, Leonard Bernstein, John Hammond, Oscar Hammerstein II, Dorothy Parker, Sam Wanamaker, and Harold Rome (Dunaway 1990; Lieberman 1995). With little involvement other than lending their names to the masthead, the existence of this board reflected PSI's self-image as a nonprofit organization as well as a bottom-up social movement.

As the two boards attest, there is a structural parallel between PSI and its constituency on the one hand and the conventional social relations between performer and audience on the other. Both involve a hierarchical relationship with one elite group endowed with talent and leadership offering a cultural object *to* a broader group for consumption. Initiative, leadership, and creativity flow in one direction, which receivers can accept or reject. The creators are trying to reach the receivers, who have veto power but only indirect feedback into the creative process. The composers, performers, and political activists on PSI's board of advisors and the illustrious musical and literary celebrities on its board of sponsors stood above its intended constituents just as a performer stands socially and often physically above his or her audience. Despite Seeger's and others' sincere desire to create singing unions and infuse music into the activities of contention, the organizational form fostered the music of performance more than participation. The vanguardist mentality can be seen even when they acknowledged that they were failing to reach their full constituency. Earl Robinson, one of their most talented composers, celebrated that many Americans were participating in singing and playing music but still felt that they needed more and better songs, encouraging PSI to bring in more professional musicians (*People's Songs Bulletin* 3, no. 1–2 [February 1949]: 2).

With $135 from members and donations, the group rented an office on West 42nd Street, drew up incorporation papers, and launched a monthly bulletin. Their hootenannies, organized for both fund-raising and outreach, outgrew apartments and moved to public auditoriums including Town Hall. Their activities were noted favorably not only by the left-wing press but also by *Time, Fortune,* and the *New York Times.* The *Christian Science Monitor* contemplated what the organization could contribute to revitalizing the American heritage of folk song and poetry ("Editorials: People's Songs" 1947). Hoping to spark a broader movement, they developed an education program with well-placed articles and pamphlets on how to organize a hootenanny, set up booking agencies, establish People's Songs branches, and lead mass singing. The *People's Songs Wordbook* preceded a full-fledged *People's Song Book* coordinated by Waldemar Hille, a former concert pianist and director of music at Elmhurst College, who had taken over responsibility for their songbooks. To facilitate group singing they created filmstrips so song leaders could project onto a screen lyrics of songs such as "Mister Congressman" and "United Nations Make a Chain" with an accompanying book of music. They also compiled a library of over ten thousand pages of folk, union, and political songs. By the end of the first year, the outlook was upbeat. Seeger shared with members an account of his national tour reaching out to branches, expressing confidence that the organization would continue to grow from its 1,700 members. Both the branches and the national office were well poised to write and distribute new songs, organize concerts, distribute film strips, and make music available to all takers. Seeger's main goals were to get better songs published in the bulletin and distribute good music to as broad an audience as possible (*People's Songs Bulletin* 1, no. 10 [November 1946]).

While music was the organization's focus, it was never divorced from political action. The new organization faced bright prospects for a broad movement marching to the sound of music. As they were setting up their office and putting out their first newsletters, America was experiencing its greatest labor unrest since the Great Depression, with two million union members out on strike. Members sang on picket lines in such actions as the Westinghouse strike in Pittsburgh and marched at rallies to save the Office of Price Administration. New York's progressive newspaper described how five thousand striking workers "whooped through the refrains and . . . laughed over the 'Westinghouse Blues'" (described in Cohen and Samuelson 1996: 28). Despite bringing music to several events, overall PSI remained marginal to the movement. Though they wanted every union meeting to include songs and saw themselves as organizers, they were musicians with political commitment more than activists with talent. Unions were becoming cool to their involvement, especially with the rise of the cold war and the expulsion of communists from the CIO. While several union education directors initially worked with People's Songs, they gradually withdrew; by 1949 only openly communist unions such as the United Electrical Workers kept in contact.

Another factor that should have facilitated a broad impact in the movement was PSI's broadening out from New York. The expertise and talent was based in the New York musical and political world but not confined to it. The founders imagined a national movement with branches and offices in major cities across the land. A mimeographed pamphlet on how to organize a local branch summarized the vision of what local branches would do: Do music. Silent on political discussions, political involvement, union organizing, and collective action in general, the authors encouraged new branches to create singing groups, booking agencies, schools for song leaders, hootenannies, songwriter committees, outlets for People's Songs records, and local radio programs. They advocated links with unions, progressive organizations such as American Youth for Democracy, and community leaders. And finally they proposed a local structure that paralleled the national organization with an executive committee, board of sponsors, and various committees (People's Songs n.d.-b).

In various forms, a loose confederation developed, linked by a general vision more than national leadership, organizational template, or active coordination. Most chapters were created by musicians with political commitment. In Detroit Barbara Dane, a young singer, American Youth for Democracy member, and fan of Pete Seeger and Leadbelly, along with a German émigré guitarist, Rolf Cahn, founded a chapter that focused on relationships with auto unions. They self-consciously sought racial balance, though without much success (Silber and Dane 2001). "Boots" Cassetta, a songwriter and founder of Charter Records, who had mulled over the idea of People's Songs with Pete Seeger when they were stationed in Saipan during the war, led the Los Angeles chapter, with many members connected to the film industry. Reaching beyond folk music to the larger music industry, a series of hootenannies and parties raised the funds to support Cassetta and a vibrant West Coast office. The chapter thrived through a symbiotic relationship with the burgeoning labor movement in the film industry and regularly provided performers for movement activities such as picket lines and demonstrations. Malvina Reynolds and Earl Robinson, who had moved from New York to Los Angeles to work on film scores, were especially active. Other participants included E. Y. "Yip" Harburg, who wrote "Brother, Can You Spare a Dime," "Only a Paper Moon," and "Over the Rainbow," the songwriting duo of Morry Goodson and Sonny Vale, who regularly contributed pieces to the *Bulletin*, calypso singer Sir Lancelot, and singer-actor Tex Ritter (Cohen and Samuelson 1996). The Los Angeles branch's Vern Partlow exemplified what PSI should be. One of the best political songwriters on the West Coast, author of "Atomic Talking Blues," he spent several weeks as an organizer in a drive to organize California canneries. The Food, Tobacco, Agricultural and Allied Workers of America (FTA-CIO) had asked specifically for a singing organizer and he obliged by singing from sound trucks, on street corners, and at union rallies. They had a regular show with union songs, Mexican tunes, and some popular stuff, including not only his own songs but some made up by the union workers (*People's Songs Bulletin* 1, no. 10 [November 1946]).

The Los Angeles chapter also illustrated a different approach to communist orthodoxy. As a national organization, the People's Songsters owed more to Alan Lomax's somewhat romantic populism than to Marxist-Leninist materialism. Harry Hay, later the founder of the nation's leading gay and lesbian organization, the Mattachine Society, offered a regular twenty-week course under the auspices of PSI's Los Angeles chapter. His mimeographed outline draws on conventional Marxist-Leninist materialism to show how class struggle historically shaped music. The course proceeded stage by historical stage as the forces and relations of production evolve to higher forms. His analysis sometimes directly reduced material forces to cultural change, as when primitive communism gave rise to music based on the work rhythms of pulling, pushing, and pounding. As the analysis moved closer to the present, the reduction became more indirect, such as the transition from feudalism to capitalism's fostering of "opposites in unity" in European baroque music, or the explanation of romanticism in terms of the conflict between empire and the petty bour-geoisie. Although Hay was familiar with the Lomax-Seeger approach to music and included many folk songs among his wide-ranging musical ex-amples, he was skeptical, based on style and theory. In fact his attitude toward folk music was closer to Charles Seeger's earlier feeling that folk music saps militancy. Still, he saw some hope in folk music, which he wrote "reveals the scope of the people's struggle against the super-imposed feudal class." Songs such as "Gypsy Laddie" and "Barbara Allen" thus do display open militant sedition, though others, such as "Pretty Boy Floyd," exemplify the "twentieth century hero ballad compounded of negative despair and adventurism action" (Hay 1948: 4-1).[4] The model Hay devel-oped was highly complex, thoroughly developed, and certainly intelli-gent. But it was also highly scholastic, pedantic, even esoteric, with a specialized argot that one had to be inside to understand. One would have to be well versed to think within the system, much less contribute to it. The system might be interpreted as idiosyncratic or as cultist; it was certainly vanguard.

The Chicago branch was managed by Ray Flerlage, a blues photogra-pher and author who organized his own tour, singing for union people in several midwestern states. Traveling on a shoestring, he sang to concert crowds, from sound trucks, in union halls, and on radio stations, includ-ing before an audience of three thousand at the UAW Local 600 in De-troit (*People's Songs Bulletin* 1, no. 11 [December 1946]). Felix Landau, one of the leaders of the Chicago chapter, reported to the readers of the *Bulletin* how they planned to organize there around performing talent. Though at first discouraged that so many local musicians had migrated to New York from Chicago, he was pleased to discover "enough talent to get started with" and set about organizing a conference. Then they tried to follow this plan: establish a center for people to come together; hold hootenannies; organize songwriters to write new songs; establish a li-brary and collect songs; mobilize songwriters and singers for local cam-paigns, demonstrations, and strikes; help organize choruses; distribute PSI material; and persuade as many people as possible to join PSI. This all required money, so the first step would be to raise funds (*People's Songs Bulletin* 1, no. 9 [October 1946]).

A San Francisco chapter worked closely with the California Labor School, which also supported a labor theater and a labor chorus. Another active chapter in the heartland was in Cleveland, which held monthly "wing-dings," worked with unions and political groups, and regularly hatched new songs. Led by Bryant French, a college English teacher, gui-tarist, and jazz pianist, its members included Norm Berman, assistant educational director of Cleveland's largest UAW local, and calypso singer and songwriter Si Kurtz. Spinning off from the Progressive Players, a writing and acting group that performed at many rallies and meetings, they often appeared at events together (*People's Songs Bulletin* 2, no. 9 [October 1947]).

To help coordinate the chapters and share ideas among them, a national convention was held in Chicago in October 1947. About forty-five delegates from nine chapters constructed a national constitution, shared experiences and ideas, and held a hootenanny at Orchestra Hall. The convention greatly facilitated communication among the chapters, with subsequent issues of the organization's bulletin full of news from the grassroots. The activities reports by the chapters suggest a variety of social relations—performers singing for audiences, music in union meetings, sing-along hootenannies, song swapping among composers, and singing on picket lines.

But most of the activities of the national office promoted activities around performance, as illustrated in their publicity manual for the branches (People's Songs n.d.-a). The pamphlet offered practical advice for attracting wider audiences to the organization's events. By definition, publicity reaches the public, not just an organization's members.

Another publication, actually printed, not just mimeographed, more fully expressed the performative dimension while emphasizing folk music in particular. In the pamphlet we find the basic steps of institution building. First there was naming work—explaining what a hootenanny is and where the term came from. The pamphlet describes the legends that had grown up around the word, noting that Pete Seeger and Woody Guthrie had learned the term in the Pacific Northwest. Then there is the creation of a collective memory, achieved by recounting the hootenanny's history and identifying iconic personages. The emblematic figures included Alan Lomax, Pete Seeger, Lee Hays, and Woody Guthrie, who were "the men who started the folk song renaissance that is now sweeping the country" (People's Songs n.d.-b: 4). Finally, documenting its acceptance by the public helps reify it as a taken-for-granted "thing" that just exists. Pete Seeger summed up the principle of the hootenanny:

Well, it's simple. People have always been singing about their work and play, their troubles and their mothers-in-law, their problems and their games. Out of the Kentucky mountains and the western plains, from the riverboats and the prison farms, from the men who fought with Washington and sought peace with Lincoln, the men who cleared the northern forests and settled the southern deserts, come thousands of folk songs that are America's proudest musical heritage. And that's a process that has never stopped. Today, as always, people are still making up songs about the things that are close to them. A Hootenanny is a meeting where people come to sing and to swap these songs. (People's Songs n.d.-b: 4)

More than other PSI publications, including their bulletin, Seeger is highlighting folk music, associating music with the American ideal—the agrarian imagery and common people, especially those who toil. The imagery of a group is tied to a temporal process emerging from the past, continuing in the present. Music thus draws together not only those who are present at its making but also symbolically those in the present join with those proud and free Americans of the past. What unites them at the hootenanny is less the common experience of collective action than the diffuse symbolic consciousness of shared orientation. It is the music itself that is expected to forge the bonds. The music expected to do that work is folk music, broadly defined here to include topical songs, those songs that people were making up at the time and feeding into the folk process through the organizational form of the hootenanny. Despite Seeger's admirably democratic vision, in fact hootenannies were rarely places where "people come together to sing and swap these songs." More often they were a place where audiences were entertained by performers who invited them to sing along. Or if they were places to swap songs, the event would gather like-minded and socially similar people together.

Still, despite the failure to live up to the inclusive vision of song sharing, the ideals articulated for the hootenanny did give substance to the democratic principle of folk music. Hootenannies were decisively different from commercial concerts, both in content and in social relationships within the audience. What made the hootenanny part of the folk process was not absence of professional performers—PSI advocated that musicians be well compensated—but the institution itself. The format was offered in the name of the people, for the people, and with the people participating, even if more music was consumed than actively shared. Although performers had some connection to the world of commercial music, at least on the margins, the hootenanny itself was an alternative to the institutional framework of commercial music.

This equivocal nature of the hootenanny reflected the contradictions of sponsoring agencies like PSI. "Hootenanny" was a mode of activity, a way of doing music that represented a microcosm of the social relations people's songsters aspired to create. Seeger retrospectively described his ideal event: "The best hoot, in my opinion, would have an audience of several hundred, jammed tight into a small hall, and seated semicircular-wise, so that they face each other democratically. The singers and musicians would vary from amateur to professional, from young to old, and the music from square to hip, cool to hot, long-hair to short" (Seeger,

Tusler, and Briegleb 1972: 328). The description evokes the New England town hall meeting both visually and interactively. Just as "folk music" was to be the music *of* the people, the hootenanny was to be an event that invited participation, an event filled with folk music and itself part of the folk process. But just as the unstated assumption of direct democracy in the town meeting was social homogeneity, the hootenanny assumes a shared culture of like-minded enthusiasts. Unlike the idealized New England town meeting, PSI did not bring together a community of peers, except for committed leftists. Even working beyond the discipline of the party hierarchy they were a musical vanguard bringing to the "people" music that neither the People's Songsters nor the workers collectively connected to. Still, they were able to attract some African Americans. Irwin Silber recalls how they held some hoots in Harlem, ending them at 10 P.M. and then bringing in a dance band for the younger folks (Silber and Dane 2001).

While the hootenannies were promoted primarily to galvanize audiences already committed to folk music, another strategy of the PSI project involved evangelizing folk music to the broader public. Lomax, Seeger, and the others promoted folk music as a new fashion, a trend that would capture the attention of the media and impart a political message. Lomax, no doubt aspiring to a self-fulfilling prophecy, wrote in *Vogue* that "Nineteen forty-six will be remembered, among other things, as the year that American folk songs came to town." *Glamour* concurred, effusing that "nobody can remember anything that's had night-clubbing cities more excited than the re-discovery of folk songs."[5] Again proclaiming "the spring freshet of enthusiasm for native balladry and folklore that is running through the country from coast to coast," Lomax gave a political spin for the readers of the *New York Times Magazine*, explaining the trend as a "longing for artistic forms that reflect our democratic and equalitarian political beliefs" and "a hankering after art that mirrors the unique life of this western continent" (Cohen and Samuelson 1996: 30).

The contradiction between the ideals in the form and the practical need to create a constituency led them in the end to compromise the vision. It seemed that the project of people coming together to share music needed to be bolstered by the gleam of star power. PSI's hootenanny pamphlet sells the idea by telling readers that "The artists that perform are nationally known, and a list of the sponsors and members of People's Songs, and its companion group People's Artists, reads like a 'Who's Who' of the entertainment world" (People's Songs n.d.-c: 5). The stature of the performers is then cited as a reason for their success, as the text drops the distinction between concert and hootenanny, noting that successful events were held in some of the grandest halls in the nation's major cities.

ORGANIZATIONAL DILEMMAS

The hootenannies crystallized one of the tensions that all social movements face: reconciling the relationship between its members and its target public. Tarrow distinguishes among three aspects of organization: formal hierarchical organizations, organization of collective action at the point of contact with opponents, and connective structures that link leaders and followers, center and periphery, and different parts of a movement sector. Criticizing utilitarian models of social movements, he maintains that the most critical challenges in mobilizing for collective action are less a matter of motivating a constituency than organizational (Tarrow 1998). PSI was a formal organization aspiring to infuse music into collective action at the point of contact with opponents but was most successful as a connective structure. Much collective action at the point of contention, notably the extended sit-downs and strikes of the 1930s, incorporated music, but the business-union strikes of the late 1940s did so less often, rarely linking leaders and followers, center and periphery, or different parts of a movement. The hootenannies tied together audiences. When those audiences corresponded to the connective structures of the movement, the movement was solidified. But too often audiences were a narrow part of the movement networks—the educated urban cultural elites, not the workers. PSI's imagined connective structure can be seen in the opening page of the first issue of their *Bulletin*, where they offer invitations "To Unions," volunteering to help them put together a songbook or record a song, "To Songwriters" offering to publish songs for them, and to "Singers, Leaders of Choruses," soliciting them to join the organization. Tying together unions, songwriters, and choruses would contribute mightily to a movement in which music was embedded into the vernacular culture. But in the late 1940s, unions were moving into narrowly construed business unionism. As Walter Sassaman, UAW-CIO regional educational director in the Midwest, explained, most local union meetings were very simple and straightforward with little opportunity for music. Members may have known a few old union songs like "Solidarity Forever" but listened mostly to popular tunes. He suggested that the way to reach them would be with parodies distributed as singles (*People's Songs Bulletin* 1, no. 3 [March 1946]). PSI was doing that, but it was not clear whether they were reaching union members. Their bulletin was filled with parodies of traditional songs, many of them reproduced as single-song broadsides, though they were prevented by copyright laws from including current tunes. "Mr. Congressman" took the tune of "Little Brown Jug," Guthrie's "Jesus Christ" was based on "Jessie James," and one issue included a parody of the theme from *Carmen*.

More important, they were going beyond just publishing by trying to construct the connective sinews that Tarrow affirms. At first they worked proactively to link these constituencies together through formal organization. A Popular Song Writers Committee, chaired by Paul Secon, met with CIO representatives to see how unions could be served, but apparently the talks went nowhere (*People's Songs Bulletin* 1, no. 2 [February 1946]).

One of the connective links that is especially problematic in cultural relations is the link between center and periphery. Like the gap between performers and audience, cultural centers like New York and Los Angeles stood above and apart from the heartland. Performers, songwriters, and other professional musicians gravitated to the cultural centers where they could be part of a creative network of professionals. If you wanted the stimulus and nurturance of a fully developed musical world, the larger the city the better. Ironically, folk music, when categorized as a special genre, is no different. Even "authentic" legends like Aunt Molly Jackson, Woody Guthrie, and Huddie Ledbetter gravitated to New York. PSI was a New York organization with an office near Times Square. But most unions were in heartland industrial centers, which were considered culturally second-rate. Thus, although the leaders of PSI defined unions and their members as the core constituencies, those on the periphery of PSI, especially in its regional organizations, had more active working relationships with unions. The New York office occasionally worked with union leaders but were hardly on the front lines. The people in chapters more often were. Rolf Cahn and Barbara Dane sang old union and popular songs for locals standing in the line during a Chrysler strike, from a sound car, at concerts, and in strike kitchens for the women. The Cleveland PSI had a mass-singing and talent-pooling session for representatives of about thirty local organizations. A Minneapolis-St. Paul chapter focused on organizing Scandinavian workers in the city and the iron range. Even when the New York–based leaders and performers such as Seeger and Guthrie performed for unions, they did so on the road, as they did for a Westinghouse strike in Pittsburgh (*People's Songs Bulletin*, passim).

PSI's orientation toward the music profession created another organizational dilemma. Adapting the performer-audience template for music, they generally treated music as something done by musicians. Even though those musicians were given the job of nurturing a musical culture, the vehicles were songwriting and song leading. Their folk music process was one steered by professional musicians. "Don't Kill the Goose" (*People's Songs Bulletin* 1, no. 2 [February 1946]: 2) pointed out that singers need income to survive and encouraged unions and other organizations that organized meetings or parties with singers to include an entertainment budget. As they explained, "Singers can't pay rent with applause."

The Communist Party generally eschewed volunteer labor on the grounds that people who provide labor should be paid a fair wage. Not only would those who do work for the movement potentially be exploited, but a reliance on volunteer labor might exclude working-class people with less leisure time than middle-class supporters.[6] But the movement had few resources to support musicians, especially as McCarthyism choked off opportunities for paid work in the music industry.

This orientation toward professionalism created an even more debilitating dilemma in PSI's internal organization. After an initial sprint of growth gave way to harder times, they responded by becoming more bureaucratized. Onetime Almanac Lee Hays initially served as executive director, but his organizational ineptness and a number of personality clashes prompted his expulsion. Twenty-one-year-old Irwin Silber eventually took the job, with Leonard Jacobson taking on the booking responsibilities and Waldemar Hille assuming full-time responsibility for the newsletter. Silber had been making a living writing for a group of trade magazines and had been active in folk music activities with American Youth for Democracy (Silber and Dane 2001). Professionalization and specialization fostered greater efficiency, along with a bureaucratic mentality reflecting their association with the party. The party was operated as a bureaucracy more than a social movement, with a clear boundary between members and non-members, a hierarchy of responsibility and authority, a clearly defined division of labor structured in formal roles, and a legal-rational set of rules and bylaws. Like the party, PSI preferred to employ a staff, both to avoid "exploitation" and to ensure accountability of those who did the work. Thus relative to other social movements, especially those of the New Left a generation later, it was highly professionalized, with managers and functionaries. Though working on a shoestring, with salaries frequently reduced or deferred, the PSI staff could competently execute the regular tasks that the organization took on. For a brief period of history, America had a vibrant formal organization dedicated to promoting folk song on behalf of a progressive political movement.

Elusive Social Foundations

As challenging as the internal dilemmas were, the organization could have survived with a more solid social base. The fundamental problem with People's Songs was that they were seeking to supply a service to organizations and groups of people without a firm footing in the social foundations of the people they were serving. Any initial opportunity disappeared when the unions, under threat of political repression, expelled the communists and adopted a trade union model. As Pete Seeger retro-spectively analyzes what he invested several years of his life doing, "How our theories went astray! Most union leaders could not see any connec-tion between music and pork chops. . . . 'Which Side Are You On?' was known in Greenwich Village but not in a single miner's union local" (Seeger, Tusler, and Briegleb 1972: 20–21). The gap between PSI and their target constituency, especially the unions, can be seen in a complaint from PSI singer Bernie Asbel, a Chicago activist who often sang at union meet-ings, lamenting that singers were too often poorly integrated into the flow of a meeting and too often a poorly presented adjunct, unappreciated and indifferently accepted by the audience who had little inkling of why they were there (*People's Songs Bulletin* 1, no. 8 [August 1946]). Folk singer and PSI activist Ernie Lieberman looked back with similar disappoint-ment, describing PSI's goal as "reaching the masses of America with our political message through the vehicle of folk songs, which were their music, only they didn't know it" (Lieberman 1995: 73).

The need for music to connect to the social base of a movement can also be seen in an important exception to PSI's failure to rally the work-ing class. The Los Angeles chapter used music not just to evangelize pro-gressive ideas, but also to galvanize collective action. Karla Duhar wrote in the *Bulletin* about how People's Songs LA helped in the Hollywood studio lockout. Women arrested on the picket lines had learned to sing in jail, where they made up new words to familiar tunes. "Cell 502 rocked from one end to the other with singing and applause," helping them keep up their morale through a hunger strike of several days. Rose Kavner echoed the sentiment, describing the six hundred jailed union activists: "We found out in those four days just how important a role songs play. Not just any old moon-June song, but the kind that have meaning and come out of the struggles of the people" (*People's Songs Bulletin* 2, no. 4 [May 1947]). People's Songsters were active in the unionization of the entertainment industry, both as participants and supporters. They would have had an advantage over those trying to instill music into industrial union efforts because the music they promoted was closer to the culture of the workers they were organizing. Easing away from the emphasis on folk music, they more unabashedly used mainstream popular music. Though factory workers may have found folk music not their music, for the entertainment workers, the songs sung by Earl Robinson, Vern Part-low, and the others, not to mention the songs the activists were making up in jail, were the music of the people. Earl Robinson was equally adept at writing "Joe Hill," the television version of *The Adventures of Huckle-berry Finn*, and songs for entertainment unions because in some sense he was writing for the same audience. So in Los Angeles, where the social distance between PSI activists and "the people" was closer, music was less about propaganda and persuasion than a source of social solidarity in collective action, much like the civil rights movement a generation later.

But the problem was not just that the masses in America did not know folk music was their music. The distance between the activists and the people is revealed in the imagery of "reaching." Reaching assures one-way action across a distance. Similar depictions of social distance between the politically engaged and the unaware can be found in PSI's pamphlet "A Condensation of Music for Political Action: A Section of PAC's New Manual of Techniques": "Ever since 'Yankee Doodle' first haunted the Redcoats, songs have been a potent political weapon. People lend willing ears to a message when it has rhythm and swing" (People's Songs n.d.-a: 3). They compare political music to the music of advertisements, where music is used primarily as an attention getter. Thus a catchy song with a clever message will be most effective, especially parodies on favorite old songs. The advice is to use music to forge a positive link on the way to delivering a message. It is incidental to the message, which can either come with the music or after the music has softened up the audience. The pervasive imagery is one of persuasion, of an enlightened group bringing others to their point of view. The music is intended to bridge an ideological gap between the performer and the audience, but they overlooked the social gap that music must first bridge.

This is not to say that people associated with the Communist Party only performed like popular stars. Pete Seeger has seen himself as much a leader of singing as a performer and credits both the Highlander School and Lee Hays for helping him hone his song leader skills. He has brought music to hundreds of sit-down strikes, picket lines, protest marches, and jail cells. But Seeger and the rest of the red musicians found themselves in the context of a vanguard political movement that structurally limited their own musical activities.

An audience, even an engaged one, is socially more distanced from a performer than a community from a song leader. Though working-class audiences may generally be less disengaged than the inert, acquiescent audiences of the middle and upper classes, they are fundamentally estranged from performers. The performer is not only culturally understood as set apart but is also physically removed, often literally above the audience. Since Western culture requires that those who perform music for audiences be especially talented—in contrast to amusing friends with a joke—those endowed with such ability are treated deferentially. Even for those whose social origins might not distinguish them from their listeners, the Aunt Molly Jacksons and Leadbellys, setting them on a stage or even the front of a union hall erects a boundary between performer and audience.

The music that would have reached ordinary people most directly, popular commercial music, was not only politically offensive but also legally elusive. Folk songs and topical songs were attractive to PSI in part because these were music that they could own, both in the proprietary sense and the figurative sense. Because folk songs were in the public domain, not under copyright control, they could be published and performed without securing permission or paying royalties. Occasionally individuals in the *Bulletin* would endorse greater use of popular music, reaching ordinary folks with the music they knew best, but even if the leadership of PSI had agreed, such songs could not have been published in the *Bulletin*, distributed as broadsides, or sung at rallies without paying royalties. More important, they felt that folk music was the music *of* the people, in contrast to commercial music composed and performed *for* the people. As Guthrie effused about the music in *Folksong USA*: "There's more real fun and human living in this book than there is in ten flatcar loads of popular, sissified, neurotic mouth frothing dished out by the rivers and by the floods by our pop houses" (*People's Songs Bulletin* 3, no. 4 [April 1949]: 4). Similar sentiments were expressed about Moe Asch's failed attempt at the Disc Company, an abortive harbinger of Folkways, that closed up in 1948. "Moe Asch wanted, and still wants to put out the Authentic, as contrasted to the Commercial in people's music. He is to be congratulated for his defeat at the hands of the major companies as well as for his significant contribution to American people's culture" (*People's Songs Bulletin* 3, no. 12 [December 1949]: 2). The focus on folk music did not entirely rule out other forms of vernacular music. Writers in the *Bulletin* often endorsed popular music, even Tin Pan Alley. Lee Hays was among the more insistent that activists should heed popular musical tastes, that "people's songs" should be interpreted literally—what the people listen to. Waldemar Hille even included religious music, which he considered part of the folk heritage, characterizing many songs in hymnals as freedom songs and songs of brotherhood. Negro spirituals, shape note songs, Christmas carols, Hanukkah songs, and religious ballads, he wrote, are a large part of American culture and speak to a social conscience (*People's Songs Bulletin* 2, no. 11 [November 1947]). One issue of the *Bulletin* included a number of Christmas carols, both sacred, such as "O Come All Ye Faithful" and secular, such as "Jingle Bells."

THE DECLINE OF PEOPLE'S SONGS

The underlying structural disjuncture between the audience for folk music and the target of left-wing mobilization, exacerbated by political repression, was experienced in the organization as financial struggle. Although they thrived the first year, during the next year poorly promoted folk music concerts in Town Hall lost money and triggered a long-term financial slide. With several "loans" secured by Alan Lomax, profits from *The People's Song Book*, and support from the Los Angeles office, they held on until 1949, when a mountain of debts—nearly $12,000—brought the organization down. Their last hurrah was the Wallace presidential campaign of 1948.

Henry Wallace was vice president under Roosevelt and secretary of commerce under Truman, who forced his resignation after the New Dealer advocated cooperation and coexistence with the Soviet Union in 1946. Promoting "progressive capitalism" and civil rights, he ran for president as a candidate of the Progressive Party. Endorsed by the Communist Party and refusing to repudiate that endorsement, Wallace and his campaign were widely painted as communist dupes or worse. Like most progressive activists, the leaders of People's Songs saw the Wallace campaign as the best hope to return to the enlightened commitments of the New Deal and a retreat from the chilling politics of the early cold war. Wallace and his party embraced the songsters, creating what Lieberman calls "the most dramatic alliance of folk music and electoral politics in American history" (1995: 130). While Wallace captured less than 2 percent of the national vote, People's Songs, Inc. devoted nearly all of its meager resources to the campaign. It paid half the salary for Boots Cassetta as the campaign's musical director, supplied singers at campaign events, and organized musical tours that traveled with the candidate. Alan Lomax handled many of the arrangements, including production and distribution of songbooks, song sheets, and records. Virtually all party events included folk song performances and mass singing, as Pete Seeger, the Industrial Workers of the World, Woody Guthrie, and others donated their time and energy. In the short run, the effect was exhilarating for the musicians and others dedicated to the campaign. As Fred Hellerman recalled, "We went into it with tremendous energy. People worked their asses off" (quoted in Lieberman 1995: 132). Participants felt that not only were they participating in an important historical event, People's Songs was being validated as the voice of the movement. As Cassetta expressed it, "I don't think ever before and certainly not since has music been used in such an intelligent, creative, exciting way as it was during the Progressive Party" (quoted in Lieberman 1995: 132). But the exhilaration was short-lived. Not only did the campaign flop at the polls, it sapped the organization's resources and aggravated its debts. Some observers, including musicians, attributed part of the failure to its music. Woody Guthrie complained, "A dozen things were wrong with our songs and in the ways we used them" (quoted in Lieberman 1995: 134), characterizing the election songs as shallow, uninspiring, and jingoistic. While some felt that the campaign had lost support because it was out of the mainstream, Guthrie lamented that the songs were not radical enough, alluding to both the content of the lyrics and the watered-down pop sounds that diluted the folk music tradition. However, Lieberman feels that the campaign did offer wide exposure for folk music and reinforced the public association between folk music and progressive politics. If there had been any ambiguity about the political connotation of folk music before the campaign, the effort indelibly stained the genre as pink.

In retrospect, one can see that the decision to devote all the organization's material resources and political capital to the Wallace campaign was a tactical mistake. A presidential campaign, especially a third-party campaign, is a weak social foundation for a serious cultural project. While the electoral cycle has fostered a political party apparatus that includes enduring cultural imagery and an ideological repertory, the musical activity of elections has been derivative, not constitutive. That is, music in electoral campaigns depends on existing musical worlds; it can do little to reconstruct musical worlds for its needs. Even such broadly celebrated songs as "Lincoln and Liberty Too" and "Happy Days Are Here Again" had little impact on later music. Not only are presidential campaigns episodic rather than enduring, they exist in a specialized social realm with relatively weak ties to the broader fabric of society. Prior to the Wallace campaign, People's Songs had aspired to be a social movement more than a narrowly political adjunct. By committing itself to the Wallace campaign, they were signaling their affiliation with their radical, intellectual, middle-class adherents more than with the unionized working class celebrated in their ideology. The CIO and most unions in their retreat from communist influence repudiated the Wallace campaign. When the choice between the unions and the middle-class radicals was unavoidable, they drifted from the unions, even if the decision was ratifying the state of affairs. "We knew the price we would pay. . . . We were losing out with the unions," explained Irwin Silber (Dunaway 1990: 129). The irony is that in choosing the broad public over the workers, they popularized folk music. The CP had not reached workers with music because folk music was not popular. So they "settled" for broadening the public appeal. Even if workers never embraced folk music, by mid-century they would have recognized it as a mainstream, though left-leaning, genre. Bess Lomax Hawes, who sang with the Almanacs and eventually was director of the Folk Arts Program at the National Endowment for the Arts, agrees. "It wasn't the working class that we were reaching. The intellectuals, the college students—the people that were feeling lost and wanted a repertoire and wanted something to represent them, so they bonded to that with great affection" (Hawes 2001).

In considering the organization's demise, Lieberman characterizes it as "a victim of the cold war and its own blind faith in the inevitability of socialism" (1995: 139). Even though Pete Seeger has downplayed the role of McCarthyism, there was little doubt that the growing intolerance of organizations and ideas associated with the party sucked dry the sea in which PSI aspired to float, especially the unions. Dunaway points out that ironically, the FBI took PSI more seriously than the party did. Yet, the organization's vision itself was not necessarily flawed. While there was constructive divergence in exactly what the organization was about, it was essentially a forum where progressive songwriters and performers could come together and link to audiences. As Lieberman writes, "People's Songs assumed that popularizing folk and topical songs would return the folk heritage to people, educate people about important issues, and encourage creativity and activism" (1995: 72). They were intentionally seeking a form of expression outside the musical world of the commercial mainstream and had succeeded in constructing folk music as that alternative. People's Songs was their attempt to build an independent musical world as part of what they hoped would be a growing left-wing political movement.[7] It had to be independent in both form and content, with an organizational basis that represented autonomy in symbol and nurtured creativity materially. When they met to charter the organization at the end of 1945, that was a realistic vision; they could not have foreseen that the prewar flowering would not pick up after the end of hostilities. When the cold war stepped up its prosecution of the left, aggravated by the party's retreat into sectarian orthodoxy, the fertile ground for a musical left dried up. People's Songs itself was the target of McCarthyism, with New York newspapers attacking the group as communist, *Life* magazine characterizing Earl Robinson's "Ballad for Americans" (sung by Frank Sinatra among others) as degenerate, and the House on Un-American Activities Committee accusing the organization's members of disloyalty. The now infamous exposé of the entertainment industry, used widely to blacklist performers and writers, listed as subversive PSI members Yip Harburg, Burl Ives, Pete Seeger, and Josh White.

Lieberman emphasizes the remoteness of People's Songs from the party, noting that most of the folk music folks had little knowledge or interest in party debates and that the party gave the organization no material support. When Seeger approached the party leadership to forge a tighter bond, he was met with indifference (Dunaway 1990). The party was reverting to a narrowly ideological view of culture as a weapon for the vanguard to educate the masses, a tool that had to be shielded from revisionism. Those who failed to submerge culture to political orthodoxy doctrine were denounced, with William Z. Foster, the new chairman, insisting on "necessary rectifications" in cultural party discourse. Though PSI vigorously debated issues such as whether political or musical criteria were more important in selecting songs for their bulletin, the organization was loose enough that pluralistic points of view were tolerated. Their executive director, Irwin Silber, remained a member of the party, but most of the others were not. The main link between the party and PSI was a Folk Music Club founded in the late 1940s as part of the Music Section of the Communist Party. Its twenty members met to discuss Marxism, current events, political theory, racism, social trends, and aesthetics but did not collude to run PSI (Reuss 1971). Lieberman noted that the organization looked to the party for political guidance but was highly independent culturally. Los Angeles member Malvina Reynolds quit the party because its leadership "had no concept of what I was doing or of what effect it would have" (quoted in Lieberman 1995: 77–78). So the wish for autonomy was mutual. The party's cultural orientation tilted toward politically explicit high culture while the People's Songsters chafed at the discipline of a tight organization. Still, the party and PSI spoke to the same constituency and were understood by friend and foe alike as part of the same social orbit. The result was that leftist politics immediately after the war was a musical high point of progressive politics.

RACE

Though the social world of radical music reached its apex in People's Songs, the potential of folk music to bridge racial boundaries remained unfulfilled. The movement was as racially progressive as any of their era. They conscientiously achieved racial diversity on their advisory board (but not their board of sponsors), their stable of musicians available for performance, and the style of songs in their bulletins. During their first year, Alan Lomax spearheaded a highly successful "Blues at Midnight," an impressive concert of renowned African American talent. "Big Bill" Broonzy, Sidney Bechet, Sonny Terry, Pete Johnson, and others entertained an audience at Town Hall. There soon followed "Spirituals at Midnight," "Calypso at Midnight," and "Ballads at Midnight" (Cohen and Samuelson 1996). Virgil Thomson's review of the first concert in the *New York Herald Tribune* found the evening "an elevating musical experience" free from commercial taint, authentic in both selection and performance (Thomson 1946).

Hootenannies, at least in New York, typically presented a diverse roster of performers. Two held in May 1946 included Josh White, Woody Guthrie, Pete Seeger, Lee Hays, Sonny Terry, Brownie McGhee, Betty Sanders, Eleanor Young, Frank Warner, and others (*People's Songs Bulletin* 1, no. 3 [March 1946]). Still emblematic of the underlying social relationships in the musical world of People's Songs, Alan Lomax served as master of ceremonies. Racial inclusiveness was confined to the terrain the people's songsters could control: the performance side. While they would have welcomed racially diverse audiences, their social base was other white, middle-class or upwardly mobile, political progressives, many of them immigrants or children of immigrants. Concerts were more likely to be in Town Hall than Harlem. The hootenanny form was unknown in the black communities, so it is not surprising that the movement made few inroads there.

AFTER PEOPLE'S SONGS

The demise of People's Songs left the movement with only a vestige of a musical infrastructure. People's Artists, a party-affiliated booking agency, struggled to find outlets for politically engaged performers with the few organizations willing and able to hire them. So they organized their own hootenannies, such as the "Peace on Earth" hootenanny on Christmas Eve 1949. The program included carols from many lands, new topical songs such as "Hold the Line," and a choral ensemble from the Grito de Lares Youth Club (People's Artists 1949b). Race, of course, continued to be an important issue, seen, for example, in People's Artists' sponsorship of Mozart's "Abduction from the Seraglio" by the Committee for the Negro in the Arts (People's Artists 1949a). The *Bulletin* was revived as *Sing Out!* Irwin Silber was deeded the now voluminous library as compensation for unpaid wages. But the social void in the movement permitted some of the performers with popular potential to reach beyond the unions, and they left intelligentsia for a broad commercial audience, presaging in the early 1950s the commercial folk revival late in the decade. The Weavers' unanticipated commercial success presented a dilemma between reaching a broad audience and building a political movement. They knew a racially integrated group would be commercially ostracized. The best they could do under the circumstances was introduce songs like Leadbelly's "Goodnight Irene" to a mass audience. The folk movement's identity may have remained racially broad, but its commercial image was increasingly white.

The story of the Weavers is well known—a group of movement veterans (Pete Seeger, Ronnie Gilbert, Lee Hays, and Fred Hellerman) catapulted onto the limelight with a series of hits, only to be shot down by the anti-communist scare. Any explanation of their rise must acknowledge the rich musical scene from which they emerged. Not only had People's Songs' hootenannies and concerts been promoted and reviewed in the mainstream press, but there was also an active night club scene, especially in New York and San Francisco, that incubated the growing genre of that oxymoronic phenomenon, commercial folk music. New York's Village

Vanguard put before upscale audiences black and white singers including Billie Holliday, Huddie Ledbetter, Josh White, Woody Guthrie, Richard Dyer Bennett, and Pete Seeger.

There were other components of a folk musical world struggling along in the early 1950s. Jac Holzman began Elektra Records in 1950 with $200 of borrowed money. After finding some success with the music of Jean Ritchie, he recorded Frank Warner, Josh White, Ed McCurdy, Sonny Terry, Brownie McGhee, and others (Brand 1962). Another new company, Vanguard, recorded the Weavers, Pete Seeger, and others before blossoming as one of the premier folk labels during the revival. All of these, plus Riverside, Prestige, and Tradition, had some connection to record producer Kenneth Goldstein, an industrial statistician who began producing folk music as a hobby, took it up as a profession, and eventually earned a degree and became a professional folklorist. He was one of the links that tied together much of the folk recording world in the 1950s and 1960s, especially with pre-revival musicians such as Ledbetter, Guthrie, McGhee, and Terry. One of his most notable discoveries was Blind Gary Davis, whom he found singing for coins on a New York subway (Narvaez 1996).

Fortified by the success of the Weavers while being contemptuous of their commercial success and compromised authenticity, folk clubs were popping up on American campuses. Joe Hickerson, eventually the librarian and director of the Archive of Folk Song at the American Folklife Center of the Library of Congress, was drawn into the folk club at Oberlin College in 1953. He remembers liking the Weavers but more for the music than the politics (Hickerson 2000). Green described how the University of Illinois even had competing folk clubs. One inspired by People's Songs met in the basement of Unitarian Church and canonized their "trinity" of Seeger, Guthrie, and Leadbelly. Green belonged to the other one, whose sanctification took the form of authenticity, mocking the political folkies, and when the commercial folk revival blossomed "reveled in the fact that we had the truth on our side, based on authenticity" (Green 2001b). In one of the earliest sociological studies of the folk revival, Arlene Kaplan studied folk clubs of the Bay Area in California. Explaining the interest in folk music as a form of alienation from mass society, Kaplan observed the tension between those who appreciated folk music mainly for its political connotations and those who were attracted to the music for its own sake. Students from San Francisco State and UC Berkeley formed a club as early as 1950, soon splitting into political and purist variants, a pattern found on many campuses over the next decade (Kaplan 1955).

Part of the movement's infrastructure played a very different function—that of socializing young people into its politics and culture. There were several left-wing summer camps, much like religious camps that many other children attended. Several former members of the Almanacs and Weavers were on the staff at Camp Wo-Chi-Ca. People's Songs, Inc. executive director and *Sing Out!* editor Irwin Silber discovered folk music there beginning in the late 1930s, when he was introduced to the music of Woody Guthrie and Leadbelly (Silber and Dane 2001). Paul Mishler has written about a camp frequented by Pete Seeger: "At [Camp] Woodland, the new vision of folk music as popular, democratic culture was put into practice. It formed the framework for the cultural life of the camp" (Mishler 1999: 105). A New York state investigation identified twenty-seven communist summer camps during the 1930s and 1940s. Some focused on Jewish ethnic identity, others on black-white relations, and some specifically on folk culture. Camp Woodland, for example, aspired to link urban radicalism and rural traditions with a full program of traditional and topical folk singing, dancing, and stories (Mishler).

FOLKWAYS RECORDS: LEFT-WING MUSIC WITHOUT THE POLITICS

Not all the elements in the left-wing folk project were explicitly political. Moses Asch, the feisty entrepreneur who had tried his hand at record companies with Disc Records and Asch Records, finally found an enduring niche with Folkways Records. Though steadfastly maintaining his lack of interest in politics, Folkways Records has done as much to cultivate the left-sponsored folk music project as anything. It was the longest-lasting component of the folk infrastructure, the one that reached the most people inside and outside the movement, and, with its acquisition by the Smithsonian Institute, the one that has the greatest legitimacy.

This musical world would have struggled along as a minor niche with or without the Weavers. But the popular success of the Weavers both attracted new listeners and performers to folk music and inserted the contentious distinction between authentic and commercial music into folk music itself. Most of the performers associated with People's Songs held in contempt normal commercial musical endeavors, convinced that the revival of interest in folk music would come through the unions. But when the organization folded and unions, wary of their pink taint, became even less welcoming, mainstream media became a more viable way to make a living and reach the people. Lee Hays had the idea of forming a group, which they decided to name after a radical play by German dramatist Gerhart Hauptmann. Seeger had a few years earlier met Fred Hellerman, who had been singing folk songs with Ronnie Gilbert. With Hellerman's skillful guitar and wide singing range, Seeger's high tenor, Gilbert's mellow contralto, and Hay's big gospel bass, they found they could give new resonance to many conventional songs. Their earlier performances and recordings were updated for more professional renditions of the Almanacs' sound—vivacious and acoustic, but professional with urban production values. Some of their recordings for Charter are folk classics, including "Wasn't That a Time," "Freight Train Blues," and most famously, "The Hammer Song" ("If I Had a Hammer"). Though not thinking in terms of commercial success, they took a nightclub gig at the Village Vanguard and found themselves popular (Seeger, Tusler, and Briegleb 1972). Though skeptical that a group of folk singers could succeed in the predominantly solo genre, the Vanguard premiered the Weavers in 1949, gaining wide public notice in part due to an effusive review by the well-known poet of Americana and onetime folk singer Carl Sandburg. "The Weavers are out of the grass roots of America. I salute them. . . . When I hear America singing, the Weavers are there" (N. Cohen 1990: 39). They then remained at the Vanguard for months (Brand 1962). After first recording for niche labels Charter and Hootenanny, they signed a deal with Decca, hitting the charts with "Goodnight Irene"/"Tzena Tzena," which sold over two million copies. The music may have sounded authentic compared to Patti Page or Frank Sinatra, but its violin and choral accompaniment owed more to Tin Pan Alley than the backwoods or cotton fields. "So Long" and "Wimoweh" were top hits with big band accompaniments. "On Top of Old Smokey" spent seventeen weeks on Cashbox's best-seller list, peaking at number two (N. Cohen 1990). From 1951 to 1953 they recorded twenty-eight songs for Decca. "Smokey" exemplifies the blending of authentic and commercial musical influences. Opening with a short banjo riff, the first verse is sung in four-part harmony, with the banjo marking the 3/4 rhythm. The next three verses bring in the chorus, but folk style, with Seeger lining each line before it is sung. Then a verse is plucked with humming in the background, with two more increasingly harmonized verses, ending in a modulated, ascending cadence. Their most saccharine release was "Goodnight Irene." Leadbelly's innocent love song opens with a sonorous violin solo, tenderly presaging the melody line, followed by the quartet with Ronnie Gilbert in the lead, over a softly harmonic orchestra. The chorus is followed by a hummed verse with rich orchestral accompaniment that would have sounded sentimental even for Doris Day or Guy Lombardo.

Conclusion

The 1950s marked the end of the influence of the American communist movement, though fear of communism persisted. But there was more continuity in politics and music than conventional histories typically imply when they contrast the placid 1950s and the tumultuous 1960s. Only three years separated the demise of the Weavers and the birth of the civil rights movement in Birmingham, and it was just another three years until "Tom Dooley" kicked off the folk song revival. More important for music and social movements, the communist era was the inspiration, a major source of songs, and the incubator for leadership for the latter movement. It was the social relationship between the movement and its base that afforded a more participatory mode of musicking and a stronger role for music to bridge social boundaries in the civil rights era. The political inspiration of the communist-led movement was also participatory music. Pete Seeger, especially, envisioned a singing movement but miscalculated what the workers would sing. Many of the songs were good songs, effectively used in both eras. "Which Side Are You On?," "Solidarity Forever," and others were highly singable, rollicking, and adaptable. As the civil rights movement unfolded, Seeger, Alan Lomax, and Irwin Silber joined a younger generation to forge a singing movement.

The communist effort vividly shows the sociological dimension of musicking in social movements. First, the relationship between a movement and its constituency must be not only in the alignment of political frames but also in the social roots of affiliation. While it is not essential that organizers and members share the same race, class, gender, or generation, mobilization is set within cultural relationships often structured along those lines. If music, art, literature, and other cultural expressions are to persuade individuals or solidify groups, they must be meaningful in form and content. Of course, people can be socialized into a movement culture as they are converted, but that is a very different process from using culture as a device for conversion, a distinction that many movements overlook. Second, the social form of musicking is more consequential than the underlying political theory or the content of the lyrics. The American Music League, the Almanacs, and the People's Songsters all aspired to participatory musicking. They even developed a new format, the hootenanny, which would get people to sing together. Song lyrics were carefully selected to be politically sound and appeal to audiences, but most of what they did was restricted to the performer-audience format. Within that framework, they succeeded in reaching audiences, but not the one they aspired to reach. Only when the Weavers sang politically innocuous, musically sweetened pop songs did they reach a mass audience. This is not to discount the achievement of a politically dedicated, highly coherent subculture. The commercial mainstream is not the appropriate criterion with which to evaluate the worth of cultural creativity. As Eyerman and Jami-

Figure 1. The oldest depiction of the banjo—an eighteenth-century depiction of music in slave culture. (*The Old Plantation*, Abby Aldrich Rockefeller Folk Art Museum, Colonial Williamsburg Foundation, Williamsburg, VA.)

Figure 2. The Fisk Jubilee Singers in the late nineteenth century.

The New Masses Presents

AN EVENING OF AMERICAN NEGRO MUSIC

"From Spirituals to Swing"

(DEDICATED TO BESSIE SMITH)

FRIDAY EVENING, DECEMBER 23, 1938

Carnegie Hall

SEVENTH AVENUE AND 57TH STREET, NEW YORK CITY

Figure 3. Program of "From Spirituals to Swing" concert,
December 23, 1938. (Carnegie Hall Archives.)

Figure 4. Woody Guthrie (left) and Huddie Ledbetter (Leadbelly) perform together in Chicago, ca. 1941. (Chicago History Museum, #1980.0058 PPL, photograph by Stephen Deutch.)

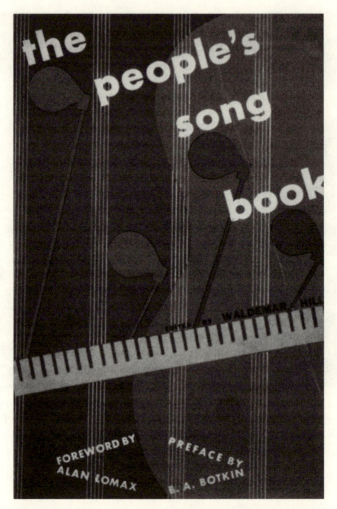

Figure 5. Songbook cover for *The People's Song Book*, 1948.

Figure 6. Members of the Student Nonviolent Coordinating Committee and Guy Carawan at Fisk University, 1960. (Wisconsin Historical Society, ID #65503.)

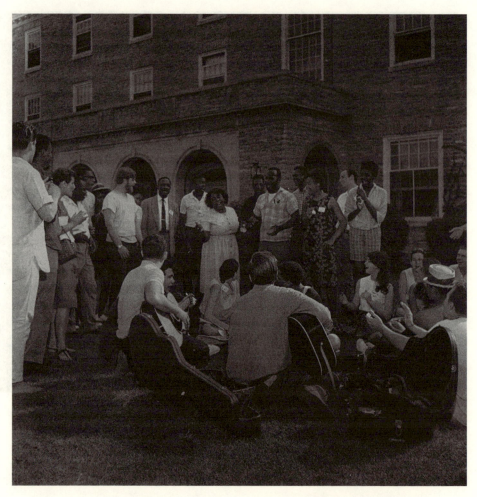

Figure 7. Fannie Lou Hamer leading students training for "Freedom Summer" at Western College for Women in Oxford, Ohio, 1964. (Photograph by George R. Hoxie; courtesy of Smith Library of Regional History, Oxford, OH.)

Figure 8. Alan Lomax and Jerome Weisner transcribing folk songs and documenting records in the Library of Congeress. (Photo by Bernard Hoffman, Time & Life Pictures, Getty Images.)

Figure 9. Pete Seeger and Bernice Johnson Reagon singing at the Poor People's March on Washington, 1968. (Smithsonian Institution, Center for Folklife and Cultural Heritage, photograph by Diana Davies, # FP-DAVI-BWPR-0399A-18.)

Figure 10. The Lumpen at a San Francisco school. (Image courtesy of It's About Time Archives, photograph by Ducho Dennis.)

CHAPTER SEVEN

The Highlander School

Though activists within the communist-influenced left led the most visible, most consequential political project for American folk music, the roots were sprouting for a very different site of musical activism. Far removed both geographically and socially from the people's songsters, the Highlander School of Monteagle, Tennessee, a small, struggling center of union and community-organizing workshops, succeeded in a different way. They never sponsored commercially successful singers or hit songs but helped make music a central activity of social movements, culminating in the freedom songs of the 1960s. The Highlander, along with similar institutions such as Commonwealth College, the John C. Campbell Folk School, and Pine Mountain Settlement, worked with unions, farmers, community groups, churches, and, later, civil rights organizations to challenge local power structures and foster indigenous empowerment. Though predominantly led by whites, the Highlander's uncompromising racial inclusiveness won the broad support of black progressives. It not only included music in its activities but cultivated music-making in the many indigenous organizations that participated in its programs of leadership training and organizational skill building. Through the early civil rights movement it eventually served as the conduit of folk music into the New Left. Thus, while the musical activities associated with the Communist Party had greater influence on popular culture, the Highlander School achieved greater success in fostering a musical movement and a more indigenous musical world.

The paradox is that the movement that was more mobilized musically was less successful in making music a part of movement practice. The movement that thoroughly made music an integral part of the movement was less musically mobilized but more embedded in the community. It is not that people's songsters were not embedded or that the Highlander did not depend on mobilization. The people's songsters were embedded in organizations that gave them access to mass culture outlets more than community organizations. Likewise, the Highlander School could have had no successful programs without an organizational infrastructure, but the organization through which music was made was found more in the groups that participated in programs than in the Highlander itself. As a transistor uses a small trace of energy to direct larger electrical currents, the Highlander facilitated leaders from other organizations toward music.

There is a second paradox. Both organizations were among the most racially progressive white-led social movements in the first half of the century. The Communist Party worked in the more racially progressive North while the Highlander School was set within the segregationist South, yet the Highlander School more successfully constructed music as racially inclusive. Though the people's songsters assiduously promoted African American musicians and frequently affirmed their commitment to racial justice, it was the Weavers rather than Leadbelly who led the organizations and had the hit songs. Though the Highlander was no less white in its leadership, including its musical activists, it was indispensable in making the civil rights movement a singing movement, providing it with music that was distinctively political—the freedom songs.

The comparison between the Communist Party and the Highlander demonstrates the importance of concrete social relations of musicking for shaping social movements. For the Communist Party, music revolved around the composer-performer-audience nexus. For the Highlander, it revolved around the song leader. While the people's songsters more actively engaged audiences than popular singers did and tried to make musical events as inclusive as possible, the context was still a performance, in which the underlying social relationship was inherently unequal and non-participatory. As a result, the people's songsters reached much vaster audiences than Highlander ever could. But the music remained peripheral to the movement, barely noticed by its leaders and often treated by members as entertainment. In contrast, the musicians of Highlander never reached mass audiences but involved the constituency on a more visceral level, making music something the movement did, a central activity. The context was less one of performer and audience than facilitator and singers.

ORIGINS OF THE HIGHLANDER SCHOOL

About the same time that the Communists were deciding that folk music was a better candidate for "the people's music" than contemporary classical music or ethnic choruses, Myles Horton, a young Presbyterian minister, made an odyssey to learn how others had empowered rural people. Beginning his quest from the Tennessee YMCA, he moved to New York's Union Theological Seminary, where he was heavily influenced by worldly theologians, such as Walter Rauschenbusch and Reinhold Niebuhr, then to the Sociology Department at the University of Chicago. He eventually found in Danish folk schools a template for the participatory, enabling process of education he was seeking. Dissatisfied with the romantic view of rural life and gradualist approach to social change in existing American settlement schools, such as the John C. Campbell Folk School (in Brasstown, North Carolina), Horton saw in the Danish commitment to socialism and cooperative agriculture a more viable exemplar for the American South. Horton was rural in origins but urban in experience. Becoming involved in the Socialist Party, he seriously read the works of both Karl Marx and John Dewey. At the University of Chicago he learned from Lester F. Ward that conflict could improve society and from Robert Park that social movements could shape history. It was there that Jane Addams encouraged him to organize a rural settlement house. But it was in Denmark that Horton developed the vision into a concrete plan (Horton 1989). The Danish schools demonstrated that the key to empowerment was balancing an unwavering commitment to social change with a respect for the students, achieved through dialogic interaction. Horton imagined a school where ordinary people engaged in collective action could come for reflection, interaction, sharing, and growth (Bledsoe 1969; Glen 1988; Horton 1989).

On returning to the United States, Horton met another young man with a remarkably similar background. Don West came from a large, poor, but politically progressive farm family in Gilmer, Georgia, and became interested in unions while in college (where he was expelled for participating in a student strike). Like Horton, his first exposure to the settlement house movement was at seminary, working at the Martha O'Brien Settlement House to pay for his study at Vanderbilt Divinity School. After a year at the Hindman Settlement School in Kentucky, West received a Vanderbilt University scholarship for a year's visit to Denmark (Wigginton 1991). With aspirations to build a Danish-style school on his return, he was soon introduced to Horton, and, with funding secured with the help of liberal theologian Reinhold Niebuhr, the two of them founded the Highlander School in Monteagle, Tennessee. West's political commitments may have inspired him to read the communist literature, but his indigenous southern identity was an enduring source of pride.

Other early staff members combined the rural roots and urban experience that facilitated the construction of a social movement possessing the rare quality of indigenous sophistication. Elizabeth "Zilla" Hawes was educated at Vassar but had spent time at the Brookwood Labor College and the John C. Campbell Folk School. Ralph Tefferteller, a native of Bount County, Tennessee, and graduate of New York's Union Theological Seminary, was instrumental in reviving square dances in the region around Highlander.

Perhaps because many of the staff members had a foot in both rural and urban worlds, the school remained doggedly non-partisan and accessible. While most rarely hesitated to proclaim their socialist sympathies or their support for southern workers, staffers affiliated with no broader organization. According to Horton, "The Highlander staff's radicalism reflected its willingness to experiment with new and unorthodox ideas, techniques, and leaders to combat the problems southern workers faced. Its primary allegiance was to the southern labor movement and to the work of the school" (1989: 44).

On the face of it, a school would seem an ill-suited institutional setting for the goals of transforming society and promoting a social-democratic vision of society, especially in the Appalachian Mountains. Many in the target constituency had little formal education and would have associated "school" less with political enlightenment than with the kind of top-down authoritarian learning that Highlander leaders eschewed, an unappealing social activity for adults. Yet other types of indigenous organizations were even less feasible. A party, especially one espousing the left-wing sentiments shared by Horton and the other early staff members, would have estranged many potential participants and invited even more repression than they faced. Except for one campaign when they backed a candidate for sheriff, staffers generally ignored the electoral process. And unlike communist and socialist parties, they did not offer memberships. Nor did their goals fit social movement organizations that worked through the legal system such as the National Association for the Advancement of Colored People (NAACP) and the Urban League. While Horton and other early leaders were affiliated with religious organizations and had strong spiritual feelings, their goals were manifestly more cognitive and emotive than religious, thereby excluding church organizations. Just as many urban settlement houses were affiliated with the YMCA and YWCA, the YMHA and YWHA, the Quakers, and the Catholic settlement movement, Horton might have opted for a stronger religious bond but elected to go a more secular route. So especially in light of Horton's and West's positive impression of the Danish settlement school, the school offered a viable template for their organization.

COMMUNITY AND RACE

The Highlander School's main activity was running workshops for activists and potential activists, typically people involved in local community organizations. "Students" would be invited to a workshop, either at the Highlander School itself or on location throughout the South. Over the course of a weekend, week, or several weeks, participants would diagnose the problems in their community or organization, brainstorm potential solutions, strategize short-term and long-term goals, and map out specific tactics. The workshops aimed to nurture empowerment: to develop a sense of efficacy and commitment to action among often poorly educated, long-oppressed southerners in a region with little collective memory of indigenous collective contention. Rather than didactic preaching, the staff used consultants, movies, audio recordings, drama, music, and written material to build on students' knowledge and present new points of view, measuring success by how well students followed up on decisions made in the workshops (Glen 1988). For example, Highlander joined with the Southern CIO regional directors for a monthlong Southern CIO School in 1944. Topics ranged from the mundane—stencil cutting and union buttons—to postwar planning and the cost of living.

In the early workshops, music, folk dancing, and group singing appeared on the program among several other recreational activities, along with volleyball and hikes. By the late 1940s, singing was playing a much larger role in the center's activities. A "Hillbilly Holiday" for union officials in 1951 combined nitty-gritty issues such as shop committee responsibility and National Labor Relations Board (NLRB) elections with broader issues such as labor and political education. Music had grown from just another recreational activity to a major feature of the events. The weeklong workshop included some form of music nearly every evening, sometimes with square dancing, sometimes with group singing, and sometimes as entertainment.

The goal of the workshops was to energize and facilitate community-based activities. The Highlander leaders carefully nurtured networks with local community organizations, drawing students from existing groups and providing those groups with allies and ideas. Staff members traveled extensively, networking, learning about progressive movements, and building bridges between groups. A 1955 trip by Henry F. Shipherd to Tuskegee, Alabama, illustrates how Highlander staffers worked through community organizations. The fact that the white staffer stayed with a black couple would have signaled to the residents a challenge to the assumptions of segregation and perhaps a courageous act of defiance. To foster development of community-based activities, Shipherd cultivated relations with local institutional leaders—faculty from Tuskegee Institute, the NAACP, an African American school principal, the local Civic Association, and several black ministers. Lewis Jones, a sociologist at Tuskegee, a member of the Highlander executive board, and a central figure in the local effort to achieve compliance with *Brown vs. Board of Education*, introduced Shipherd to the local leaders. Feeling that the key to desegregation was the school superintendent, they strategized on how to attract superintendents to Highlander, discussed plans to use the university, a boycott, and meetings with local white leaders, and drew lessons from the experience of similar efforts in other southern cities. During his visit Shipherd also recruited more potential community leaders, especially ministers and teachers, to participate in workshop programs. All these activities illustrate the tight bond between the work of the Highlander and the activities of the local community organizations. The local leaders knew they were part of a larger movement engaged in the historically vital project to desegregate southern schools and welcomed the opportunity to learn about the experiences of other communities and meet with activists from other places. Though the movement was regional, the real action was clearly rooted in the local community.

Working through the community was an effective strategy for building a broad network, but it did not always mobilize the most progressive segments. If there was tension between permeating the fabric of the community and coalescing with the most politically like-minded partners, Highlander opted for the former and the Communist Party for the latter. But the community often meant the elite, both white and black. Connecting to the community did not necessarily mean mobilizing them, a source of frustration for Highlander leaders. One report from a Highlander staff member (probably Myles Horton) visiting Louisville in the late 1950s offers a discouraging assessment of the prospects for mobilizing the local black community.

> About the group—The middle class Negro group is complacent prestige conscious, generally well-heeled, and unaccustomed to the idea of giving for the cause, as over against giving for the purpose of achieving personal status. They seem to feel no particular connection with Negroes, as a whole, or with responsibility for problems that face the deep south. (I consider this a natural and wholesome way to be, and a tribute to the way in which Negroes have progressed in this area.) My impression is that deep south problems are too near to look like "foreign missions" and, too far to offer immediate pressure.

But the author still felt that Highlander could get Louisville blacks interested in the school with patience and continuous contact. He or she also suggested that since Louisville liked to party more than most places, Highlander might organize a musical event similar to one they had held at Carnegie Hall in New York, proposing that Guy Carawan could help organize such an event. Thus music was proposed as a way to bridge the class divide within the black community as well bridge the racial divide.

This basic model of activism characterized the Highlander throughout its existence and was applied to three substantive foci: unions in the 1930s and 1940s; civil rights, especially school desegregation, in the 1950s and 1960s; and Appalachian development and anti-poverty efforts thereafter. The fact that the organizational form of activism remained stable suggests that it is more fundamental than the content of the issues being addressed. Music was part of this strategy. Cognizant that collective action, especially in conflict with volatile organizations and individuals, could incite violence, the Highlanders knew that solidarity, trust, and commitment to each other had to be nurtured. Making music together is one means, in the context of intense political work, of doing that.

During the 1930s and 1940s, when left-wing politics in the United States was virtually synonymous with the labor movement, both Highlander and the Communist Party (CP) focused their energy on unions, making the labor movement their top priority. The Highlander adopted a dual strategy, developing leadership skills among workers who could then lead organizing efforts throughout the South, and participating in strikes and other local events as they erupted.

Both the communists and the Highlanders aspired to transcend the moderate unionism that had been ascendant for most of the twentieth century. The CP challenged business unionism by fostering a strong sense of class identity that could fortify militancy. The Highlanders, in contrast, sought to make unions community organizations, not just narrowly economic entities. During the war period, the link between community and unionization became more overt when the Highlander began to offer workshops for union leaders on union involvement. In these workshops, community relations were defined as ongoing relationships with racial groups, business and professional groups, churches, news media, businesses, social agencies, and charities. The conception of the community here is a web of organizations. Unions were encouraged to seek representation on organizational boards and committees. Representatives were to be selected from the union rank and file, both to relieve leadership of further burdens and to use such relationships to cultivate new leadership. The leader of Highlander's first Community Relations Workshop wrote, "As the union's primary function has expanded from that of securing higher wages to one of broader scope concerned with the entire life of its members as part of the community, the union must assume some responsibility for integrating its members within the community" (Hart 1944). Greater integration into the community was intended both to expand workers' rights of citizenship and to educate others on what unions contribute to the general welfare. Although the CP and the Highlander had different approaches, both worked primarily with CIO unions. A 1945 press release boasted that they were virtually the CIO's southern training center (Haessler 1945).

The songs the Highlander School used during this period reflected involvement in the labor movement. Their parodies of well-known songs were songs that people could sing. "Old McDonald" became "John L. Lewis Had a Plan," with the refrain "CI-CIO." The Pentecostal hymn "I Shall Not Be Moved" was adapted into the more collective "We Shall Not

Be Moved." Even the Confederate anthem "Dixie" could be made progressive with the refrain "Look Ahead, Working Men." While Myles Horton joined in organizing drives and strikes, his wife, Zilphia, sang at union meetings, workers' educational conferences, rallies, and strikes.

During this period, the Highlander leaders were fully committed to racial justice, but they tried to work within the constraints of southern realities. They generally obeyed the laws that prohibited integrated facilities but attempted to include African Americans in their workshops and actively promoted racially inclusive unionization efforts. Highlander leaders actively encouraged participating unions to send racially inclusive delegations, with mixed results. Sometimes unions would agree to include African Americans in their delegation but only in a token fashion. For example, the CIO regional director agreed to include two African Americans in the 1945 CIO workshop but found any greater representation inadvisable.[1] Thereafter they explicitly directed anyone involved in recruiting to inform potential participants that workshops would be integrated and made plans to deal with troubled white participants. Elaborate plans were devised to minimize racial tensions. Although sessions were integrated, whites were given the option of staying in a "white-only" cabin and bathing in a "white-only" facility. To ease interaction, they insisted that everyone address each other as "Brother" and "Sister" and avoid "Mister" or "Miss," salutations some whites would have resisted when addressing African Americans. White staff members made a point of sitting with African Americans at meals, even as they ensured that tables without African Americans had open seats available.

A 1944 session titled "Things CIO Unions Can Do on Racial Discrimination" in a community relations class suggested a variety of tactics to facilitate integration. Unions could institutionalize the issue of race by forming committees on racial discrimination. They could reach out into the community and form bonds with local black leaders. Union members were encouraged to educate themselves by reading books and magazines on African American life. Leaders were encouraged to monitor racist language and jokes in their unions. This was a more sophisticated approach than merely preaching at unions that they should integrate. It thus may have been naive to assume that workshop participants would be personally sympathetic and willing to educate others. Or they may have been confident their audience was made up of progressive southerners. By the mid-1950s, the Highlander was remarkably integrated for a southern organization. Not only had they adopted school integration as their major goal, their union-organizing activities were generally integrated. A photo in their 1954–55 annual report shows a thoroughly integrated group attending a workshop for the United Furniture Workers Union (Highlander Folk School 1955).

MAKING MUSIC WITH THE MOVEMENT

Four factors stimulated the use of music at the Highlander. First, vernacular music was a deeply embedded element in southern popular culture. Insofar as the school's organizers aspired to ground political movements in the local culture, music was a salient mode of sociality. Second, the Danish schools that had served as models for Highlander self-consciously used music to culturally empower the Danish people. Third, most of the early leaders of Highlander were closely affiliated with mainstream Protestantism, which in twentieth-century America was the most important sponsor of noncommercial music. Finally, the Highlander had the good fortune of musical leadership by two remarkably energetic and influential movement entrepreneurs, Zilphia Horton and Guy Carawan, who, over two generations, fostered music-making throughout the nation.

The Highlander was located in the Appalachian region and its leaders and staff shared a strong regional identification. But that does not mean that the social milieu conformed to the stereotype of the isolated mountaineer in a cabin up the hollow plucking a banjo. While the region was poor, with few cities of any size, people were generally not isolated from the outside world. Even before the turn of the century, a northern sociologist would write in the *American Journal of Sociology*, "We had heard so many stories of the ignorance of the mountaineers that we were somewhat disappointed by their familiarity with a good many things we had expected them not to know" (quoted in Whisnant 1983: 17). More important, the Highlander's constituency was not the isolated mountaineer but the deeply embedded community organizations located in towns and cities. Southern urban life, as it was everywhere, was woven together in extensive webs of political, religious, fraternal, labor, and civic associations. It was the organizational leaders that the Highlander sought to mobilize.

It is hard to say whether the South was objectively more musical than the rest of the country. Certainly Kansas farmers had hoedowns and Pennsylvania miners had their ballads. Most Americans who attended church sang regularly in services. But it does seem that music was more commonly used for identity work in the South, especially to fortify regional identity. Not only did the legacy of the Civil War feed cultural polarization on both sides of the Mason-Dixon Line, but Appalachian resentment of coal and textile companies gave class conflict a regional flavor. Regional identity in culture was also reinforced by the "discovery" of southern culture in literature and folklore. Whisnant sets the "discovery" of indigenous culture in the context of other processes at the end of the nineteenth century. Economic colonization by northern capitalists was changing the physical landscape and social relations, sparking spo-radic worker and farmer resistance. And northern cultural missionaries were helping shape and disseminate images and artifacts of an isolated though quaint hillbilly. The settlement schools of the early twentieth cen-tury selected particular customs and artifacts to symbolize Appalachian culture for northern consumption (Whisnant 1983). The settlement schools also served as focal points for newly established folklore societies and collectors like Cecil Sharp to gather songs they could present, not as one regional music in a diverse society but as the remote vestige of a by-gone era. Even if labeled American folk music, the music of the region was being set off as distinctive and thus put into the cultural repertoire as a potential symbol of regional identity. For the Highlander then, using this indigenous music was not just getting people to sing the music they knew—though the indigenous roots were important—they were continu-ing the process of inventing tradition and drawing on a cultural reper-toire that imbued the music with political overtones.

Myles Horton and Don West saw in Denmark not only a general model for adult education but a cultural parallel of a disempowered people. Like the people of Appalachia, the people of Denmark had been margin-alized from the centers of power and had lost appreciation of their own culture. Just as the nationalist folk projects of other European countries had affirmed national identity by embracing myths of people in music, poetry, and lore, the Danish schools offered folk culture to empower. West was quite explicit about how the Danish model influenced the Highlander.

> It helped to restore to the Danish people a feeling of self-assurance and human dignity. Here in Appalachia, I've always felt that we needed that. We need that restoration. We still need it as badly as we've ever needed it. We have had our heritage destroyed in many ways and so many of our people have no knowledge of it at all. They became ashamed in the mountains here of being mountain people. Our music suffered. Much of our folk music was considered inferior and not fit to be played, and mountain people in general were, and still are, ridiculed and caricatured. All that caused many mountain people to lose confi-dence in themselves as a people. (Wigginton 1991: 70)

Culture empowers most effectively when it is culture that people do, not just when its content affirms people. Self-assurance and dignity are felt when people own culture, and there is no more effective way of owning it than doing it. But doing culture must be cultivated in experience. For most southerners, the experience of doing music was developed in the church.

Both Myles Horton and Don West were raised in the southern church and both attended divinity school, Horton at Union Theological Seminary in New York and West at Vanderbilt. Not only are American Protestant denominations heavily musical, the structuring of music in American religion is decidedly egalitarian and participatory. Membership in the religious community involves singing regardless of musical talent or inclination (Wuthnow 2003). Thus the form and often the content of music at Highlander mirrored congregational singing. The form was based on a leader coordinating a group in song. As for content, many of the songs sung at Highlander, including the most famous and influential song to circulate from the school, "We Shall Overcome," had religious roots. Zilphia Horton's collection of songs at the Highlander included a liberal sprinkling of hymns such as "Break Thou the Bread of Life" and "The Church in the Wildwood."

The social organization of music at Highlander was very much like congregational music in the Christian churches that the school's founders grew up in. A group leader would guide the collectivity in songs they knew, though often with new lyrics, reaffirming group values and fostering a sense of belonging. Like the clergy in churches, the school's leadership provided the group leader and gathered a repertoire of songs that they printed in songbooks distributed for regular congregational gatherings. And as in many churches, the result was greater enthusiasm and a heightened sense of solidarity than what listeners might experience when listening to what they deemed fine music, at least as measured by conventional aesthetic standards—more for singing than for listening. When the occasion called for harmonious music, adaptations were necessary. To create a record for unions to use in their local settings, Zilphia Horton once took a group of students to record in a Nashville studio, but the group found it challenging to practice, sing, watch for signals, and sing on cue, the basic fundamentals of performance. As often as they may have made music together, they were not accustomed to performing.

The final ingredient securing the place of music at the Highlander was the presence of two dynamic, talented, and committed individuals who served as movement entrepreneurs, the "Johnny Appleseeds" of folk and topical music in the South. Zilphia Horton was the daughter of an Arkansas mine owner and majored in music at College of the Ozarks, where she became an accomplished classical pianist. When she became interested in the labor movement, her father kicked her out of the house, but Myles invited her to Highlander in 1935 as a scholarship student. Although initially disdainful of country music, Zilphia soon learned to appreciate the music that the people of the region enjoyed (Bledsoe 1969). Soon after taking over as cultural director in 1938, she began to develop parodies of well-known songs to use in workshops and organizing efforts. The Highlander began mimeographing song sheets, which were carried on field trips and distributed to striking mill workers. In workshops, students were encouraged to share songs from their own backgrounds, to write songs, and to lead songs. Many students learned to be group leaders. The center's growing reputation led to invitations from unions to lead singing at meetings and conferences, including the constitutional convention of the Textile Workers Union of America (TWUA) in Philadelphia. A few months later, the TWUA published Zilphia Horton's *Labor Songs*, with introductory remarks by John L. Lewis, Sidney Hellman, and Emil Rieve (Horton 1989). During her years at Highlander, they published ten songbooks and mimeographed hundreds of songs (Glen 1988). As important as these organizational achievements are, the legend of Zilphia Horton, attested to by anyone who has ever written on Highlander, is based on her remarkable gift for group singing. She had an infectious enthusiasm, a trained voice that sounded natural, and a commanding presence that invited participation. As Zilla Hawes Daniel, an early staffer, described it, "You weren't on the outside as a spectator, you became wholeheartedly involved with the moment. And that was singing either one of the traditional labor songs, which spoke of the struggle of years past and had application to today, or a new song that had been brought in by a participant in one of the workshops, which was then ingested and became a part of the collective material and would eventually appear in print as a part of a little songbook" (quoted in Wigginton 1991: 114).

After Zilphia Horton died in 1956, her role as music leader at Highlander was taken over by a California native, Guy Carawan. Guy had grown up on the West Coast and had earned a master's degree in sociology at UCLA. But unlike Zilphia, he did not have to struggle to learn to appreciate the vernacular music. Even as a youth his politics took musical form and his musical interests expressed themselves politically. While a teenager, he met Pete Seeger, a man who would have a profound effect on him for the rest of his career. The merging of his musical and political interests found a home in the local branch of People's Songs, spawning a group called the Sierra Folk Singers. As a member of the UCLA folk club, his role was helping others develop their talents, while working up songs so that the vocal range, harmonies, and instrumentation could encourage as many people as possible to join in singing. In the early 1950s he moved to New York City and became part of the Village folk scene where he was heavily influenced by African American musicians such as Leadbelly, Rev. Gary Davis, Big Bill Broonzy, and Brownie McGhee. The political influences he felt in New York were the remnants of People's Songsters, Inc.—Pete Seeger, Earl Robinson, Lee Hays, and Abel Meeropol, who wrote

"Strange Fruit." Among Carawan's musical outlets was a multiracial choir, the Jewish Young Folksingers. Living with a left-wing Yiddish family deepened both his musical understanding and his political maturation. In Pete Seeger, Carawan found a new kind of role model, someone who aspired to be a song leader, not just a performer. But feeling the call of his southern roots, he embarked on a southern odyssey with singers Frank Hamilton and Jack Elliott, making a living singing wherever it offered a salary, a commission, or handouts. A suggestion from Pete Seeger prompted a visit to the Highlander School that not only would change his life but also profoundly influence the relationship of music to political protest more generally (Carawan and Carawan 2001).

Carawan originally called Myles Horton asking if he could use Highlander as a base of operations, and Horton said only if he took over Zilphia's job as coordinator of musical activity. When he began at Highlander, blacks in civil rights meetings had lost their tradition of spiritual singing and were singing songs like "Onward Christian Soldiers" and "The More We Get Together, the Happier We'll Be." When he was invited to workshops for civil rights organizations, he introduced songs like "We Shall Overcome," "Keep Your Eyes on the Prize," and "We Shall Not Be Moved." Like Zilphia, Carawan mimeographed songs as fast as he could and passed them out wherever he could. As the civil rights movement blossomed, he used a broad variety of media to spread the music, including three LP records: *The Nashville Sit-In Story*, *We Shall Overcome*, and *Freedom in the Air, Albany, Georgia*, which documented the movement's events and sounds. A songbook, *We Shall Overcome*, was widely distributed through the movement and in folk song circles. And he traveled extensively promoting music as an integral part of collective action.

The social relationships around the music paralleled the social relationship in the Highlander's workshops, which reflected the way Highlanders conceived of the relationship between leaders and the movement. Though Guy Carawan had performed before joining the staff at Highlander, he did not see himself primarily as a performer: "I started off around little circles of people who liked to sit and play, and sit there and look at each other, play and get those sounds, that was the most fun. It didn't start out as a performance, but just liking the sound of the guitar. You liked the songs, you did it for your own satisfaction, then you could play with other people, blues, gospel, somebody could add things, a mandolin, or you might have a great bass player, just all different possibilities" (Carawan and Carawan 2001). So he fit in well at the Highlander, where his role was to be a song leader and trainer of song leaders. Rather than demonstrate how good a singer he was, his job was to find out what songs a group knew and loosen them up to sing. He compared it to the workshops, in which leaders were to facilitate discussion so people could find the solutions within themselves. It was also a mode of interaction he identified with the black church, in which anyone can raise a song, sparking the congregation to join in, elaborate, and make music together. Whether in a workshop or in music-making, the leader would respond to a suggestion from the group, set the tempo, orchestrate an accompaniment, help blend the voices, and express the group's sensibility. In both cases, the group process simultaneously fostered the creation of a "product" and a sense of belonging. The workshop produced programs for the participants to develop or ideas for the participants to take home. The music-making group produced a song. In the overall mobilization process, group solidarity was as important as the product. Moreover, as pointed out by Guy Carawan's wife, Candie, the leaders at Highlander were aware that they were dealing with oppressed people (white and black), people who had learned to believe that their culture was inferior. Collectively sharing their culture valorized it and thereby empowered them (Carawan and Carawan 2001).

Carawan self-consciously developed the use of folk music in the civil rights movement. Because of its roots in African American churches, the movement had always been musical, but with little distinction among religiously rooted music, folk music, and popular music. Committed to the idea that a movement should "sound like a movement," Carawan promoted music with a religious and folk basis, that is, music whose musical and lyrical connotations signified moral righteousness and cultural authenticity. While parodies of rock and roll songs cemented a sense of togetherness, Carawan helped create a new genre—freedom songs—that expressed the movement's association with Christianity and, as a form of black spirituals, its African American heritage and roots in slave culture.

Always conscious of his position as a white man in a movement dedicated to the freedom of black people, he adopted the position of a teacher, giving workshops, sharing songs, and performing, but he was careful that the music came from the movement. Bernice Reagon, one of the most musically active participants in the movement, credits Carawan with adding spirit to the music. Before the era of the movement, music sung by black college students tended to be formal and uninspired, distancing them from their rural roots. Speaking of a 1961 workshop after the beginning of freedom rides, she writes, "At the beginning there was singing and you would have never believed it was the same people. Guy was leading the singing and they would sing 'We Shall Overcome.' The students asked Guy to came to Nashville to sing on the picket lines. They realized the value of music, but they hadn't got into it. That's why they asked Guy to help, because Highlander was the only place they knew that sung any kind of songs" (1975: 112). This is an important observation, a useful anecdote challenging essentialized assumptions about the relationship between the races in the movement. Many accounts of freedom songs facilely associate the energetic spirit, bodily participation, and cultural authenticity with the evangelical tradition of black church music. And while the tradition of black evangelical music did eventually energize freedom music, the relationship was not automatic or unproblematic.

A series of workshops titled "Sing for Freedom" embodied the Highlander approach to music and collective action. Music was used to galvanize solidarity in the movement, reaching across the races to involve people in the act of making music. The workshops first and foremost served song leaders and choir directors and, secondarily, singers, appealing to those who identified with the movement for freedom in the South. Brochures promised that the group would learn song-leading techniques and how to use music at mass meetings, prayer vigils, poster walks, and other meetings. The workshops were not framed in terms of folk music itself but in terms of the songs of the movement, emphasizing the process of doing music, both the rituals of inclusion and the creative process of making up new songs. But the organizers emphasized that new music should be suitable for various forms of social gatherings, organizational meetings, and demonstrations. This was not a place for singer-songwriters to hone their creative skills or cultivate talent for self-expression as much as a place to cultivate the use of music in collective action.

The first in the series, "Sing for Freedom—in the Community—on the Campus," held in 1960, was structured around different modes of collective action. A session titled "Songs of the Sit-Ins" provided practical activities for sit-in organizers while one on the Montgomery Bus Boycott drew lessons from that multifaceted mobilization. Another on school desegregation connected the participants to extended community campaigns. "Songs of Faith, Determination, and Christian Non-Violence" drew on the religious background of members and joined the movement with the organizational foundation of the movement in many southern communities. "Brotherhood Songs for Children (for the Class Room and Sunday School)" incorporated another set of songs and raised participants' consciousness about the long-term goals of the movement. Such sessions on explicitly religious themes both drew on the religious roots of the movement and reinforced the church's role in it (Archie Green Folio).

One of the unintended consequences of these workshops was the creation of a canon of freedom songs, a set of songs that were sung widely throughout the movement and that were associated with the movement. Not only did song leaders and singers learn from each other at the actual workshop, but organizers would gather songs to mimeograph or occasionally publish. At the 1960 workshop, there was not yet a standard repertoire. Though music was common at movement activities, the styles ranged from topical songs based on current popular songs to religious hymns to old union songs. Within a few years, a more or less standard repertoire had been established and canonized in Carawan's *We Shall Overcome* collection, though, of course, many singers departed from it, and new songs were cropping up all the time. An examination of sixteen songbooks containing songs of the civil rights movement showed sixteen songs that appeared in at least four books. All of the most commonly printed songs were group songs not very suitable for individual performance. The three most popular songs, "We Shall Overcome" (eleven books), "Oh, Freedom" (nine books), and "Which Side Are You On?" (eight books), were zipper songs—songs of short repeating verses in which new lyrics can be easily invented for specific occasions.

The canon of freedom songs, which has endured as the sound track of our collective memory of the civil rights movement, succeeded in embodying a culture that affirmed African American pride, music they owned by doing it. But it was more strictly the culture of a racially inclusive movement than the culture of a people, a bridge between races erected by black and white activists working together. Its status as African American culture was ambiguous and increasingly contested. Similarly, the relationship of traditionally black culture to the movement became an object of contention that began to flare up in the Highlander School just as the civil rights movement was reaching its height.

A second "Sing for Freedom" workshop four years after the previous one exposed the first cracks of what would become a cultural chasm. Billed as a "Festival of Negro Folk Music and Freedom Songs," workshop sessions helped song leaders develop a broad repertoire, learn song-leading techniques from masters such as Bernice Johnson Reagon and Fannie Lou Hamer, and develop songwriting techniques for use in the movement. There were workshops oriented toward performance, but for groups, not individuals. Choir directors could acquire arrangements from the Birmingham Movement Choir and the SNCC (Student Non-Violent Organizing Committee) Freedom Singers. The only workshop on songs that took music away from a movement context was one on traditional Negro folk music, teaching "some of the best old songs that are meaningful today" ("Sing for Freedom" brochure, Highlander School Archives, reel 31). However, the workshop did not unfold smoothly, exposing important conflicts in different people's understanding of music and tension between traditional folk music and the music of political commitment. While some song leaders emphasized that traditional music embodied values and identities that the movement affirmed, others saw the movement as a break with tradition, an attempt to break with the past. The conflict shows that the affinity of folk music to political contention is not inherent but must be constructed through active work. When the Sea Island Singers demonstrated some songs dating back to slave times, Charles Sherrod, one of SNCC's most active music promoters, challenged them, "Why? Why sing those songs here?" sparking a debate over the relevance of old music. Some echoed Sherrod's perspective and found little relevance to the current struggle for freedom of music from the era when blacks were a subjugated people. African Americans, they said, had been brainwashed about what were essentially sentimentalized and complacent cultural forms, reminiscent of Charles Seeger's early characterizations of folk music in the 1920s. In contrast, others expressed a strong racial identity with the music, finding inspiration in the creativity of African Americans under the most brutal conditions, claiming the music as their music. After several sharp, sometimes personal exchanges, the meeting reached a dramatic climax when Amanda Bowen, a physically delicate girl who spoke with the cultural authority of someone who had spent two months in an Americus, Georgia, jail, exclaimed, "I'm tired of going to church and listening to teen-agers giggle and laugh when the old songs are sung. I want to know what the old songs are. I want to sing them. I want to know that my parents were working for 15 cents a day. What these songs are is what most of this means!" (Dunson 1964). Andrew Young, secretary of the Southern Christian Leadership Council (SCLC), made explicit the link between traditional music and political commitment: "We all know you can't trust a Negro on a negotiating committee who doesn't like his people's music," adding that they had learned from practical experience that traditional music was an effective organizing tool, especially in small towns (Dunson 1964).

Josh Dunson concluded his report on the second Highlander workshop in *Broadside*: "The singing of freedom songs has ceased to be solely a means for strength and unity in the face of brutality and harassment. It is slowly becoming a wedge with which the treasure chest of Afro-American culture is being opened" (Dunson 1964). There are multiple ironies here. The wedge would open not just the treasure chest of Afro-American culture but also splinter the racial solidarity of the movement. As African Americans discovered pride in their culture and learned to affirm what had been earlier shunned, the movement was beginning to crack along racial lines, with solidarity becoming intra- rather than interracial. When freedom songs were primarily a means for strength and unity, they reached across racial boundaries. As a source of racial pride, they became the property of African Americans, relinquished by white radicals when they moved from the civil rights to predominantly white movements of the late 1960s.

The changing meaning of music was even more visible at a third workshop held the following year in Edwards, Mississippi, jointly sponsored by the Highlander School and the Delta Ministry of the National Council of Churches. Organized to train a group of young Mississippi volunteers, the focus was changing from music as a cement for movement solidarity to music as an expression of cultural pride, a means to convince indigent people that they have something special to offer culturally as well as politically. The Newport Folk Foundation made it possible for the Sea Island Singers, Ed Young, and Alan Lomax to attend the workshop. At a time when white men routinely lectured African Americans on their own culture, Lomax concluded the workshops with a presentation titled "Negro Folk Songs and the Freedom Movement." Not surprisingly, he approached the music as a musicologist, articulating the relationship between the music and the people, rather than as an activist, who might have approached music as a way to solidify commitment. The emphasis was on the "folk" in folk music. Echoing Herder, Percy, and Sharp, who treated music as a source of identity and pride, Lomax was defining a people by its music. For him, this was the music of a race more than the music of a movement: "The Negro folk singers and musicians of the South have created music in ragtime, the blues, jazz and the spirituals which today is loved by the whole world. A few of these songs have served the Negro people directly in the freedom movement; they have been transformed into the 'freedom songs' which provide the morale for the integration movement" (A. Lomax 1965). Lomax wanted African Americans to be proud of their musical heritage, reasoning that because everyone in the black community was likely to be involved in music, music could be a means to bring everyone together. He proposed that communities organize musical festivals both to give an entrée for political activists into the community and to ensure the preservation of African American culture. Missing was any consciousness about the social context of the freedom songs, an especially noteworthy omission for someone who advocated attention to music's social roots. He made the sociologically naive assumption that the social basis resides in the music itself rather than the social relations within which people do music. So people could affirm blackness by performing or listening to black music. Unlike the Carawans, a white couple for whom music was a tool to mobilize a movement, for Lomax, the community was a forum in which to make music. While one would expect a musicologist to hold this attitude, those who made him a keynote speaker at a workshop on organizing were unintentionally reshaping the role that music played in the movement. Lomax hoped that "The Negro community would learn to be proud of all its musical talent, and of itself." The seeds of identity politics were being cultivated, ironically, by a white southerner.

The irony is deepened by the fact that by the time of Lomax's exhortation to the black community to embrace their traditional music, folk music as a popular genre had been bleached of its African American roots and thoroughly identified as white, whether in the commercial hits of the Kingston Trio, Peter, Paul and Mary, and Bob Dylan or in the putatively authentic Appalachian sounds of the New Lost City Ramblers and Doc Watson. Despite two generations' attempts to make folk music a bridge to bring black and white people together, just when America had a realistic chance to end legal segregation, folk music was becoming bifurcated across racial boundaries.

I am not criticizing Lomax or the African American community for using music to bolster solidarity or racial pride. The doctrine of Black Power and the identity politics that followed were an appropriate response to deeply embedded structures of white supremacy that pervaded American society. My interest here is more analytical than judgmental—how to explain the shift in the meaning that music had and the contradictory relationship between folk music and racial identification, how a genre that was politicized because it was racially inclusive bequeathed the music of freedom to African Americans while the vessel of the genre itself became appropriated so thoroughly by the white majority.

From the vantage of several decades' retrospection, Lomax's admonishment to the civil rights activists was perfectly reasonable. Music did play a special role in the African American community and was an effective means of galvanizing solidarity and collective pride. But the message also included the medium—a white man prescribing what blacks should do to fight racism, exhorting the audience that "SNCC, composed as it is of individuals who are unashamed and flexible and unhampered by stuffy middle class prejudice, must provide the leadership and sponsorship that will nurture this cultural movement" (Highlander School n.d.). Within a year, SNCC officially adopted the mantle of Black Power and rejected the notion that whites could tell them what they "must" do. So Lomax, in preaching to the civil rights movement how they should mobilize the African American community by using folk music, was solidifying the association between folk music and white paternalism. The next conference, instead of bringing together activists to learn how to use music, brought together musicians with roots in indigenous music. In October 1965, six months after the conference in Edwards, Bernice Reagon and the Carawans organized the Conference for Southern Community Cultural Revival at the Highlander. An article in the *Southern Patriot*, using Alan Lomax as the main informant, emphasized the revival of true African American folk music. The perspective is very much what Eyerman and Jamison would adopt a generation later, that politics fosters cultural effervescence. Civil rights activists were given credit as the "moving force" and their politics accorded a source of cultural authenticity. As the magazine phrased it, "Possessed of an inner freedom and sense of dignity won in struggle, they no longer feel ashamed of traditions of the past and have suddenly discovered a beauty and strength in the culture of their forefathers" ("The Movement Stirs Folk Revival" 1965). It was probably not coincidental that the cultural turn appeared when the political movement itself was fading into the background. The conference participants discussed how to keep the old cultural forms alive and give them meaning for contemporary times, targeting the black community, and planned a series of cultural festivals like the one held earlier in Milestone, Mississippi. A manifesto from the conference framed the cultural movement as an extension of the civil rights movement, going beyond simple integration to resist assimilation into the "sterile ways of Main Street America." The focus was also shifting from the movement context within which music was made toward the cultural meaning of the music itself.

Not only did the Highlander School facilitate the use of folk music in the civil rights movement, they publicly articulated the connection between folk music and racial integration. Their discourse specified that it was folk music in particular that could bring races closer together. "Folk Music," read a headline in the *Southern Patriot*, reprinted in a Highlander fund-raising brochure, is "a bridge toward prideful and democratic meeting ground for Negro and white people of the South." The article cited a Highlander statement that "In Southern folk-lore there has never been a Jim Crow line. Songs, stories, traditions and dialects were swapped back and forth between the two peoples" ("The Movement Stirs Folk Revival" 1965). Not only did the music contribute to the freedom movement; the article noted how the freedom movement affected the way that white people heard traditional music. The music that some had considered nationalistic was now widely understood as reaching across the racial divide. Thus the discourse reinforced the boundaries around the musical genre to erode the boundaries between the races; the distinction between folk music and other music was framed as a distinction between nonracist and racist southern culture. An article like this, especially one in a journal published by a progressive organization such as the Southern Conference Education Fund, was as much prescription as description, as much an active contribution to a movement as an account of it, an action in a cultural project to define southern culture as racially inclusive.

Social movements are episodic activities with life spans more often in years than decades or centuries, occurring in cycles or spurts. Tarrow (1998) reviews several factors that affect the demobilization phase of social movement cycles, emphasizing that these are not inevitable tendencies but variable influences. Internal processes include exhaustion and polarization. The exhilaration of social movements is both a strength, attracting participants to the rush of action, and a vulnerability, difficult to sustain and apt to evoke disillusionment. The waning of exhilaration can often spark polarization as those with lukewarm commitment drift off and the more militant core escalate confrontational tactics. Polarization often takes the form of a conflict over violence and institutionalization. Some prefer to consolidate gains and seek broader support while others prefer to challenge the system as directly as possible. The dynamics of violence and institutionalization are related to the responses of the authorities through facilitation and repression, both of which can, under some conditions, reinforce demobilization. Some movements have achieved their goals and have no reason to continue in their original form, as did the abolitionists, prohibitionists, and suffragettes. Others win limited concessions and become becalmed, working within the system for reform, as did the NAACP, the environmental movement, and the more moderate branch of the gay rights movement. But states more often raise the cost of collective action through selective repression of some contenders. Occasionally providing a common target for activists to rally against, more frequently repression provokes activists to polarize between more and less militant factions.

As elaborated in the next chapter, the transformation of the civil rights movement around the issue of Black Power splintered it into separatist or black nationalist, forsaking white support, and integrationist branches. The rise of the Black Power doctrine in the African American movement created a dilemma for the Highlander. All white liberal and radical activists had to reassess their place in the movement when many of the most visible and active organizations adopted a more militant stance. SNCC and CORE (Congress of Racial Equality) abandoned the nonviolent philosophy that had been the tactical and the moral core of the movement. While many white leaders sympathized with the escalation of militancy, the Black Power concept left little room for them.

An undated Highlander document, probably by Myles Horton, exposes the dilemma felt by white activists in the face of the Black Power movement. The author expresses support for the sentiment that blacks should control their own destiny, an idea at the heart of American thought, embraced by successive generations of categorically defined social groups. The writer affirms black pride and admonishes paternalistic whites who feel threatened. But it was clear that the role previously played by Highlander was being foreclosed, not the least with its music. Julius Lester had written that "the days of singing freedom songs and days of combating bullets and billyclubs with love are over. 'We Shall Overcome' sounds old and dated. Man, the people are too busy getting ready to fight to bother with singing anymore" (cited in Highlander School n.d.). Where did that leave an organization that sought a better world through dialogue, education, community organizing, and music? As the document put it, "At one time, black people desperately wanted to be American and to communicate with whites, to live in the Beloved Community. Now this is ir-relevant." What did this sentiment imply for the role of whites in the creation of a racially just society? Many black leaders were saying that they no longer aspired to an integrated society, that the movement was shifting toward the development of black pride and militant self-defense. Black power, of course, means many things to many people, from a sim-ple affirmation of self-respect to electoral clout to armed resistance. This Highlander document notes several of them, reassuring an implicit white audience, perhaps the Highlander staff, that neither the doctrine nor its advocates threatened white safety. But it is silent about what to do, ac-knowledging only that past solutions had been rendered obsolete (High-lander School n.d.). From the Highlander's point of view, the message was clear. The civil rights movement was saying to them, "Highlander, you are a nice place, thanks for your help, but we are going to take care of our own business" (Carawan and Carawan 2001).

Black power not only splintered the civil rights movement internally; it fortified the reactionary assault on the movement's organizations and their supporters. The *Knoxville Journal*, which had long red-baited the Highlander and supported their repression, published several stories link-ing the Highlander to Stokely Carmichael, the most visible spokesperson for Black Power. One charge, also published in the conservative *National Review*, was that Carmichael stated he had gotten the Black Power con-cept from Myles Horton. Besides making the racist assumption that only a white person could have formulated such a powerful concept, the arti-cle attributed to Horton a level of militancy foreign to his deeply rooted commitments. Responding put Horton in a bind, forcing him to either align himself with Carmichael, who had become an icon of violent upris-ing, or distance himself from the movement for racial justice. The High-lander issued press releases in which Horton denied coining the term "Black Power" but clarified that Carmichael had been present at work-shops affirming the right of self-determination and collective pride. Edu-cation and violence, he insisted, are by nature incompatible, though dis-advantaged groups did often require power or leverage to make progress.

Though the leaders of Highlander respected the impulse of black activ-ists to seek self-determination and ethnic pride, they did not immediately change their program. While Horton lamented that "When these pro-grams dead-ended for the Negro masses, we had nothing more to offer," he pondered, "If we went with the militant Negroes (as Foreman sug-gested), is a revolutionary educational program compatible with our present one?" (Horton 1967). In the end he could only strategize that they continue to offer what they had been offering, an integrated pro-gram along with workshops for African American candidates.

When the civil rights movement splintered along racial lines, the Highlanders, like most white activists, moved onto other projects, in their case Appalachian community organizing. Poor whites in the region lacked both economic skills and a cultural sense of worth. Just as Lomax encouraged civil rights activists to use music to foster community among African Americans, the Highlander School used music to promote community among poor whites and validate a culture that the mainstream mocked and derided. In place of the musical workshops for civil rights workers of the early 1960s, in the second half of the decade the Highlander organized workshops for mountain music. The practices of musicking and the structure of the workshop continued. They focused on group singing, both for leaders and songwriters, with a much greater inclusion of dancing. Like the earlier workshops, they recruited people working in the community who wanted to bring people together with music—singers, song leaders, musicians, and potential song leaders. But the music was different. The political content was barely visible, either in the content or use of the music. Instead of the freedom songs and topical songs, this workshop emphasized Appalachian folk music. Instead of the picket lines and jail cells, the locus shifted to the community center and public picnic. But the goal remained the same—fostering in the community the fortitude to resist the powers that be, whether a predatory factory owner or a reckless development project.

The irony is that the Highlander was recapitulating the music made famous by Cecil Sharp. But while Sharp embraced the music because it connoted racial superiority, the Highlander was now seeking to empower white Appalachians who had been told their only source of pride was their whiteness. The music was to be part of a strategy to give Appalachians pride in something more than their whiteness. This required affirming their culture without invidious comparisons to non-white culture, convincing them that their culture was due respect not because it was white but because it was theirs. The language and concepts available to the Highlanders would have been borrowed from Sharp and the other early folklorists, but in the half century since then, it had been refracted through people's songsters and the Freedom songs.

CONCLUSION

Both the Communist Party and the Highlander turned to music as a mobilizing tool and an expression of solidarity. But their contrasting organizing strategies created different social contexts for African-derived and European-derived music. The Highlander philosophy was bottom-up, the center catalyzing indigenous movement by training leadership and building organizational skills. The musicians on the staff—primarily

Zilphia Horton and Guy Carawan—acted more as teachers than performers, helping organizers learn to lead community singing and distributing songs that had been effectively used in movements. The African traditions of leader-and-response singing, the freedom of improvisation and adaptation to context, and the liberal use of repetition in lyrics all fostered an affinity between black musical forms and the Highlander use of music. Thus the Highlander use of music conformed to the folk process—a collective effervescence sharing music and indigenous singers drawing on traditional forms, but changing the music to fit new circumstances. And the folk process worked because the style of organizing meshed with the social relations of the music. The "folk" in folk music was not just a reference to the sonic qualities of a musical genre but a bond tying together those making music. For once, "folk music" was not someone else's music.

In contrast to Highlander, the Communist Party vanguard strategy dictated that music would take the form of performers using music as a propaganda weapon to mobilize the masses. While for the Highlander, the target of musical expression was the community, for the Communist Party, it was an audience. Even though they actively engaged the audience in participation, an audience is not a community. The relationship of performer to audience was less egalitarian, with performer and audience sharing merely a symbolic link. While a common background or codes of authenticity can create some sense of sharing, the bond pales next to the tuning in of making music together. But even Woody Guthrie and Aunt Molly Jackson (after moving away from Kentucky) assumed a vanguard role relative to their audiences, bringing the truth to the untutored. The structure of their mobilizing activities had a greater affinity with music of European roots than African. The emphasis on performer and performance, the social distance between the performer and the audience, the identification of meaning with lyrics, the relative complexity of lyrics and limited use of repetition, and the congealing of music into fixed, repeated, and mimicked songs gave their musicking a whiter flavor. While there is no reason to think that the commitment of communists to racial unity was any less sincere or intense than the commitment of the Highlanders, their strategy of organizing was less suitable for African-rooted music. That is not to belittle the success they did have. Folk music sustained a racially ambiguous identity in the public mind. But while the Highlander use of music incorporated the folk process, the communist use of folk music was about the discursive meaning of "folk." They used "folk" to depict the music and the musicians—music that came from "the people" and was performed for "the people." Songs were categorized as folk songs or not more on style or provenance than whether people listened to or ever sang the songs.

In the last decade or so sociologists have cogently affirmed some of the ways that the cultural activities of social movements have influenced the larger culture (Aminzade et al. 2001; Darnovsky, Epstein, and Flacks 1995; Eyerman and Jamison 1998; Flacks 1988, 1999; J. Gamson 1997; Goodwin and Jasper 2003; Jasper 1997; Mattern 1998; Roscigno and Danaher 2000). Indeed, Eyerman and Jamison (1998) argue that social movements have exerted greater impact on the cultural arena than politics or economics. It is clear that the strategic choices that social movements make about their cultural activities reverberate long after the marchers have disbanded and the social movement organizations have folded up. For example, the programmatic goal of the abolitionists was eclipsed when slavery was ended a century and a half ago, but their introduction of slave music to the white North not only established the quintessential mode of African American music—the Negro spiritual—but established a mode of pervasive thinking by which the authenticity of culture is validated by the suffering of its artists, what Jon Cruz calls "ethnosympathy" (1999).

Yet most of the scholarship on the cultural life of social movements has focused on the content of the culture, employing cultural analysis of meanings and fathoming the sensibilities of participants. The research agenda of effects has followed an influence model—the extent to which the content of the movement's culture is propagated to others. In contrast, the agenda here has focused on the social contexts within which culture is enacted, exploring how they influence the extent to which culture creates bridges or boundaries among a movement's constituent groups. Movements make strategic choices about how they will do culture—what the social relationships among the performers and audiences will be, the kind of activities within which culture will be enacted, and the structures through which culture will diffuse. The social relations of culture then affect the relations among constituents. Though not really independent of content, the effects are not reducible to content.

The Communist Party succeeded in changing the general understanding of American folk music, introducing to society in general what had been an academic concept and giving a progressive connotation to the notion of authenticity. Woody Guthrie, Leadbelly, Pete Seeger, and others became cultural icons largely through efforts of people associated with the party. But the People's Songsters' reliance on performative music constrained the party's musical activities. Insofar as audiences were racially segregated, songs about racial equality, regardless of the race of the performer, could have limited effect on racial relations. In contrast, the Highlander School, by promoting freedom songs in racially diverse contexts, helped make music a bridge between races even if that bridge was eventually fractured. Guy Carawan, a white who learned music from blacks and

CHAPTER EIGHT

Music at the Heart of the Quintessential Social Movement

The mid-century American civil rights movement was the quintessential social movement, forming the image of the social movement against which others have been compared. The paradigm now called the "classic" theory of social movements (McAdam, Tarrow, and Tilly 2001) was developed by analyzing it. More important, perhaps, it was the spring from which flowed virtually all American social movements since then. Other ethnic-racial movements, the women's movement, the Vietnam antiwar movement, the environmental movement, the gay rights movement, and the student movement were direct offshoots. Many of the early leaders of those movements were first radicalized by their experience in the civil rights movement, where they learned what a social movement was all about. The repertoire of collective action, including demonstrations, sit-ins, marches, and so forth, was imported from the civil rights movement. And the discourse of equality and rights shaped the ideologies not only of subsequent social movements but of politics in general, being adopted by other racial, ethnic, and gender groups, the disabled, and on behalf of the unborn and the non-human. The United States now has a president whose ascendency is often interpreted through the prism of that movement. Even white males now gather in rallies, march in the street, and protest that their rights have been violated.

Among the distinctions enjoyed by the mid-century civil rights movement was a remarkable incorporation of music. In no other social movement has music enjoyed such a pervasive presence. Not only was music present at meetings, at demonstrations, at marches, and in jails, but music has remained a symbolic icon of the movement. Rarely do commemorative activities of the movement take place without the freedom songs. Virtually all accounts of the movement describe the extensive use of music, the role of music as a glue of social solidarity, a siren's song beckoning new recruits, and a cultural underpinning expressing the yearning for freedom and equality. Typical is Charles M. Payne's richly textured *I've Got the Light of Freedom*: "Then, too, there was the music. It would be hard to overestimate the significance of the music of the movement. The changing fortunes of the movement and the morale of its participants could have been gauged by the intensity of the singing at meetings" (1995: 261).

The three most important reasons why the civil rights movement was so much more musical than subsequent American social movements were history, social context, and agency. First, the rich musical heritage of the Old Left described in previous chapters created a historical legacy for the civil rights movement to build on. The civil rights movement inherited the vision of what music can do for a movement, a shared aesthetic and ideology concerning folk music in particular, and a repertoire of specific songs. The link was quite direct through people like Pete Seeger and indirect through organizations like the Highlander School. Second, the southern African American communities, especially the black church, provided a context for the organizational model and much of the leadership. Third, the agency of leaders built a solid noncommercial musical infrastructure. By mid-century, the social organization of music had been reduced to profit-making enterprise throughout virtually all of society except in four institutions—the church, schools, the organized left, and the family. The civil rights movement was able to draw on three of those institutions— the church, schools, and the organized left—to develop its own network of song leaders, practices, and canon of songs.

Music, like all culture, requires a material and organizational foundation for the history, context, and agency to stand on (Becker 1982; DeNora 2000; Finnegan 1989). Throughout the twentieth century, that foundation came chiefly from profit-making enterprise, so much so that many accounts of music discuss only the music produced by for-profit enterprise. But there is a great deal of not-for-profit musicking. Professional musicians are sustained for nonprofit entities subsidized by the wealthy, especially in classical music, educational institutions, religious organizations, and occasionally civic organizations. Most of the music people hear the majority of the time is transmitted through commercial transactions—people buy a CD, listen to a commercial radio station, or pay for a ticket to a live performance. Though more and more music is mediated through commercial transactions, other institutional structures of music persist, even if they also use commercial transactions themselves. Children learn to play musical instruments in school, in private lessons, and, as teenagers, often from each other. Music is an essential part of virtually all religious life. Millions of Americans sing in community choirs or play in private bands. And many family gatherings, often in conjunction with educational, religious, or community musicking, feature musical activity. Although the mass media have successfully conveyed the impression that all music is commercial music—or perhaps that the only music that matters is commercial music—other institutional forms endure, inspire listeners, and occasionally thrive.

Like music, social movements have institutional bases. Sociologists have long emphasized that collective action requires an institutional and organizational base, both in the social movement organizations themselves and in the broader social context. Mao Tse-Tung's metaphoric sea that buoys social movements includes not only individual fish but institutional reefs. Social movement theory has emphasized the role of institutional foundations for members and resources, or occasionally the cultural roots of social movement frames (W. Gamson 1975; Klandermans 1992; McAdam 1982; McAdam 2001; Morris 1981; Tarrow 1998; Tilly 1978; Zald and McCarthy 1979). Other institutions such as political parties, religion, education, volunteer organizations, and communities serve social movements as recruiting grounds, training sites, meeting places, material support, and consciousness-raising centers.

The institutions that social movements draw on, such as religion and education, also serve as organizational and ritual templates for social movements (DiMaggio and Powell 1983; Polletta 2002). Social movements draw their repertoire of collective action not only from earlier social movements but also from organizations participants have experienced. Modes of leadership, definitions and responsibilities of membership, construction of boundaries, and rituals of solidarity are typically imported from other groups. These are the taken-for-granted aspects of what an organization is and does. Just as nineteenth-century laborers brought secret rituals, mystical symbolism, and representations of manhood from fraternal organizations into early unions, African American activists brought congregational singing and charismatic leadership into the civil rights movement and consciousness of racial identity in music from historically black colleges and universities. Which institution a social movement uses as a template shapes the social relations within which music is done and thus what music does for the movement.

BLACK CHURCHES

African American churches served the civil rights movement not only as a recruiting ground and a source of cultural repertoire but also as a place where the movement met, a place where participants were used to making music collectively. Churches provided a model for leadership, a sense of identity, and a culture of shared symbols and rituals (Morris 1984). It was the "free space" where blacks could congregate and strategize with a modicum of autonomy (Evans and Boyte 1987). Morris (1984) emphasizes two points that are especially important to understand how music was a part of the movement. First, the church was tightly linked to historically black colleges. They channeled promising young men to the colleges, many of whom returned to local churches as ministers, trained in theology and leadership skills. Thus when religious leaders formed the leadership corps of the movement, they were able to collectively recruit from both colleges and local churches. Second, black churches knitted together a common culture throughout the African American community. While there were differences between the more evangelical and the more mainline churches, the commonality was strong enough to bridge class, region, and rural-urban boundaries. Ministers' councils tied people together and served as a channel for disseminating information throughout communities. As long as the movement remained close to the church, religious leaders were able to minimize the effect of cleavages and conflicts. The eventual splintering of the movement was both a cause and a result of secularization.

In the early period of the civil rights movement, before freedom songs were widely known and sung, it was religious music that bound the participants together in solidarity. From its birth, the movement was bathed in the music of the church. The Montgomery Bus Boycott of 1955, generally considered the movement's inaugural event, had music at its meetings, in car pools, and at demonstrations. Martin Luther King described the singing of the old hymn "Onward Christian Soldiers" at the first mass meeting of the boycott, held at Holt Street Baptist Church: "When that mammoth audience stood to sing, the voices outside swelling the chorus in the church, there was a mighty ring like the glad echo of heaven itself" (King 1958). Before "We Shall Overcome" became the anthem, "Onward Christian Soldiers" was the movement's marching song with lyrics that expressed the will to fight and a martial cadence to forge a collective sense of unity (Reagon 1975). Unlike the sit-ins and freedom rides in which students played leading roles, the bus boycott was a community affair, and for the black population of Montgomery, the community meant the church.

Reagon notes that most of the songs of the Montgomery movement were group songs, typically led by song leaders, many of them elementary school girls. Mary Ethel Dozier, a member of the Montgomery Gospel Trio, remembers singing such songs as "This Little Light of Mine" and "We Are Soldiers in the Army": "In church, at the mass meetings you would sing songs that would give you strength to face the streets" (cited in Reagon 1975: 97).[1] Guy and Candie Carawan discuss how Rev. Ralph Abernathy first introduced "Ain't Gonna Let Nobody Turn Me Round" to a meeting at the Mount Zion Baptist Church in Albany, Georgia (Carawan and Carawan 1963).

Holding civil rights meetings in churches and using religiously inspired music helped create a sense of religious commitment and belonging. John Lewis described to Bernice Reagon the impact of "Amen" in the Nashville movement: "This song represented the coming together, you really felt it—it was like you were part of a crusade, a holy crusade. You felt uplifted and involved in a great battle and a great struggle. We had hundreds and thousands of students from the different colleges and universities around Nashville gathering downtown in a Black Baptist Church" (Reagon 1975: 102). The power of the "Amen" song did not come from the lyrics, which only repeated the title word five times (and in subsequent verses single words such as "freedom"). The song's harmonic richness lends itself to gospel-style participation and its straight-on rhythm invites group clapping.

The style of music and, more important, the mode of participation would have been very familiar to African Americans and southern whites raised in Protestant churches. The very act of collective musicking is difficult to evoke without participants who are comfortable doing it. While most Americans have participated in collective singing as children, there are few social settings where adults sing together except in performance situations. Occasionally concerts, especially folk music concerts, invite participation and adults may occasionally sing holiday songs or "Happy Birthday." But religious congregations are the main sites by which Americans are socialized into the practices that distinguish musical performance from musical participation.

The African American church introduced the widely used leader-and-response format into the movement. One of Africa's main contributions to American song, the leader-and-response format permeated other African American genres such as work songs and field songs and would have been familiar to the activists in the 1960s through the churches. This format creates a social relationship around music that transcends content; people are drawn into the group under the loose coordination of a leader while fully participating in the collective activity. A song leader lines a verse and congregants complete it. Some songs would be structured around alternating lines, with the singers responding to the leader. Others would have repeating lines, perhaps with a final line that contrasts, so that the leader would begin a phrase and the singers would join in as soon as they realize which previously known verse is being sung. "Oh, Freedom," for example, repeats the title phrase three times followed by "And before I'll be a slave, I'll be buried in my grave, and go home to my Lord and be Free." Subsequent verses substitute phrases like "No more hatred," sometimes adding words appropriate to the occasion, such as "No more, Pritchett," sung about the Albany, Georgia, sheriff.

Many in the movement, both black and white, were highly musical, often from the experience of growing up in the church. Bernice Robinson, an activist from Johns Island, South Carolina, who later worked on the staff at the Highlander School, had aspired to be a musician. With her father a church choir leader, and with an organ in the house, music was a formative family activity (Wigginton 1991). Many others in the movement were not especially musical but had grown up in churches where they were exposed to noncommercial music and collective musicking. Even those who grew up in staid mainstream denominations participated in congregational singing and listened to choirs and cantors, developing an intuitive sense of the role that music can play in cementing a sense of belonging. Guy Carawan, who was so important in spreading music throughout the civil rights movement, attended Christian Science Sunday school as a child but, with his singing partner Frank Hamilton, would visit black churches in Los Angeles because that was where "you could hear the power" (Carawan and Carawan 2001).

BLACK COLLEGES AND UNIVERSITIES

If some churches were more musical than others, the musical exposure people got in colleges varied even more. Historically black colleges and universities were another institutional template for the musical activity of the civil rights movement. Although religious singing was especially important in leading participants to collective music, colleges fostered noncommercial performative music, especially the heritage of American Negro spirituals. The musical practices established by groups such as the Fisk Jubilee Singers marked a strong tradition. Even if students never attended a choir concert, they would have learned that vernacular music embodied black identity.

Since the time of emancipation, music had been highly valued among the black middle class. Following the international acclaim of the Fisk Jubilee Singers, most black colleges and universities developed active music programs and highly visible choirs. In cities with sizable populations there were music festivals, segregated orchestras and choirs, and subscription as well as public concerts. For example, an Atlanta Colored Music Festival was organized in 1910 by the local black elite when they were excluded from Metropolitan Opera performances. Supported as an opportunity to display black classically trained talent, the event featured the work of black composers and was headlined by the Jubilee Singers, baritone Harry T. Burleigh, and violinist Joseph Douglass. White leaders were invited but required to sit in a segregated section. The *Atlanta Constitution* widely publicized the festival, praising the organizers as "the hope of the entire race" (G. Campbell 1999). While events like the Atlanta festival focused on classical music, spirituals constituted the specific music of the black middle class, a polysemous and sometimes controversial genre that gave African Americans an identity through their own music while being used to win white respectability.

Stimulated by the work of black composers such as John Wesley Work III, Henry Burleigh, and William Arms Fisher, middle-class African Americans could find examples of success in the musical world more frequently than in most of the other arts. With the church and colleges as incubators of talent, African Americans faced less discrimination in music than in other realms. During the first half of the twentieth century, African Americans composed works played by major symphony orchestras, appeared in major opera companies, and conducted major orchestras. By 1941 three of the ten most highly paid concert performers were African American (Southern 1983). Roland Hayes, an internationally famous tenor, Marian Anderson, the first African American to sing a leading role in the Metropolitan Opera, and Paul Robeson, the most politically committed of the classical stars, not only served as role models for middle-class African American youth but actively supported aspiring musicians and helped open doors for the most talented. Successful conductors and composers such as Florence Price, a 1906 graduate of the New England Conservatory, wrote prize-winning compositions performed by such mainstream orchestras as the Chicago Symphony Orchestra. William Grant Still continues to be widely considered one of the premier American composers of the twentieth century. An alumnus of the Oberlin Conservatory and the New England Conservatory of Music, his compositions blended African American, classical, jazz, and popular genres with a serious music framework. His *Afro-American Symphony* (1930), though not as renowned as Gershwin's *Rhapsody in Blue*, was one of the most successful attempts to incorporate African heritage material into high art music, one of the compositions that inspired Leopold Stokowski to describe Still as "one of our greatest American composers" (Southern 1983). The appreciation of music extended beyond the elite. Small describes African American culture from the slave period forward as imbued with music, a subculture in which it was assumed that everyone is musical; music was not the property of a talented few (Small 1987). In 1819, John F. Watson, a white Methodist minister, marveled at slaves' enthusiasm for music: "I have known in some camp meetings, from 50 to 60 people crowd into one tent, after the public devotions had closed, and there continue the whole night, singing tune after tune (though with occasional episodes of prayer) scarce one of which were in our hymn books" (quoted in Small 1987: 89).

Even before the Civil War, the piano was a symbol of middle-class respectability among both black and white middle classes and continued to be so well into the twentieth century. Although many early jazz and blues singers fit the stereotype of the untutored musician playing only by ear, others, including Louis Armstrong, Sidney Bechet, and Jelly Roll Morton (born Ferdinand Joseph La Menthe), were classically trained. Though the social gap between vernacular music and "serious" music widened among African Americans, as it did among European Americans, the cultural roots of music bridging class divisions had established a solid legacy for subsequent collective action. This wide distribution of musical knowledge and appreciation has sometimes been stereotyped as a natural quality, invidiously demeaning the cultural roots of music and underestimating the work that individuals invest in their talent. The stereotype of musically talented black folks that has pervaded American culture from minstrelsy to hip-hop is thus not entirely the fantasy of racist imaginations. What makes the stereotype racist is the attribution of musical talent to nature, not the observation of musical talent in the black population. If we treat the important role of music in black culture as genetic endowment, not a historical fact, we beg the question of cause and effect. Why has music thrived in black culture and what effect has it had?

Like church choirs, singing groups at colleges and universities formed a relationship between performer and audience different from that of commercial musicians. The singing group symbolized the institution, its members elevated above ordinary students to broadcast the exceptional essence of the institution. Performers and audiences were reminded that music is more than entertainment; it also embodies values and identities. The Fisk Jubilee Singers and similar groups explicitly affirmed that the singers embodied the caliber of their race, not only in the talent in their performance but also in the character of the people. Music was treated as not only the offering of individual singers to an audience but the expression of collectivity, the music of a people. W.E.B. DuBois was moved by the Jubilee singers when they were new: "To me Jubilee Hall seemed ever made of the songs themselves, and its bricks were red with the blood and dust of toil. Out of them rose for me morning, noon, and night, bursts of wonderful melody, full of the voices of my brothers and sisters, full of the voices of the past" (DuBois 1989 [1903]). Half a century later, Candie Anderson (later Carawan), who helped Guy Carawan spread the music throughout the civil rights movement, was also inspired by the music at Fisk. Speaking of her experience as a white student at Fisk, she recalled, "When I got to Nashville and first of all I was in the choir there, which was a completely different experience from being in the choir at Pomona College, I can assure you; the Jubilee singers were part of the choir, but this was the a cappella choir. We began to have mass meetings at church after church in Nashville, and music just took on a whole different kind of life for me, because the music was part of the community and it was building on music that had been in the community for generations, and it just had kind of a power and connection that nothing in my previous experience had ever had" (Carawan and Carawan 2001). Such musical experience could never be achieved with commercial music, no matter how brilliantly composed and performed because it was based on the social relations within which music is practiced.

Not only did Fisk students directly cultivate music in the movement, but Fisk was also instrumental in crystallizing, codifying, and preserving African American music. In addition to the Jubilee Singers, musicologists and sociologists, most notably John W. Work III, collected a wide variety of secular and sacred music, interpreted African American music to white and black audiences, and mediated between "the folk" and "the public." His books included *American Negro Songs* (1998) and *Folk Song of the American Negro* (1969). Nashville was also the home of the American Baptist Seminary, where the members of the Nashville Quartet were students, and Tennessee State University. Matt Jones, from an educated family and kin to Paul Robeson, attended Tennessee State before becoming a SNCC field secretary. At the request of James Forman he joined SNCC Freedom Singers, continuing to perform activist music to raise awareness for such issues as Northern Ireland and South Africa (Seeger and Reiser 1989).

This is not to say that black colleges aspired to steep their students in African American heritage. Most black colleges aimed to culturally incorporate young African Americans into the black middle class, which meant defining traditional culture as backward, ignorant, and uncouth. Most of the cultural education was distinctly framed in white standards—Shakespeare, Melville, and Mozart. The primary exceptions were some of the writers of the Harlem Renaissance and black spirituals. Though nurtured on campuses to present an "acceptable" version of black culture to white audiences, and captured within the confining strictures of conductor-dictated uniformity, spirituals embodied an identifiably black music with an audibly distinct sound outside commercial genres. For the acculturated middle-class African American students, the spirituals sung by the college choirs may have been a stepping-stone into black identity, a music that had been refracted through European aural aesthetics but was still understood as expressing the spirit of the slave heritage.

Although black colleges were primarily oriented toward acculturation into the dominant middle class, at times movement themes were incorporated into university-sponsored cultural presentations. J. P. Cochran, a drama instructor at Atlanta University's Spellman College, directed a production, *Sit Down Train*, mostly written by Julian Bond,[2] that included Georgia Brenda Gibson's takeoff on the well-known Ray Charles hit, "Tell Me What I Say." The new lyrics were direct and to the point: "Oh segregation—it ain't no good! And I won't stop fightin' till integration is mine" (Reagon 1975).

The use of the Ray Charles hit illustrates one of the ways that the movement bridged religious and educational institutions. Whereas the music from the religious roots of the movement were hymns and spirituals, many of the songs from the student culture were secular, especially popular rhythm and blues tunes. Four student activists from the American Baptist Theological Seminary created the Nashville Quartet, which supplied new lyrics to current hits. Little Willie John's "You Better Leave My Kitten Alone" mocked white attitudes as "You Better Leave My Segregation Alone." One of the more popular rewritten hits was "Get Your Rights, Jack," based on Ray Charles's "Hit the Road, Jack." The secular basis of this music was institutional and situational more than a difference in the kinds of people that wrote or sang them. Raised with church music and involved in demonstrations and meetings where hymns like "Amen" were sung collectively, these seminarians chose to perform secular music.

Whereas some of the religious music in the black community, especially spirituals, expressed collective themes, the popular music, which typically addressed individual issues like love and work, often required more extensive adaptation for movement use. Revising popular songs like "Hit the Road, Jack, and don't come back no more" into "Get your rights, Jack, and don't be a 'Tom' no more" parsed easily and spread rapidly throughout the movement. Nonetheless, as Reagon points out, the shift was a matter of changing the relationship between actors and the objects of action while preserving the underlying feel. "Hit the Road, Jack" expresses the sentiments of a lover who has had enough, telling the partner in no uncertain terms that the old relationship is over. "Get Your Rights, Jack" also redefines a relationship, though a social rather than an individual one. Both kinds of songs involved an adaptation of the music from institutions the activists were embedded in, not just the casual appropriation of songs they happened to be familiar with.

The fact that the civil rights movement derived its music from churches and colleges is more than an incidental aspect of its history. The role that the black churches and colleges played as templates for music-making accounted for much of the power that the movement drew from music, helping freedom songs become one of the formidable cultural developments of the mid-twentieth century. The importance of the religious and educational institutional base became evident in the shift to black power. When the movement fractured after the mid-1960s, a new generation of activists without church or black college backgrounds entered the movement with no experience of vernacular musicking. Whites gravitated toward the antiwar, women's, gay rights, and environmental movements while a younger generation of African Americans pushed for black power and identity issues. Many African Americans who in an earlier generation would have enrolled at historically black colleges and universities selected historically white institutions where they pressed for educational reform with non-musical tactics, or they attended metropolitan colleges like Oakland City College where Bobby Seale and Huey Newton met and founded the Black Panther Party.

POLITICAL ROOTS

Churches and schools were institutional templates for vernacular music that created solidarity by doing, but they did not endow music with political meaning or offer a model for social movement ritual. To fully explain how the civil rights movement adopted music as a specifically political activity that signified a boundary between the movement and the opposing establishment requires identifying the genealogical organizational roots of political musicking: who brought musical ritual into the movement and helped develop it as a site of political music-making?

Three interrelated sets of organizations provided the civil rights movement with political music: the Highlander School, unions, and the Communist Party, all of which had inherited musical traditions from the antislavery movement and the IWW, and topical songs from partisan politics. The particular songs, song styles, and repertoire of musical activities were inherited from these three sets of organizations.

The issue addressed here is not just what the musical precedents were but, more important, the concrete relationships through which a musical heritage of movement music was transmitted. It is often noted that many of the freedom songs, including "Solidarity Forever," "We Shall Overcome," and "Which Side Are You On?" were previously union songs (Carawan and Carawan 1963; Denisoff 1971; Eyerman and Jamison 1998; Reagon 1975). But it was not unionists who brought the songs into the movement.

Not only did the religious, educational, and social movement institutions affect the social form that musicking took, but they also contributed particular songs to the civil rights movement. Spirituals and hymns that had evoked otherworldly promises were reworked to galvanize commitment to change in this world. The spiritual "I'm gonna sit at the Welcome Table" easily lent itself to verses such as "I'm gonna sit at Woolworth's lunch counter."[3] The "light" in "This Little Light of Mine" shifted from a spiritual to a political beacon. Some of the union songs used by the Old Left, both at Highlander and in the North, were picked up by the movement. "We Shall Not Be Moved" was one of the most popular songs in both eras, as was "Solidarity Forever." The lyrics of "Which Side Are You On?" are appropriate for nearly any political confrontation and its repeating line, engaging melody, and strong rhythm have made it a perennial sing-along in various movements.

It is well known that the songs of the civil rights movement were inherited from the union songs of the 1930s and 1940s and the music of the African American church. But there has been little systematic comparison of the relative contribution of each. A rough picture of the social roots of the civil rights music can be seen in the songs published in songbooks and anthologies. Of the 280 songs that appeared in 16 civil rights songbooks, 28 percent appeared in at least one book or anthology of union songs while 11 percent had religious content. (See the appendix for methods.) If we identify any songs in three or more of the 16 civil rights collections as part of the movement's canon, there were 28 songs in the canon. Of these, 68 percent, or two-thirds, were found in at least one union collection. The canonical union songs included the best known of the civil rights songs—"Ain't Gonna Let Nobody Turn Me Round," "The Hammer Song," "Oh, Freedom," "We Shall Not Be Moved," "We Shall Overcome," and "Which Side Are You On?" In contrast to the two-thirds of the canonical songs with union roots, only a quarter (25 percent) had any religious roots. Included were many of the most popular songs, including "We Shall Overcome," "This Little Light of Mine," "Wade in the Water," and "Certainly Lord."

These important results indicate that it was not so much the particular songs that were rooted in the black community, but the mode of making music, the social relations in musicking. The canonical songs drawn from the union heritage were similar in form, with short repeatable verses—zipper songs capable of new verses made up on the spot—and strong rhythm that invites clapping. Many of them could be easily lined, with a song leader or group participant initiating a verse that the group could easily pick up and repeat, a call-and-response format well known to people with experience in the black church.

The preponderance of union songs also indicates the importance of mediators who spanned the generations from the Old Left to the civil rights organization, notably Guy Carawan, who inherited Zilphia Horton's union-oriented repertoire and hung around with the remnants of the Old Left in New York, and Pete Seeger, the main link between the People's Songsters and the New Left. These union songs did not magically appear in Birmingham, Nashville, and Albany, but were infused by workshops—especially at Highlander—interpersonal networks, and occasionally records or books.

The song most deeply associated with the movement, "We Shall Overcome," was a religious song popular in black churches, refracted through the southern union movement, shared at the Highlander School, and popularized in the 1960s by Guy Carawan. Originally "I'll Overcome Someday," a hymn written in 1900 by Charles Tindley, it was given a collective meaning as "We Will Overcome" in the southern textile strikes of the late 1920s (Reagon 1975). Occasionally it would be included in union songbooks over the next two decades, but was not widely known. Zilphia Horton slowed the tempo and added new verses. When *People's Songs Bulletin* published "We Will Overcome" in 1948, she wrote, "Its strong emotional appeal and simple dignity never fails [*sic*] to hit people. It sort of stops them cold silent" (Lieberman 1995). It was intermittently recorded by such labor troubadours as Joe Glazer, who learned it from a friend who had picked it up at the Highlander (Glazer 2001). In the late 1940s Pete Seeger learned it at the Highlander and changed the title to the more mellifluous "We *Shall* Overcome." As it spread throughout the civil rights movement, it took on a ritual quality, typically sung with participants gathered in a circle with arms crossed and linked together, people swaying with the flow of the music. A simple, repetitive structure (AAABA) made it easy to learn and improvise new lyrics in the midst of the action. For example, when the Highlander School was raided by the Tennessee state police, as the demonstrators were being led away to the waiting paddy wagons, they began singing the song and someone added, "We are not afraid . . . today," thereafter an often repeated verse. The song's pulsing but relatively slow beat and basic chord structure invited harmonizing, elaboration, and embellishment. Reginald Robinson, a SNCC field secretary, explained that "The tone of our 'We Shall Overcome' is quite different from the way it was in union days. We put more soul in it, a sort of rocking quality, to stir one's inner feeling. You really have to experience it in action to understand the kind of power it has for us. When you get through singing it you could walk over a bed of hot coals, and you wouldn't feel it" (Reagon 1975).

The song has unequivocally been the best-known symbol of the movement, not just its most visible song. Scores of books, records, and visual pieces have taken the title. Rare is a documentary account of the movement that does not include it. Its universal appeal can be attributed not only to its exceptional beauty as a song, its ritual performance at formal gatherings and demonstrations, and its self-conscious promotion by Pete Seeger and the Carawans, but also to its stirring but multivocal message. The obstacle to be overcome is like a Rorschach inkblot, an image that the viewer can see for him- or herself—segregation, racism, capitalism, apathy, sin, hate, or the white race. Who can be against "overcoming"?

The Social Relations of Musicking in the Movement

If music is an activity, not just a thing, the activity of musicking must be consistent with the full set of activities one is doing. Whether the musicking is part of a performance that hermetically isolates non-musical activities, an action in a religious service, a secret revelry in the shower, or a diversion while walking through the city, the social relations in the activity of musicking must be consistent with its larger context. The practice of group singing had a structural and a cultural affinity with the nonviolent strategy of the civil rights movement. Structurally, the tactics of nonviolent civil disobedience included moderate numbers of people publicly disrupting racially segregated activities. In contrast to the large demonstrations such as the March on Washington, which lent themselves to performative music, direct action tactics such as sit-ins or freedom rides ritualistically dramatized situations that patently contradicted core social values. Groups ranging from ten to thirty activists, most of them trained in movement workshops, could readily sing together. Moreover, civil disobedience events were charged with tension, often with a threat of violence and/or arrest. Music could ease the tension and strengthen the sense of community. In her autobiography, *Coming of Age in Mississippi*, Anne Moody recounts an incident like countless others during the early 1960s. After an NAACP-sponsored demonstration at Tougaloo College, two police cars holding arrested students were surrounded by a large hostile crowd. With two policemen locked inside their cars, fearful of what might happen next, someone began to sing "We Shall Overcome," which was immediately taken up by the crowd. When the song ended someone suggested they go to the football stadium for a rally, where more freedom songs were sung and speeches given. In a case like this, the effect was not specifically to incite or mollify the crowd so much as to engage a script of collective action. Singing signaled what kind of collective action was unfolding. With singing, the event was being defined as neither a riot nor a retreat, but as a known type from the broader repertoire of collective action events.

Yet the use of music to signal the type of collective event was not an arbitrary code. Nonviolent civil disobedience is based on a stance of moral rectitude. People who violate laws and disrupt daily life in pursuit of justice evoke a higher authority than legal codes or social mores. The act of singing signifies not only a sense of abstract solidarity but also a moral community, especially in the context of a movement rooted in the Christian church. The moral dimension of singing together was further reinforced in the lyrics, which also explicitly referenced higher moral authority. Freedom song lyrics often articulated such sentiments. From the earliest events of the movement, religious songs expressed the transcendent meaning of what the movement was doing. At the meetings to coordinate the Montgomery Bus Boycott, "Onward Christian Soldiers . . . With the Cross of Jesus" symbolically linked the participants not only to the broader African American religious fabric but to the long lineage of disciples for justice. Another song from Montgomery changed "Old Time Religion" to sing, in part, "We will all stand together / Until we all are free" (Reagon 1975). "We Shall Not Be Moved" gives a visual image of the nonviolent squadrons, holding their ground for the cause of freedom. And, of course, "We Shall Overcome" connotes a transcendent vision, both a prediction and a commitment.

Sit-ins, marching, and civil disobedience with mass arrests facilitate collective music-making. Meetings with speakers, the use of media, support for cultural activism, and hierarchical organizations are more likely to stimulate performer-audience forms of musicking. The civil rights movement's promotion of music-making took root in fertile social ground. The particular repertoire of collective action in the movement tended to bring people together with tight proximity, treacherous environments, and unstructured time. Riding a bus for days through the hostile South was perhaps the ideal setting for collective singing. The Freedom Rides, most of which took place in 1961, included long stretches of relatively empty time, both on the buses and in jail. Intended to focus public attention on segregated transportation and to pressure the federal government to assert its jurisdiction over interstate travel, they set out from Washington, D.C., headed for New Orleans, taking them through the Deep South. When one bus carrying seven black and six white passengers was burned in Anniston, Alabama, and a second faced a mob in Birmingham, they decided it was too dangerous to continue. Veterans of the sit-ins from Nashville then decided to pick up where the others had left off, starting in Birmingham and getting arrested in Jackson, Mississippi, where they were sent to the notorious Parchman Penitentiary. These events gave rise to some of the best-known and most enduring freedom songs of the movement, including "If You Miss Me from the Back of the Bus" and "Freedom's Comin' and It Won't Be Long," an adaption of Harry Belafonte's "The Banana Boat Song" (T. Glazer 1970; Reagon 1975).[4] While in the Hinds County Jail (in Jackson), James Farmer wrote new lyrics for the popular labor song "Which Side Are You On?" raising issues relevant to that movement, redefining the choice of participants from striker versus scab to activist versus racist. The collective nature of the musicking can also be seen in the numerous parodies of familiar tunes that were crafted for a particular event. "Yankee Doodle" was sung as "Freedom Riders came to town / Riding on the railway, / Mississippi locked them up / Said you can't even use Trailways." "On Top of Old Smokey" became

"Way down in Old Parchman." Additionally "The Battle Hymn of the Republic," "Frere Jacques," "Streets of Laredo," and even "Dixie" were rewritten for the occasion (Carawan and Carawan 1963).

When music was planned, the decision to do music and the type of music used were considered with a strategic eye toward the goals of collective action. The earliest sit-ins were conducted in silence, the organizers reasoning that they did not want to unnecessarily provoke hostile crowds or give an excuse for arrest. If they were sitting at a counter asking for service, they wanted to make it unambiguous that they were denied service because of their race. When they were arrested and jailed, the songs would begin. Many published recollections of the movement express warm nostalgia for the music-making in the jails, where long hours could be filled with the sounds of freedom. "Oh Pritchett, Oh Kelly" about the Albany chief of police and mayor, was sung after the marchers were jailed and told not to sing. The lyrics included self-referential lines such as "I hear God's children prayin' in jail" and "Bail's gettin' higher" (Carawan and Carawan 1963).

Reagon notes that the experiences in the Hinds County Jail and Mississippi State Prison, popularly known as the Parchman Farm, inspired one of the greatest creative bursts of the movement, searing into the movement's culture both the music inherited from the labor movement, including "Which Side Are You On?," "We Shall Not Be Moved," and "We Shall Overcome," as well as adapted R&B and gospel songs from the Nashville singers. She tells of a song, "Dogs," created by James Bevel and Bernard Lafayette, that questioned the segregation system: "Dog, Dog, Dog, Dog / My dog loves your dog and your dog loves my dog / Then why can't we sit under the apple tree." Cordell Reagon recalled, "In Mississippi it was sung more than anything else because everybody or about 85 percent of the people in jail were Southerners. We had shared the same experience and we knew what that song was about" (Reagon 1975).[5]

MUSIC AT THE GRASSROOTS

The participants in the Freedom Rides of 1961 became a core network of the civil rights movement. Many of the students did not return to school that fall, becoming full-time organizers for CORE, SCLC, and especially SNCC, for whom sixteen became field secretaries. SNCC in those years focused on voter registration and direct action in the Deep South, especially in small communities. Freedom songs became a basic tool of organizing: "No mass meeting could be successfully carried off without songs led by strong leaders" (Reagon 1975). Field secretaries often were song leaders, training local residents to the skill, teaching them techniques that enhanced participation and the growing repertoire of movement music.

Albany, Georgia, was one such place. A small town in the black belt of south Georgia and home of Albany State College, itself a target of black activism in that period, Albany was the site of one of the first attempts to dismantle the entire institutional spectrum of segregation. Morris (1984) describes structures and events in that historic Albany movement. Following the successful bus boycott in Montgomery and the flush of activism in the sit-down protests that had radiated across the Deep South, SNCC decided to send two field secretaries, Cordell Reagon and Charles Sherrod, to the small Georgia town where college students had begun to mobilize the community. Unlike earlier attempts at desegregation, the Albany movement aspired to coordinate an assault on segregation as a system from public transportation to schools, restaurants, and swimming pools. Both direct action against these institutions and the political clout of voter registration would be used to reinforce each other.

Initially mobilizing students and ministers, the movement soon coalesced in the formation of an organization named the Albany Movement, whose affiliates included groups as diverse as the Ministerial Alliance, the Federation of Women's Clubs, the Negro Voters' League, the Criterion Club, and the NAACP along with its Youth Council. Led by a young doctor new to the city, the Albany Movement was hardly a hotbed of radicalism. But relative to the southern racial codes of conduct, the actions were militant indeed. As Morris explains it, the transformative impetus was a new attitude toward incarceration. Previously the threat of jail was one of the most powerful weapons in the white arsenal, since jail time not only disqualified a person for many jobs but also was a social stigma in the black community. Reagon and Sherrod, by their example, showed that jail was neither as fearsome nor as shameful as commonly assumed. As the community mobilized, the confrontation unfolded. Blacks and their allies demonstrated at segregated facilities and were arrested, only to be replaced by others. As the jails filled, demonstrators were released to make room for more, only to return to the demonstrations. The city was paralyzed for about a month, forcing the white leadership to enter into negotiations with the Albany Movement, an unprecedented concession.

At this point, the events became more complicated. The movement was wearing down from fatigue and lack of resources to defend the demonstrators. The white sheriff, citing national publicity that had won widespread sympathy for protesters violently beaten in other southern cities, tactically decided to refrain from violence, depriving the movement of a moral advantage they had capitalized on in places like Birmingham and Montgomery. With hundreds in jail without legal assistance and a loss of momentum, the head of the Albany Movement, against the opposition of SNCC and other members of the coalition, invited Dr. Martin Luther King Jr. After his arrival, he, along with his associate Ralph Abernathy, the head of the local organization, and two hundred others were arrested. With King pledging to stay in jail until their demands for desegregation were met, the local authorities agreed to release the protesters and return all bond money, desegregate bus facilities immediately, and create a permanent commission to desegregate other facilities. Once King agreed and left the city, the white leadership reneged. He returned the following year, and was again jailed, vowing to escalate the conflict. But a federal injunction banned picketing, congregating, or marching in the streets. Because King felt that the federal judiciary was a necessary ally, he refused to violate the injunction, mortally weakening the Albany activists and ensuring their short-term failure. Although desegregation did not come to Albany until later, the movement there was a model for the civil rights movement throughout the South, both as an inspiration of the possibilities for full social mobilization and for the tactical lessons they learned (Morris 1984).

One of the most influential features of the Albany experience was the music. "Albany was the first singing movement. Every song that entered Albany was changed in the process, for here the whole community sang—a community dominantly influenced by the older church traditions" (Dunson 1965). Cordell Reagon, a song leader in the Nashville Student Movement, and Charles Sherrod brought a consciousness of music as an inherent part of what a movement does. Among their first activities was teaching the "proper" way to sing "We Shall Overcome," not the warmed-over hymn that local residents had adopted after seeing it sung on television. People were to cross their arms, join hands, and change "I'll Overcome" to "*We* Shall Overcome." The song was becoming a ritual that defined membership in the movement. Bernice Johnson, an Albany native who later married Cordell Reagon, explains that the song also was developed in new ways there. Black churches in that region were musically highly developed, with sophisticated skill at choral singing. Members knew how to take melodies, elaborate the melodic structure, embellish the harmonies, complicate the rhythms, and embroider the lyrics with phrases like "I know that" or "I do believe" (Reagon 1975).

Meetings create a context for different kinds of musicking, ranging from musicians playing or singing for passive audiences to leaders prompting collective singing to spontaneous audience-initiated song. Organizing in Albany involved many meetings to educate people about what had happened in other communities, train them in the techniques of nonviolent civil disobedience, build individual courage, forge a sense of community, and respond to arrests. Which type of music is found at any particular meeting is a function of the cultural practices of the audience, the musical history of the particular collectivity, and the immediate dynamics of the meeting. The meetings of the civil rights movement provided ample opportunities for collective musicking. The cultural practices of the participants included experiences in religious services, especially the southern black church. When large groups of people gathered in a ritual manner, music was a familiar expression of unity. In Albany people knew they were part of a musical movement, and the immediate dynamics of meetings were arranged to include collective musicking. As people gathered in churches or church-like halls, song leaders intentionally encouraged participation, and song sheets were often distributed. Such a setting also influenced the selection of songs to sing since some felt it inappropriate to sing rock and roll type songs like "Dogs" or "You Better Leave Segregation Alone" in church.

It was at mass meetings that the call-and-response format was most congruent with social setting. A mass meeting is structured around single (or occasionally group) leaders speaking to a relatively undifferentiated audience. Communication from the audience to the speaker is typically thin in its information—affirmation through applause or crisp phrases such as "Amen, brother," disaffection through booing or heckling. The call-and-response format allows a leader to initiate and coordinate musicking in large groups. When audiences are musically savvy, they can elaborate the response, adding harmony, countermelodies, and variations. Many songs have simple verses that can be made up on the spot. Several radiant call-and-response songs came from Albany. "Sing Till the Power of the Lord Comes Down" was an old song familiar to many residents but imbued with new meaning. The leader offers, "Now let us sing," holding the last note while the audience replies, "Sing till the power of the Lord comes down." After repeating that interaction, the leader and audience exchange shorter phrases, setting up a verse that ends "I will overcome some day." Another call-and-response song was adapted as "I'm on My Way to the Freedom Land," whose lyrics connect the biblical image of deliverance, the African American flight from slavery, and the contemporary promise of freedom. Similar emancipatory imagery was found in another song popular in Albany, "Oh, Freedom." Its simple repetitive lyric, forceful message, easy adaptability to many situations, and ready harmonization helped make it one of the most widely used songs of the movement. Because verses could be quickly picked up by singers, leadership could pass through the group on each verse, with singers introducing a verse signaling to the group that they wanted to lead. Similarly the well-known freedom song "Ain't Gonna Let Nobody Turn Me Round" was adapted to local conditions. After a federal judge issued an injunction against demonstrations in Albany, participants at a mass meeting began singing "Ain't Gonna Let No Injunction Turn Me Round." Other verses attested that singers would not be turned around by "Nobody," "Chief Pritchett," "Jail House," and "Mayor Kelly." After Albany, it became one of the most popular freedom songs, a powerful song, with a strong, clappable beat, repetitious lyrics, and ready adaptability for local circumstances (Reagon 1975).

Albany, like the Freedom Rides before, not only was important as a site where activists and community members creatively elaborated modes of musicking in collective action but quickly became a model for others to follow. The concept of "freedom songs" was becoming crystallized as a particular type of song and way of doing music. Promoting music as a project of the civil rights movement, activists and their chroniclers in the mass media actively publicized the musicking of the Albany movement. As a result freedom songs became more solidly ensconced as a fundamental item of the repertoire of collective action for the movement and came to represent its spirit in the mainstream media and, presumably, the public mind.

Three sets of actors were especially important for publicizing the musical dimension of the movement. The mainstream media, most notably Robert Shelton, folk music critic of the *New York Times*, constructed a media frame of heroic songsters for freedom. Guy and Candie Carawan, whose entrepreneurial energy had been so important in incubating music in the movement, celebrated Albany as a model for emulation. And movement leaders decided to capitalize on the publicity by creating a performing troupe to carry the message and raise funds in northern cities. Though short-lived, the period from 1962 to 1965 saw the belated culmination of the second folk music project, as blacks and whites self-consciously used music to bridge racial boundaries.

Just as the Albany students had learned "We Shall Overcome" from watching television, media coverage of Albany fused a symbolic association between the civil rights movement and music. Prior to the Albany events, the phrase "freedom songs" had not appeared in the *New York Times* (at least not enough to be noted in its online index). Robert Shelton visited Albany and wrote several articles about music that appeared in northern and national publications. His front-page article, "Songs a Weapon in Rights Battle," fashioned the media frame on the music of the movement, treating freedom songs as both fad and inspiration. Ignoring the union roots of many of the songs, he opened the article highlighting its black religious and folk roots: "Negro folk music, which has been singing of the promised land since the days of slavery, has become a vital force in the attempt to fulfill that promise in the South today." Specifically citing Albany, this text made the politics inseparable from the music: "A new tributary of 'freedom songs,' bold words set to old melodies, is making the deep river of Negro protest in song run faster." Music was described as powerful, a means of bringing people together and giving them hope, an essential ingredient of the movement. SNCC worker Charles Jones was quoted, "There could have been no Albany Movement without music. . . . We could not have communicated with the masses of people without music" (Shelton 1962). Shelton's most pervasive theme was that the music fortified their courage and alleviated their fear. The spirit in the music was seen as so persuasive that it sometimes softened the hostility of southern police and jailers. Albany police chief Pritchett recalled that guards were singing and humming with the prisoners. But the spirit is framed as most definitely African American, rooted in slave spirituals, passed on through the black church, and resonating with specifically black cultural practices such as congregational participation in religious services. Apparently to legitimize the music with the northern audience of the *New York Times*, the article concluded by noting that its influence was being felt beyond the South, exemplified by a young singer-songwriter named Bob Dylan, who had written a song about "patience and dignity" called "Blowin' in the Wind."

Shelton also helped canonize "We Shall Overcome" as the anthem of the movement. Though the song had already become the most often sung and probably the most revered song in the movement, it had not yet become the singular symbol of the movement to northern whites when Shelton penned an entire article on it for the *New York Times*.[6] "Rights Song Has Own History of Integration" recounted the history of how the song passed from African American to white singers and back again. Unusual for a newspaper, the article included a facsimile of the music itself, even with guitar chords, no doubt helping spread knowledge of the song even further.

The *New York Times* coverage was indicative of the faddish tenor of social movements more generally, quickly rising and falling in sync with what were considered newsworthy trends (Gitlin 1979). Stories about freedom songs spanned the middle years of the decade, jumping from five stories in 1962 to 31 the following year, falling slightly and peaking in 1965 at 49. The following year they carried only 16 stories, none of them by Robert Shelton, though 50 of his 408 stories managed to mention Bob Dylan. Of the 16 stories on freedom songs, only one was by a critic of any sort and that concerned the actor Godfrey Cambridge. By 1967, stories about freedom songs virtually disappeared with only six articles, none by critics of any sort.[7]

While non-activist writers such as Shelton can only tangentially be considered part of the folk song project of the civil rights movement, activists such as the Carawans promoted musicking in and beyond the movement. The Carawans' compilation *We Shall Overcome! Songs of the Southern Freedom Movement* was published by Moses Asch and Irwin Silber's Oak Publications while the memories of Albany were still fresh in the minds of anyone who paid attention to the news.[8] With songs grouped by phases of the movement, beginning with "Sit-ins" and moving on to "Freedom Rides," "Albany, Georgia" earned its own subject heading, including some of the songs now remembered as classics of the era, including "Ain't Gonna Let Nobody Turn Me Round" and "Oh, Freedom." The Congress of Racial Equality (CORE) also distributed a songbook and a stereophonic album of sit-in songs (Congress of Racial Equality 1962).

Albany spawned one of the best-known and most historic attempts to reach out from the movement to a broader audience, the SNCC Freedom Singers. When the civil rights activists did perform music away from direct action or mobilization activities such as meetings, it was primarily for fund-raising. After the Albany campaign died down, SNCC field organizer Cordell Reagon got the support of executive director James Foreman to form a singing group that could tour the North and raise funds. Joined by Rutha Harris, Bernice Johnson, and Charles Neblett, the SNCC Freedom Singers took to the road to spread freedom songs and gather money. Their first attempt at Chicago's McCormick Place was a financial disaster. A month later, in November 1962, the group held a more successful joint concert with Pete Seeger, then toured the country in a Buick station wagon to raise funds and educate northerners about the movement. They were supposed to be paid $10 per week, but more often it was $20 per month, and they often accepted free room and board where they performed (Dunson 1965). Bernice Johnson Reagon attributes part of their appeal to the folk music revival. This is an important point that must be put into historical context. While a cappella style was very folk-like in virtually all definitions of the term, the topical songs, soulful harmonies, and lively rhythms would have been understood as folk music only after the People's Songsters had broadened and politicized the genre a generation before. Being identified as a folk group certainly made the SNCC Freedom Singers more appealing to white audiences. With their success in fund-raising growing to the point that they were raising four to five thousand dollars a week, they increasingly defined their mission as outreach, frequently appearing on college campuses and at folk festivals (Seeger and Reiser 1989). Altogether they netted $45,000–50,000 (Dunson 1965). Mahalia Jackson, commenting on a Carnegie Hall recital in the *New York Times*, described them as "the ablest performing group to come out of what is perhaps the most spontaneous and widespread singing movement in the world today" (Reagon 1975: 141). As personnel turned over, they were joined by Matthew Jones, the secretary of SNCC and a jazz songwriter. Without abandoning the older participatory freedom songs, they added contemporary songs by Jones, Bob Dylan, Tom Paxton, Gil Turner, and even the Beatles. But the Freedom Singers were not just reaching out to white audiences. They also helped SNCC forge links with other black organizations. For example, Malcolm X invited them, along with Fannie Lou Hamer, to sing at a meeting of the Organization of Afro-American Unity in New York in 1964 (Carson 1981).

When the tactics of the movement changed, so did the mode of music-making. In Albany, where direct action tactics and mass arrests predominated, the singing was congregational. A year later in Birmingham, a coordinated attempt to end racial segregation in all public arenas, including schools, public accommodations, and public service jobs, sought to learn from the Albany experience, including their use of music. But the larger scale of the movement and the city fostered a more performative kind of music, especially in mass meetings. With three thousand people crowding into venues such as the Sixteenth Street Baptist Church, the halls rang with the sounds of "We Shall Overcome" and "Ain't Gonna Let Nobody Turn Me Round" (Seeger and Reiser 1989). The Birmingham Movement Choir, led by Carlton Reese, drew on the strong gospel tradition of the region to infuse all the activities with music (Reagon 1975). In addition to the choir, meetings included parodies of old songs, such as Ernie Marrs's takeoff of "Down in the Valley" as "Bull Connor's Jail," which began "Down in Alabama, in the land of Jim Crow / There is a place where lots of folks go." Guy Carawan came with his repertoire of old and new songs, bringing songs from Nashville, Albany, and other sites of the movement. And as in other places, old hymns and spirituals were revitalized as freedom songs. Newer gospel songs could also be used. Carlton Reese's composition "Ninety-Nine and a Half [percent] Won't Do" pulsed to a strong beat, "Oh, Lord, I'm runnin'" as the audience responded "Lord, I'm running,' tryin' to make a hundred." When the audience roared "Five, ten" the leader countered, "No, no," counting on up, back and forth, to "I got to make a hundred" (Carawan and Carawan 1963). One of the most historical events, a children's march, invoked another kind of sonic tactic—silence. Instructed by one of the leaders, Rev. Fred Shuttlesworth, to refrain from singing or chanting lest they provoke retaliation, they were to sing only after being arrested. When the crowd was met with fire hoses and one thousand were arrested in view of national news cameras, the images shocked and appalled northern white audiences. The Birmingham jails became filled and surrounded with song as those inside were joined by those marching in support outside (Seeger and Reiser 1989).

In contrast to the multifaceted Albany and Birmingham campaigns, the movement in the majority-black Alabama town of Selma focused on voter registration. But severe repression led to an escalation and broadening of goals. The local authorities responded to the voter registration drive with many arrests and unprovoked violence, including the death of local resident Jimmy Lee Jackson, who was shot by police while trying to defend his mother as they were beating her. After a plan to march to Birmingham was repelled by police, people began to gather from around the country. When Jim Reeb, a white Unitarian minister from Boston, was killed by a policeman who cracked his skull with a club, the press coverage made Selma a national focal point of the movement. Three thousand marchers set out for the Alabama capital of Montgomery, fifty miles away, though only three hundred were allowed on the narrow, two-lane highway.

There is probably no better context for making music than a long march. Mass meetings are mainly for speeches and dialogue; freedom rides have groups of people thrown together for long periods of empty time, but also allow individual activities like reading. Marching not only gathers large groups for long periods but invites the entraining coordination of chants and songs. Thus the Selma march displayed to a nation the movement at its most musical. Pete Seeger described the musicking thus: "The songwriters and the young singers of Selma were creating one great song after another right before our eyes. One woman saw me trying to notate a melody and said, smiling, 'Don't you know you can't write down a freedom song?' All I can do is repeat what my father once told me: 'A folk song in a book is like a photograph of a bird in flight'" (Seeger and Reiser 1989). In its musicking, the microcosm of the freedom march is not unlike that of soldiers training, though one is framed in the discipline of nonviolence and the other intended to foster the discipline of violence. McNeill (1995) has described the bodily entrainment, what he calls "muscular bonding," roused by chanting and singing together in such diverse settings as training soldiers, dancing, calisthenics, and marching bands. So it is not surprising that the deft song leaders on the march would fashion new musical styles for the long march. As Len Chandler describes, "We were marching along and some old army guys were calling cadence: 'Hup hip, to your left, to your left, right left.' I started thinking it wasn't quite right. The word 'right' is affirmative. We want to get to Montgomery, right? So I said, 'Why don't we accent on the right foot?' And so 'a-right, right,' and then we could put together verses, and the answers from the group would be 'right, right.' And so I started singing" (Seeger and Reiser 1989).

On reaching Montgomery, a very different kind of music happened at the rally, with folk stars Harry Belafonte, Joan Baez, and Peter, Paul and Mary performing. Activist and singer Len Chandler led the group in "Do What the Spirit Say Do" and "Which Side Are You On." Later that night Viola Gregg Luizzo, a white mother of five and wife of a Detroit teamster, was killed by Klansmen after driving a group of marchers back to Selma. President Johnson went on television to calm the nation and announce his Voting Rights Act of 1965, ending his speech with the phrase, "We Shall Overcome." In retrospect, we can see that this gesture of reconciliation and co-optation both signaled the success and heralded the decline of the movement. The goal of the movement had been to end the system of legal segregation, which rested on the disenfranchisement of African Americans. Selma was the crest of the wave that goaded the federal government to begin dismantling de jure racism. When major legislation was passed the immediate goals were fulfilled, leaving the next steps on the road to racial justice to be contested within the movement. Those later steps would rarely be marked by music. As Bernice Johnson Reagon describes it, "To a large extent, President Lyndon B. Johnson's use of 'We Shall Overcome' ended the effectiveness of that song as the theme song of the civil rights movement. The 'Selma to Montgomery' March and its after effects signaled a turning point in the ideology, tactics, and direction of Black struggles. Musically, this trend was reflected by the decline in the use of songs and singing as an integral part of the continuing struggle" (Reagon 1975). Thus 1965 marked the culmination, success, and end of the classic civil rights movement.

The classic civil rights movement was also the apex of music in social movements. As such, it is important to specify what the music did in the movement. Rather than convert new recruits or persuade the skeptical, music induced participation through the act of doing it. Not the meaning, but the motion, people singing together, brought people together. Freedom songs, like the larger movement, were moral statements, but they did not propagate unfamiliar ideas or seek to convert the uninformed. Racial prejudice and discrimination were patently out of step with core American values, and the movement's rhetoric was aimed more at highlighting obvious injustice and fortifying the disenfranchised than convincing anyone that change was desirable. Thus the movement had little need to educate the naive or persuade the skeptical. Music was more a vehicle of cementing solidarity among the committed than of recruiting new adherents. Education was strategic and tactical, convincing people that change was possible and most feasible through nonviolent collective action. Music contributed to this by reinforcing the social relations in which it was made, embodying solidarity by the act of doing music together. That is not to say that the movement lacked propaganda songs or individual performers. White performers singing to white audiences were especially important in highlighting what many Americans had conveniently ignored. Pete Seeger, Joan Baez, Peter, Paul, and Mary, even Bob Dylan vocalized a consciousness that the times were indeed changing.[9]

Insofar as the lyrics of the freedom songs had any impact, it would have been very general. Most of the songs evoked only diffuse commitments to freedom, victory, or the movement. Of the 45 songs in Carawan and Carawan's canonic collection, *We Shall Overcome*, nearly all evoked commitment but generally, as in the title song, more inclusive than specific. Other songs were equally general—"Ain't Gonna Let Nobody Turn Me Round," "Certainly Lord," or "Keep Your Eyes on the Prize." Fewer than half (19 of 45) made any reference to segregation, desegregation, integration, or Jim Crow, and several of them were only passing references such as the line "I'm gonna sit at Woolworth's lunch counter" in "I'm Gonna Sit at the Welcome Table." Only nine made any reference to race as an issue, or specific black or white races, with inclusive sentiments, as in "Blacks and whites together," a verse of "We Shall Not Be Moved." The rare references to white racism or white racists mentioned specific individuals or groups. "Get Your Rights, Jack," for example, describes as a racist Mississippi governor Ross Barnett. But there is nothing that challenges or prods the many white liberals who had signed on to the movement.

The greater lyrical attention to diffuse commitments and the movement itself rather than specific references to desegregation or race may also reflect the fact that there was a greater need for empowerment than conversion. Few southern blacks would have doubted the injustice of the system they lived under. Black compliance since the end of slavery depended more on the violence of repression and lack of alternatives than any false consciousness about the benevolence of the Jim Crow social order. Yet movements of defiance require not only a sense of injustice but the collective will to defy authority. The work of the movement throughout the South was that of galvanizing the previously compliant residents with the black and white outsiders into a disciplined collectivity that could meet, march, picket, and survive jail without turning on each other or striking back violently. Polletta describes how the meetings in many southern communities helped empower people to participate in decision-making and emboldened them to act for their rights. She quotes Bob Moses about his work in Mississippi: "People learned to stand up and speak. . . . The meeting itself, or the meetings, became the tools. . . . People were feeling themselves out, learning how to use words to articulate what they wanted and needed. In these meetings, they were taking the first step toward gaining control over their lives, by making demands on themselves" (quoted in Polletta 2002: 69–70). For many, singing in the group would be a prelude to speaking up.

While earlier generations of left-wing activists had found it politically meaningful to embrace topical music under the umbrella of "folk" music, few African American leaders or musicians framed the music of the civil rights movement as "folk." Bernice Johnson Reagon, for example, in her dissertation about music in the movement frames her analysis in terms of oral history and folklore but does not refer to the music as folk music. She places the music in two categories, group participation songs and topical songs (Reagon 1975). Both types are explicitly linked with African American culture. Group participation songs derive from the call-and-response practices of slave music and later spirituals, topical songs from the nineteenth-century anti-slavery movement (as well as the Wobblies and later unionists).

The Carawans used the term "folk," but only as one of many types of songs that freedom songs drew on, along with hymns, spirituals, gospel songs, popular music, and union songs. In the introduction to *We Shall Overcome*, they note that many educated blacks had learned to scorn African American folk culture, but the term carries no special meaning, analytical weight, or emotional charge (Carawan and Carawan 1963).

THE MUSICAL INFRASTRUCTURE OF THE CIVIL RIGHTS MOVEMENT

The musical infrastructure of the civil rights movement fell between the highly organized, disciplined, formalized model of the Old Left and the reliance on the commercialized popular culture pattern of the later New Left. Using the churches and schools as musical training grounds, enhanced by Old Left veterans and commercial singers, the music spread by networks and diffusion facilitated by a core of musician-activists such as Bernice Johnson Reagon and Guy Carawan.

In contrast to People's Songs, Inc., which served as a booking agency for leftist musicians and an educational apparatus for topical songs, or Folkways, which distributed the music of Leadbelly and Woody Guthrie, the civil rights movement had no single focal point of music. The closest analogy is the Highlander School, but it operated through workshops and networking more than direct organizing of chapters or canonizing music in songbooks.

Indicative of the difference was the reliance on the mimeograph rather than the printing press. People's Songs published a regular magazine and two collections of songs. Printing magazines and books is a more centralized process, takes more resources, has a longer turnaround time, and elicits a firmer image of finality. A mimeograph is more decentralized—by the late 1950s virtually all churches had them, along with many schools and moderately well-organized social movement organizations. Unlike printing, which required professional typesetting, anyone could cut a mimeograph stencil in a typewriter or etch it by hand. When printed, a mimeographed document seemed temporary, a disposable paper distributed for a particular event. Activists would have been used to getting mimeographed church bulletins, school examinations, meeting fliers, or commercial advertisements. Moreover, the mimeograph was a wholly local medium. Because only hundreds of pages could be printed from any one stencil, it was used primarily for modest-sized events. National organizations with large constituencies typically depended on printing presses to dispense their literature.

Singing at movement events was typically orchestrated by song leaders and frequently coordinated by mimeographed song sheets, usually with words only. The mimeographed song sheet made it possible to bring songs from other events, allowing quick diffusion throughout the South, either through informal networks or facilitated by musical activists like Guy Carawan. Verses could be added for the occasion or words changed, such as James Farmer's adaption of the classic "We Shall Not Be Moved," which added verses like "They say in Hinds County, no neutrals have they met / You're either for the Freedom Ride or you 'tom' for Ross Barnett" (Carawan and Carawan 1990). As mimeographed sheets, songs could be easily distributed, and when the events were over, they could be discarded, passed on to others, or saved for memory.

Thus, the freedom songs had their own folk process, taking songs, passing them from hand to hand, adapting them for new circumstances. Some of their songs were inherited from the society at large—consider all of the songs that have been derived from "John Brown's Body," from the "Battle Hymn of the Republic" to "Solidarity Forever" to "Move on Over," written by Len Chandler in 1963. Many were updated from spirituals and other African American music, such as the way "I'm Gonna Sit at the Welcome Table" took on a new meaning at the lunch counter sit-ins. Songs from the movement's left-wing tradition were similarly reshaped. For example, "Keep Your Eyes on the Prize" is credited in one printed collection as "Words adapted by Alice Wine & the Civil Rights Movement" (Carawan and Carawan 1990). Others were composed anew, often with little memory of composer or adapter.

The performative music also required infrastructure. Many SNCC organizers could not separate their musical activities from their organizing activities. Cordell Reagon was a highly talented performer who toured with the SNCC Freedom Singers and also worked as a SNCC field organizer in Albany, Georgia. Others, such as Len Chandler, were primarily performers. A rally could include both performers and group singing. At the historic March on Washington for Jobs and Freedom in 1963, the official program included mostly performers known more for their musical gifts than their political involvement. Marian Anderson sang the national anthem, the Eva Jessye Choir performed "Freedom Is the Thing We're Talking About," and Mahalia Jackson offered "I Been 'Buked and I Been

Scorned." The official program ended with the crowd of nearly a quarter million people joining together in "We Shall Overcome." As a coalition of diverse organizations including the NAACP, the National Urban League, CORE, SNCC, the National Catholic Conference for Interracial Justice, the National Council of Churches, the United Auto Workers (UAW), and SCLC under the leadership of A. Philip Randolph, the program represented the most mainstream group of speakers and performers. Singers with strong political associations or who were seen primarily as entertainers were not included. Anderson, Jessye, and Jackson were more in the tradition of the Fisk Jubilee Singers and William Grant Still than Leadbelly or Paul Robeson.

The pre-march rally was a different story, with a much broader political and musical range of performers, including Joan Baez ("Oh, Freedom"), Peter, Paul and Mary ("Blowin' in the Wind"), Odetta (four songs), Bob Dylan ("Only a Pawn in Their Game"), and Pete Seeger ("The Hammer Song"), priming the participants to sing collectively along the route, reliving the spirit of sit-ins, freedom rides, and local demonstrations (Reagon 1975). Here were the stars, each of them sincere in their commitment to the cause, performing as stars. Significantly, most of the performers at the 1963 pre-march were white. It was the white singers who had the greater commercial success as political musicians, who could get the media attention, and who sang more of the popular hits that the crowd would be familiar with. The SNCC Freedom Singers had been added as an afterthought, brought to Washington on a chartered plane sponsored by Harry Belafonte.

CONCLUSION

The cultural success of a social movement can mean many things to many people. For many scholars and writers, cultural success means changing the popular culture that most people are exposed to through the mass media. A movement is successful when television, radio, recording companies, newspapers, and popular magazines cover the movement or its cultural products. The popular culture approach to social movement music is as much a methodological orientation as a substantive one. Regardless of what scholars may say in the abstract, if their evidence is drawn primarily from mass media sources, they are implicitly adopting a popular culture perspective. Eyerman and Jamison, for example, programmatically emphasize the importance of the social context in which music is produced, but much of their evidence is drawn from mass media sources. Thus Bob Dylan and Jimi Hendrix overshadow Bernice Reagon

Johnson or the SNCC Freedom Singers. Musical activists like Guy Cara-wan are mentioned only in passing. They have very little discussion of demonstrations or other movement events except broad generalizations and a few references to the 1965 March on Washington, which featured commercially successful performers (Eyerman and Jamison 1998).

From the popular culture perspective, the folk revival of the 1950s and 1960s began with the Kingston Trio's hit single "Tom Dooley" and ended with Bob Dylan's conversion to the electric guitar, and expressed middle-class youth alienation and longing for authenticity (Cantwell 1998). The media are treated not just as informants about a reality accessible through a variety of sources but as verification of what is real or important. Bluestein (1994) makes the link between popular culture and folk culture explicit, arguing that in a society dominated by mass media, there is no folk culture as traditionally understood—the noncommercial, entirely in-digenous, unwritten, and anonymous music and lore. Popular culture and folk culture have become synthesized, he argues, into "poplore." The mu-sical styles and forms played on commercial outlets have their roots in indigenous music. And it is popular music that ordinary people embrace as their own; when they make music in non-institutionalized settings—outside churches, choirs, and bands—they take the music they know from commercial outlets and apply the folk process. They adapt the music and pass it along by oral as well as written means. While Bluestein underesti-mates the extent to which people embrace noncommercial forms of music, he does not conflate vernacular or indigenous music and popular music. Despite misjudging the ability of people to make music outside the parameters of mass media, at least he problematizes the relationship. Un-like the commercial folk revival that made icons out of Bob Dylan and Joan Baez, the freedom songs fit the more traditional use of folk music as music embedded in noncommercial social relationships. Insofar as social movement success depends on collective action—actions of an indigenous collectivity in which people are fortified against the established powers by their reliance on each other—the freedom songs were an indispensable part of America's archetypical movement.

What lessons can be drawn? The civil rights movement suggests broader generalizations for the kinds of movements that use music as part of their collective action. Movements that adopt decentralized structures conduct activities together in unstructured time, and produce moral statements about obvious grievances that are more likely to include rituals of soli-darity than are movements that are hierarchical, conduct highly structured activities, or educate potential recruits about the existence of grievances.

The civil rights movement was a decentralized movement. The sit-ins, freedom rides, bus boycotts, and other activities emerged in local settings by local initiative and diffused by imitation among loosely structured networks. National organizations such as SNCC, SCLC, and CORE were primarily federations of autonomous, local chapters, and served to facilitate the diffusion of events, enhance communication among activists, and provide spokespersons for the national media. Music spread throughout the movement in the same way as activities—through diffusion and informal networks, with national organizations playing a coordinating role more than directing by fiat. The Highlander School's workshops and traveling song leaders and the SNCC Freedom Singers' inspirational model of emulation worked at the ground level to foster musicking among the rank and file. As the sit-ins, freedom rides, and bus boycotts spread throughout the South, music spread with them.

The national organization of SNCC, for example, was indifferent to music, at least in its public stance. Its national newsletter had virtually nothing about music as a feature of collective action. The few references to the SNCC Freedom Singers focused more on their fund-raising function than on their musical contribution to the movement. Thus the organizational basis for music was a broad grassroots network, rooted in the African American religious community and cultivated by a few important individuals.

Insofar as music is a social activity that can be embedded within a variety of social relationships, the particular social relations music takes reflect the social context in which it is set. Whether a social movement does music within a performer-audience setting or a collective musicking setting depends both on the strategic commitment of the leaders and the kinds of social relationships that pervade the movement. Different kinds of collective action constitute different kinds of social relationships that can foster different kinds of music-making.

While the civil rights movement has served as a template for virtually all American left-wing movements (and many right-wing movements) since the 1960s, its musical practices have been adopted only as a faint echo. The women's movement, antiwar movement, ecology movement, gay rights movement, anti-globalists, and even the animal rights movement have widely adopted the core repertoire of collective action. Activists organize demonstrations to focus public attention on the plight of an aggrieved population; the most highly committed risk arrest and bodily harm to disrupt the normal operation of an oppressive institution; governments are implored to intercede between oppressed and oppressors; demands are framed in terms of traditional American values, especially equality and rights. Yet music, which was at the heart of the ritual life of the civil rights movement, has been primarily an afterthought if it appears at all. Demonstrations typically include chanting, often trite and unimag-

CHAPTER NINE

A Movement Splintered

After 1965, the American left splintered and its music changed in both social context and content. The civil rights movement endorsed the rallying cry of "Black Power," asserting independence from white allies who turned to other issues in which they could take the role of the aggrieved. But where other American movements sprang from the root of the civil rights movement, there was a consequential difference between the primogenitor and the offspring. A united movement to eradicate the most glaring and immediate instance of injustice in American society evolved into a loose and sometimes contentious amalgam of constituent-based movements. In the early 1960s, the well-publicized movement for desegregation in the rural South had existed alongside the militant urban black movement, which was largely beyond the gaze of the white media. By the end of the decade militants had transformed several of the best-known civil rights organizations, and white activists had turned their attention to student rights, women's rights, gay rights, and especially the war in Vietnam. Militant urban movements that spurned integration replaced the nonviolent civil rights movement in the mainstream.

Most accounts of racial movements in the 1960s describe a shift in goals from integration to Black Power. This is only half true. Two of the best-known organizations, SNCC and CORE, did adopt the rhetoric of Black Power. But even there the shift was as much turnover in generations as a change of philosophy. Though the mainstream media and many historical accounts track the lineage from the civil rights movement to black militancy, groups such as the Black Panther Party (BPP) were organizationally distinct and based in different social circumstances. Urban movements such as the BPP may have originally drawn some inspiration from the southern rural civil rights movement, but they faced different problems with different ideologies and strategies.[1] The media shifted its attention from the rural South where desegregation was the first order of business to the urban North and West where deep inequality belied the nominally equal legal system. After the reporters packed up and left the Deep South and the cameras showed Black Panthers toting guns in Oakland in place of Bull Connor beating up protesters, the people who lived in small southern towns continued to tangle with local authorities over the right to vote, have their votes counted, and run for office while keeping pressure on the remaining bastions of segregation such as the University of Alabama (Andrews 2004; Gaillard 2004; Lehman 2006; Mills 1993; Payne 1995).

With the splintering of the original movement, the social organization of musicking reverted from participation to performing-listening. Neither the black militants nor the predominantly white New Left included very much music in collective action. For both, music, when included in movement activities, was more often sung or led by performers and less often a matter of participants doing music collectively. Like the Old Left, the politics of music became more a matter of its content than its context. Whereas any song sung as part of the collective action of the civil rights movement had been political, whether "We Shall Overcome" or "Michael Rowed the Boat Ashore," the political nature of music in the late 1960s became measured by the militancy or politics of the lyrics. James Brown's "Say It Loud—I'm Black and I'm Proud" was the music embraced by the Black Panther Party while the Jefferson Airplane's "Gotta Have a Revolution" became the music of the white New Left. In both the black and white movements, political commentary in both mainstream and activist media embraced political content in music and maintained that it prodded commitment. But it was increasingly a spectator sport. Bob Dylan, once an occasional visitor to civil rights events in the South, became a media superstar, an iconic figure like the Beatles. On the basis of politically ambiguous hits such as "Blowin' in the Wind" or "The Times They Are A-Changing" and a few hard-hitting songs like "Masters of War" the media anointed Dylan as the musical voice of his generation.

This is not to say that music with political content was not a part of movement culture. On the discursive level, soul music and funk were cited to affirm black pride while "protest songs" fortified a sense of historical mission for whites. Marvin Gaye's "What's Going On?" and Phil Ochs's "There But for Fortune" were listened to and discussed as activists worked to make sense of an alternate vision of what society could be. But it is important to emphasize that the shift was not just a change from one set of symbolic icons to another but a change in the social organization of music in the movement. Instead of an activity that the movement shared, music became a commodity that movement members consumed and that movement intellectuals discussed. Music became less an inherent part of the collective action itself and more an activity that activists enjoyed in their leisure. Insofar as music was important to the left of the late 1960s, it was primarily symbolic in terms of what it stood for rather than what it did or what people did with it. Since later movements spun off the civil rights movement, it is puzzling why they did not include the movement's mode of musicking among the many features they borrowed.

Three factors help explain why music receded from a form of collective activity to a form of consumption. First, the nature of collective action changed from activities that required medium-sized organizational meetings and long periods of congregation to activities of two sorts, neither of which fostered much musicking. Militant confrontations with authorities such as the Black Panthers wielding guns at the Oakland courthouse and anti-draft activists blocking a troop train escalated confrontation beyond what was feasible for music. Similarly, huge demonstrations with thousands of participants such as the massive antiwar demonstrations often featured performers, some of whom led group singing.

Second, contrary to popular media images, white New Left activists typically conceptualized politics and culture as dissonant to each other. While the mass media lumped activists and hippies together, the two groups tended to distance themselves from each other. Activists generally saw the hippies as hedonistic, frivolous, and apolitical, identifying cultural critiques of the system with the hippies. Hippie types tended to see the activists as straight, moralistic, and heavy-handed. Although the New Left had a formidable infrastructure of media organizations, including underground newspapers, film groups, and radio groups, it did very little to promote its own music, conceding the making of music to commercial recording companies. Unlike the Old Left of the 1930s and 1940s, they had little commitment to doing culture themselves, choosing to focus on the more "serious" side of political activism. Only the women's movement, which proclaimed the unity of the personal and political, produced their own culture.

Third, the understanding that Americans had of folk music as someone else's music hampered groups engaged in constituency-based social movements from "discovering" their own music. While identity-politics movements later in the 1970s often affirmed their folk roots while making claims of selfhood, often groups in the late 1960s had no basis for any such claims. The freedom songs of the civil rights movement no longer appealed to black or white offshoots. Blacks generally associated freedom songs with the earlier integrationist phase of the movement, with the ideals of nonviolent civil disobedience, and with moderate leaders such as Martin Luther King Jr. White activists deferred cultural proprietary rights to African Americans and would have been loath to "steal" the music from them. Insofar as they had a music of their own, it was rock and roll, which was embedded in commercial, not movement, institutions.

The Discursive and Organizational Basis of Black Music

Though a full analysis of the reasons why the civil rights movement splintered in the late 1960s is beyond the scope of this work, the basic facts are well-known. As the movement moved into the second half of the decade, militant rhetoric and confrontational tactics reflected escalating dissatisfaction with the principles and tactics of nonviolent civil disobedience. In 1966 several major civil rights organizations endorsed the principles of "Black Power" and articulated stronger sentiments of black nationalism. The inclusive goal of racial integration was displaced by the more divisive goal of Black Power, as young radicals vexed both moderate organizations like the SCLC and NAACP and white participants.

The greater emphasis on Black Power, black identity, and racial pride might have implied a stronger motivation for blacks to own their own music. Discursively, that did indeed happen. The period of the late 1960s is generally remembered as a period when popular music expressed intense black pride and fortified militant social movements. Aretha Franklin, James Brown, and even the manicured sounds of Motown were embraced as signifying blackness, as music that belonged to the black race.

"Soul" became a trope that captured a particularly black way of talking, walking, dressing, dancing, and making music. As Ward summarizes it, "Soul music ultimately served as a sort of cultural cement for the mass of black Americans in much the same way that freedom songs served to unite and fortify those at the forefront of civil rights activities in the South" (1998: 202). While there may be an affinity between the racial pride found in soul music and political action, the relationship is more discursive than concrete. Though activists may have personally embraced manifestly "black" music and a few African American musicians may have made overtly political overtures, neither was the movement very musical nor the musicians very activist. While some of the biggest stars in soul or rhythm and blues released songs that overtly affirmed black pride, they were not deeply involved in political organizations or even very political as individuals. James Brown's "Say It Loud—I'm Black and I'm Proud" was just another hit along with "I Got You (I Feel Good)" and "Get Up (I Feel Like Being a) Sex Machine." Similarly Sam Cooke's "A Change Is Gonna Come" was less popular at the time than his "You Send Me" and "Wonderful World." Both were performers, not activists. Observers, both at the time and retrospectively, have claimed a symbolic bond between the movement and the music. But the connection is easily overstated, as in Ogbar's unsupported claim that "One of the most pervasive influences of the Black Power movement was the popular music of the era" (2004: 100). However, the concrete linkages on the ground are rarely spelled out. For example, music critic Larry Neal discusses the rise of the Black Panther Party and the strong racial identity found in popular music, establishing their relationship by referring to them in consecutive passages. The links between them are assumed in the amorphous public culture, where political movements and music were both "voices." Neal framed it this way: "As the organized struggles for African American empowerment intensified and subsequently migrated North to urban centers, the black popular music tradition began to convey the urgency of its historical moment" (1999: 61). He ignores the fact that the movements themselves were abandoning music, except to occasionally use musical events for fund-raising and to participate in discourse about music. Music was no longer a part of their collective action.

But the discourse about music did not match what black movements were doing with music. One reason that the movements for racial justice abandoned music was that the social basis of the movement shifted. Several important civil rights organizations experienced extensive turnovers in leadership and membership, leading to new goals and tactics. SNCC's full-time staff in 1965 grew to more than two hundred (Payne 1995) while CORE was managing a million-dollar budget (Meier and Rudwick 1973). SNCC in particular moved from its base of southern, rural, religiously raised students to northern, urban, secular activists. Its roots in black churches and black colleges where music enveloped collectivity were increasingly irrelevant. Other organizations also lost touch with the social base in the South. CORE, a national organization with its basis in the North, which had jumped on the opportunity to participate in the southern civil rights movement, reverted to community organizations and urban anti-poverty efforts (Meier and Rudwick 1973). Even SCLC was turning its attention to northern cities and the issue of poverty.

As the movement sought to progress beyond its integrationist phase, the SNCC freedom songs became a rhetorical symbol of accommodation instead of defiance. When Lyndon Johnson used the phrase "We Shall Overcome" in promoting his voting rights bill, the movement's musical symbol of unity was sapped of its potency (Reagon 1975). The readers of *Sing Out!* may not have agreed but they would have understood why Julius Lester would write in its pages in 1966, "Now it is over. The days of singing freedom songs and the days of combating bullets and billy clubs with Love. 'We Shall Overcome' (and we have overcome our blindness) sounds old, outdated and can enter the pantheon" (1966: 22). Or Malcolm X could invite Fannie Lou Hamer and the SNCC Freedom Singers to a meeting and lecture, "I'm not one who goes for 'We Shall Overcome.' I just don't believe we're going to overcome, singing. If you're going to get yourself a .45 and start singing 'We Shall Overcome,' I'm with you. But I'm not for singing that doesn't at the same time tell you how to get something to use after you get through singing" (quoted in Mills 1993: 144).

Unfortunately, the vitality of movement music declined when it could have contributed the most to solidarity. In the first half of the decade, there was a broad consensus in the movement over goals and tactics.

Virtually all movement participants agreed that nonviolent civil disobedience could achieve racial integration. But in the second half of the decade there was consensus on neither. McAdam's analysis showed that from 1961 to 1965, participants appealed for integration in 56 percent of all movement-initiated events. But from 1966 to 1970, even though integration was an issue more often than anything else, in only 12 percent of events did claimants cite it. It was an issue just barely more often (11 percent) than internal dissent. "Other" and "Too vague to be coded" accounted for over 40 percent of all events (McAdam 1982: 187). Because music can be multivocal in its message, music could have solidified activists when the movement's goals were becoming contested. But it did not. The white establishment was a common enemy and groups gave lip service to solidarity among progressive movements, even as bitter infighting among leaders undermined joint actions. The kinds of coalitions that had sponsored such activities as the Mississippi Freedom Summer and the Selma march were less and less tenable. Within the major organizations, there was increasing tension, especially at the national level. Mary King reflected on the deterioration of personal relationships: "Until late 1965 it was possible to disagree in SNCC and yet not feel reviled, because the underlying bonds were strong. Personal hostility was now being expressed. This did not feel like SNCC to me. It was foreign—dissonant" (quoted in Payne 1995: 368). So even if activists had been inclined to sing together, there were fewer opportunities to do so.

While Black Power organizations made some use of music, primarily to raise money or recruit members, it was always peripheral to their main activities. The Black Panther Party released an album by Elaine Brown, *Seize the Time*, in 1969 and later organized the Lumpen, a group of professional musicians who wrote some of their own material, recorded an album, and performed an hourlong choreographed show at clubs, community centers, and colleges in the San Francisco Bay area, with one national tour. Like the SNCC organizers who led freedom songs in the rural South, they were fully active party members (Torrance 2007). After several members were arrested for singing while selling the BPP newspaper, a report declared that "The singing of revolutionary songs is a very effective form of education for Black people, because they relate very heavily to music" (quoted in Ward 1998: 413). But the Ministry of Information made it clear that music was only a vehicle for a message. "We like the beat of James Brown, we say the Temptations sound great, but if we try to relate what they are saying to our conditions we'd end up in a ball of confusion. . . . So now when we hear the Temptations song, 'Old Man River,' tell them to keep the sound, but to borrow the words from the Lumpen and sing 'Old Pig Nixon'" (quoted in Ward 1998: 414). Like the Communist Party of the 1930s and 1940s, music was primarily a propaganda weapon. It was never an integral part of their collective action, whether organizing free breakfasts for poor children or brandishing weapons on the steps of the state capitol.

While organizations like the Black Panther Party used culture as a propaganda weapon to fortify their political and economic programs, cultural nationalists treated culture as the core of the struggle for racial justice. Asserting that liberation could be achieved through cultural empowerment, they promoted an African-inspired aesthetic to free blacks from the culture of slavery. New styles of art, music, literature, dress, and demeanor became fashionable, as adherents adopted African names and donned dashikis. A new holiday, Kwanzaa, was introduced as a winter holiday with African-inspired symbols and ritual. While African music was seen as a source of pride, cultural nationalists tended to reject the music and dance enjoyed by African Americans most of the time. Some intellectuals like playwright-activist Ronald Milner embraced jazz because it was the "blackest" form of music; John Coltrane was "a man who through his saxophone before your eyes and ears, completely annihilates every single western influence" (quoted in Ward 1998: 409). Imamu Amin Baraka called for art that would completely get away from white people. Maulana Ron Karenga, one of the most visible cultural nationalists, disavowed the blues as invalid because "they teach resignation, in a word acceptance of reality—and we have come to change reality" (quoted in Werner 1999: 119).

POLITICS VERSUS CULTURE IN THE WHITE NEW LEFT

Even though the white New Left was at least as much a spin-off of the civil rights movement as the urban black movement, initiated by movement veterans, adopting its basic repertoire of collective action, incorporating its rhetoric of rights, and for many even its style of speech and dress, the predominantly white New Left abandoned the earlier mode of musicking.

Given that imitation is a major mechanism guiding the selection of social movement strategies and tactics (Strang and Soule 1998; Tilly 2004b), especially when leaders of new movements come from similar movement backgrounds, we might expect new movements to imitate the civil rights movement's musical practices. The New Left's failure to include musicking in its collective action was especially puzzling, given its formidable media infrastructure. Two factors were important. The organizational context of the infrastructure, notably the underground newspapers, oriented them more toward mass popular culture than movement-based culture. And a festering tension between the movement's cultural and political segments, known to each other as hippies and politicos, discouraged cultural practices within collective action activities.

It is not surprising that as members of the baby boom generation staked out a chunk of the political landscape, some people, both inside and outside the movement, would associate the music of the generation with the culture of the movement. But the leaders of the movement were divided and often ambivalent. Although the mass media, both then and now, lumped the countercultural displays of the hippies with the radical political movements against the war, university administrations, and patriarchy, participants in both were mutually suspicious of each other. At the risk of polarizing what was a complex interplay of political and cultural meanings or drawing too broad a categorical distinction between what was more accurately a continuum from political to cultural poles, we can characterize two types of activists. The politicos viewed hippies as hedonistic, lazy, and often narcissistic, adding up to a conclusion that they were undisciplined or, in the language of the time, "too fucking flaky." Even when politicos shared the hippie critique of mainstream America as commercialized, plastic, and alienating, they felt that a deeper quality of life required overturning the structures of power, not just adopting alternative lifestyles. Todd Gitlin, an early politico and founder of SDS, criticized those who claimed that a rock concert was a political event.

> Dots on the periphery of a large circle, with the music at the center. Dots on the periphery don't establish relations with each other. They relate to the center. A crowd of dots. Dots will not take responsibility for each other. Dots will crawl over each other to get a better piece of the real action—the "really heavy music." Dots with long hair and dots stoned on who knows what—still dots. Dots invented by the elite of mass communications. Dots turned on not to each other, not to the communal possibilities, but to the big prize, the easy ticket, the "good trip." (quoted in Armstrong 1981: 178)

Gitlin here is applying a sociological analysis similar to that in this book, examining the social relationships in which music is being done. Members of an audience are being described as unconnected dots, linking only to the performer. But he goes beyond a concern with atomization to impute their state of mind: an aspiration for the "good trip." Journalist Jack Newfield, writing in *The Nation*, expressed the tension between politicos and hippies more directly: "They [hippies] lack the energy, stability and private pain to serve as 'the new proletariat' that some of the New Left perceive them to be. Bananas, incense and pointing love rays toward the Pentagon have nothing to do with redeeming America. . . . The whole hippie contagion seems to be a recoil from the idea of politics itself; it is not merely apolitical but anti-political" (1967: 809).

Hippies tended to view politicos as puritanical, zealous, and short-sighted. In their eyes, political revolution would be fruitless; the politicos were just "too fucking heavy!" Real change, they felt, had to come from challenging the system by transcending it, abandoning traditional values, renouncing hypocrisy, and living now the lifestyle of freedom and fulfillment. Political movements without free cultural expression only mirrored the bureaucratic, alienated system they were trying to change.

These tensions were played out in the diverse and often chaotic setting of movement cultural organizations, which could have fostered musicking within collective action but more often validated commercial culture or neglected music altogether. Popular retrospective accounts of the 1960s, and even some academic ones, often neglect the formidable cultural infrastructure that the New Left mobilized. There were serious organizations that emerged in virtually all media, including print, visual, and auditory. The most visible were underground newspapers, which ranged from simple mimeographed handouts struggling to survive for weeks or months to glossy, multisectioned moneymakers that thrived beyond the era. The University of Oregon Knight Library has a microfilm collection of "Underground Newspapers" published between 1965 and 1971 with over 460 papers.[2] There was *Ain't I a Woman* from Iowa City, Iowa, the *Albany (NY) Liberator*, the *Boston Free Press*, *Los Muertos Hablan* from El Paso, Texas, the Spokane, Washington, *Provincial Press*, and the St. Louis *Xanadu*, just to name a few. Underground newspapers sprouted up in prisons, military posts, and high schools, some to expire as a seedling and some to blossom.

The underground newspapers were simultaneously a representative voice of the nebulous tumult known as "the sixties" and autonomous participants in the movement to which other activists were responding. More than anything else, casual activists, journalists, and too often historical chroniclers have taken the underground press as their eye on the movement. It is primarily from them that the image of the New Left as a musical movement arose. It is from the underground papers, filtered through the media mainstream, that the images of SDS marching to the beat of rock and roll and Bob Dylan capturing the spirit of a generation became a part of the collective memory. But the underground papers constructed a very particular connection of music to politics that reflected their structural position vis-à-vis the music world and the political part of the movement. They could readily imagine a unity of politics and music because both were floating in their imagination. The world of music and the political movement were easier to harmonize in the discursive venue of the underground papers than were the strained relationships of hippies and politicos. As journalists, underground news people could mix and match any symbolic material as a hybrid, declaring that politics were musical and music was political, constrained only by others in the discursive field. So the first issue of Detroit's *Fifth Estate* could carry a lead story on Bob Dylan and dedicate the issue to an antiwar activist who burned himself to death outside the office of the secretary of defense, symbolically marrying commercial performative music to politics (Hippler 1992; Tilly 2004b). While there is no reason to believe that the journalists who ran the underground newspapers were less than genuinely sincere in their politics and commitment to music, there was also a structural factor that reinforced the union of a particular political agenda and a particular mode of musicking. Newspapers require concrete resources. While a few such as the *Black Panther Party* could eke by from sales, most depended on advertising, either from personal ads, which many eschewed because of the high number of sexual inquiries, or counterculture capitalism, especially record companies.[3] Thus could Columbia Records in 1968 widely publish an advertisement boasting that "The Man Can't Bust Our Music" (Armstrong 1981; Peck 1985). Morris Baumstein, advertiser for CBS Records Division, explained the affinity between his company and the underground papers: "The underground press is probably the least professional effort in publishing. But they are a highly logical medium for us. The people who read the papers are the ones who include music as essential to their way of life. It is simply a part of their bag" (quoted in Lloyd Ellis 1971: 115). But this intimate relation between the underground papers and large corporations also reinforced many activists' suspicion of culture. Hippies and the counterculture, including their music, were seen as eroding discipline, easily co-opted, and unserious—in a word, flaky.

While underground newspapers shared a structural position dependent on advertisers and participated in the same discursive field, they varied along the political-cultural continuum. Some stalwart political newspapers eschewed hippies while other countercultural newspapers expressed contempt for heavy-handed political movements. Participants' retrospective accounts often recall the tension between political and cultural types. A few managed to embrace both. Sally Gabb described her experience with the Atlanta *Great Speckled Bird*: "The early issues of the Bird reflected the student politics of its founders: the civil rights fervor of white supporters; the growing outrage at the war in Vietnam; the connection between discrimination, economic oppression, and war through history and in the present. As Bird staffers, we always prided ourselves on expressing both 'alternative lifestyles' (we were indeed . . . and proudly . . . 'hippies') and our independent New Left politics" (1992: 44). But the balance was always unstable, as recounted by Ed Falien about a Minneapolis newspaper he was involved in: "Two strains always coexisted in the page and on the staff of *Hundred Flowers*: the political and the cultural. They didn't always rest easily, and eventually they were the reason we fell apart. I was one who wanted to publish stories about resistance struggles, and some of the others wanted to publish photos of themselves with LOVE written on their foreheads. We did both. The result was a bit schizophrenic but, in the early days, our differences were our twin pillars of strength" (1992: 309). So as a group they aspired to cover the war in Vietnam along with the movement against it, give favorable coverage to minority movements, challenge racism, sexism, and imperialism, while at the same time reviewing rock and roll, extolling psychedelic drugs, and snubbing their noses at the uptight mainstream.

This tension between culture and politics existed on two levels.[4] At the level of meaning, the love, peace, drugs, and sex of those who reveled in culture grated with the conflict, discipline, and rationality of the political types. The politicos' suspicion of the hippies' "flakiness" and the hippies' impatience with the politicos' "heavy" seriousness permeated the decade's imagery, language, and ideals. But the level of meaning was plastic enough to permit some convergence. Both tendencies shared a common adversary—the "establishment," "system," or "status quo." It was the same police who broke up political demonstrations and conducted drug busts, the same universities that enforced curfews and conducted research for the Pentagon, the same parents who condemned premarital sex and supported the war in Vietnam. But ultimately the "Turn On, Tune In, Drop Out" culture of the hippies increasingly clashed with the confrontational politics of the left.

The second level was organizational. Though it is beyond the scope of this work to conduct a systematic study, an impressionistic examination suggests that underground papers with links to SDS or other political organizations were more political while those founded and sustained by journalists tended toward the cultural end of the spectrum. The Jackson, Mississippi, *Kudzu*, for example, was founded by David Doggett, an organizer for the Southern Student Organizing Committee. While they certainly covered sex, drugs, and rock and roll, they were very self-conscious about politics, especially the place of the South (Doggett 1992).

The conflict between the politicos and hippies was especially vivid in the organization that tried to speak for and to all the underground newspapers. Liberation News Service (LNS) was founded in 1967 by Marshall Bloom and Raymond Mungo, a couple of college journalists excommunicated from the College Press Service. From offices in Washington and New York, twice a week they sent out packets to underground newspapers with much of the content drawn from their member newspapers. Harvey Wasserman, who typed rock lyrics in the margins of the pages, gives a flavor of the style: "The news service was colorful, lively, obscene, and funny. Feature stories included demonstration scorecards, exposés of the insidious tentacles of foreign and domestic imperialism, caricatures of official buffoonery both local and national, denunciations of drug laws, true tales of military insubordination, and long tomes of righteous doctrine" (1992: 52). But the content was heavily political and the organization eventually fractured in the 1970s along the cultural-political divide. Bloom and Mungo hijacked the equipment and for a year issued their own heavily cultural LNS from a farm in Massachusetts. Afterward, Lloyd Ellis reported "much discontent with the Service because of its devotion to SDS-oriented politics and confrontation strategy that is not consistent with the philosophies of all the undergrounds" (1971: 110). Not only did many of the staff keep an ongoing relationship with SDS, but the organization was able to secure funding from influential supporters such as political journalists I. F. Stone, Jack Newfield, and Nat Hentoff, who along with radical lawyer William Kunstler published an appeal for funds in the *New York Review of Books* (Stone et al. 1972). With independent funding, they were less dependent on the full panoply of culturally and politically oriented underground papers.

While the ease of paper publications made the underground newspapers the most fully developed part of the media infrastructure, activists formed organizations in other media. The largest film group was Newsreel. With loosely affiliated branches in New York, San Francisco, Detroit, Boston, Kansas, Los Angeles, Vermont, and Atlanta, Newsreel collectives produced and distributed films on third-world issues, racism, sexism, university issues, movement events, and work. A few of the groups still exist. But they did little on music, arts, literature, or drama (Armstrong 1981).

There was even a glossy monthly, *Ramparts* magazine, with feature articles, color photos, and well-known authors, the movement's equivalent to *Harpers* or *Atlantic Monthly*. Founded by a benefactor as a voice for liberal Catholic laypeople, it became an outlet for mainstream journalists to reach a broad left-wing audience. For example, *New York Times* reporter Seymour Hirsch, unable to get his employer to print stories about the massacre of innocent Vietnamese civilians at My Lai, distributed the story through the Dispatch News Service. *Ramparts* picked up the story and published it with a photo, later widely circulated as one of the most memorable and searing posters of the decade, of a country road littered with bodies, many of them small children, and overlaid with the words, "And babies?" on top and "And babies" at the bottom.[5] Such articles pumped the circulation to as high as 250,000. Eldridge Cleaver, later known for his vivid memoir *Soul on Ice* and as the 1968 presidential candidate for the Peace and Freedom Party, became senior editor in 1966. Other editors included Robert Scheer, later a liberal syndicated columnist for the *Los Angeles Times*, and born-again paleo-conservative writer David Horowitz.

The organization that had perhaps the greatest aptitude for distributing musical material was Radio Free People (RFP).[6] RFP was a collective of about a dozen people founded in a Brooklyn apartment in 1966, where it operated for a few years until building a small but professional recording studio in Manhattan. Their primary activity was producing and distributing radio programs to New Left organizations and independent radio stations. Their underlying conception of media eschewed "mass" media in favor of media-based organizing tools. Rather than produce programs on abstract topics such as "imperialism" that might radicalize individuals listening in isolated settings, they worked with specific organizations, including the Black Panthers, women's movements, and Vietnam Veterans Against the War. Aiming less at the solitary individual, they produced programs solidifying the commitment of members and facilitating collective reflection. Though the organization was never as well known nationally as Newsreel or as visible as underground papers, it was an important component of the New Left's media infrastructure and tied into the social networks of the media organizations. And because of its small size and good luck in the chemistry among personalities, it was never hobbled by the fractious ideological disputes that struck many movement organizations.

Although it produced a few tapes of poetry, most notably by Marge Piercy and Diane DiPrima, a few scripted documentaries, and a handful of musical tapes, most of its programs were "talking heads." Programs included "Interview with Angela Davis," "Paul Goodman on Compulsory Education," "Seize the Time: The Panther Manifesto" (issued from jail by the Panther 21), "Free Our Sisters, Free Ourselves!" "Letters from POWs," "The Farm Workers Union: An Emancipation Proclamation," "Bay Gio Hoa Binh" (from the Winter Soldier Investigation where 150 Vietnam veterans testified about atrocities they committed or witnessed), and "Bernadette Devlin: Class Struggle in Northern Ireland." Their catalog at one point listed nearly 100 programs available for purchase on reel-to-reel or cassette tape.

Yet Radio Free People missed an opportunity to foster a richer musical life for the movement. They had the hardware to record individuals and small ensembles but only occasionally did so. First and perhaps most important, they saw themselves more as serving the movement than directing. If other New Left organizations had done more musicking, RFP would have happily documented it for distribution. In this, the failure of RFP to distribute music reflected the lack of music in the movement. Second, they never aspired to mass distribution of anything. Their own facility consisted primarily of a half dozen reel-to-reel recorders that could copy one program at a time. They contracted larger-scale cassette recordings of some of their more popular programs but still mailed them by hand. Given their commitment to collectivity, they would have been reluctant to contract out broader distribution. As long as they were distributing primarily to organizations and radio stations, the small-scale setup worked efficiently and smoothly. Third, its members shared the left's general suspicion of cultural politics. Although several were individually drawn to art, literature, and music, collectively they were committed to "serious" politics.

The music that RFP did distribute can easily be categorized between "our music" and "their music," that is, between music that brings people together under a common identity and music that builds empathetic support and political solidarity for a group that includes neither the singer nor the listener. Their 1973–74 catalog included eight programs of songs, of which only one cannot be easily distinguished as one type or the other. "Our music" songs were all by women singers. *Beverly Grant: Chain Reaction* and *Ruthie Gorton: This Bird Is Learning How to Fly* included songs of feminist consciousness. Interestingly, Gorton had a second tape of "their" music, described in the catalog as songs of solidarity with Irish, Vietnamese, African American, and African liberation movements. Other tapes of solidarity included Will Street singing Appalachian folk songs, *Quilapayun* (Chilean singers), and *Loi Ca Giai Phong: Liberation Songs from North Vietnam*. Though the performers were playing or singing their own music, most American listeners would have heard it as the music of others. The only ambiguous tape was *The Red Star Singers in Concert*, described as "music which relates to what we feel are real conflicts in our lives and those of other people."

Although RFP aspired to create tools for specific organizations, the music tapes were performed by free-floating musicians, some of whom certainly were active in organizations but none of whom was identified with any affiliation. Thus the music was political by virtue of its content rather than its context. Even Will Street, singing songs of his native Appalachia, was billed as singing about miners' struggles, the Vietnam War, and the problems of veterans, Indians, and the hypocrisy of his hometown. Only the music of oppressed groups—Chilean Indians and Vietnamese—could stand on its own without an explicit political message, though each included songs of struggle as well as traditional folk music.

Given their experience in erecting a cultural infrastructure, it is not surprising that veterans of the Old Left built organizations for distributing music during the era of the New Left. *Sing Out!*, the successor to *People's Songs Bulletin*, rode the crest of the folk revival wave and continued to publish some topical songs. Although it tilted to the left while regularly covering political singers and reprinting songs with political lyrics, it was clearly a magazine about folk music that happened to have a political slant more than a political magazine that included music. That role was taken up by *Broadside*, a magazine created in 1962 and edited by former Communist Party members Gordon Friesen and Sis Cunningham. Singer-songwriter Malvina Reynolds, with support from Pete Seeger, had the idea to distribute songs too radical for the mainstream press and too new for *Sing Out!* The idea was as much to stimulate people to write topical songs as to distribute existing songs. Several of the founders aspired to spark the kinds of topical songs regularly coming out of Britain (Dunson 1965). Implicitly distinguishing themselves from *Sing Out!*, their first issue explained that "*Broadside* may never publish a song that could be called a 'folk song.' But let us remember that many of our best folk songs were topical songs at their inception" (quoted in R. Cohen 2000: 11). People gathered monthly in Friesen and Cunningham's New York apartment to sing into a microphone so songs could be transcribed and printed on a mimeograph machine abandoned by the American Labor Party. Early participants included Phil Ochs, Tom Paxton, Len Chandler, Bonnie Dobson, Peter LaFarge, Mark Spoelstra, and Bob Dylan, whose "Blowin' in the Wind" was first distributed in its pages. Other notable songs found in its pages included Ochs's "Links on the Chain," Paxton's "What Did You Learn in School Today?," Janis Ian's "Society's Child," Pete Seeger's "Hard Rain's A-Gonna Fall," Nina Simone's "Mississippi Goddam," Malvina Reynolds's "Little Boxes," and Rev. F. D. Kirkpatrick and Jim Collier's "Burn, Baby, Burn." Folkways began to distribute collections of *Broadside* recordings, and many of their songs found their way to commercial release or widely distributed cover versions by such stars as Joan Baez and Peter, Paul, and Mary. The New York group inspired other clusters of topical singers to pop up as *Broadsides* groups around the country. There was enough interest in topical songwriting to hold a workshop in 1964 that included former People's Songster Barbara Dane, Phil Ochs, Tom Paxton, Bernice Johnson Reagon, Len Chandler, Pete Seeger, Buffy Sainte-Marie, Jack Elliott, and Julius Lester (R. Cohen 2000). Always struggling to survive, the editors decided in the early 1970s to become more radical and lost the support of some of their liberal supporters though the magazine was able to hang on until 1988. A commemorative book and CD collection was released by the Smithsonian Institution in 2000.

Just as Old Leftists founded *Broadside* to publish music to the left of *Sing Out!*, two People's Songs veterans founded a record company during the 1960s to the left of Folkways. Irwin Silber and Barbara Dane's contribution to the cultural infrastructure included Paredon Records. Over the next decade and a half, they released over fifty records capturing music of liberation and leftist movements around the world, including

Vietnam, Chile, Angola, and Cuba. While much of the music carried a political message, its main political significance lay in the affiliations of its performers. Though never visible in the mainstream media, Paredon infused a radical internationalism into the American left. It, too, was later purchased by the Smithsonian, which now distributes many of its releases.

Even when the left press gathered to coordinate and exchange experiences, the tension between the politicos and the hippies surfaced. A 1970 Alternative Media Conference at Goddard College in rural Vermont brought together all the groups identifying with the nebulous theme. A New York coalition that included the Committee to Defend the Panther 21, Newsreel, Radio Free People, *The Guardian*, Liberation News Service, Media Women, and *The Rat* constructed a packet of mostly political publications with a cover page titled "Whose Alternative Media" illustrated by the RCA Victor logo of a dog listening to a gramophone with its familiar caption, "His Master's Voice." Implicitly rebutting the belief that media could transform society merely by presenting countercultural content, they asserted that "All media are political. The same forces control the media that control all other institutions. True alternative media do not undermine the people's culture by making the culture a commodity. True alternative media undermine the institutions of oppression." The sponsoring groups in the coalition were all themselves media organizations that created their own content and for the most part carried on active relationships with direct action groups. Their statement fused the political content with the organizational form. The language used terms like "struggle," "forces," "commodity," "oppression," and "the people," not "culture," "freedom," "liberate," or "love." Throughout the four days of the conference, the conflict between politicos was just one of several conflicts that riveted the sessions—men versus women, homosexuals versus straights, electronic media versus print media, even New Yorkers versus non–New Yorkers.

FROM DOING TO PERFORMING AND LISTENING

This quick survey shows that in the New Left, culture, especially music, was seen more as a form of consumption than of participation. The primary social axis was between performers and listeners, a paradigm taken from mass culture. Even when culture was understood to represent a new lifestyle, a criticism of mainstream America, and a radical transformation, the politics were expressed in the content more than the context. The political activity around music was one of signification more than collective action. Music was more important for the New Left, both the political and cultural strains, as a discursive world of semiotic codes. Discussion focused more on what bands and music signified than what music did. Music was treated as a "statement" typically fashioned by critics and debated by spectators. The symbolism of whether music or musicians were radical or establishment, authentic or sellout, black or white, swirled through the discursive field.

That is not to say that the New Left was oblivious to the social relations of music but that the issue remained primarily at the discursive level. Radical critics frequently went beyond the music itself to the social relations within which the music was exchanged—business. Michael Lydon wrote in *Ramparts* that "From the start, rock has been commercial in its very essence. An American creation on the level of the hamburger or the billboard, it was never an art form that just happened to make money, nor a commercial undertaking that sometimes became art. Its art was synonymous with its business" (1969: 21). He did not dispute the talent of the musicians or the pleasure of their entertainment, only the claim that they had any political impact. An anonymous article in the Washington, D.C., underground newspaper *Quicksilver Times* also addressed the fundamental conflict between "our groovy 'alternate' subculture" and corporate capitalism. The article distributed by LNS not only reiterated the common complaint that capitalists were getting rich off the movement but also lamented the social distance between performer and audience when musicians become stars. Unlike the pervasive aesthetically oriented criticism in the underground press, an article in *Quicksilver Times* went beyond denunciation to advocate that the movement take back control: "As a first step toward revolutionary music, let's decentralize the music that we have, make it real on the local level" ("Cultural Capitalizers" 1969: 15). At the other end of the spectrum, some saw music as an engine of revolution, not just for its lyrics but also for the social relations it engenders. John Sinclair, head of Michigan's White Panther Party, proclaimed that "Music is revolution . . . because it is immediate, total, fast-changing and on-going. . . . At its best music works to free people on all levels, and a rock-and-roll band is a working model of postrevolutionary life" (quoted in Peck 1985: 172).

The debates over whether particular music or musicians were radical or whether music itself served capitalism more than it undermined the system belied concurrence on the New Left's approach to music. Both sides made discourse the terrain upon which music was approached in the New Left. Music was more akin to a sound track of the 1960s than a marching song for the movement. A sound track tunes in spectators to the emotional overtones of what they are viewing; a marching song synchronizes collective activity. Because the New Left abandoned control over doing music to the commercial sector, it could never be more than a sound track. There is a certain irony in this. As the movement drifted from the issue of race toward the war and the universities, the music drifted from folk and freedom songs to rock and roll. Though historically an amalgam of African American rhythm and blues and white southern country music, rock and roll genuinely belonged to white youth, at least in terms of content and consumer power. Perhaps for the first time in American history, a generation could claim a genre as truly "our" music. Reproached by their parents, condemned by politicians and other authority figures, teenagers and young adults, with their purchasing power, had staked out a big chunk of the cultural landscape (Cantwell 1998).

THE YIPPIES: A BRIDGE TOO SHORT

The group best known for bridging the hippies and politicos vividly illustrates the adage that the exception proves the rule. Combining political and cultural radicalism proved to be an effective media ploy, provoking heated controversy and contributing many of the era's iconic images in our collective memory. But the bridge remained more symbolic than operational. The Yippies (Youth International Party) were basically a media concoction of Abbie Hoffman, Jerry Rubin, and Paul Krasner. Though they created a putative formal organization based on SNCC (without dues or formal membership), the main activity was staging public events. The trio were especially media-savvy promoters of public events dramatizing opposition to the system, with such capers as dropping dollar bills from the spectators' balcony at the New York Stock Exchange. Or there was the time that Hoffman appeared before the House Committee on Un-American Activities dressed as an Indian with feathers, hunting knife, and a bullwhip. With an electric yoyo, he performed for the committee tricks such as "Around-the-Capitalist-World," "Split-the-Southern-Cracker," and "Burning-Down-the-Town." The event that drew the most media attention, and perhaps cemented the Yippies' place in history, was their attempt to organize a "Festival of Life" at the 1968 Democratic Convention in Chicago. The antiwar movement had planned an elaborate set of demonstrations, hoping to unite all antiwar activists. The Yippies wanted a large rock concert and a counterconvention where they would nominate their candidate for president, a pig named Pigasus. When they introduced Pigasus to the country, the pig and its owners were taken into custody. The pig was never heard from again, but Hoffman and Rubin became two of the "Chicago Eight," who were involved in one of the most infamous political trials of the twentieth century.

The Chicago Eight included David Dellinger, a longtime peace activist, Rennie Davis and Tom Hayden, leaders of SDS, and Black Panther Bobby

Seale. The Yippies' frequent theatrics, such as showing up dressed in American flag shirts, got full media coverage, helping cement in the American mind the counterculture with the New Left. But inside the movement, the relations were more strained. Michael Rossman, a veteran of the Berkeley Free Speech Movement, wrote an open letter to Jerry Rubin, published in the *Berkeley Barb* and distributed across the country by Liberation News Service before the Chicago events. Questioning the political mileage of an event aimed at the media, he feared for the safety of naive flower children in "the nation's richest pool of uptight bad vibes, set to flash" (1968: 1).

Rossman's letter reflects a widespread feeling among the politicos: "The Yippie thing really troubles me, man, because it's deeply and dangerously irresponsible" (1968: 2). Then he offered Rubin a general critique of the Yippie strategy: "The brilliant formless Yippee publicity, in building the magical beckoning symbol of our Music, projects an image which is recklessly and dangerously slanted, however well it's meant. It promises grooving and warmth, and does not warn that joy there must be won from within—not absorbed from others—in a landscape of total hostility whose ground condition may well be the terror and death of one's brothers" (1968: 2).

Rossman was especially concerned about the safety of naive participants, concerned that young innocents would be drawn to Chicago by fun and games, finding themselves instead the victims of police violence. He pleaded with Rubin to act responsibly so that youthful sentiments would be channeled into constructive protest rather than reckless frenzy. It was not that Rossman was insisting on a peaceful, orderly demonstration so much as he was asking that participants be aware of what they were facing, including the possibility of violence. He wanted not a festival but a political confrontation, in which participants could relish the drama and make a public statement. Speaking of the polarity between political and cultural activism, he advocated that "the warring strands of our nature must come together. The politicos make no provision for the nature of joy there. You [Rubin] are mirroring their mistake, seeking too easy an alternative: the joy and the politics must be fused." Rossman agreed that music was necessary but suggested that they play from sound trucks "without all this Festival bullshit" (1968: 5). Thus the issue was less one of culture/no culture than the social context of culture and the relationship between the political and cultural activities of the movement. The fear was that a music festival, even in the context of the Chicago demonstrations, would vitiate the political significance of what was happening. Whether or not a music festival would have dampened the political significance of the Chicago demonstrations, Rossman's missive reflects an assumption that culture and politics conflicted. It was that chasm that the

Yippies aspired to bridge, but the fact that they could do so only as a media spectacle indicates how broad the gap was.

Conclusion

The quick eclipse of participatory music in the civil rights movement reveals how fragile an achievement it was. In our society "music" is equated with highly skilled performers making explicitly composed intonation for audiences either directly in specialized performance settings or mediated by specialized technologies usually sold as commodities. This is the taken-for-granted meaning of music and virtually all institutional underpinnings of music operate according to this meaning of music. In a society dominated by this mode of musicking, constructing a musically active social movement is a formidable but tenuous achievement. If the experience of the Old Left showed that an inspired vision is insufficient to create a musical movement without the institutional underpinnings, the experience of the civil rights movement showed that when the institutional underpinning erodes, the way that the movement does music can quickly revert to forms of the broader society. The unique musical life of the civil rights movement grew out of its roots in southern black religion and black colleges manifested in a particular repertoire of collective action in the rural South. When secular northerners took over the movement and shifted its focus to urban forms of collective action, the music that had bridged the racial boundaries ceased to be a part of the movement.

Without the underlying social foundation and an explicit conception of participatory music, the music of the left reverted to its social default—a division between performance and audience, most often mediated by commercial products. Both the soul music embraced by post–civil rights black activists and politically tinged rock acclaimed by the left drew inspiration from the freedom songs but contributed more to a zeitgeist of rebellion than they fortified actual protest. The freedom songs themselves became part of the mainstream media, less as freestanding performance than as background music for collective memory. They remain part of our culture but as part of neither collective nor commercial hits. Rarely are they heard outside a very few settings—classroom lessons on the history of the movement, especially during February (Black History Month), documentary and feature films on the movement, and museums commemorating the movement. As background music for our collective memory of the movement, they come to be seen as the background of the movement itself. They still inspire, and not just for graying participants but also for those born after its demise. So people wonder why social movements today are not more musical. Why isn't there a sound track to contemporary collective action? But since the freedom songs are heard as the sound track to collective memory rather than as an integral part of the collective action itself, we underestimate how difficult it was to mobilize a truly musical movement and how fragile it was. The fact that black and white leftist movements borrowed so much from the civil rights movement but did not borrow the mode of musicking tells us something about the relationship of music to society, including how difficult it is to sustain a musical movement.

CHAPTER TEN

How Social Movements Do Culture

Social movements do culture. Not just in the sense of culture as a shared orientation toward the world but in the more vernacular sense of art, music, drama, literature, and dance. People joining together to right social wrongs and weaken abusive power create posters, music, murals, plays, poetry, and fiction, and orchestrate gala celebrations. In the 1920s, John Reed Clubs and their offshoots attracted groups of poets, novelists, painters, sculptors, actors, photographers, filmmakers, ballet dancers, labor balladeers, classical musicians, and composers. The Harlem Renaissance of the same period included some of America's most creative minds—writers such as Langston Hughes and Nora Zeale Hurston, performers as renowned as Paul Robeson, painters as influential as Jacob Lawrence, and of course their musical outpouring included a "Who's Who" of artists from Billie Holiday to Louis Armstrong. Similarly the women's movement of the 1960s and 1970s inspired, nurtured, and created opportunities for poets like Diane diPrima, Adrienne Rich, Nikki Giovanni, and Toni Morrison. Feminist artists created images that challenged basic assumptions about the meaning of gender and the political dimensions of relations within and between genders. Gender relations were similarly interrogated in drama on the street, in theaters—wherever women (and sometimes men) gathered.

Reading the social science literature on social movements, you only get a faint whiff of creative mobilization. The sociological literature on culture and social movements that offers overviews of the field tends to omit art, literature, music, drama, and other creative endeavors (see, for example, Johnston and Noakes 2005; McAdam 2000; Meyer, Whittier, and Robnett 2002; Polletta 2008; Swidler 1995). Thus T. V. Reed could introduce his 2005 book, *The Art of Protest*, as the first book of comparative movement analysis to focus on the cultural creativity movements.[1] Social movement scholars have focused much more on such vital issues as why people join social movements, why social movements proliferate and dwindle when they do, and how they operate as organizations. When scholars address the topic of how social movements relate to creative culture, they typically examine the relationship of the issues that social movements address to cultural content (Berezin 1994; Eyerman and Jamison 1995; Hanson 2008; Lipsitz 2000; McAdam 1994; Steinberg 2004;

Zolberg 1997). Indeed, social movements have been remarkably effective at injecting their themes into American popular culture. Abolitionists introduced African American spirituals into white mainstream culture, laying the groundwork for the racially hybrid music at the core of all popular music thereafter. Leftist artists helped foster realism in American painting and sculpture and challenged theater to address real-life issues of ordinary people. Latino activists inspired and facilitated a now common art form in the urban landscape—the mural. Over the second half of the twentieth century social movements have compelled the leaders of American popular culture to include images of people much closer to the composition of the American visual arts than the white male monopoly that had dominated for so long.

As important as the content of cultural forms is or the impact that social movements have had on American culture, this book takes a different approach. What matters is not only the culture that social movements *have* but also how they *do* culture. The basic argument is simple but far-reaching: The effects of culture—illustrated here with music—depend at least as much on the social relations within which culture is embedded as on its content. We need to move beyond attending to the *content* of music, drama, literature, and so forth to examine how people are relating to each other while *doing* it. We need to recognize that the social relationship by which one person or group has a monopoly on creativity, which they disperse to audiences—the relationship of performers to audiences—is only one kind of social relationship for culture. The preceding chapters have demonstrated that many people *doing* music, not just consuming it, is an extraordinarily powerful mode for both solidifying commitment to collective action and for helping collectivities achieve their goals.

This argument has been elucidated with a comparison of two social movements that self-consciously used American folk music but with contrasting results. The communist-led movement of the 1930s and 1940s developed the most extensive and elaborate cultural infrastructure of any movement in American history, with influence in every aesthetic realm from fine literature to Hollywood cinema (Denning 1996). Its adherents successfully catapulted folk music from an esoteric preoccupation of academics and antiquarians into a genre of popular music. But they fell short of reaching their target audience—the working class. One major reason is that they never transcended the conventional social relationship that prevails in Western creative culture, that of performer and audience, even though many of them earnestly tried to make music participatory. In contrast, the civil rights movement of the 1950s and 1960s is well known as one of the most musical moments in American history. For a shining moment at least, music fortified the movement, welding solidarity among the participants, and, with songs that had strikingly thin political content, stirred the public imagination. The more powerful role that music played in the civil rights movement is explained less by the music itself, much of which was inherited from the Old Left, than by the social relationships within which it was done. For the civil rights movement, music was less a matter of a performer singing for an audience than part of the collective action itself. At the lunch counter, on the picket line, on the bus rides, and in jail, they made music collectively. Unless we attend to the social relations within which people are doing culture, we will be unable to explain the different effects music had for these two movements. We can explain how the civil rights movement was able to be the fulfillment of the vision inherited from the People's Songsters through the kinds of social relations that underlay the movement and in which music was done.

It is the social relationship among the participants that is missed when scholars focus on the content—or, more specifically, the relationships of culture are displaced. In analyzing cultural content the analyst adopts the standpoint of the audience. The totality of the social relation is assumed to be the content of communication between the performer and the audience. The analyst summarizes the content, explains how it relates to broader cultural meanings, probes beneath the surface to excavate latent meanings or presuppositions, extrapolates implications beyond overt claims, evaluates aesthetic qualities, or extends the meaning to the analyst's own agenda. These models of analysis all depend on putting oneself in the social role of the audience. More often than not taking the role of the audience is simulated and after the fact. The analyst typically has access only to mediated artifacts of cultural activities—reports, audio and video recordings, books, recollections, and other reproductions. Of course, the overwhelming volume of historic evidence of cultural activity takes these forms. Since sociology's cultural turn of the 1990s, sociological analysis of social movement culture has become increasingly refined, insightful, sophisticated, and nuanced (Aminzade et al. 2001; Berezin 1994; Goodwin and Jasper 2003; Goodwin, Jasper, and Polletta 2001; Jasper 1997; Johnston and Klandermans 1995; Johnston and Noakes 2005; McAdam 2000; Polletta 2002, 2006; Steinberg 1999; Swidler 1995). But it has made less progress in conceptualizing the social relations within which culture is done.

When the analyst steps into the role of the audience, he/she reduces his/her relation to the author and masks the relationship of the creator to the audience in real life. "Which Side Are You On?" sung at the Gastonia textile strike, in a hootenanny, at a Town Hall concert, on an Albany, Georgia, picket line, at a Friends of SNCC fund-raiser, or in a college lecture on twentieth-century history are all lumped together. The fact that the music is allaying fear and empowering action in Gastonia, fostering an educated middle-class subculture in New York, bringing blacks and whites together in the Deep South in Albany, raising money for a movement fund-raiser, or giving students a bit of cultural capital on the campus cannot be fathomed by attending only to the song's content. There are matters of how culture is done.

To examine how social movements do culture, it is necessary to think about what social movements do in general and how their activities affect their success (W. Gamson 1975). In conventional sociological accounts social movements succeed by adding members; members decide to join and participate on the basis of alignment between their meaning systems and those of the social movement. Culture is important to social movements because it helps them attract, retain, and engender commitment from members. So a social movement can grow and thus succeed by articulating meanings close to potential constituents or by doing the cultural work of converting potential constituents to their ways of seeing the world. As a close parallel to the way that some religious organizations grow, we might call this the evangelical model of movement building. What becomes sociologically at stake in this perspective is what content of ideas, symbols, ideologies, narratives, and, in recent scholarship, frames most effectively convert recruits into apostles. The recruit is assumed to be mainly a culture processor, taking in ideas, symbols, ideologies, narratives, and frames, and responding with support, indifference, or hostility on the basis of a preexisting mental state. The typical event in this process is the culture-driven decision.[2] And that culturally driven decision to participate or not is often prior to and analytically divorced from the recruit's actual participation in the social movement itself. Though eschewing the autonomous decision-maker of rational choice theory, cultural theory too often substitutes a culturally informed decision-maker. Both assume an autonomous actor soaking up input, digesting it internally, and outputting a decision. Missing from the model is the kind of social relationship within which culture is performed and the effect that such relationship might have on the movement. As important as the content of culture is, the same words, symbols, images, narratives, and frames can have very different effects depending on the qualities of relationship within which they occur. This is what a relational approach can bring to the table.

This model is most explicit in the sociological writing on framing. Frames are schemata of interpretation that render events meaningful by organizing experience and guiding action (Benford and Snow 2000). People are drawn to social movements when their personal frames are aligned to that of the social movement or when the movement is able to transform the individual's frame through conversion (Snow et al. 1986). When recent social movement analysis is summarized, framing theory is typically cited as the core of cultural dynamics. Even when sociologists move beyond framing theory, when they analyze cultural objects or creative activities, they generally focus on the content of what producers create and audiences consume.

In contrast, the relational approach focuses on the qualities of interaction itself. It is the sound of two hands clapping, which can never be reduced to the qualities of each hand separately. In a relational perspective, the focus is on qualities that can only be ascertained in terms of two or more actors. Of course, each actor brings attributes, dispositions, and resources to a relationship, but the relationship can never be reduced to what any one actor brings. For example, equality is a relational quality, irreducible to the amount of goodies held by either party but found only in the relationship of parties to each other.[3]

THE DISTINCTIVENESS OF SOCIAL MOVEMENTS

The analysis of music in the People's Songs movement and the civil rights movement highlights two foundational characteristics of social movements and how they do culture. While hardly original to this book, these features are often neglected or elided. But if we are to understand how social movements use culture to influence society, we need to keep them in mind. First, social movements necessarily involve conflict, typically against the state or other authorities. Though not always involved in outright uprising, by definition they are making claims that if realized will threaten the interests of others (Tilly 2004b). The communists in the 1930s and 1940s sought better pay and working conditions that would have cost employers and ultimately wanted to displace the employers altogether. African Americans in the 1950s and 1960s sought to dismantle a system based on white privilege. Second, social movements to some degree or another attempt to embody within themselves the world they are trying to create; that is, they are prefigurative (Polletta 2002). Certainly movements vary between those who are content to postpone elevating their internal relations until after the revolution at one end of the spectrum to those who feel that the most effective change comes from within at the other. Still, social movements generally tend to be more attentive to the consonance between their values and how they manage their affairs than many kinds of organizations. Thus, social movements must attend to the potential tension between meeting their goals and the means by which they build and sustain the movement. What makes this especially challenging for social movements is the first issue—that they are involved in inescapable relations of conflict. Thus both the dynamics of conflict within which social movements find themselves and the challenges of prefiguring a better world within one's own activities shape the form in which social movements do culture and the effectiveness of achieving their goals.

CULTURE AND CONFLICT

In reaction to theories of social movements that treated them as displaced reflexes to exceptional circumstances, sociologists have emphasized the similarities between contentious politics and ordinary politics, pushing the stark reality of conflict into the background. The focus on how social movements mobilize material resources to grow, on the relationship between their cultural frames and dominant values, and on how political opportunities affect their rise and fall—the overriding themes of social movement scholarship for the last several decades—has sometimes muted the fundamental feature of social movements as relationships of conflict. The way that conflict is structured and managed can influence how social movements do culture both in terms of the message communicated and the forms adopted.

The way that social movements engage in conflict by doing culture helps explain why folk music was adopted as the people's music. The goal was more than finding music that people enjoyed. Popular music would have fit that bill. While other genres may have been equally vernacular, folk music was attractive to both the People's Songsters and the civil rights movement because the discourse around it carried a critique of modernity. The People's Songsters thus embraced "the people's music" as the embodiment of class conflict in which "the people" stood in for workers. The distinction between folk music and commercial music was seen as an indictment of capitalism and the culture it created.

Even though the folk making the music may have been oblivious to the connotations others would attribute to it, the scholars and antiquarians who "discovered" folk music, codified its significance, and defined its canon were establishing a genre based on who did it rather than its sonic qualities or social functions. It was the music of the people displaced by time and space from modern, urban, industrial—that is, contaminated—society. But they were people who embodied the pure essence of peoplehood. By making folk music the music of a national-ethnic folk, they invited conflict over who counted as the folk. When the first folk project proclaimed that America did indeed have folk music and that it was Anglo-Saxon, they excluded not only the newly arrived European immigrants but also the long-resident African Americans. But when the second folk project challenged the boundaries of who counted as folk, anointing black spirituals as the most distinctively American folk music, the left (many of them recent European immigrants) could embrace folk music as the people's music, overtly incorporating African Americans into "the people." The contested genre boundaries around folk music were thus projected to the social conflict between the people (workers) and the powers (capitalists).

Still, the actual music of the People's Songsters included much more than the music that the folk were doing. Because the left saw culture as a weapon of propaganda, they felt obliged to offer a more explicit political message, making the music speak through its lyrics, not just its form. They saw the conflict as one of a battle over consciousness in which every available weapon including—perhaps especially—culture would be wielded to capture hearts and minds.

As a vanguard movement, the content of the propaganda weapon would be aimed from the leaders to the rank and file. Granted, cultural creators in general were much less accountable to the hierarchy than other party activists, but the general orientation toward cultural content equated audiences with teachable masses. The culture was to prepare the masses for the real conflict, whether it was an impending strike or the eventual revolution.

In contrast, for the civil rights movement the conflict was immediate, and culture, especially music, was an essential element in facing the foe. They, too, shared the assumption that folk music embodied a distinction between the people and the elites. But unlike most of the Old Leftists, for whom folk music was always someone else's music, the music of the civil rights movement was the music of the participants. It was not that these were their songs; in fact, many were inherited from the Old Left. But through collective singing, the songs became theirs. Doing music on the picket line, on the bus, or in jail, especially when done in racially mixed groups, made music an act of defiance against the system of segregation. The music was not just about conflict; it was a form of conflict. A population that for four hundred years had been forced to bow and scrape in deference before any white person was redefining the relationship between races, not just by articulating a demand for freedom but also by acting it out socially. Doing music was *doing* a new relationship.

What this implies is that the cultural activities set within the overt relations of conflict with authority are likely to contribute more directly to the achievement of goals than those that are merely about conflict. Conventionally, the most common mode of analyzing the role of culture in social movements is analyzing its content. The semantics of lyrics, the meaning of visual symbols, and the representation of society or actors is distilled into prosaic discourse expressing political ideas. Art, music, literature, or drama is treated merely as a vehicle to communicate content, like speeches, newsletters, protest demands, petitions, or interviews. Hermeneutic, semiotic, or interpretive analysis is applied to understand how social movements make meaning or connect to the meaning sets of constituencies. As Swidler describes the cultural role of social movements, "Even without conscious efforts at publicity, one of the most important effects social movements have is publicly enacting images that confound existing cultural codings" (1995: 33).

PREFIGURATIVE CULTURE

The ways in which social movements prefigure the social worlds they aspire to create is typically analyzed in terms of broad features of society such as democracy or equality (see, for example, Polletta 2002). But we can also parse out more analytical dimensions of the social relationships within which culture is enacted, focusing on music but extending examples to other arts. Some of the analytical dimensions that are especially relevant to our case are the division of labor, the dynamics of power, the way that people are tuned in, and the way culture is embedded.

The contrast between the communist-inspired movement of the 1930s and 1940s and the civil rights movement of the 1960s illustrates these four dimensions. The social relations within which culture was enacted help explain the differential effect that it had on the movement and the broader society—why the People's Songsters succeeded more at making folk music a well-known form of popular music than bringing together the broad range of people included in the "folk," and why the civil rights movement was able to forge a racially diverse movement that served as a model for subsequent movements.

The Division of Labor

For Western music, labor is divided among composer, performer, listener, and interpreter, though other societies have very different divisions of labor (Feld 1984). The folk music process, as idealized by scholars, embodies a very different division of labor in which performers collectively appropriate the composer's role to the point that individual composers are rendered irrelevant (Kittredge 1932 [1904]). The hootenanny fuses the roles of performer and audience, especially when audience members can introduce songs for all to sing. Some forms of street theater attempt to break down the wall between performer and audience by enticing bystanders to participate in the unfolding drama.

For social movements doing culture, the division of labor in cultural activities parallels the division of labor in the movement. A division of labor among creators, performers, and audience means that those roles are also found in the movement. If there is no such division of labor, if ordinary members make music as well as listen to it, music can inscribe a relationship that minimizes the difference between leaders and followers. If ordinary members can create music on the spot, for example, making up new verses of "zipper songs," doing culture is a part of making the movement.

There are, of course, other aspects to the division of labor. Similar to the relationship between creating, performing, and receiving is the degree to which culture is done by specialists or generalists. Song leaders can be organizational leaders trained to lead songs, as many ministers in the civil rights movement were, or musicians who have a commitment to partici- pation, like Pete Seeger. In most cases, we would expect generalists to be more effective at integrating culture into the full range of movement ac- tivities, but as Pete Seeger's amazing career shows, this is not always the case.

As committed as the People's Songsters were to participatory musick- ing, they found it difficult to transcend the conventional composer- performer-audience division of labor. Although the earliest communist- inspired music was found in popular choruses, mostly singing in languages other than English, the composers, song collectors, and performers who promoted folk music in the 1930s and 1940s tended to fall back into a performance mode. Although the movement's most visible advocate, Pete Seeger, aspired to something more collective, actively pushing hootenan- nies and singing unions, the movement's social context overwhelmingly adopted the composer-performer-audience division of labor. Seeger and Guthrie could write songs that politically committed audiences relished, especially when singing them in hootenannies, but "the people" were more accustomed to listening than singing together, affording the movement its greatest opportunity for success. The movement virtually invented the urban folk singing ensemble with groups such as the Almanacs and the commercially successful Weavers, but failed to foster the singing unions they had hoped for. The conventional composer-performer-audience divi- sion of labor was also reinforced by the organizational infrastructure developed by party members and sympathizers.

When the young Communist Party self-consciously used culture as a weapon in the class struggle, they assumed a division of labor between those who wielded the weapon and the targets of the weapon. Art, litera- ture, and music were more often created for than by the working class. From the John Reed Clubs of the 1920s to the flowering of all the arts in the Popular Front era, the movement mostly adopted the division of labor common in the broader society. Doing so facilitated the construction of the left's formidable infrastructure in which critics, performers, writers, editors, and audiences could plug into familiar roles substituting radical content for what was offered in the mainstream. People's Songs, Inc. drew together progressive musicians from the party fringes, New Deal activists, unions, and college campuses. By publishing books and magazines, sponsoring events, creating forums for interaction, and linking to other producers and distributors of left-wing music, they gave folk music a greater presence both in the media and the movement at large.

The civil rights movement did maintain some division of labor between the specialist trainers such as the Carawans and generalist organizers or between song leaders and participants, but in practice it muddied the conventional distinction between composer, performer, and audience. Meetings were modeled after the template of the black church where members were accustomed to congregational singing. While some major events such as the celebrated 1963 March on Washington followed a conventional performer-audience model, most of the collective action events in the movement had no single person presiding. Sit-ins, picketing, bus riding, marching, and the like involved organized crowds. Like the conventional roles that the People's Songsters borrowed from their milieu, the musical division of labor between the leader and group was a well-known relationship in black communities. Though the Highlander School refined the roles in their workshops, the basic division of labor was already comfortable to many participants.

Power

Whatever the division of labor among people doing culture, there is variation in the power structure that describes the relative distribution of influence among different actors within art worlds (Becker 1982). In classical music, for example, music directors select the repertoire for programs, composers dictate the notes played, conductors shape how the notes are played, and listeners influence trends through their choices of patronage. Similarly, the relative power of artists, patrons, critics, brokers, and consumers varies in different societies and in different kinds of art.

In thinking about how power is relevant to the social relations of doing culture, it is important to distinguish between power over cultural activity and the power that cultural activity has. The relationship among creator, performer, and receiver concerns power within the cultural activity itself. When songwriters such as Woody Guthrie decided to write about some issues rather than others or when the Almanacs changed their messages about World War II in response to Communist Party directives, relations of power are shaping culture. But when listeners deemed some of Guthrie's songs as trite or when independent activists became disillusioned by the Almanacs' transparent flip-flop, the limits of cultural power over the movement were exposed. Conversely, when the power over the doing of culture was the most subtle, as in the civil rights movement, the power that culture—especially music—exercised over the movement was most potent.

The vanguard strategy of the Old Left, manifested in a hierarchical party structure, contrasted with the leadership and empowerment orientation by which the civil rights movement did culture. Though the artists and musicians associated with the party exercised considerable autonomy, the party did authorize the broad parameters of cultural form and content. A vanguard is a group that takes responsibility for educating masses. Under its guidance, culture is a means to communicate its understanding of truth. So the Almanac Singers, who were hardly party stalwarts, reversed their earlier antiwar lyrics after Hitler invaded the Soviet Union, parroting the party's fresh pro-Roosevelt belligerency. In contrast, the civil rights movement was always highly decentralized, both organizationally and culturally. Song leaders were accountable only to other organizers. They were trained at transitory events such as workshops at the Highlander School and communicated with each other through mimeographed songbooks and gathering at demonstrations. Thus the music could more easily serve to create solidarity among people than to carry a message from a central leadership.

Tuning In

Schutz (1964) has described how music has the ability to synchronize people's consciousness into a sense of sharing that transcends the meaning it might have for any solitary listener. McNeill (1995) has argued that the synchronization of drilling, chanting, and singing fortifies collective efforts, including war. While auditory media like music, poetry, and chanting have obvious qualities of tuning in because they are set in real time, visual arts also vary in the extent to which people experience them collectively or individually. For example, Chicano activists have self-consciously created murals as group projects to foster solidarity (Reed 2005). Many accounts have described how the Chinese Cultural Revolution in the late 1960s was fanned by the crowds who gathered around poster walls.

Tuning in has been seen as the basis for close social relations in both neurological and sociological mechanisms. Neurologist and musician Daniel Levitin has argued that the cohesive effect of music is hard-wired in the human brain. Singing together releases oxytocin, a chemical promoting trust. Thus the social roots of musicking are very deep: "I believe that synchronous, coordinated song and movement were what created the strongest bonds between humans, or protohumans, and these allowed for the formation of larger living groups, and eventually of society as we know it" (2008: 50).

Sociologically, tuning in is necessary for all social relations. Fundamental components of social relations such as turn-taking, repairing breaches in conversation, a shared orientation to each other, and a common definition of the situation must be achieved in order for social relations to achieve anything (Schegloff 2007).

Music always involves some sort of tuning in (Schutz 1964). And virtually all social movements that use music are attentive to its ability to create solidarity as well as carry a message (Eyerman and Jamison 1998; Rosenthal and Flacks 2009). But the social relations within music affect the ways in which people are connected to each other and thus what is political about the culture. For the Old Left, politics was first and foremost in the lyrics. So tuning in took the form of frame alignment (Benford and Snow 2000; Gamson et al. 1992; Johnston and Noakes 2005; Snow et al. 1986). People were considered close to each other to the extent that they were "on the same page." Cultural activities were considered successful insofar as they raised people's consciousness. To extend the metaphor of tuning in, resonance was defined in terms of political agreement. In contrast, for the civil rights movement, tuning in was based more on common participation in making music. They were able to achieve what the Old Left had aspired to, creating a singing movement. SNCC organizer Charles Sherrod has described how when he first arrived in Albany, Georgia, people had learned to sing "We Shall Overcome" from seeing it on television, but it was stiff and passive. So he taught them how to join arms, sway, and harmonize, binding the participants into a collectivity (Reagon 1975).

Embeddedness

Western society is distinctive in the extent to which it has framed culture as putatively pure form, denigrating art, music, literature, and drama that is supposedly compromised by "using" culture for non-artistic purposes. As this study illustrates, social scientists are moving beyond the simple issue of whether "pure" culture is ever possible. Rather than treating culture and society as levels, systems, or entities that can be autonomous or interrelate, they are now also investigating the relation between cultural and other social relations by studying what people are doing when they do culture. In this sense the performance of a Mozart symphony is just as social as a protest song because we can analyze the social relations involved in doing either. This is not just a question of motivation or intention. Even when people understand themselves as doing pure culture, they are doing other things. Small (1998), for example, has ethnographically described how the classical music concert is a site of displaying and reproducing middle-class respectability. Other studies more explicitly have investigated the relationship between cultural objects and religion, politics, sports, relaxing, making love, education, and of course social movements. While many of these studies focus on the content, others have analyzed how the culture is embedded in social relations (Berezin 1994; DeNora 2002; Du Gay 1997; Ikegami 2005; Leblanc 1999; B. Martin 2004; Reed 2005; Rosenthal and Flacks 2009; Zolberg 1997). Analyzing the embeddedness of culture means suspending the distinction between pure and pragmatic culture or between aesthetic and social dimensions to focus on what people are *doing* when they enact culture. Futrell, Simi, and Gottschalk describe the music of the White Power movement as prefigurative in that its members use music to create a microcosm of the white world they aspire to live in. Musical events "are among the few face-to-face contexts in which activists live and feel the types of experiences and relationships that reflect the society the movement seeks to build, if only for a few hours or days" (2006: 289).

Music for the Old Left was embedded in a political party aspiring to change people's consciousness. Much of their music was overtly political, which in Western society creates a tension with aesthetic standards of "pure" culture. When activists became performers, they thus distinguished between their political songs and their popular songs, as the Almanac Singers did when they intentionally balanced their repertoire with political and folk songs (Lieberman 1995). When they tried to embed music in forms other than political parties, such as unions, they found mixed success. They did find a ready audience when they performed for Progressive candidate Henry Wallace in the 1948 presidential campaign, although the effort bankrupted the sponsoring organization, People's Songs, Inc. But the hootenannies, summer camps, and choruses helped create the rich cultural milieu that Lieberman (1995) describes so vividly.

For the civil rights movement the music was embedded in the collective action itself, in meetings, picketing, riding on buses, sitting in, and passing the time in jail. These were activities in which a crowd of people, often confronted with hostile authorities, engaged in drawn-out activity that required tight coordination and communal movement. Their repertoire of collective action was ideal for making music together. And music was the ideal medium for reinforcing and empowering these forms of collective action. Tellingly, when the movement abandoned nonviolent civil disobedience and its related repertoire of collective action, they also abandoned music in the movement and, like the Old Left before them, embraced music for its content.

Beyond Music

Both the Old Left and the civil rights movement were musically successful on their own terms. American folk music developed from a category
comprehensible mainly to academics and antiquarians into a mainstream
genre. People associated with the folk music project of the 1930s and
1940s created a set of musical codes and a canon of songs that erupted in
the 1960s with a new revival. And American folk music, even when divorced from activism, would carry a leftist overtone. The civil rights
movement not only ended de jure segregation, its number-one goal, but
also has offered the template of collective action for all sorts of rights-
based movements since then, even those on the right.

The lessons can be extended beyond music. The social relations within
which social movement culture is enacted are shaped by both cultural
medium and the designs of the activists. For the women's movement of
the 1970s, poetry was a major activity in consciousness-raising groups,
both its writing and reading. It was a medium for women to articulate
problems they had intuitively felt but for which they lacked a language.
Women used poetry as a means to communicate with other women in
their consciousness-raising group and to collectively connect the personal
to the political (Reed 2005). Both music and poetry have a strong metric
component, a pre-cognitive tuning in that transcends the literal meaning
of the words. Through the social process they were also making the personal collective, taking a medium usually assumed to be the epitome of
personal expression and individuality and using it to both capture and
deepen the consciousness of a group. Similarly, the Chicano collaborative
creation of murals collectivizes what is usually considered an individualistic medium. Though there is a division of labor between production and
consumption of murals, the producers remain part of the public whose
space is transformed by the mural.

Reed has described how gay activists, led by ACT UP, used their decentralized, anti-hierarchical organization to launch a blitz of creative inter-
ventions that captured media coverage, challenged corporations, led artistic exhibitions, and used advertising to redefine the relationship that
gays had with society. Instead of hiding in the closet or emphasizing their
normalcy, they defiantly projected their distinctiveness and their pride. It
was not only the content of their cultural expression but the social relations in which the culture was done that made it effective. ACT UP was
organized in small affinity groups with little oversight. So instead of any
single mode of expression, the result was a broad variety of messages and
forms, ranging from outrageous public displays to scholarly mobilization
of scientific knowledge (Epstein 1996; Reed 2005).

Thus examining the social processes by which people *do* culture can deepen our understanding of how social movements operate. Recent work, such as Polletta's pathbreaking analysis (2002) of participatory democracy in movement organizations, has focused on the internal dynamics of how social movements operate, shifting attention away from the perennial issue of why people join. We can move beyond the evangelical model of social movements to see what explains the internal social relationships with movements and how those social relations help shape the broader effects that social movements have on society. The division of labor within which culture is enacted, the power dynamics among those doing culture, the way that culture tunes in people involved in culture, and the activities within which culture is enacted transcend its content and explain the effects of culture on social movement dynamics and consequences in a way that analyzing the content of culture inevitably misses.

The Future of Music in American Social Movements

Unfortunately the conditions for social movements to deeply embed music in their collective action as did the civil rights movement are today not propitious. Or to state it more hopefully, if inventive social movements such as those of gays, environmentalists, immigrants' rights groups, or anti-globalization activists extensively do music, it will be constituted within in a very different set of social relations. First, most constituents have grown up relating to music almost solely as mass media. Even Christian churches include more performative music and less congregational singing (Wuthnow 2003). Children reaching maturity today have had fewer opportunities to participate in music-making than previous generations had as schools have cut back on all arts education. Thus, music is increasingly something you buy more than something you can imagine participating in.

Second, it is unlikely that any socially coherent group will have the respect and influence to shape any movement's culture independent of the mass media in the way that blacks did in the civil rights movement. Beyond the critical core that grew up singing in churches, participants from other cultural backgrounds entered a movement in which the culture of the black church and the black colleges presented a template respected by all. Only ethnically based groups today have a culturally homogeneous leadership that offers a model for doing culture.

Third, there is little cultural infrastructure in today's movements—no unifying party such as the communists had, no national organizations like People's Songs, Inc., no training facilities like the Highlander School, no record companies like Folkways. Some movements are very informal and decentralized, like ACT UP, while others are highly professionalized and bureaucratic, as is much of the environmental movement. And while there is much cultural expressiveness mostly oriented to the mass media, there is relatively little cultural infrastructure. One notable exception is a movement dedicated to undoing the movement this book has treated as the model for collective musicking: the American White Power movement. Futrell, Simi, and Gottschalk insightfully describe the extensive musical infrastructure of the White Power musical scene, including White Power bands (more than a hundred of them in the United States), record companies, music festivals, and Web sites. In an important article they address an agenda very close to mine—how social movements use music. Their answer is similar to mine—that the effect of music is mainly a matter of the social relations within which it is found, though they do not state it quite that way. What is distinctive to their analysis of social movements and music is their focus on music scenes, which, they emphasize, create a holistic sense of belonging for participants that goes beyond the content of lyrics or the meaning of particular rituals.

Finally, collective action itself has lost the tradition of doing music. In marches, chants have replaced songs. Demonstrations only occasionally have music, almost always as performance without participation. The songs of an earlier generation are considered old-fashioned and none has taken their place.

Yet, there are glimmers of hope. New electronic technologies allow music to be made much more easily than ever before. The Internet offers great possibilities for musicking but in a very different form than that of past movements. Especially if we broaden the making of music beyond singing and playing an instrument to include mixing, synthesizing, and sampling, there are new opportunities for movements to do music. The technology is now widely available for people of relatively modest musical and technical training to express themselves musically and reach an audience more extensively than anyone but major stars could reach previously. Not only mass networking sites like YouTube but also issue-oriented sites such as Earthman make it possible to do music as part of a movement.[4] It may be that there is now a greater abundance of politically oriented music in circulation than ever before. The main difference between this musicking and the musicking of organizations like the civil rights movement is that the social relations are mediated by technology. It is not making music together. While the power relations may be more egalitarian than some other forms of music, the division of labor between performer and listener is more remote, the tuning in is less synchronized, and the embedding is more disjointed from other activity. That is not to say that musicking mediated by the Web cannot foster effective social movements but that if it does, it will work through very different relationships involving very different social mechanisms. At the very least the Web can be the institutional basis of new movements to the extent that it can be thoroughly integrated into other aspects of life in the same sense that black churches and black colleges were integrated into the lives of many civil rights activists. The potential that the Web offers for decentralized movements in general equally applies to music and other culture.

Music has an essential quality that will always make it potent: its ability to inspire passion. The poets who embrace the transcendental spirit of music, the throngs who venerate the latest pop icon, the worshipers who use music to touch their own souls, and the lovers who set the stage for intimacy with music all share a passion with the strikers who march to the tune of "Solidarity Forever" or the picketers who join arms and sway to "We Shall Overcome." The passion that people have for music is not just the euphoria of hearing the sounds wrought by genius; it is the collective bonds of shared experience. Many people care about music and about the others with whom they share it. A force that can ease the tedium of working together, enrich the awe of worshiping together, and sweeten the ecstasy of making love together always has the capacity to foster the pursuit of justice together.

The People's Songsters in the first half of the twentieth century and the civil rights movement in the second half can offer inspiration for activists of the future. And by learning from the history of these movements' social relations as well as their content, they can make their own history that reshapes the world.

Coding of Songbooks and Song Anthologies

All songbooks and song anthologies from the University of California combined campus library catalog (MELVYL) and other sources I encountered that included American social movement and protest songs from the 1930s to the 1960s were incorporated into a SAS data set. There were 12 books of union songs and 16 books of civil rights songs. Variables included the title, the type of book or anthology, whether the collection was framed as union songs or civil rights songs (a dummy variable for each type), and whether the song had religious themes (dummy variable). Any song with a reference to God, Jesus, heaven, salvation, the cross, joy, spirit, sin, soul, or Shalom, or any song known to be a spiritual (for example, "Get On Board Little Children"), or any song known to have religious text (for example, "Turn, Turn, Turn") or religious origins (for example, "We Shall Overcome") was coded as religious.

The songs analyzed here were the 281 songs found in any of the 16 civil rights songbooks. A little over three-quarters (77 percent) of them were found in only one book. The songs found in more than five books, listed in order of frequency, are presented below.

Song	Number of Books
We Shall Overcome	10
Oh, Freedom	8
Which Side Are You On?	8
Get On Board Little Children	7
This Little Light of Mine	7
We Are Soldiers	6
We Shall Not Be Moved	6

Notes

1. The music of real experiences also included topical songs, rejected by purists as impure because they were new, but welcomed by the left as the voice of the people about things that mattered.

2. This tendency to emphasize goals and recruitment can be attributed to the desire of resource mobilization advocates to show that social movement organizations are rational goal-seeking entities more than symptomatic expressions of stress.

3. Gamson, for example, found that centralized social movement organizations were more likely to achieve success in meeting goals and gaining recognition by authorities than were decentralized organizations (1975). But the generalization is hotly debated. Piven and Cloward (1979) contend that organization tends to suppress militancy and engender co-optation.

4. The main exception was activities aimed at youth, the goal of which was to cultivate commitment more than achieve operational goals. Summer camps, clubs, and specifically social activities often included active musicking, dancing, drama, and art.

5. Cultural projects more generally promote the creation, development, or transformation of a genre such as classical music (DiMaggio 1982b), rock and roll (Ennis 1992), or country music (Peterson 1997a).

6. There may be instances where it is obvious that a movement is only persuading an audience, especially if the audience is considered hostile, or only recruiting, if they assume the audience already agrees with them. But the line between cultural work that persuades outsiders and that which attracts new members is indistinct at best. Activists usually assume that the difference between agreeing and joining is a matter of degree. Joiners just need more persuasion than do supporters.

7. In 1971, Richard Reuss completed his dissertation on music and the Old Left, a rich resource for subsequent scholars. After his untimely death, his wife, Joanna, revised it for publication (Reuss and Reuss 2000). Both are cited in this work. The published version is cited when appropriate, but there are a few facts or quotations that were included only in the dissertation.

8. After the initial phase aimed at ending legal segregation, the rise of black pride, especially in colleges and universities, spawned a broad variety of cultural projects, rivaling the communists' efforts of the 1930s and 1940s.

9. Bohlman (1999) also mentions an ontology he calls adumbration, whereby music is not directly present but recognizable by its effects or absence, as when music is negated or excluded. For example, Islamic thought claims that the recitation of the Koran is not music, thereby fortifying the reality of other sound production that is understood as music.

10. DeNora elaborates a similar conception, explicitly approaching music so-

ciologically when she analyzes music as a device of social ordering: "Music may be employed, albeit at times unwittingly, as a means of organizing potentially disparate individuals such that their actions may appear to be intersubjective, mutually oriented, co-ordinated, entrained and aligned" (2000: 109).

11. These issues, of course, presuppose ontological issues. It is impossible to find meaning in music unless music is seen as an object. But the converse does not necessarily follow. Treating music as an object does not necessitate that meaning is in the music. One can treat music as an object and posit meaning in the discourse around it rather than in the music itself.

12. Even Denisoff, whose analysis focuses on the different functions of lyrical content, doubts whether the political messages of protest music make much difference: "If the power and quality of song were social determinants of political power then the Black man [sic] would have overcome decades ago; and the Industrial Workers of the World, not the CIO, would have unionized factory workers and the 'Masters of War' would not have led a nation into a foreign jungle entanglement" (1983: viii).

13. It is my suspicion that lyrics are studied more than sounds or contexts because they are more easily accessible.

14. The emphasis on function does not imply functionalism. Functionalism holds that specific parts of society are explained by their functioning in the larger social system. I make no such claim.

15. The people who were active in the Old Left musical activities, especially listeners, were more racially homogenous. Those who grew up attending hootenannies and attending concerts where the Weavers led group singing report warm feelings of solidarity and fondly recall the music they made together. But they were mostly middle-class whites.

16. The distinction between culture and society here is of course merely analytic since the very constitution of social categories is inseparable from cultural distinctions. For example, blackness and whiteness are defined in part by what music people listen to. Still, the concept of alignment permits the examination of the role of culture in constituting, reinforcing, and destabilizing categorical differences.

17. Some theorists approach homology from the perspective of the society as a whole, positing that different types of society give rise to different types of music. Lomax, for example, has argued that societies with simple social structures tend to create simple music, while complex societies tend to have more complex music (1962). Weber adopted a similar logic, detailing how music became rationalized as society in general rationalized (1958). The principle of homology can be seen in Adorno's theory that commercialization of culture destroys music's vitality and its potential to elevate the human spirit (2000).

18. Averting a sentimental interpretation of music in social movements, Rosenthal and Flacks are also attentive to the dysfunctions of music in social movements. Music can reinforce prevailing values, especially in lyrics. Following Adorno, they note that the form of music can divert activists from the cause, amusing rather than arousing them. There is always the danger that music can develop a star system that corrodes egalitarian values in a movement. One of the chief benefits of music, the enforcement of solidarity can also become a liability,

insulating activists from their constituency. And finally music can create a safety valve in the face of oppression (Rosenthal and Flacks 2009).

19. But there is often ambiguity about whether essentialism characterizes analysts or the subjects of their research. The confusion occurs when analysts observe or write that people out there (composers, performers, and audiences) hold essentialist ideas and react to music and to each other as though there were fixed, rigid expressions of racial identity. Some other writers then often write as though those who observe essentialism are themselves essentialist. They often seem to assume that if they advocate a fluid, polysemic, multicultural way of thinking it will somehow achieve that reality.

20. The metaphor is not accidental. Pete Seeger's longtime column in the folk magazine *Sing Out!* is titled "Appleseeds."

Chapter 2. Music and Boundaries: Race and Folk

1. Odum was one of the earliest and most active scholars to extend the concept of folk music to African Americans (1911). A southerner whose attitudes toward blacks might charitably be described as paternalistic (Sanders 2003), his commitment to objective social science dictated that he give broad voice to blacks he studied (Odum and Johnson 1925, 1926).

2. Different institutions can have different relationships with genres. There is probably more variation in production of music than in distribution. Classical music and popular music or rock are produced in very different kinds of organizations; symphony orchestras cannot exist without patronage and rarely take the form of profit-making enterprises. Rock bands are almost always profit oriented. But within distribution organizations, genre differences are based on sonic differences more than organizational ones. Concert tickets, CDs, radio stations, and now music downloading handle classical and rock music similarly.

3. Scholars have debated whether spirituals are more European or African, but virtually all agree that the idiom blends both, differing only in their relative influence (Cruz 1999; DuBois 1989 [1903]; Jackson 1933; Johnson and Johnson 1925; Laubenstein 1930; Perkins 1922).

4. http://www.iath.virginia.edu/utc/abolitn/absowwba2t.html.

5. It noted, however, that the individual songwriters ("poets") were of humble station, such as the informant who rowed a boat for a living.

6. Cruz argues that ethnosympathy has two main features. The first is antimodern disenchantment, Thoreau's legacy to the abolitionist movement. The second is an objectivist, scientistic view of the subordinate group. William Francis Allen's introduction to *Slave Songs of the United States*, for example, contains detailed descriptions of the slave dialects with extensive examples and analytic generalization.

7. A decade later, Henry E. Krehbiel, a musicologist who generally wrote about the European canon, not only argued that spirituals qualified as American folk music but described folk music in terms that often specifically applied to spirituals—that folk music comes from suffering, has "peculiar" rhythms, expresses a racial or ethnic temperament, and generally adopts minor modes (1914).

8. Lyrics included: "About my color I'm feeling mighty blue. I'm having lots of trouble, I'll tell it all to you. I'm certainly clean disgusted with life and that's a fact. Cause my hair is all wooly and my color it is black."

CHAPTER 3. THE ORIGINAL FOLK PROJECT

1. Pete Seeger pointed out that his father, Charles Seeger, also preferred the term "vernacular" to folk (P. Seeger 2001).

2. Alan Lomax file, Archives of American Folk Life, Library of Congress.

3. While some versions of particular ballads clearly share common roots, some versions seem quite different from each other.

4. Bluestein rebuts those who interpret Herder as a nationalist chauvinist. While some subsequent writers have cited Herder's writings to bolster chauvinist and racist claims, Herder strongly opposed racist ideas and insisted that all societies were of equal merit. Volk was an ethnic, not a racial term. He similarly rejected the idea of superman and master race: "Domination or persecution of any kind, whether of man by man, or of one nation by another, was abhorrent to his very being" (Bluestein 1994: 31).

5. Peter Buchan, a Scottish collector of the early nineteenth century, was important as much for his supposed shortcomings as the content of his works. Often maligned by critics for having no standards for what he collected, he was one of the few collectors to present his material without editorial "improvement," thus leaving more highly accurate songs than many of his more renowned contemporaries (Lomax n.d.).

6. An exception is Louis Pendleton's "Notes on Negro Folk-Lore and Witchcraft in the South" in 1891, in which he addressed "the present belief among savages that spirits dwell all about them in the very material atmosphere" (Pendleton 1891: 207).

7. Unlike some interpreters who associate Herder with reactionary nationalism, Bluestein (1994) emphasizes Herder's democratic sympathies. Contrary to the tenets of national chauvinism, Herder insisted that each culture has its own independent value and gains national character from its peasantry. What he was arguing against was the Enlightenment premise that civilization had reached its apogee, as manifested in the high culture of the elite.

8. Academic folklorists were keenly interested in American Indian culture, as the pages of the *Journal of American Folklore* attested, but treated it as entirely partitioned from white mainstream national culture.

9. Letter dated September 14, 1927, Gordon correspondence file, Archive of American Folk Life, Library of Congress.

10. The folk revival of the 1960s fundamentally changed the relation of promoters and musicians. Instead of collectors, academics, and antiquarians collecting the music of people very different from themselves, folk music has become a genre of singer-songwriters and preservationist-performers.

11. For example, Annie Williams, an informant in Friars Point, Mississippi, when asked to "sing like old folks sing," included songs learned from her grand-

mother, from sheet music, from hymn books, and from church (AFS 6642B 1942). Others interspersed songs learned from the radio or medicine shows.

Chapter 4. White and Black Reds: Building an Infrastructure

1. I use the word "hegemony" here quite intentionally to denote both the relative power of the commercial recording industry and the taken-for-granted association between music, or at least "popular music," and the products of the recording music industry. Too many histories of non-classical American music in the twentieth century exclude all noncommercial forms such as political music, church music, or community bands and choirs.

2. Of course, as McLuhan contended, the medium constrains the message, so the distinction between form and content is often ambiguous (1965). Still, it remains important to distinguish between content providers and medium of content.

3. The only substantial left-wing radio presence in the United States had different political roots. The Pacifica Foundation was organized in 1946 by pacifists and within a few years had broadcast stations in five major cities, continuing to the present day.

4. Some documents and sources spell his name "Lahn Adohmyan" and he sometimes used that spelling as a byline in the *Daily World*. But the majority of sources use "Adomian," which was the spelling used in his numerous compositions and film scores.

5. This quotation should not be interpreted to indicate that Seeger accepted the conventional whiggish view of a progression from primitive folk to sophisticated serious music. From his first year at Berkeley, he questioned the conventional teaching of music in these terms and included the folk songs of many nations in the courses that had previously included only European serious music (Pescatello 1992).

6. Some participants later recalled that singing old ballads like "Barbry Allen" in jail fostered a profound sense of solidarity, but the northern activists highlighted mainly the explicitly political songs like "Mill Mother's Lament" and "Solidarity Forever" (Roscigno and Danaher 2004).

7. Larkin later married Albert Maltz, subsequently a member of the "Hollywood Ten" screenwriters who went to jail for refusing to testify about their political activities. Seeking political refuge in Mexico, she worked as a research assistant for anthropologist Oscar Lewis on his studies of culture and poverty and wrote two novels.

8. The period of the 1930s–1940s was racially one of the most polarized in the history of popular music. Most record companies dropped the race record lists in the 1930s as predominantly white swing style by big bands became the overarching mainstream. Other genres with black participants such as jazz were also marginalized. By the postwar period, popular music was unambiguously white as an oligopolistic record industry promoted such white singers as Frank Sinatra, Patti Page, and the occasional "smooth" sounds of African Americans like Nat "King" Cole.

CHAPTER 5. MOVEMENT ENTREPRENEURS AND ACTIVISTS

1. Much of the following material on Lomax's life is taken from Porterfield's thoroughly researched and even-handed biography. Lomax's very influential daughter, Bess, became Bess Lomax Hawes. She was a performer (with the Almanacs, among others), an activist, a government official (most notably with the National Endowment for the Arts), a scholar, and a college professor. She is not included in this chapter because most of her impact came after the period covered here.

2. Most of the songs came in the mail from friends, associates, and people who answered his advertisements in local newspapers and magazines. Several had been previously published. Only a few came from the lips of cowboys (Porterfield 1996).

3. While the foundations certainly facilitated his work, it would be misleading to infer that Lomax ever worked at their behest or that they can claim credit for the growth of American folk music. Lomax was very much on a personal mission, grateful for the support when he got it but determined to proceed without it (Porterfield 1996).

4. Recognizing Lomax's contribution to folk music, even his bridging black and white music, neither ignores nor condones his personal racism. I recognize that my analysis focuses more on his achievements than his pernicious views on race. That is because for me as a sociologist, it is important to separate the consequences of action from individual motives, whether lofty or sordid.

5. Mexican Americans were also a part of this vision. For example, on their 1939 recording expedition, John and Ruby Lomax collected over one hundred Spanish-language songs in Texas (http://memory.loc.gov/ammem/lohtml/lorecexp .html).

6. Lomax-Ledbetter Correspondence, Archive of Folk Culture, Library of Congress, Washington, DC.

7. His name was found at http://www.websters-online-dictionary.org/definitions/ PL/PLATT.html (accessed June 5, 2007).

8. Later in his career, after the folk revival capped the project of making folk music a truly popular genre, Alan turned his attention to academia, developing systematic modes of musical analysis, especially cantometrics, a theory and quantitative method to identify recurrent relationships between social structures and song structures (Lomax 1962).

9. Of course, not everyone was as laudatory, at least in private. John Greenway, author of American Songs of Protest and editor of the Journal of American Folklore, wrote Archie Green, "Something else you should be wary about is Alan Lomax's one talent: conning people. I have no academic respect at all for Alan Lomax, and not a hell of a lot of personal respect" (Greenway to Green, January 18, 1967, Archie Green Papers, Collection 20002, University of North Carolina, Southern Folklore Collection, series 1, General Correspondence and Related Items, file 142).

10. Anthony Seeger, personal correspondence with the author.

11. Of course, Seegers besides the father and sons have been important to the history of folk music. Charles's first wife, Constance Edson, was a violinist and his second wife, Ruth Crawford, was a respected composer who had worked with Carl Sandburg on *The American Songbag* and often participated in musical evenings singing folk music at the Sandburg home (Pescatello 1992; Tick 1997). Charles and Ruth's daughter Peggy has for decades been a popular singer of folk songs on both sides of the Atlantic. This section focuses on Charles and Pete because they were the most active in the left-wing folk music project of the 1930s and 1940s.

12. Some authors have proposed revising this categorical scheme by lumping folk and popular music together as "vernacular," arguing that the packaging of music as a commodity does not fundamentally affect the music, and that music learned orally from friends and relatives is no more music of the people than music heard on the radio or playback machine (Green 2001a; Small 1987).

13. In addition to the easy access through Proquest (http://www.proquest.umi .com/), the *New York Times* is a bellwether of American news coverage in general. Less prominent news organizations typically take their cues from the *New York Times*, and it is very unlikely that a public figure would be nationally known without coverage in the paper.

14. It's not that he was unknown before the HUAC hearings. There were occasional references to the Almanacs or Weavers or articles that featured him but did not headline him. At the height of the Weavers' popularity, a *Newsweek* article echoed *Variety*'s hype of the group as "The hottest singing-instrumental group around today" but featured none of the singers ("Weavers' Yarn" 1951). Even when he was the focus of coverage, as in a 1955 piece in the *Detroit Free Press*, "Folk Singer Boasts Revival-Tent Fervor" (April 11), he lacked the name recognition to identify without a description.

15. Retrospective accounts such as Cantwell's portray the folk revival as the dramatic and surprising rupture of the Kingston Trio into the world of rock and roll (1998). Articles like this suggest that the narrative of the abrupt folk revolution may be based more on number-one songs than on a broader reading of the musical terrain.

16. http://www.youtube.com/watch?v=3YlLtmMV8zs.

As I went walking I saw a sign there
And on the sign it said "No Trespassing."
But on the other side it didn't say nothing,
That side was made for you and me.
(http://www.woodyguthrie.org/Lyrics/This_Land.htm)

CHAPTER 6. ORGANIZING MUSIC: THE FRUITS OF ENTREPRENEURSHIP

1. After their CBS broadcasts, Decca Records made overtures for a contract but withdrew after red-baiting press coverage.

2. Though widely accused—both at the time and in subsequent histories—of

reversing their attitudes in response to the CP's new party line, Seeger has pointed out that virtually all progressives reversed course and supported the war. He insists that no one, CP or otherwise, told them to change their songs (Seeger interview with Reuss, April 9, 1968).

3. Even though several of these later recanted their political commitments, they did make a meaningful contribution to the movement.

4. It would have been interesting to see how he used the dozen or so musical examples included in each class. For example, how would his playing of Bach's "Little Fugue in G Minor" validate his attribution to Bach of the "final synthesis of the Absolute Central Idea of Feudalism" (Hay 1948: 10-1) or his contention that the concerto embodied "the cultural censoring intentions of the Counter-reformation . . . transformed into its deadly opposite" (Hay 1948: 11-1).

5. There were even voices that presaged the surge of popular singing in the folk revival of the late 1950s and early 1960s. Courtlandt Canby, reviewing *The Fireside Book of Folk Songs* in the *Saturday Review*, described the popularity of ordinary people singing: "Young people with a guitar singing together the cowboy ballads or the songs of the Spanish Civil War, the 'aficionados' of the ballad-singer cult, the more staid discoverers of English folk songs, the blues devotees, the college and school glee clubs with their arrangement of songs from many lands—all have helped to pull us out of the nineteenth-century slough of sentimentality and cheapness" (quoted in Cohen and Samuelson 1996: 30).

6. A viable case could have been made within Marxist theory to rely on volunteers for music. Treating all effort as labor commodifies it, as though it were part of capitalist relations of production. Marx was highly critical of tendencies to transform all social relations into capitalist relations, to commodify all effort as paid labor. The party ironically eschewed the social relations of a communist system by insisting that labor be treated as a commodity. Instead they decided to undermine capitalism by mirroring it.

7. Oscar Brand (1962) gives a somewhat different account, downplaying the politics of the organization and describing the organization and its activities as a mere extension of the magazine. While acknowledging that the mood of the country was progressive, he says little about any vision of a broad political movement.

CHAPTER 7. THE HIGHLANDER SCHOOL

1. Paul R. Christopher to Carey E. Haigler, April 28, 1945, Highlander Archives, box 60, folder 1.

CHAPTER 8. MUSIC AT THE HEART OF THE QUINTESSENTIAL SOCIAL MOVEMENT

1. The trio later went to the Highlander School and appeared at a Carnegie Hall benefit for the Highlander in 1961.

2. Bond was later an activist in the movement, a congressman, and the president of the NAACP.

3. Other songs, especially those from the black churches, had no explicit political lyrics but were accorded political connotations from their use in the movement. For example, the mistreatment sung of in "I've Been 'Buked, and I've Been Scorned," once thought of as personal mistreatment, was interpreted anew as racial injustice.

4. Sweet Honey and the Rock sang "Calypso Freedom," essentially the same song with additional verses, with writing credit given to Cynthia Tierney.

5. The song was later recorded by Harry Belafonte, *Belafonte on Campus*, RCA LSP-779.

6. Stories in other newspapers were using the song as representative of music in political events but were not taking it for granted that audiences would know it. A story in the *Los Angeles Times* in the summer of 1963 described a Baltimore demonstration in which protesters were singing the song, "their favorite demonstration song" ("Head of Presbyterians Seized in Racial March" 1963).

7. ProQuest Historical Newspapers, *New York Times* (1851–2001), http://www.proquest.umi.com/.

8. Carawan's *Freedom Is a Constant Struggle* was the only other compilation of civil rights songs actually published during the integrationist phase of the civil rights movement (1960–66), as documented in the Library of Congress catalog "African Americans' Civil Rights Songs and Music" (http://www.catalog.loc.gov).

9. Few of their songs addressed racial issues in their lyrics. Baez's "Ghetto" was explicit as any but was not nearly as well-known as her rendition of Phil Ochs's "There But for Fortune," which readily lent itself to a racial interpretation. Her concerts and albums also included such freedom songs as "Oh, Freedom" and "We Shall Overcome," exposing non-activist listeners to the music of the movement in contexts other than newscasts or documentaries.

CHAPTER 9. A MOVEMENT SPLINTERED

1. Several SNCC chapters became affiliated with the Black Panther Party, but the alliance lasted only five months (Stoper 1989).

2. http://libweb.uoregon.edu/govdocs/micro/uginv.htm.

3. Other high-resource organizations such as Newsreel depended on sales and donations. A factor that made the underground papers more rooted—their localism—also made them more dependent on capitalist enterprise.

4. If we switch from using "cultural" to mean arts, music, and literature to the anthropological use to mean the symbolic level of reality, and from using "political" as organized mobilization in relationship to the state to mean social relationships of coalition and conflict, these two levels could be characterized as the cultural level and the political level.

5. R. L. Haeberle (photographer) and Peter Brandt (designer); Art Workers Coalition.

6. The author was a member from 1969 to 1971.

CHAPTER 10. HOW SOCIAL MOVEMENTS DO CULTURE

1. The claim should be a bit more qualified, perhaps describing itself as one of the first. There were a few earlier comparative studies of social movement culture. See, e.g., Mattern 1998.

2. While there is no reason why sociologists could not study iterative processes by which previous cultural work changes social movements or recruits, setting the stage for later culturally informed decisions, this is rarely done. However, see Pedriana and Stryker (1997) for an effective analysis of how discourse at one point in time can influence later discursive interaction.

3. A relational approach to social movements can take at least three forms. The most common is the network approach (Andrews and Biggs 2006; Diani and McAdam 2003; Gould 1995; Klandermans and Oegema 1987; Marwell, Oliver, and Prahl 1988; Snow, Zurcher, and Ekland-Olson 1980). Here the content of cultural work is refracted through the structure of relationships within which a recruit is embedded. Such factors as the unanimity of influence, the number of people that influence a recruit, and the extent to which interaction partners interact with each other all have an effect on how people make decisions. A second relational approach focuses on various enduring qualities of interaction among people. Trust, emotional bonds, and solidarity among people enable cultural work, making potential recruits more open to influence (Jasper 1998; Stepan-Norris and Zeitlin 1989; Tilly 2005). A third approach, which is emphasized here, focuses on the social dynamics of the interaction as it happens, examining how the nature of what is going on at the time of the interaction affects the consequences of *doing* culture. For example, the social relationships in a classical music performance are shaped by such factors as the architecture, physical layout, performance practices, norms of audience comportment, and the division of labor among composer, performer, conductor, and audience (Small 1998). Similarly, DeNora (2000) describes how the activities that people do *to* music shapes not only the meaning of the music but the activities being done, whether solitary listening, aerobics, shopping, making love, or raving. The social relations interact with the sonic qualities to shape the experience, as music *affords* or lends itself to different ways of experiencing.

4. http://www.earthman.tv/2004/index.html.

References

Adorno, Theodor W. 2000. *On Classes and Strata: Music, Culture, and Society*. New York: Oxford University Press.

AFS 6642B. 1942. The Library of Congress/Fisk University Mississippi Delta Collection. Tape 420. Lwo No. 4872.

Alexander, Jeffrey C. 1996. "Collective Action, Culture and Civil Society: Secularizing, Updating, Inverting, Revising and Displacing the Classical Model of Social Movements." Pp. 205–34 in *Alain Touraine*, ed. Marco Diani and Jon Clarke. London: Falmer Press.

Allen, William Francis, Charles Pickard Ware, and Lucy McKim Garrison. 1971. *Slave Songs of the United States*. Freeport, NY: Books for Libraries Press.

"American Songs Are Played and Sung for King and Queen." 1939. *New York Times*, June 9, p. 5.

Aminzade, Ronald, Jack A. Goldstone, Doug McAdam, Elisabeth J. Perry, William H. Sewell Jr., Sidney Tarrow, and Charles Tilly. 2001. *Silence and Voice in the Study of Contentious Politics*. Cambridge: Cambridge University Press.

Anderson, Benedict. 1991. *Imagined Communities*. New York: Verso.

Andrews, Kenneth T. 2004. *Freedom Is a Constant Struggle: The Mississippi Civil Rights Movement and Its Legacy*. Chicago: University of Chicago Press.

Andrews, K. T., and M. Biggs. 2006. "The Dynamics of Protest Diffusion: Movement Organizations, Social Networks, and News Media in the 1960 Sit-Ins." *American Sociological Review* 71:752–77.

Archie Green Folio. "A Carter Family Bibliography." Southern Folklore Collection, University of North Carolina, Chapel Hill.

Armstrong, David. 1981. *Trumpet to Arms: Alternative Media in America*. Cambridge, MA: South End Press.

Barlow, William. 1989. *"Looking up at Down": The Emergence of Blues Culture*. Philadelphia: Temple University Press.

Becker, Howard S. 1982. *Art Worlds*. Berkeley: University of California Press.

Benford, Robert D., and David A. Snow. 2000. "Framing Processes and Social Movements: An Overview and Assessment." *Annual Review of Sociology* 26: 611–39.

Berezin, Mabel. 1994. "Cultural Form and Political Meaning: State-Subsidized Theater, Ideology, and the Language of Style in Fascist Italy." *American Journal of Sociology* 99:1237–86.

Blacking, John, and R. Byron. 1995. *Music, Culture & Experience: Selected Papers of John Blacking*. Chicago: University of Chicago Press.

Bledsoe, Thomas. 1969. *Or We'll All Hang Separately: The Highlander Idea*. Boston: Beacon.

Bluestein, Gene. 1994. *Poplore: Folk and Pop in American Culture*. Amherst: University of Massachusetts Press.

Bohlman, Philip V. 1999. "Ontologies of Music." Pp. 17–34 in *Rethinking Music*, ed. Nicholas Cook and Mark Everist. Oxford: Oxford University Press.

Bourdieu, Pierre. 1984. *Distinction: A Social Critique of the Judgement of Taste*. Cambridge, MA: Harvard University Press.

Bowker, Geoffrey C., and Susan Leigh Star. 1999. *Sorting Things Out: Classification and Its Consequences*. Cambridge, MA: MIT Press.

Brand, Oscar. 1962. *The Ballad Mongers: Rise of the Modern Folk Song*. New York: Funk & Wagnalls.

Brazier, Richard. 1968. "The Story of the I.W.W.'s Little Red Songbook." *Labor History* 9:91–106.

Browder, Earl. 1968. "Interview with Earl Browder by Richard Reuss 2/12/68 at His Home in Princeton, NJ." Southern Folklore Collection, University of North Carolina, Chapel Hill.

Bryson, Bethany. 1996. "'Anything But Heavy Metal': Symbolic Exclusion and Musical Dislikes." *American Sociological Review* 61:884–99.

———. 2001. "Working Definitions: A Symbolic Boundaries Approach to the Meaning of Multiculturalism." http://peregrin.jmu.edu/~brysonbp/symbound/papers2001/Bryson.html (accessed 2009).

Campbell, Gavin James. 1999. "Music and the Making of a Jim Crow Culture, 1900–1925." Ph.D. diss., University of Georgia.

Campbell, John L. 2004. *Institutional Change and Globalization*. Princeton: Princeton University Press.

Cantwell, Robert. 1998. *When We Were Good: The Folk Revival*. Cambridge, MA: Harvard University Press.

Carawan, Guy, and Candie Carawan. 1963. *We Shall Overcome! Songs of the Southern Freedom Movement*. New York: Oak Publications.

———. 1990. *Sing for Freedom: The Story of the Civil Rights Movement through Its Songs*. Bethlehem, PA: Sing Out Corp.

———. 2001. Interview by the author. July 17. Riverside, CA.

Carson, Clayborne. 1981. *In Struggle: SNCC and the Black Awakening of the 1960s*. Cambridge, MA: Harvard University Press.

Cerulo, Karen A. 1995. *Identity Designs: The Sights and Sounds of a Nation*. New Brunswick, NJ: Rutgers University Press.

Clayton, Martin, Rebecca Sager, and Udo Will. 2005. "In Time with the Music: The Concept of Entrainment and Its Significance for Ethnomusicology." *ESEM CounterPoint* 11:3–75.

Cohen, Norm. 1990. *Folk Song America: A 20th Century Revival*. Washington, DC: Smithsonian Collection of Recordings.

Cohen, Ronald D. 2000. "*Broadside* Magazine and Records, 1962–1988." Pp. 11–17 in *The Best of Broadside, 1962–1988: Anthems of the American Underground from the Pages of Broadside*, ed. Jeff Place and Ronald D. Cohen. Washington, DC: Smithsonian Folkways Recordings.

Cohen, Ronald D., and Dave Samuelson. 1996. *Songs for Political Action: Folk Music, Topical Songs and the American Left, 1926–1953*. Hambergen: Germany: Bear Family Records.

"Composers Collective." 1936. *Daily World*, p. 7.

Congress of Racial Equality. 1962. *Sit-In Songs*. Congress of Racial Equality.

Cooke, Deryck. 1959. *The Language of Music*. New York: Oxford University Press.

Courlander, Harold. 1992. *Negro Folk Music U.S.A.* New York: Dover.

Cruz, Jon. 1999. *Culture on the Margins: The Black Spiritual and the Rise of American Cultural Interpretation*. Princeton: Princeton University Press.

"Cultural Capitalizers." 1969. *Quicksilver Times*, August 26–September 9, pp. 14–15.

Darnovsky, Marcy, Barbara Epstein, and Richard Flacks. 1995. *Cultural Politics and Social Movements*. Philadelphia: Temple University Press.

Denisoff, R. Serge. 1971. *Great Day Coming: Folk Music and the American Left*. Urbana: University of Illinois Press.

———. 1983. *Sing a Song of Social Significance*. Bowling Green: Bowling Green State University Popular Press.

Denning, Michael. 1996. *The Cultural Front: The Laboring of American Culture in the Twentieth Century*. London: Verso.

DeNora, Tia. 2000. *Music in Everyday Life*. New York: Cambridge University Press.

———. 2002. "Music into Action: Performing Gender on the Viennese Concert Stage, 1790–1810." *Poetics* 30:19–33.

———. 2003. *After Adorno: Rethinking Music Sociology*. New York: Cambridge University Press.

Diani, Mario, and Doug McAdam, eds. 2003. *Social Movements and Networks: Relational Approaches to Collective Action*. New York: Oxford University Press.

DiMaggio, Paul. 1982a. "Cultural Entrepreneurship in Nineteenth-Century Boston, Part I: The Creation of an Organizational Base for High Culture in America." *Media, Culture, and Society* 4:33–50.

———. 1982b. "Cultural Entrepreneurship in Nineteenth-Century Boston, Part II: The Classification and Framing of American Art." *Media, Culture, and Society* 4:303–22.

DiMaggio, Paul J., and Walter W. Powell. 1983. "The Iron Cage Revisited: Institutional Isomorphism and Collective Rationality in Organizational Fields." *American Sociological Review* 48:147–60.

Doggett, David. 1992. "*The Kudzu*: Birth and Death in Underground Mississippi." Pp. 213–32 in *Voices from the Underground: Insider Histories of the Vietnam Era Underground Press*, ed. Ken Wachsberger. Tempe, AZ: Mica's Press.

Douglass, Frederick. 1997 [1845]. *Narrative of the Life of Frederick Douglass: An American Slave. Written by Himself*. New York: Signet Classic.

DuBois, W.E.B. 1989 [1903]. *The Souls of Black Folk*. New York: Bantam.

Du Gay, Paul. 1997. *Doing Cultural Studies: The Story of the Sony Walkman*. Thousand Oaks, CA: Sage.

Dunaway, David King. 1980. "Charles Seeger and Carl Sands: The Composers' Collective Years." *Ethnomusicology* 24:159–68.

———. 1990. *How Can I Keep from Singing: Pete Seeger*. New York: Da Capo Press.

Dunson, Josh. 1964. "Slave Songs at the 'Sing for Freedom.'" *Broadside*, no. 46.

Dunson, Josh. 1965. *Freedom in the Air: Song Movements of the Sixties*. Westport, CT: Greenwood Press.

"Editorials: People's Songs." 1947. *Christian Science Monitor*, March 4.

Edmands, Lila W. 1893. "Songs from the Mountains of North Carolina." *Journal of American Folklore* 6:131–34.

Eisler, Hanns. 1938. "Speech to the Choir of the International Ladies' Garment Workers Union." http://unionsong.com/muse/unionsong/reviews/eisler1.html (accessed July 9, 2004).

Ennis, Philip H. 1992. *The Seventh Stream: The Emergence of Rocknroll in America*. Hanover, NH: Wesleyan University Press.

Epstein, Steven. 1996. *Impure Science: AIDS, Activism, and the Politics of Knowledge*. Berkeley: University of California Press.

Evans, Sara M., and Harry C. Boyte. 1987. *Free Spaces: The Source of Democratic Change in America*. New York: Harper and Row.

Eyerman, Ron, and Andrew Jamison. 1991. *Social Movements: A Cognitive Approach*. University Park: Pennsylvania State University Press.

———. 1995. "Social Movements and Cultural Transformation: Popular Music in the 1960s." *Media, Culture, and Society* 17:449–68.

———. 1998. *Music and Social Movements*. New York: Cambridge University Press.

Fabbri, Franco. 1982. "A Theory of Musical Genres: Two Applications." In *Popular Music Perspectives*, ed. Philip Tagg and David Horn. Gothenburg and Exeter: IASPM.

Feld, Steven. 1984. "Sound Structure as Social Structure." *Ethnomusicology* 28:383–409.

Feld, Steven, and Aaron A. Fox. 1994. "Music and Language." *Annual Review of Anthropology* 23:25–53.

Felien, Ed. 1992. "Let a Hundred Flowers Blossom, Let a Hundred Schools of Thought Contend: The Story of *Hundred Flowers*." Pp. 305–12 in *Voices from the Underground: Insider Histories of the Vietnam Era Underground Press*, ed. Ken Wachsberger. Tempe, AZ: Mica's Press.

Filene, Benjamin. 1991. "Our Singing Country: John and Alan Lomax, Leadbelly and the Construction of the American Past." *American Quarterly* 43:602–24.

———. 2000. *Romancing the Folk: Public Memory & American Roots Music*. Chapel Hill: University of North Carolina Press.

Finnegan, Ruth. 1989. *The Hidden Musicians: Music-Making in an English Town*. Cambridge: Cambridge University Press.

Flacks, Richard. 1988. *Making History: The American Left and the American Mind*. New York: Columbia University Press.

———. 1999. "Culture and Social Movements: Exploring the Power of Song." Paper presented at the Annual Meeting of the American Sociological Association, Chicago.

Flores, Angel. 1935. *Latin American Folk Festival*. Festival program.

"Folk-Lore Collected." 1928. *Daily Worker*, January 13, p. 6.

"Folk Singing." 1962. *Time*, November 23.

Foner, Philip S. 1975. *American Labor Songs of the Nineteenth Century*. Urbana: University of Illinois Press.

Forten, Charlotte. 1864. "Life on the Sea Islands." *Atlantic Monthly*, May and June.

Frith, Simon. 1989. "Towards an Aesthetic of Popular Music." Pp. 133–49 in *Music and Society: The Politics of Composition, Performance and Reception*, ed. Richard Leppert and Susan McClary. New York: Cambridge University Press.

———. 1996. *Performing Rights: On the Value of Popular Music*. Cambridge, MA: Harvard University Press.

Frith, Simon, Stuart Hall, and Paul Du Gay. 1996. "Music and Identity." Pp. 108–27 in *Questions of Cultural Identity*, ed. Stuart Hall and Paul Du Gay. Thousand Oaks, CA: Sage.

Futrell, Robert, Pete Simi, and Simon Gottschalk. 2006. "Understanding Music in Movements: The White Power Music Scene." *Sociological Quarterly* 47:275–304.

Gabb, Sally. 1992. "A Fowl in the Vortices of Consciousness: The Birth of the *Great Speckled Bird*." Pp. 41–50 in *Voices from the Underground: Insider Histories of the Vietnam Era Underground Press*, ed. Ken Wachsberger. Tempe, AZ: Mica's Press.

Gaillard, F. 2004. *Cradle of Freedom: Alabama and the Movement That Changed America*. Tuscaloosa: University of Alabama Press.

Gamson, Joshua. 1997. "Messages of Exclusion: Gender, Movements, and Symbolic Boundaries." *Gender & Society* 11:178–99.

Gamson, William A. 1975. *The Strategy of Social Protest*. Homewood, IL: Dorsey.

———. 1992. *Talking Politics*. New York: Cambridge University Press.

Gamson, William A., David Croteau, William Hoynes, and Theodore Sasson. 1992. "Media Images and the Social Construction of Reality." *Annual Review of Sociology* 18:373–93.

Gates, David. 1990. "The Voices of America." *Newsweek*, 116:60.

Geismar, Maxwell, and Joseph North. 1969. "Introduction." Pp. 5-13 *in New Masses: An Anthology of the Rebel Thirties*, ed. Joseph North. New York: International Publishers.

Gilroy, Paul. 1993. *The Black Atlantic: Modernity and Double Consciousness*. Cambridge, MA: Harvard University Press.

Gioia, Ted. 2006. *Work Songs*. Durham: Duke University Press.

Gitlin, Todd. 1979. *The Whole World Is Watching: Mass Media in the Making and Unmaking of the New Left*. Berkeley: University of California Press.

Glazer, Joe. 2001. *Labor's Troubadour*. Urbana: University of Illinois Press.

Glazer, Tom. 1970. *Songs of Peace, Freedom, and Protest*. New York: D. McKay Company.

Glen, John M. 1988. *Highlander: No Ordinary School*. Lexington: University of Kentucky Press.

Goodwin, Jeff, and James M. Jasper. 2003. *Rethinking Social Movements: Structure, Meaning, and Emotion*. Lanham, MD: Rowman and Littlefield.

Goodwin, Jeff, James M. Jasper, and Francesca Polletta. 2001. *Passionate Politics: Emotions and Social Movements*. Chicago: University of Chicago Press.

Gould, Roger V. 1995. *Insurgent Identities: Class, Community, and Protest in Paris from 1848 to the Commune*. Chicago: University of Chicago Press.

Green, Archie. 1993. *Wobblies, Pile Butts, and Other Heroes: Laborlore Explorations*. Urbana: University of Illinois Press.

————. 2001a. *Torching the Fink Books & Other Essays on Vernacular Culture*. Chapel Hill: University of North Carolina Press.

————. 2001b. Interview by the author. February 27. Oakland, CA.

Haessler, Carl. 1945. *Highlander Folk School Activity Double Last Year's*. Detroit: Federated Press Central Bureau.

Hanson, Michael. 2008. "Suppose James Brown Read Fanon: The Black Arts Movement, Cultural Nationalism and the Failure of Popular Musical Praxis." *Popular Music* 27:341–65.

Harker, Dave. 1985. *Fakesong: The Manufacture of the British "Folksong": 1700 to the Present*. Milton Keynes, IL: Open University Press.

Hart, Virginia. 1944. "Report on Community Relations Class of CIO Term." Highlander School Archives, box 59, folder 14, Monteagle, TN.

Hawes, Bess Lomax. 2001. Interview by the author. March 28. Northridge, CA.

Hay, Harry. 1948. "Music . . . Barometer of the Class Struggle." Lecture notes. Los Angeles.

"Head of Presbyterians Seized in Racial March." 1963. *Los Angeles Times*, pp. 1, 12.

Hebdige, Dick. 1979. *Subculture: The Meaning of Style*. New York: Routledge.

Hemingway, Andrew. 2002. *Artists on the Left: American Artists and the Communist Movement, 1926–1956*. New Haven: Yale University Press.

Hickerson, Joseph. 2000. Interview by the author. August 9. Washington, DC.

Highlander Folk School. 1955. "Annual Report." Highlander Folk School, Monteagle, TN.

Highlander School. n.d. "Black Power." Highlander School Archives, reel 37, Monteagle, TN.

Hippler, Bob. 1992. "Fast Times in the Motor City: The First Ten Years of the *Fifth Estate*, 1965–75." Pp. 9–36 in *Voices from the Underground: Insider Histories of the Vietnam Era Underground Press*, ed. Ken Wachsberger. Tempe, AZ: Mica's Press.

Horton, Aimee Isgrig. 1989. *The Highlander Folk School: A History of Its Major Programs, 1932–1961*. Brooklyn, NY: Carlson Publishing.

Horton, Myles. 1967. "Notes to Himself." in Papers 1851–1990, vol. Box 1-18 MAD2M/26/S4-6. Madison, WI: Wisconsin Historical Society.

Ikegami, Eiko. 2005. *Bonds of Civility: Aesthetic Networks and the Political Origins of Japanese Culture*. New York: Cambridge University Press.

Jackson, George Pullen. 1933. *White Spirituals in the Southern Uplands*. Chapel Hill: University of North Carolina Press.

Jasper, James M. 1997. *The Art of Moral Protest: Culture, Biography, and Creativity in Social Movements*. Chicago: University of Chicago Press.

————. 1998. "The Emotions of Protest: Affective and Reactive Emotions in and around Social Movements." *Sociological Forum* 13:397–424.

Johnson, James Weldon, and J. Rosamond Johnson. 1925. *The Book of American Negro Spirituals*. New York: Viking Press.

Johnston, Hank, and Bert Klandermans. 1995. *Social Movements and Culture*. Minneapolis: University of Minnesota Press.

Johnston, Hank, and John A. Noakes, eds. 2005. *Frames of Protest: Social Movements and the Framing Perspective.* Lanham, MD: Rowman and Littlefield.

Kahn, Ed, and Ronald D. Cohen. 2003. Pp. 1–8 in *Introduction to Part I: 1934–1950: The Early Collecting Years.* New York: Routledge.

Kane, Anne. 1991. "Cultural Analysis in Historical Sociology: The Analytic and Concrete Forms of the Autonomy of Culture." *Sociological Theory* 9:53–69.

———. 1997. "Theorizing Meaning Construction in Social Movements: Symbolic Structures and Interpretation during the Irish Land War, 1879–1882." *Sociological Theory* 15:249–76.

Kaplan, Arlene E. 1955. "A Study of Folksinging in a Mass Society." *Sociologus* 5:14–28.

Karpeles, Maud. 1932 [1904]. Preface to *English Folk Songs from the Southern Appalachians.* Vol. 1. London: Oxford University Press.

Kelley, Robin D. G. 1990. *Hammer and Hoe: Alabama Communists during the Great Depression.* Chapel Hill: University of North Carolina Press.

Kennard, James K., Jr. 1996 [1845]. "Who Are Our National Poets." Pp. 50–63 in *Inside the Minstrel Mask*, ed. Annemarie Bean et al. Hanover, NH: Wesleyan University Press.

Kent, Robert. 1934. "Singing for the 'Daily.'" *Daily Worker*, January 17, p. 5.

King, Martin Luther, Jr. 1958. *Stride toward Freedom.* New York: Harper and Row.

———. 1963. *Why We Can't Wait.* New York: Harper and Row.

Kittredge, George Lyman. 1932 [1904]. Introduction to *The English and Scottish Popular Ballads*, ed. Francis J. Child. New York: Houghton Mifflin.

———. 1965 [1882]. "Biographical Sketch of Professor Child." Pp. xxiii–xxxi in *The English and Scottish Popular Ballads*, vol. 1, ed. Francis J. Child. New York: Dover.

Klandermans, Bert. 1992. "The Social Construction of Protest and Multiorganizational Fields." Pp. 77–103 in *Frontiers in Social Movement Theory*, eds. Aldon D. Morris and Carol McClurg Mueller. New Haven: Yale University Press.

Klandermans, Bert, and Dirk Oegema. 1987. "Potentials, Networks, Motivations, and Barriers: Steps towards Participation in Social Movements." *American Sociological Review* 52:519–31.

Klein, Joe. 1980. *Woody Guthrie: A Life.* New York: Delta.

Krehbiel, Henry E. 1914. *Afro-American Folk Songs.* New York: G. Schirmer.

Lamont, Michèle, and Marcel Fournier. 1992. "Introduction." Pp. 1–20 in *Cultivating Differences: Symbolic Boundaries and the Making of Inequality*, ed. Michèle Lamont and M. Fournier. Chicago: University of Chicago Press.

Lamont, Michèle, and Virág Molnár. 2002. "The Study of Boundaries in the Social Sciences." *Annual Review of Sociology* 28:167–95.

Larkin, Margaret. 1929. "Ella May's Songs." *The Nation*, pp. 382–83.

Lasswell, Harold D. 1936. *Politics: Who Gets What, When, How.* New York: Whittlesy House.

Laubenstein, Paul Fritz. 1930. "Race Values in Aframerican Music." *Musical Quarterly* 16:378–403.

Lawless, Ray M. 1960. *Folksingers and Folksongs in America.* New York: Duell, Sloan and Pearce.

Leblanc, Lauraine. 1999. *Pretty in Punk: Girls' Gender Resistance in a Boys' Subculture*. New Brunswick, NJ: Rutgers University Press.

Lehman, Christopher Paul. 2006. "Civil Rights in Twilight: The End of the Civil Rights Movement Era in 1973." *Journal of Black Studies* 36:415.

"Lenin Meetings Hear New Songs and Fine Pageant." 1923. *Daily Worker*, p. 2.

Lester, Julius. 1966. "The Angry Children of Malcolm X." *Sing Out!* October–November, pp. 21–24.

Levine, Lawrence W. 1977. *Black Culture and Black Consciousness: Afro-American Folk Thought from Slavery to Freedom*. New York: Oxford University Press.

———. 1988. *Highbrow, Lowbrow: The Emergence of Cultural Hierarchy in America*. Cambridge, MA: Harvard University Press.

Levitin, Daniel J. 2008. *The World in Six Songs: How the Musical Brain Created Human Nature*. New York: Dutton.

Lhamon, W. T., Jr. 1998. *Raising Cain: Blackface Performance from Jim Crow to Hip Hop*. Cambridge, MA: Harvard University Press.

Lieberman, Robbie. 1995. *"My Song Is My Weapon": People's Songs, American Communism, and the Politics of Culture, 1930–1950*. Urbana: University of Illinois Press.

Lipsitz, George. 2000. *Time Passages: Collective Memory and American Popular Culture*. Minneapolis: University of Minnesota Press.

Little, Paul H. 1956. "Seeger Helps Restore American Folk Heritage." *Down Beat*, May 30, p. 16.

Lloyd Ellis, Donna. 1971. "The Underground Press in America: 1955–1970." *Journal of Popular Culture* 5:102–24.

Lomax, Alan. 1942. "Fisk University Mississippi Delta Collection." Washington, DC: Library of Congress.

———. 1959. "Folk Song Style." *American Anthropologist* 61:927–54.

———. 1960. *The Folk Songs of North America*. New York: Doubleday.

———. 1962. "Song Structure and Social Structure." *Ethnology* 1:1–27.

———. 1965. "Negro Folk Songs and the Freedom Movement." Highlander School Archives, reel 31, Monteagle, TN.

———. 1968. *Folk Song Style and Culture*. Washington, DC: American Association for the Advancement of Science.

———. 2003a. *Alan Lomax: Selected Writings, 1934–1997*. New York: Routledge.

———. 2003b. "Folk Music in the Roosevelt Era." Pp. 92–96 in *Alan Lomax: Selected Writings, 1934–1997*, ed. Ronald D. Cohen. New York: Routledge.

———. n.d. "A History of the English Ballad-Controversy." Alan Lomax Collection, file 19, Archive of Folk Culture, Library of Congress, Washington, DC.

Lomax, Alan, and R. Rudd. 1976. *Cantometrics: A Method in Musical Anthropology*. Berkeley: University of California Extension Media Center.

Lomax, John A. 1934. "'Sinful Songs' of the Southern Negro." *Musical Quarterly* 20:177–87.

Lomax, John A., and Alan Lomax. 1934. *American Ballads and Folk Songs*. New York: Macmillan.

———. 1946. *American Ballads and Folk Songs*. New York: Macmillan.

———. 1947. *Best Loved American Folk Songs (Folk Song: U. S. A.)*. New York: Grosset and Dunlap.

Lomax, John Avery, Alan Lomax, Ruth Crawford Seeger, and Harold William Thompson. 1941. *Our Singing Country: A Second Volume of American Ballads and Folk Songs*. New York: Macmillan.

Lopes, Paul. 2002. *The Rise of a Jazz Art World*. New York: Cambridge University Press.

Lott, Eric. 1993. *Love and Theft: Blackface Minstrelsy and the American Working Class*. New York: Oxford University Press.

Lydon, Michael. 1969. "Rock for Sale." *Ramparts* 19:21–24.

M. M. 1936. "Festival of Music League to Open Here Tomorrow." *Daily Worker*, p. 7.

Martin, Bradford D. 2004. *The Theater Is in the Street: Politics and Performance in Sixties America*. Amherst: University of Massachusetts Press.

Martin, Peter J. 1995. *Sounds and Society: Themes in the Sociology of Music*. Manchester: Manchester University Press.

Marwell, Gerald, Pamela E. Oliver, and Ralph Prahl. 1988. "Social Networks and Collective Action: A Theory of the Critical Mass, III." *American Journal of Sociology* 94:502–34.

Mattern, Mark. 1998. *Acting in Concert: Music, Community, and Political Action*. New Brunswick, NJ: Rutgers University Press.

McAdam, Doug. 1982. *Political Process and the Development of Black Insurgency*. Chicago: University of Chicago Press.

———. 1994. "Culture and Social Movements." Pp. 36–56 in *New Social Movements: From Ideology to Identity*, ed. Enrique Larana et al. Philadelphia: Temple University Press.

———. 2001. "Culture and Social Movements." Pp. 253–68 in *Culture and Politics: A Reader*, ed. Lane Crothers and Charles Lockhart. New York: St. Martin's Press.

McAdam, Doug, Sidney Tarrow, and Charles Tilly. 2001. *Dynamics of Contention*. New York: Cambridge Universtity Press.

McClary, Susan. 2000. *Conventional Wisdom: The Content of Musical Form*. Berkeley: University of California Press.

McKim, James Miller. 1862. "Negro Songs." *Dwight's Journal of Music*, August 9.

McLuhan, Marshall. 1965. *Understanding Media*. New York: McGraw-Hill.

McNeill, William H. 1995. *Keeping Together in Time: Dance and Drill in Human History*. Cambridge, MA: Harvard University Press.

Meier, August, and Elliott M. Rudwick. 1973. *CORE: A Study in the Civil Rights Movement, 1942–1968*. New York: Oxford University Press.

Meyer, David S., Nancy Whittier, and Belinda Robnett. 2002. *Social Movements: Identity, Culture, and the State*. New York: Oxford University Press.

Mills, Kay. 1993. *This Little Light of Mine: The Life of Fannie Lou Hamer*. New York: Dutton.

Mishler, Paul. 1999. *Raising Reds: The Young Pioneers, Radical Summer Camps, and Communist Political Culture in the United States.* New York: Columbia University Press.

Morris, Alden. 1981. "Black Southern Sit-In Movement: An Analysis of Internal Organization." *American Sociological Review* 46:744–67.

———. 1984. *The Origins of the Civil Rights Movement: Black Communities Organizing for Change.* New York: The Free Press.

Motherwell, William. 1873 [1827]. *Minstrelsy, Ancient and Modern.* Paisley, Scotland: Alex. Gardner.

"The Movement Stirs Folk Revival." 1965. *Southern Patriot.*

Narvaez, Peter. 1996. "A Tribute: Kenneth S. Goldstein, Record Producer." *Journal of American Folklore* 109:450–51.

Neal, Mark Anthony. 1999. *What the Music Said: Black Popular Music and the Black Public Culture.* New York: Routledge.

Negus, Keith. 1996. *Popular Music in Theory: An Introduction.* Hanover, NH: Wesleyan University Press.

Negus, Keith, and Patria RománVelázquez. 2002. "Belonging and Detachment: Musical Experience and the Limits of Identity." *Poetics* 30:133–45.

Newfield, Jack. 1967. "One Cheer for the Hippies." *The Nation* 204:809–10.

Odum, Howard W. 1911. "Folk-Song and Folk-Poetry as Found in the Secular Songs of the Southern Negroes." *Journal of American Folklore* 24:255–94, 351–96.

Odum, Howard W., and Guy B. Johnson. 1925. *The Negro and His Songs: A Study of Typical Negro Songs in the South.* Chapel Hill: University of North Carolina Press.

———. 1926. *Negro Workaday Songs.* Chapel Hill: University of North Carolina Press.

Ogbar, Jeffrey, and Ogbonna Green. 2004. *Black Power: Radical Politics and African American Identity.* Baltimore: Johns Hopkins University Press.

Payne, Charles M. 1995. *I've Got the Light of Freedom: The Organizing Tradition and the Mississippi Freedom Struggle.* Berkeley: University of California Press.

Peck, Abe. 1985. *Uncovering the Sixties: The Life and Times of the Underground Press.* New York: Pantheon Books.

Pedriana, Nicholas, and Robin Stryker. 1997. "Political Culture Wars 1960s Style: Equal Employment Opportunity–Affirmative Action Law and the Philadelphia Plan." *American Journal of Sociology* 103:633–91.

Pendleton, Louis. 1891. "Notes on Negro Folklore and Witchcraft in the South." *Journal of American Folk-Lore* 3:201–7.

People's Artists. 1949a. "CNA Workshop Makes Bow with Mozart Opera." In People's Songs Collection, box 21-1, Archives of Labor & Urban Affairs, Detroit.

———. 1949b. "'Peace on Earth' Hootenanny for Christmas Eve." Press release, Archie Green Papers, University of North Carolina, Chapel Hill.

"People's Songs." 1946. *People's Songs* 1:1.

People's Songs, Inc. n.d.-a. *A Condensation of Music for Political Action: A Section of PAC's New Manual of Techniques.* New York: People's Songs, Inc.

———. n.d.-b. *Organize a People's Songs Branch*. New York: People's Songs, Inc.

———. n.d.-c. *How to Plan a Hootenanny for People's Songs Branches*. New York: People's Songs, Inc.

Perkins, A. E. 1922. "Negro Spirituals from the Far South." *Journal of American Folklore* 35:223–49.

Pescatello, Ann M. 1992. *Charles Seeger: A Life in American Music*. Pittsburgh: University of Pittsburgh Press.

Peterson, Richard A. 1997a. *Creating Country Music: Fabricating Authenticity*. Chicago: University of Chicago Press.

———. 1997b. "The Rise and Fall of Highbrow Snobbery as a Status Marker." *Poetics* 25:75–92.

Piven, Frances F., and Richard A. Cloward. 1979. *Poor People's Movements: Why They Succeed, How They Fare*. New York: Vintage.

Polletta, Francesca. 2002. *Freedom Is an Endless Meeting: Democracy in American Social Movements*. Chicago: University of Chicago Press.

———. 2006. *It Was Like a Fever: Storytelling in Protest and Politics*. Chicago: University of Chicago Press.

———. 2008. "Culture and Movements." *Annals of the American Academy of Political and Social Sciences* 619:78–96.

Porterfield, Nolan. 1996. *Last Cavalier: The Life and Times of John A. Lomax*. Urbana: University of Illinois Press.

Pound, Louise. 1917. "The Beginnings of Poetry." *PMLA* 32:201–32.

Radano, Ronald. 2003. *Lying up a Nation: Race and Black Music*. Chicago: University of Chicago Press.

Ramsey, Guthrie P. 2003. *Race Music: Black Cultures from Bebop to Hip-Hop*. Berkeley: University of California Press.

Reagon, Bernice Johnson. 1975. "Songs of the Civil Rights Movement, 1955–1965: A Study in Culture History." Ph.D. diss., Howard University.

Reed, T. V. 2005. *The Art of Protest: Culture and Activism from the Civil Rights Movement to the Streets of Seattle*. Minneapolis: University of Minnesota Press.

Reuss, Richard A. 1971. "American Folklore and Left-Wing Politics, 1927–1957." Ph.D. diss., Indiana University.

Reuss, Richard, and Joanna C. Reuss. 2000. *American Folk Music and Left Wing Politics: 1927–1957*. Lanham, MD: Scarecrow Press.

Roscigno, Vincent J., and William F. Danaher. 2001. "Media and Mobilization: The Case of Radio and Southern Textile Worker Insurgency, 1929–1934." *American Sociological Review* 66:21–48.

———. 2004. *The Voice of Southern Labor: Radio, Music, and Textile Strikes, 1929–1934*. Minneapolis: University of Minnesota Press.

Rosenberg, Neil V. 1993. *Transforming Tradition: Folk Music Revivals Examined*. Urbana: University of Illinois Press.

Rosenthal, Robert, and Richard Flacks. 2009. *Playing for Change*. Boulder, CO: Paradigm.

Rossman, Michael. 1968. "I Don't Believe Yip Can Legislate Participation Any Better Than LBJ Can." Liberation News Service, March 31, pp. 1–5.

Roy, William G. 2001. *Making Societies: The Historical Construction of Our World*. Thousand Oaks, CA: Pine Forge Press.

———. 2004. "'Race Records' and 'Hillbilly Music': The Institutional Origins of Racial Categories in the American Commercial Recording Industry." *Poetics* 32:265–79.

Sandburg, Carl. 1927. *The American Songbag*. New York: Harcourt, Brace.

Sanders, Lynn Moss. 2003. *Howard W. Odum's Folklore Odyssey: Transformation to Tolerance through African American Folk Studies*. Athens: University of Georgia Press.

Schegloff, Emanuel A. 2007. *Sequence Organization in Interaction: A Primer in Conversation Analysis*. New York: Cambridge University Press.

Schutz, Alfred. 1964. "Making Music Together." Pp. 157–78 in *Studies in Social Theory*, vol. 2. The Hague: M. Nijhoff.

Scofield, Ronald D. 1953. "John Jacob Niles Sings Sweet, True." *Santa Barbara News-Press*, October 23.

Seeger, Anthony. 2004. *Why Suyá Sing: A Musical Anthropology of an Amazonian People*. Urbana: University of Illinois Press.

Seeger, Charles. 1934. "On Proletarian Music." *Modern Music* 11:121–27.

———. 1957. "Music and the Class Structure of the United States." *American Quarterly* 9:281–94.

Seeger, C., A. G. Tusler, and A. M. Briegleb. 1972. *Reminiscences of an American Musicologist: Charles Seeger/Oral History Transcript*. Los Angeles: Oral History Program, University of California.

Seeger, Pete. 2001. Telephone interview by the author. July 29.

Seeger, Pete, and Bob Reiser. 1989. *Everybody Says Freedom*. New York: Norton.

Sharp, Cecil J. 1916. *One Hundred English Folksongs*. Boston: O. Ditson Company.

———. 1927 [1908]. *Folk-Songs from Various Countries*. Book IV, *Folk-Songs of England*. London: Novello and Company.

———. 1932. *English Folk Songs from the Southern Appalachians*. London: Oxford University Press.

Shelton, Robert. 1962. "Songs a Weapon in Rights Battle." *New York Times*, August 20, p. 1.

Shepherd, John, and Peter Wicke. 1997. *Music and Cultural Theory*. Malden, MA: Polity Press.

Shepherd, John. 1989. "Music and Male Hegemony." Pp. 151–72 in *Music and Society: The Politics of Composition, Performance and Reception*, ed. Richard Leppert and Susan McClary. New York: Cambridge University Press.

Silber, Irwin, and Barbara Dane. 2001. Interview by the author. Oakland, CA.

Simmel, Georg. 1955. *Conflict and the Web of Group Affiliations*. New York: The Free Press.

Small, Christopher. 1987. *Music of the Common Tongue: Survival and Celebration in Afro-American Music*. New York: Riverrun Press.

———. 1998. *Musicking: The Meanings of Performing and Listening*. Hanover, NH: University Press of New England.

Snow, David A., E. B. Rochford Jr., S. Warden, and R. D. Benford. 1986. "Frame Alignment Processes, Micromobilization, and Movement Participation." *American Sociological Review* 51:464–81.

Snow, David A., Louis A. Zurcher Jr., and Sheldon Ekland-Olson. 1980. "Social Networks and Social Movements: A Microstructural Approach to Differential Recruitment." *American Sociological Review* 45:787–801.

Sohrabi, Nader. 2005. "Revolutions as Paths to Modernity." Pp. 300–332 in *Remaking Modernity: Politics, History, and Sociology*, ed. Julia Adams et al. Durham: Duke University Press.

Solomon, Mark. 1998. *The Cry Was Unity: Communists and African Americans, 1917–1936*. Jackson: University Press of Mississippi.

Southern, Eileen. 1983. *The Music of Black Americans: A History*. New York: Norton.

Steinberg, Marc W. 1999. *Fighting Words: Working-Class Formation, Collective Action, and Discourse in Early Nineteenth-Century England*. Ithaca: Cornell University Press.

———. 2004. "When Politics Goes Pop: On the Intersections of Popular and Political Culture and the Case of Serbian Student Protests." *Social Movement Studies* 3:1, 3–29.

Stepan-Norris, Judith, and Maurice Zeitlin. 1989. "'Who Gets the Bird?' or, How the Communists Won Power and Trust in America's Unions: The Relative Autonomy of Intraclass Political Struggles." *American Sociological Review* 54: 503–23.

———. 2003. *Left Out: Reds and America's Industrial Unions*. New York: Cambridge University Press.

Stone, I. F., Jack Newfield, Nat Hentoff, and William M. Kunstler. 1972. "LNS." *New York Review of Books* 19 (September 21).

Stoper, Emily. 1989. "The Student Nonviolent Coordinating Committee: Rise and Fall of a Redemptive Organization." Pp. 1041–62 in *We Shall Overcome: The Civil Rights Movement in the United States in the 1950's and 1960's*, vol. 3, ed. David J. Garrow. Brooklyn, NY: Carlson Publishing.

Strang, David, and Sarah A. Soule. 1998. "Diffusion in Organizations and Social Movements: From Hybrid Corn to Poison Pills." *Annual Review of Sociology* 24:265–90.

Swidler, Ann. 1995. "Cultural Power and Social Movements." Pp. 25–40 in *Social Movements and Culture*, ed. Hank Johnston and Bert Klandermans. Minneapolis: University of Minnesota Press.

Tarrow, Sidney. 1998. *Power in Movement: Social Movements, Collective Action and Politics*. 2nd ed. New York: Cambridge University Press.

Thomson, Virgil. 1946. "Differentiated Counterpoint." *New York Herald Tribune*, November 11.

Tick, Judith. 1997. *Ruth Crawford Seeger: A Composer's Search for American Music*. Oxford: Oxford University Press.

Tilly, Charles. 1978. *From Mobilization to Revolution*. Reading, MA: Addison-Wesley.

———. 2000. "How Do Relations Store Histories?" *Annual Review of Sociology* 26:721–23.

———. 2004a. "Social Boundary Mechanisms." *Philosophy of the Social Sciences* 34:211–36.

———. 2004b. *Social Movements, 1768–2004*. Boulder, CO: Paradigm.

———. 2005. *Trust and Rule*. New York: Cambridge University Press.

Toll, Robert C. 1974. *Blacking Up: The Minstrel Show in Nineteenth Century America*. New York: Oxford University Press.

Torrance, Michael. 2007. "The Lumpen: Black Panther Party Revolutionary Singing Group." http://www.itsabouttimebpp.com/Our_Stories/The_Lumpen/the_lumpen.html (accessed September 18, 2007).

Treitler, Leo. 1997. "Language and the Interpretation of Music." Pp. 23–56 in *Music and Meaning*, ed. Jenefer Robinson. Ithaca: Cornell University Press.

Trumbull, Eric Winship. 1991. "Musicals of the American Workers' Theatre Movement, 1928–1941: Propaganda and Ritual in Documents of a Social Movement." Ph.D. diss., University of Maryland.

Wald, A. M. 2007. *Trinity of Passion: The Literary Left and the Antifascist Crusade*. Chapel Hill: University of North Carolina Press.

Ward, Brian. 1998. *Just My Soul Responding: Rhythm and Blues, Black Consciousness, and Race Relations*. Berkeley: University of California Press.

Ware, Vron, and Les Back. 2002. *Out of Whiteness: Color, Politics, and Culture*. Chicago: University of Chicago Press.

Wasserman, Harvey. 1992. "The Joy of Liberation News Service." Pp. 51–62 in *Voices from the Underground: Insider Histories of the Vietnam Era Underground Press*, ed. Ken Wachsberger. Tempe, AZ: Mica's Press.

"Weavers' Yarn." 1951. *Newsweek*, August 6, p. 88.

Weber, Max. 1958. *The Rational and Social Foundations of Music*. Carbondale: Southern Illinois Press.

Weinstein, James. 1975. *Ambiguous Legacy: The Left in American Politics*. New York: New Viewpoints.

Werner, Craig. 1999. *A Change Is Gonna Come: Music, Race and the Soul of America*. New York: Plume.

Whisnant, David E. 1983. *All That Is Native and Fine: The Politics of Culture in an American Region*. Chapel Hill: University of North Carolina Press.

Wigginton, E. 1991. *Refuse to Stand Silently By: An Oral History of Grass Roots Social Activism in America, 1921–64*. New York: Doubleday.

Wolfe, Charles K., and Kip Lornell. 1992. *The Life and Legend of Leadbelly*. New York: HarperCollins.

Work, John Wesley. 1969. *Folk Song of the American Negro*. New York: Negro Universities Press.

———. 1998. *American Negro Songs*. Mineola, NY: Dover.

"Workers Music." 1931. *New Masses*, May, p. 13.

Wuthnow, Robert. 2003. *All in Sync: How Music and Art Are Revitalizing American Religion*. Berkeley: University of California Press.

Zald, Mayer N., and John D. McCarthy. 1979. *The Dynamics of Social Movements: Resource Mobilization, Social Control, and Tactics*. Cambridge, MA: Winthrop.

Zerubavel, Eviatar. 1991. *The Fine Line: Making Distinctions in Everyday Life*. New York: The Free Press.

Zolberg, Vera L. 1997. *Outsider Art: Contesting Boundaries in Contemporary Culture*. Cambridge: Cambridge University Press.

Index

PRINCETON STUDIES IN CULTURAL SOCIOLOGY

Paul J. DiMaggio, Michèle Lamont, Robert J. Wuthnow, Viviana A. Zelizer, *series editors*

Weaving Self-Evidence: A Sociology of Logic by Claude Rosental, translated by Catherine Porter

Economists and Societies: Discipline and Profession in the United States, Great Britain, and France, 1890s to 1990s by Marion Fourcade

Reds, Whites, and Blues: Social Movements, Folk Music, and Race in the United States by William G. Roy